UNM-GALLUP
ZOLLINGER LIBRARY
200 COLLEGE ROAD
GALLUP, NEW MEXICO 87301

1. Books may be checked out for 28 days with no renewals.

2. A fine is charged for each day a book is not returned according to the above rule. No book will be issued to any person incurring such a fine until it has been paid.

3. All injuries to books beyond reasonable wear and all losses shall be made good to the satisfaction of the Librarian.

4. Each borrower is held responsible for all books charged on his card and for all fines accruing on the same.

Aransas

A Naturalist's Guide

ARANSAS

Wayne H. McAlister and
Martha K. McAlister

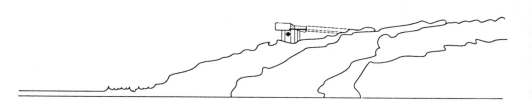

UNIVERSITY OF TEXAS PRESS
AUSTIN

This guidebook is dedicated to the late E. Frank Johnson, eleventh manager of the Aransas National Wildlife Refuge, 1973–1986.

Requests for permission to reproduce material from this work should be sent to Permissions, University of Texas Press, Box 7819, Austin, TX 78713-7819.

∞ The paper used in this publication meets the minimum requirements of American National Standard for Information Sciences—Permanence of Paper for Printed Library Materials, ANSI Z39.48-1984.

Library of Congress Cataloging-in-Publication Data

McAlister, Wayne H.
    [Guidebook to the Aransas National Wildlife Refuge]
    Aransas : a naturalist's guide / Wayne H. McAlister and Martha K. McAlister.
        p.   cm.
    Originally published: Guidebook to the Aransas National Wildlife Refuge. Victoria, Tex. : Mince County Press, © 1987.
    Includes bibliographical references and index.

    ISBN 0-292-75171-0 (alk. paper). — ISBN 0-292-75172-9 (pbk. : alk. paper)
    1. Natural history—Texas—Aransas National Wildlife Refuge.
    2. Aransas National Wildlife Refuge (Tex.)   I. McAlister, Martha K.
    II. Title.
    QH105.T4M37   1995
    508.764'122—dc20   94-41619

Contents

Preface

This guidebook is intended to provide general orientation for a visitor to the mainland portion of the Aransas National Wildlife Refuge. The Matagorda Unit is covered in a companion volume (*Matagorda Island: A Naturalist's Guide,* by McAlister and McAlister, Austin: University of Texas Press, 1993). Written with an ecological theme, this book not only names the various species of resident plants and animals but also offers insight into their natural relationships. Space has been allotted to various creatures according to their general interest and their ecological significance: an entire chapter to the whooping crane, several paragraphs to the live oak tree, only a passing mention to the common sootywing.

We must stress what the guidebook is *not.* It is not a definitive identification manual. The task of field identification is adequately handled by an array of well-written and well-illustrated field guides. Some of these are for sale at the Wildlife Interpretation Center (or WIC, called "the Wick" by refuge personnel) on the refuge. Others can be obtained at any well-stocked bookstore. Most come in economical paperback format. A selection of titles is listed in the bibliography. In addition, refuge personnel or qualified volunteers are on duty at the information desk in the WIC, and they occasionally conduct guided tours to help visitors identify and appreciate the creatures they see.

We have limited our presentation to ecological commentary and remarks about the life history of the included biota. Admittedly, this approach puts the burden of identification on the visitor. To take fullest advantage of your visit to the Aransas it is best to read beforehand the section of the guidebook that interests you. All creatures are referred to by their accepted common names, and Latin names are listed in appendices D, E, and F. You can look organisms up in the appropriate field guide. Check their fieldmarks and study their pictures. Then when you visit the refuge you will be fully prepared for a rewarding outdoor experience. If, after all your diligent homework, the first creature you see on the refuge is completely unknown to you and is nowhere mentioned in this guidebook—welcome to the intrigue and the challenge of the Texas out-of-doors!

We believe that the staff of the Aransas National Wildlife Refuge is

Oak with hawk

outstanding. From maintenance man to manager, all have courteously and enthusiastically assisted us in the preparation of this guidebook. This willing team effort is doubtless in large part a result of the instruction and example set by the late E. Frank Johnson, former refuge manager, who extended us every assistance and many solicited and unsolicited personal favors. His successor and the current manager, J. Brent Giezentanner, has continued that hospitable tradition. Ken Schwindt, assistant manager, and Tom Stehn, refuge biologist, willingly shared their professional knowledge with us. Beverly Fletcher, refuge ranger, helped us scour the refuge's extensive historical files and photo albums, and Claude Lard, former refuge manager, provided us with additional historical records. Melvin Maxwell and Ellen Michaels, outdoor recreation planners, extended us every courtesy. Without their generous co-operation and that of the rest of the Aransas staff, this guidebook could not have been written.

We published a version of this book in 1987, to commemorate the golden anniversary of the establishment of the Aransas National Wildlife Refuge. Although the refuge has expanded in size in the interim, it is gratifying that there have been no major changes in either policy or facilities. The land and the wildlife are still there, as is the opportunity to enjoy them.

Introduction

The Aransas National Wildlife Refuge lies in the center of the Texas Coastal Bend about 140 miles south of Houston and 50 miles north of Corpus Christi. Because of its inherent value to both wildlife and man, and especially because of its crucial role in the struggle to save the whooping crane, the Aransas is known worldwide.

Whether you are a newcomer or an old friend, the mood of the Aransas creeps up on you en route. You will have traveled for miles across the flat Coastal Plain on highways busy with automobile and truck traffic in this densely populated sector of the state. The congestion eases when you get onto the midsection of the picturesque hug-the-coast State Highway 35. Finally you are among occasional petrochemical plants, grain elevators, small towns, and generous voids of pasture and crop lands. By this time you will feel the insistent nudge of the steady southeast breeze, and you will probably be treated to a magnificent display of billowing Gulf clouds, a welcome third dimension in this flat terrain.

If you are coming from the south, turn coastward off State 35 onto FM 774 about twelve miles beyond the causeway outside Rockport-Fulton. From the north take FM 239 two miles outside Tivoli. Either way, just follow the brown refuge signs. Both routes eventually join FM 2040 for the final seven miles to the refuge gate.

As you speed along, the rows of enormous fields of grain and cotton fan by until the land turns sandy and the plowed furrows give way to mottes of scrubby live oaks and widespread mesquite trees scattered among short-cropped bunchgrasses. Thickets of groundsel and dark mounds of spiny aster guard the roadside ditches, while stunted netleaf hackberries and prickly ashes mark the fencelines. Grazing cattle ignore your passage. A flock of great-tailed grackles bats the wind. A great egret startles up. You glimpse a western coachwhip snake streaking arrow-straight across the road. All are harbingers of what lies just ahead.

Finally you crest a low sandy ridge and abruptly behold San Antonio Bay spread out to the horizon. The stiffened breeze, laden with the heavy organic odors of the sea, bears tidings from the terns and gulls that cruise over the nearby shallows. Pale stalks of silverleaf sunflowers

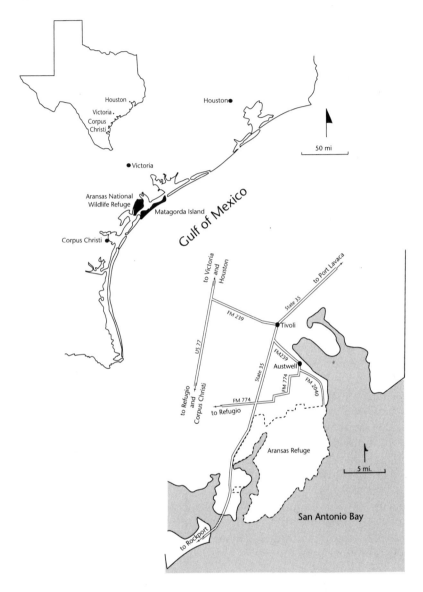

Figure 1. Location of the Aransas National Wildlife Refuge in the Coastal Bend of Texas.

SHELL RIDGE COMMUNITY. View is to the south on the Heron Flats Trail. On the right, the higher middle ridge of oystershell supports scrub live oaks, tanglewood, prickly pear, and Spanish dagger. On the left, the lower outer ridge supports mesquite, seashore dropseed, and marsh hay cordgrass. The ridges are separated by Muskgrass Slough.

TIDAL FLAT COMMUNITY. The boardwalk passes over a succession of salt-tolerant plants, criss-crossing animal tracks and tidal pools en route to the edge of San Antonio Bay.

OAK-BAY FOREST COMMUNITY.   View is to the north toward Dagger Point along the margin of San Antonio Bay. Dense foliage is composed of live oak, laurel oak, and red bay. Isolated trees on the point are live oaks.

SALTMARSH COMMUNITY. View is across Mustang Lake from the observation tower. Marsh rice rats, clapper rails, and saltmarsh snails inhabit the dense low growth of smooth cordgrass, glassworts, and maritime saltwort. Dabbling ducks frequent the shallow open water, while herons and egrets stalk the vegetation line.

RIDGE-AND-SWALE COMMUNITY. Wind-pruned and stalwart, this motte of live oaks provides food and shelter to a variety of wildlife and shade-loving plants.

RIDGE-AND-SWALE COMMUNITY. A variety of grasses and sedges form open glades between clumps of oaks and thickets of yaupon. Such a mosaic of vegetation provides multiple habitats for the diversity of wildlife on the Aransas.

RIDGE-AND-SWALE COMMUNITY. Chest-high thickets of scrubby live oaks laced with thorny greenbriars create a nearly impenetrable brushland across many acres of uplands on the Aransas. This portion of the community is periodically burned to inhibit its spread into grasslands. The bright patches of sand along the edge of the thicket are pocket gopher mounds.

The western cottonmouth moccasin is the most common poisonous snake on the Aransas. This individual is displaying its do-not-tread-on-me trademark.

The arched neck, depressed ears, and stiff-legged stance indicate that this white-tailed buck is threatening a rival male during the rutting season.

A tranquil moment in 1916 at the home of John Brundrett on the west side of Blackjack Peninsula.

In the early days, man sweat and mule power were used to scrape out catchments for fresh water on Blackjack Peninsula.

Three generations of Brundretts on the front gallery of their house built in 1905 on Blackjack Peninsula.

In 1939, this supply building (foreground) and barracks served the men in the Civilian Conservation Corps who labored on Blackjack Peninsula. The site is on the edge of San Antonio Bay near the current picnic area.

A CCC crew attempts to disinter a Speeder dragline from the coastal mire while excavating a freshwater canal on Blackjack Peninsula in 1940.

rise over hillocks of sand; depressions are lined with black willows and choked with cattails and bulrushes. Rounded copses of coastal live oaks are laced down with scrambles of mustang grape vines. Mexican hats and Indian blankets sprinkle a bright garnish along the roadside. Before you can catch your breath you are through the refuge gate, and you will likely spot your first tourist-wise white-tailed deer and admire the grove of wind-sculptured live oaks.

By the time you have registered at the Wildlife Interpretation Center (WIC), the full impact of the Aransas should be upon you. It fosters a paradoxical mix of relaxation and exhilaration, of wanting to sit quietly in one place while feeling the urge to trek about so you do not miss anything. Hopefully you will have time to do both, and while you pleasantly exhaust yourself you will come to appreciate that the Aransas is not only a refuge for harried wildlife—it is a haven for harried people as well.

It is easy to extol Nature on the Aransas National Wildlife Refuge: the oblate sun clearing the dawn mists over San Antonio Bay; a bright roadside ribbon of crimson and yellow Indian blankets; the faint norther-tossed gabble of geese reckoning on instinct in a dark and ragged sky; the poetic poise of a whitetail buck with head up and ears flared; the rugged mix of sand, oak, and sea—all so different from the straight-edged and shiny civilized world.

Yet, for all its sublimity, Nature alone does not make a refuge. The plants and the animals and the vagrant breezes simply survive and exist. They do not comprehend themselves or each other. Only people do. Today it takes people to ensure that these wild things have the opportunity to persist in their wild way. Wherever a wildlife refuge exists, it stands in evidence that someone cares.

"We the people" have dictated that this particular lonely stretch of Texas coastline shall remain forever untamed. Our collective concern is as vital to the Aransas Refuge as is the haunting bugle of the giant white birds that have for ages made it their winter home.

In 1903, appalled by the wholesale slaughter of waterbirds for the millinery trade, President Theodore Roosevelt designated three-acre Pelican Island in Florida a federal bird sanctuary. It was the beginning of the nation's wildlife refuge system, which today spans the country, numbering more than 500 units and encompassing 92 million acres.

The Aransas National Wildlife Refuge was established on December 31, 1937. It is one of fifteen such federal sanctuaries in Texas. All are administered by the U.S. Fish and Wildlife Service (USFWS), Department of the Interior, for the purpose of protecting and conserving the nation's wildlife resources.

In today's busy world every wildlife refuge is a critical meeting ground of demands, frequently contradictory demands. The wildlife require a complicated fund of resources that will provide food, shelter, and freedom so that they may roam and rest unmolested. Yet, people desire access to observe and enjoy the wild creatures in their natural haunts. For some, that enjoyment means the simple liberty to stroll, perhaps with binoculars or camera; others require a rifle. There are demands of other sorts, such as the indispensable Gulf Intracoastal Waterway that passes directly beside the vulnerable marshes and tidal flats on one margin of the refuge, and the rights of prior landowners to exploit minerals on the refuge. Wildlife disturbance caused by roaring airboat traffic around the periphery of Blackjack Peninsula is yet another concern. The USFWS attempts to conciliate these demands by subtly managing both wildlife and people. People management is by far the more difficult task.

First priority is given to wildlife by the protection of vital habitat. This means designating and patrolling refuge boundaries and letting natural events transpire within them. But because even a large refuge is only a relatively small and isolated segment of Nature and because populations of many kinds of wild creatures are precariously low, habitats must be manipulated to some extent. Vegetation is burned or mowed; some animals are culled while others are given support; occasionally individual animals are transferred from one refuge to another to invigorate inbred bloodlines; soil erosion is checked; air and water pollution are monitored—all with the hope of not upsetting the natural cycles or significantly altering the natural appearance of the area.

People are manipulated on a wildlife refuge by restricting their access and by exposing them to a vigorous program of environmental education. Brochures, films, guided tours, and special visitor centers are used to inform the public about both the delight and the plight of our wildlife heritage. Visitors contact wildlife in native habitat on designated walking and driving routes and through closely scrutinized hunting and fishing programs. Unlike a national park, a national wildlife refuge is dedicated to the wild creatures and natural habitat within its boundaries. On a refuge people come second.

In addition to the general charge of protecting and conserving native creatures within its bounds, a wildlife refuge may assume special responsibilities. The Aransas Refuge was established for the benefit of migratory waterfowl passing along the Central Flyway, and in fact it was initially called the Aransas Migratory Waterfowl Refuge. The $463,500 purchase price came from the sale of migratory bird stamps. Management of habitat for ducks, geese, and shorebirds remains a primary local objective.

Shortly after World War II, when the impending extinction of the whooping crane was fully appreciated, it was realized that by happy coincidence, the tidal flats of the Aransas Refuge included the last significant wintering ground of this stately bird. Since then, the fate of the whooping crane and the renown of the refuge have been inextricably joined.

Besides waterfowl and whooping cranes, the Aransas Refuge hosts a lengthy list of endangered and threatened animals. Equally important, it has a generous sampling of the wonderful diversity of common kinds of plants and animals representative of the wild biota of the Texas Gulf Coast. Today's enlightened habitat approach to wildlife management is very different from the predator eradication concept of the Roosevelt days and from the notion of a game animal farm that was prevalent until only a few decades ago. Today, all organisms—the ordinary and the seldom seen, the rare and the commonplace, the beneficial, the pestiferous, and the indifferent, the game and the nongame, the great and the small—are making good their claim upon a place in the Texas sun.

Today the Aransas National Wildlife Refuge complex consists of five units. The Main Unit occupies Blackjack Peninsula, an isolated neck of land bounded by St. Charles Bay on the west and San Antonio Bay on the east, sixteen miles long and two to seven miles wide. As originally established in 1937, the entire refuge was contained in these 47,261 peninsular acres, and this is still the site of Refuge Headquarters, most visitor facilities, and paved roads for public access.

In 1967, the Tatton Unit, a contiguous 7,568-acre stretch of coastal grassland lying between Highway 35 and the west shore of St. Charles Bay, was added by donation. The Lamar Unit is a disjunct 734-acre tract of live oak upland and salt marsh located on the west bank of St. Charles Bay midway between the Tatton Unit and Goose Island State Park at the tip of Lamar Peninsula. It was leased from The Nature Conservancy of Texas in 1987, and arrangements for purchase were completed in 1991. The 3,000-acre Myrtle Foester Whitmire Unit is a valuable coastal wetland added to the refuge system in 1993. It is located 22 miles north of Blackjack Peninsula on Powderhorn Lake near the historic townsite of Indianola. Future purchase or lease arrangements may increase the size of this unit to 5,000 acres. The 60,000 acres of these four combined units constitute the mainland portion of the Aransas Refuge.

In 1971, the Matagorda Unit was established when the refuge assumed management of 19,000 acres of federal land on Matagorda Island, a barrier island five miles from Blackjack Peninsula across San Antonio Bay. In 1982, negotiations were completed to incorporate that land formally into the refuge and to bring nearly 26,000 acres of surrounding state-owned salt marshes and Gulf beaches under federal wildlife management responsibility. When the remaining 11,500 acres

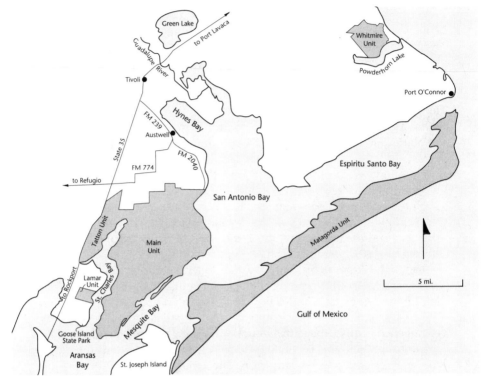

Figure 2. Five units make up the 115,000-acre Aransas National Wildlife Refuge complex.

of Matagorda Island were purchased from The Nature Conservancy of Texas in 1988, the Matagorda Unit included the entire island and its associated tidal marshes—some 56,500 acres.

In round figures, then, as of 1993, the Aransas National Wildlife Refuge complex encompassed about 115,000 acres of prime coastal mainland and barrier island real estate. In addition, the USFWS has jurisdiction over 13,000 acres of open bay waters established by presidential proclamation as a buffer zone around the margin of Blackjack Peninsula. The personnel of the Aransas are thus stewards of the largest block of wildlife habitat remaining in the Coastal Bend of Texas.

The major public access to the mainland portion of the refuge is the 5,000-acre wildlife interpretive area on the north end of Blackjack Peninsula, seven miles southeast of Austwell. Despite its relative isolation, this site lies within a four-hour drive for more than 2.5 million people, and it hosts about 65,000 visitors annually. Most people come to the

Aransas on weekends or holidays, and as Figure 3 shows, the refuge is most popular during the cool months when whooping cranes are in residence and saltmarsh mosquitoes are subdued.

Facilities in the interpretive area include

- the headquarters complex, with offices, residences, and service area
- the Wildlife Interpretation Center, which includes an information and registration desk, wildlife displays, slide and film presentations, and a bookshop
- the forty-foot-high observation tower overlooking Mustang Lake
- the boardwalk across the tidal flat adjacent to the observation tower
- elevated observation platforms at Heron Flats and Dagger Point
- observation decks at Jones and Hog lakes
- the public picnic area
- the Youth Environmental Training Area (YETA), available by reservation for educational groups
- the Tour Loop, a sixteen-mile paved vehicle loop with six wayside exhibits
- eight self-guided walking trails
- various overlooks and sites of special interest.

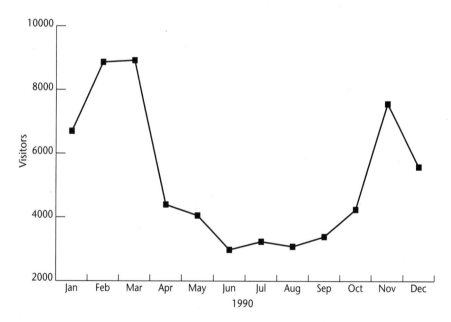

Figure 3. In 1990 more than 63,000 people visited the Main Unit of the Aransas National Wildlife Refuge. The monthly pattern of visitation is typical of most years. Data are from the files of the ANWR.

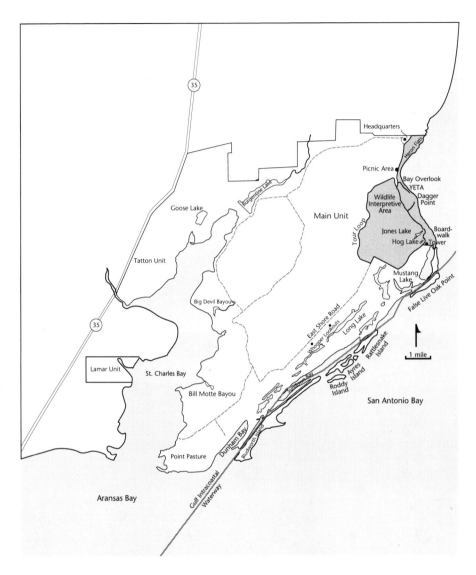

Figure 4. The mainland portion of the Aransas National Wildlife Refuge. The Whitmire Unit (not shown) lies 22 miles north.

There are no concessions or gasoline stations on the refuge, and no camping is allowed except by special arrangement for educational groups. Although gasoline can be purchased at Hopper's Landing, 2 miles outside the refuge gate, the nearest full-service gasoline station is in Tivoli (14 miles north); complete facilities are available in Rockport to the south and Port Lavaca to the north (each about 35 miles distant).

The refuge gate is open from sunrise to sunset the year round. The WIC is open daily from 8 to 5 except Thanksgiving day and Christmas day. There is no entrance fee, but all visitors are required to register (one member may register for a group). During open hours, registration is handled at the desk in the WIC; otherwise visitors sign in at a station outside the entrance to the WIC. Information may be obtained in advance by writing to Refuge Manager, ANWR, P.O. Box 100, Austwell, TX 77950, or by calling 512-286-3559.

Most of the mainland portion of the Aransas is not open to routine public access. Except for the wildlife interpretive area, Blackjack Peninsula is devoted to the management and preservation of wildlife, especially migratory waterfowl and shorebirds and the flock of winter-resident whooping cranes. The Tatton Unit is where the Aransas' dwindling flock of Attwater's prairie chickens is making its last stand. The Lamar Unit was acquired to allow for expansion of whooping crane habitat. The centerpiece of the Whitmire Unit is a 700-acre freshwater lake that supports a myriad of winter waterfowl.

By arrangement with the state of Texas, public access to the northern two-thirds of Matagorda Island—some 44,000 acres—is administered by the Texas Parks and Wildlife Department (TPWD) as the Matagorda Island State Park and Wildlife Management Area. The 7,300-acre state park has a year-round visitation program, and the wildlife management section (37,000 acres) is open for limited recreational use. No motor vehicles are allowed on the island. All access is by boat, private or charter, or the pedestrian ferry, which runs from the dock in Port O'Connor on weekends and holidays. Information can be obtained from the TPWD office in Port O'Connor, at South Sixteenth Street and Maple Avenue; by writing P.O. Box 117, Port O'Connor, TX 77982-0117; or by calling 512-983-2215.

Hunting for white-tailed deer and feral hogs is allowed each fall on selected portions of Blackjack Peninsula, and bank or wade fishing is permitted in specified areas from mid-April to mid-October. Contact the refuge manager for details. Hunting and fishing privileges on Matagorda Island are monitored by TPWD.

The Aransas National Wildlife Refuge operates on an annual budget of approximately $900,000. The staff includes about a dozen full-time professionals plus several part-time employees, clerical help, and a cadre of maintenance workers. In addition, the refuge annually benefits from several thousand hours of volunteer work. Each summer the Aransas hosts a group of Youth Conservation Corps youngsters who labor in the heat and humidity on various outdoor construction and general maintenance projects.

U.S. Fish and Wildlife Service Refuge Manager Service Roll Aransas National Wildlife Refuge

James O. Stevenson	1938–1941
Earl W. Craven	1942–1945
Charles A. Keefer	1945–1949
Julian A. Howard	1949–1956
Claude F. Lard	1956–1959
Huyson J. Johnson	1959–1964
Robert H. Shields	1964–1966
Phillip S. Morgan	1966–1968
Gordon N. Hansen	1968–1970
Robert C. Brown	1971–1972
E. Frank Johnson	1973–1986
J. Brent Giezentanner	1987–

CHAPTER 1

The Land — How It Came to Be

An inquisitive person can hardly gaze across San Antonio Bay from Dagger Point or marvel at the mighty live oaks along the Big Tree Trail without falling into a reflective frame of mind. How and when did this tangled web of nature come to be? By what forces? What came before?

Good questions. They impel us to put our scattered observations into an orderly scheme. They are good also because if we can fathom how this land came about, then we will be in a better position to ensure its continued well-being.

Over the more than 100 million years that have passed since early Cretaceous times, the Aransas area has been beneath the sea much more than above it. During that early era the arc of today's coastline was an undistinguished part of the ocean floor; the shoreline of the shallow Cretaceous sea lay 130 miles inland, along the present-day Balcones Escarpment, a cliff face of varying height that can be traced across the central part of the state from San Antonio through Austin and northward past Waco and Dallas.

From time to time, the writhing of deep tectonic forces elevated the land, pushing back the sea's edge. Significant pauses in this marine recession are marked by three low escarpments—the Bordas, Reynosa, and Oakville—lying in a crescent about midway between the Balcones and the present coastline. Rivers, pursuing the retreating shoreline, spilled their loads of sediment across the recently exposed marine shelf and laid the foundation for the modern, gently tilted Coastal Plain. Through it all the Aransas area remained submerged.

The Ice Ages

About one and a half million years ago the first of four major glaciations that marked the Pleistocene epoch began. Although no glacier pushed so far south as Texas, these great ice sheets had important impacts on local landforms. First, the buildup of glaciers incorporated enormous

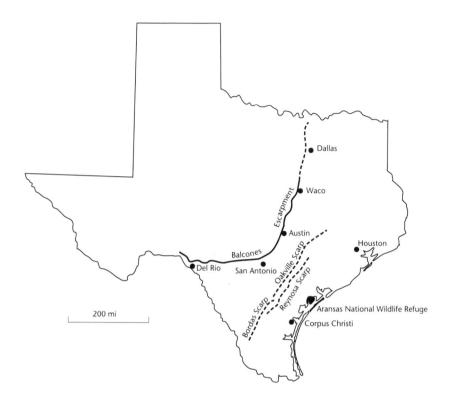

Figure 5. The Balcones Escarpment marks the shoreline of the Cretaceous sea in Texas. Smaller escarpments indicate retreating shorelines.

quantities of water, causing a drop in sea level. At their peak, great ice shields spanned the northern third of the continent with a burden of ice and snow nearly two miles thick at their centers. The retreat of the glaciers not only caused a compensating rise in sea level but also initiated widespread flooding and erosion as the surge of meltwater drained off the continent. Throughout the early Pleistocene the locale of the Aransas Refuge was alternately exposed and submerged according to the vagaries of the ice sheets and of the tectonic forces that affected the elevation of the Coastal Plain. All the strata formed at this time lie deep beneath the surface. They are the platform upon which the modern stage is set.

In late Sangamon time (120,000 years ago, just before the final push of the glaciers) the local shoreline lay approximately where it does today. Events of that time formed the substrate for the modern Aransas Refuge and its environs. The Sangamon was a period of deposition. Material eroded from the highland interior of Texas was transported by large primordial rivers already identifiable as the ancestors of the modern Nueces, Aransas/Mission, San Antonio/Guadalupe, Lavaca/Navidad, Colorado, and Brazos. Sediments were heaped across the flat land and into the local marine embayments. Each river system dumped its burden of sand, mud, and silt to create a broad delta complete with meander loops, oxbows, levees, lakes, and fresh, brackish, and salt-water marshes. Vast splays of muddy sand were shoved about, buried and disinterred, sorted and resorted, as the streams cut new channels and reoccupied old ones.

These late Pleistocene fluvial deposits eventually compacted into the black, waxy Beaumont clay from which came rich Victoria-Orelia topsoils. The final approach to the refuge passes through stretches of these dark-land fields, tilled by the local grain and cotton farmers into mile-long furrows.

Ingleside Barrier

Sea level oscillated continually during the late Pleistocene. During one of its prolonged high phases in the Sangamon about 135,000 years ago, the sea pushed the shoreline several miles inland of its modern position. Waves, longshore currents, tidal surges, storms, and the omnipresent coastal winds began to rework the recently submerged deltaic sediments. Water smoothed the finer silts and muds across the continental shelf and heaped the coarser sand into windrows along the shore, while wind piled the dried sand into a long ridge parallel to the shoreline.

Remains of that Pleistocene sandbar, which averaged three miles across and ranged from 10 to 25 feet high, can be traced from Alazan Bay south of Corpus Christi around the margin of the Gulf, disappearing into the bowels of the great delta of the Mississippi River. Locally, portions of the relict strandplain are exposed as the Encinal Peninsula (Flour Bluff), Live Oak Ridge (Aransas Pass), Live Oak Peninsula (Rockport), Lamar Peninsula (Goose Island), Blackjack Peninsula (the Aransas Refuge), and Calhoun Peninsula (Port O'Connor).

Geologists named this unassuming ridge of sand the Ingleside Barrier. Some contend that it was actually an island, fronting the sea and backed by a continuous inland lagoon quite comparable to modern barrier islands like Matagorda and St. Joseph. However, recent interpretation suggests that the Ingleside Barrier was a strandplain—a windrow

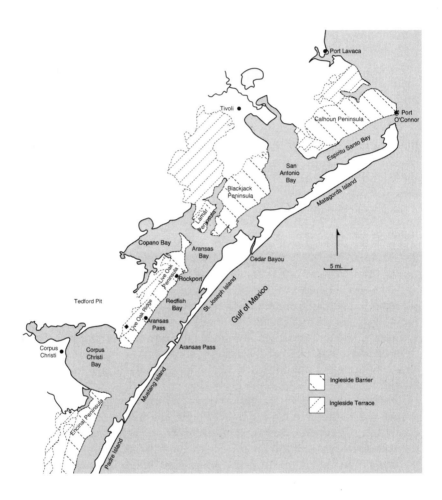

Figure 6. The Ingleside Barrier and the Ingleside Terrace were laid down about 120,000 years ago. The barrier is the remains of a late Pleistocene sand bar; the terrace was marsh land behind the bar. Note the Tedford Pit on Live Oak Ridge, from which many mammalian fossils have been recovered. Modified from *Environmental Geologic Atlas of the Texas Coastal Zone.* (Austin: University of Texas, Bureau of Economic Geology, 1976).

of sand heaped up directly on the unprotected shoreline, cut across by major river drainages and backed with a broken series of marshes, lakes, and brackish bays. Either way, the Ingleside environment must have been quite similar to that on our modern barrier islands.

Whether continuous or fragmented, the eight-to-ten-mile-wide swath of rich sediment that accumulated just inland of the Ingleside Barrier is called the Ingleside Terrace. It is the basis for the dark, fertile agricultural land that borders the coast.

One hundred thousand years ago the last of the Pleistocene glaciers began to build, and the sea embarked on its last significant retreat. By the time the Wisconsin ice shield had reached its peak the local shoreline was nearly fifty miles gulfward of its present position, and the Ingleside Barrier was left high and dry. To reach the sea, the several rivers were obliged to gouge their valleys through the exposed continental shelf. To attain grade level some streams scoured basins and channels as much as eighty feet below the level of the Ingleside strata and on out across the Pleistocene Coastal Plain. At that time the local area must have resembled the terrain as it now appears near Beeville and Goliad fifty miles inland of the refuge, but it was more broken and had deeper drainage channels.

Then, 18,000 years ago, the melting of the Wisconsin glaciers and the final advance of the sea marked the end of the Pleistocene epoch and the onset of the latest geological age, the Holocene. Natural forces began to erase much of their late Pleistocene work. The sea advanced into the river valleys and scour basins, turning them first brackish and then marine. Wave and current action caused the submerged valley walls to cave in and fill the old channels. All the while the rivers, swollen with their latest surge of meltwater, were building new deltas by unloading huge burdens of sediment into the advancing sea.

Action of wave and current on the resulting mix of marine and fluvial deposition, and general compaction and subsidence of the malleable coastal margin, finally produced the modern landform. Ten thousand years ago, as the sea filled the old scour basins, the outlines of the local bays became recognizable. At the same time the modern river deltas and estuaries stabilized and various fragments of the Ingleside Barrier became peninsulas protruding into the inland edges of the bays.

Four thousand years ago the sea reached its current level and the coastal margin took on its modern aspect. The flow of water in the river systems diminished to today's levels, while continued submarine erosion and deltaic filling reduced the depth of the bays to less than twenty feet. Meanwhile typical coastal vegetation secured the land.

As the Gulf waves rolled shoreward across the shallow shelf, they pushed sand into submarine bars paralleling the shoreline. Eventually the shoals coalesced and broke the surface. Then the wind dried the sand and piled it higher. Once begun, this accretion progressed rapidly. Smoothed by the wind and profiled by waves and longshore currents, the progenitors of the modern barrier islands came into being.

These islands took the brunt of the energy of the Gulf on their surf sides, leaving the lee-side tidal flats, bays, and estuaries in relative serenity. Passes, cut through the islands by the major rivers, allowed a mixing of the two aquatic systems, and gradients of salinity and temperature developed from estuary to Gulf.

So we have Blackjack Peninsula, a surviving fragment of the Ingleside Barrier, situated about eight miles from the open Gulf of Mexico. It is lapped by the shallow waters of St. Charles, Aransas, and San Antonio bays, themselves flooded river basins. These bays lie behind the protective influence of Matagorda and St. Joseph islands.

This brief geological story brings the Aransas up to date, but it is certainly not the end of the tale. Every seacoast exists in dynamic equilibrium, with active phases of accretion and degradation separated by intervals of relative stability. Locally the mainland shore is relatively fixed, although the barrier islands and passes exhibit perceptible changes. Storm breach, wind erosion, and the damming of rivers and erection of marine breakwaters are the significant factors affecting local cycles of erosion and accumulation of sand. Generally speaking, we live in a fairly quiet interglacial period; the level of the sea has not changed significantly for 3,000 years. However, if recent predictions of global warming prove true, the ocean may be gathering itself for yet another assault on the Coastal Plain.

A Geological Tour

Maybe you are interested in some firsthand evidence of the development of Blackjack Peninsula. Although they are not dramatic, clues lie everywhere. Perhaps the most telling is a handful of soil. Regardless of where you scoop it up, the substrate is likely to be sandy; often it is nearly pure sand. These much-abraded grains of silicon dioxide have had a long and tortuous history: loosened by weather, pummeled by water, driven by wind, dragged by gravity, buried and exposed thousands of times until you hold them in your palm. Dribble them back to continue on their endless journey.

More than two dozen low ridges trending northwest by southeast have been charted across the peninsula. As you drive around the Tour Loop you will occasionally be aware of this subtly corrugated topography. As the late Pleistocene sea drew back, the coastal breeze heaped up these parallel bands of Ingleside sand. The Dagger Point Trail me-

Dagger Point oak

anders across the most recent exposure of this stratum. If you walk the Yellow Route along the edge of San Antonio Bay you will gain one of the highest points on the refuge, a less-than-dizzying elevation of 45 feet. You will be standing on top of a wind-deposited sandpile, rendered the more impressive by its sheer, wave-cut eastern face.

Continue on the Yellow Route down to the point. Here, where Blackjack Peninsula absorbs the brunt of norther and storm-driven waves off San Antonio Bay, erosion has been rapid. To see geology in action, watch one wave leave its ripple mark amid the wrack and sediment on the shore. Then let your imagination ramble backward across the centuries to appreciate the cumulative effect of persistent, everyday processes.

Since 1860, Dagger Point has lost an average of five to ten feet a year to the sea, mostly catastrophically during storms, but the wear and tear never ceases. Until 1961, a house with a pier and a boat dock protected by a low seawall stood here, just inland of the live oak trees at the current shoreline. In that year Hurricane Carla pounded and scoured the point into its present conformation, destroying the house and its pier. You can still see some of the rockwork of the seawall just offshore.

In 1967, in an effort to prolong the life of the oak trees that make Dagger Point one of the most picturesque sites on the Refuge, bulldozers were used to shove the concrete rubble of the house to the bay side of the oaks. Soil was packed over the debris and the mat of exposed oak roots. Then ryegrass was sown to hold the patch in place. Despite the attention, though they have survived several more hurricanes, the live oaks seem to be slowly dying.

Stand at the end of the observation platform on the bay shore near the Dagger Point parking lot and gaze along the calving shoreline cliffs; you can see live oak and red bay trees in all stages of demolition. The rubble of trunks and branches at the water's edge suppresses the erosive action somewhat, but when the waves are pounding this cliff, you can get a good view of geological havoc in progress.

A concrete revetment was poured at the picnic area to protect the rapidly disappearing shoreline from the persistent action of waves coming in off the open bay. Between that buttress and the Bayfront Overlook volunteers from the U.S. Soil Conservation Service and local Boy Scouts planted smooth cordgrass in the shallows to stabilize the slumping shoreline after it was racked by Hurricane Gilbert in 1988. To temporarily protect their work from the waves, they staked strips of surplus parachutes several feet offshore. You can still see the stakes and the strands of tattered nylon, lingering reminders of an attempt to slow geological activity.

Just south of the Youth Environmental Training Area, the waves are busy grinding a rare outcrop of sandstone back into sand—again, geology in action.

Try sampling the soil along the first half of the Heron Flats Trail. It will be rather difficult to scrape up because it contains considerable organic matter as well as abundant oystershell. The shell came from offshore Holocene reefs and was thrown into several low ridges by storm tides. The firm limy base allowed a singular assemblage of woody and herbaceous growth to get established. Decay of the plants enriched the substrate to provide one of the refuge's few significant soil profiles.

You can get a feel for what the early Ingleside Barrier was like by driving to nearby Mustang Island State Park or Padre Island National Seashore. Or you might arrange a boat trip to Matagorda Island. On your way to and from the Aransas Refuge, watch for changes from black land to sandy land and back again as your route takes you across exposures of the Ingleside Barrier, the Ingleside Terrace, and lobes of the Pleistocene river deltas.

Ancient Life

What weird and wonderful creatures roamed Blackjack Peninsula in bygone ages? Such a question is intriguing, but before calling up visions of Coal Age scale trees and of lumbering dinosaurs, recall one salient fact: the Ingleside Barrier is only 120,000 years old. By the time this mound of sand was ready for occupancy much of the early drama of the evolution of life on land had transpired, and many spectacular prehistoric species were already extinct.

What might you have seen on the local Coastal Plain in the late Pleistocene some 75,000 years ago? The sparsely vegetated Ingleside sand ridge would front the sea. Behind the sand there would be a maze of fresh and brackish marshes and lakes—the Ingleside Terrace—interrupted by river deltas. The Coastal Plain that stretched inland would look much as it still does today in less trammeled spots: a bountiful prairie of knee-high grasses dotted with clumps of oaks and glades of sedges and laced with a dendritic pattern of forested drainage courses.

The casual observer would notice that the vegetation was more lush than it is today; the forests, for instance, would remind us of those we now see in East Texas. Partly this is because the landscape was pristine, but also the climate was warmer and more moist. Still, to any but the professional eye, all of the plants would appear quite modern.

What of the animal life? Mostly, it too would be disappointingly familiar. The insects, the shoreline crustaceans, even many of the backboned creatures were essentially as we find them today. You could have found a thoroughly modern specimen of bullfrog, water snake, alligator, sea gull, sparrow, vulture, white-footed mouse, coyote, bobcat, cottontail rabbit, raccoon, opossum, striped skunk, and white-tailed deer in this Pleistocene landscape. Here and there, however, you would encounter creatures that definitely belonged in the weird-and-wonderful category, and most of these would be mammals.

Our best insight into the late Pleistocene mammalian fauna of the local area comes from a fossil site known as the Tedford Pit, located 25 miles down the coast near the town of Ingleside. Here paleontologists from the University of Texas unearthed the remains of 42 species of vertebrates, including a remarkable diversity of now extinct mammals.

They found a rich array of large mammalian plant eaters: seventeen species compared to the current four. Among them were everyone's favorites, the Columbian mammoth and American mastodon. Mammoths were huge elephants standing fourteen feet at the shoulder; mastodons were shorter, stocky cousins with flat-browed heads carried high on nearly neckless forequarters. The many-tiered grinding teeth of the grazing mammoths are very different from the high-cusped molars of the mastodons, which browsed on coarser vegetation. A third species of elephant, with a curious spiral twist in its long tusks, also occurred at Ingleside.

Judging from the abundance of their remains, herds of wild horses of several species were common on the Pleistocene prairie. They were smaller than zebras, being more like wild asses in body size and probably in general behavior.

Small groups of camels browsed on the edge of the prairie. Although larger, they resembled modern dromedaries. The camels had a more

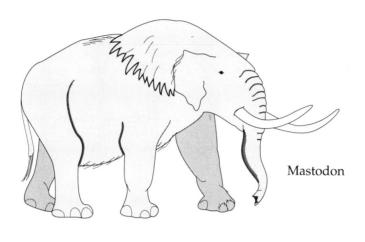

Mastodon

Horses

prolific cousin that ranged out across the grassland in fleet-footed flocks. These alert cameloids resembled llamas with exceptionally long necks.

No North American Pleistocene prairie would be complete without its nomadic herds of bison. The Ingleside boasted the ponderous, shaggy-coated *Bison antiquus*, which carried more beef than two modern bison and had a horn spread of three feet. Doubtless it influenced the ecology of the land just as the American bison did during its heyday.

Some herbivores were restricted to the forest. One of the most spec-

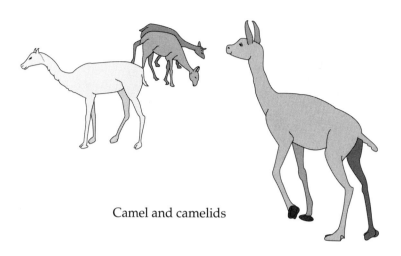

Camel and camelids

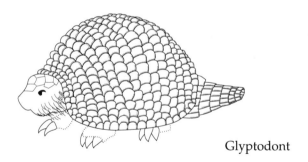

Glyptodont

tacular was the giant ground sloth. Two species of the ox-sized, bearlike creatures were recovered from the Tedford Pit. The powerful forelegs and strong claws of these mild-mannered ground sloths were used to rake a tangle of vegetation into their maws, but the same appendages could mount a telling defense against predators.

Two species of armadillos occupied the early forests. One closely resembled our modern armadillo, and it probably led the same sort of snuffling existence. But the glyptodont was something else: an ani-

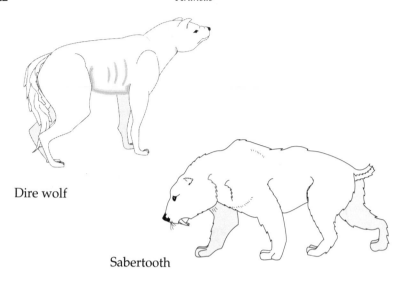

Dire wolf

Sabertooth

mated tank with a massive domed shell nearly five feet high and nine feet long. This shell, with a rigid roof of hundreds of interlocking bony scutes, accounted for most of the animal's weight of a ton and more. The passive glyptodont apparently spent its time chomping through streamside vegetation where it was more in danger of bogging down than of being attacked by any would-be predator.

The forest during Ingleside time also supported foraging groups of evil-looking flat-headed peccaries, an occasional tapir, and a herbivorous bear that resembled the modern black bear.

Where there are herbivores in such variety, there will be carnivores to eat them. Certainly the most devastating meat eater of the region was the dire wolf. With its wolf build, wolf wile, wolf endurance, and better-than-wolf size, plus a fearful hyenalike turn of mind, this animal was made to order to terrorize the hoofed fauna of the land. It was the dire wolf that perfected the art of hunting in packs, of cutting one prey animal aside, hamstringing it and eating it from one end before it had fully expired on the other, and crushing its bones for their marrow.

Prides of lions stalked the big game of this late Pleistocene Coastal Plain. They resembled the modern African lion so closely that only a paleontologist can detect skeletal differences between the two.

The tapirs and the peccaries were surely aware of another predator that lay in silent ambush beside their forest trails. Even young mastodons were regularly pulled down by the sabertooth cat. This was an especially powerful, stump-tailed animal with enlarged canines, bulging neck muscles, and heavy forequarters geared to its particular mode of assassination. The sabertooth was the master of the patient stalk, the swift leap, and the dagger thrust into the neck, accompanied by a bull-dog grip and raking, disemboweling hind claws.

What became of them all? Even paleontologists are not sure. Wide-spread extinction swept through all of the large North American mammals in the late Pleistocene. Some investigators suggest a nebulous "shift in climate and vegetation" as the cause, but their primary grounds are simply that the animals disappeared. Lately a less pleasing but very credible disruptive force has been proposed: the coincidental appearance in North America at just this time of early man with his cunning and his hunting technology. Did prehistoric men wipe out the Pleistocene herds? It is a sobering suggestion.

You will probably not find evidence of ancient life on the Aransas. Despite the yield at the Tedford Pit, the young coastal sands are ill-suited to mineralizing organic remains and so are not particularly fossiliferous. You might be alert for a fossil horse tooth washing from the shoreline of the bay, but your chances of success are so slight that it is better to count on looking at the display of fossils in the WIC. However, keep your eyes open. In 1992, a group of visiting schoolchildren discovered huge bones washing out of a clay bank on the bayshore near the Bay Overlook. (Imagine their delight!) The find has not been completely analyzed, but it includes the limb bones and tusk of a mastodon, the bones of a mammoth, the remains of two kinds of ground sloths and a large terrestrial tortoise, and scattered teeth of horses and bison. Perhaps this rich concentration of carcasses was deposited in the sediments of a prehistoric river after the animals were drowned in a flood. Eventually the fossils will be displayed in the WIC.

Of course, most of the fragmented oystershells along the Heron Flats Trail date from the late Pleistocene or Holocene, so they are of fossil age, but they are hardly inspiring to observe. Excellent displays of the prehistoric life of Texas can be viewed at the Texas Memorial Museum in Austin, and there are some exhibits of coastal fossils in the Natural History Museum in Corpus Christi.

CHAPTER 2

The Land — Where It Fits

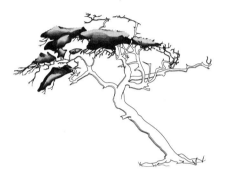

The Aransas National Wildlife Refuge is centered at 96°48′ west longitude and 28°16′ north latitude and makes up portions of Aransas, Refugio, and Calhoun counties in the state of Texas. The location of the refuge at the southern end of the Great Plains, which sweep down across the continent from Canada, has much to do with its ecology. The site straddles a critical transition zone on the east-to-west moisture gradient across the state, and it is near the middle of the north-to-south shift from temperate to tropical temperature regimes.

Because of its proximity to the Gulf of Mexico, the Aransas harbors a fluctuating combination of terrestrial and aquatic communities across a salinity gradient, from fresh through brackish to marine and even to hypersaline. The position of the refuge in the arc of the Gulf shoreline (the Coastal Bend) has implications for the water circulation in the surrounding bays, the degree of wind-generated sand erosion, and the subtle thinning of the coastal vegetation. Its position relative to the Gulf of Mexico and to the tropics makes the Aransas a critical bottleneck along the great Central Flyway, the ages-old route for millions of migratory birds. This coincidence of geography and ecology has prompted biogeographers to regard the Aransas and its environs as a veritable biological crossroads where a wonderful diversity of plants and animals meet and mingle, migrate and reside.

Physiography

The Aransas Refuge lies on the outer perimeter of the Coastal Plain Physiographic Province, that vast outwash of imperceptibly tilted land stretching south and east from the Balcones Escarpment to encompass over a third of Texas. Much of this open country originally supported unbroken tall- and mid-grass prairie and a thin hardwood savannah.

The Aransas Refuge is included in the subdivision of the coastal plain designated the coastal prairie, a strip of land paralleling the coast and spreading inland about forty miles. It stretches from the Louisiana border to Baffin Bay below Corpus Christi. Although interrupted by riparian forests and indented by marshland, this flat coastal sector is basically grassland. The immediate shoreline and the offshore barrier islands are under the direct influence of the Gulf of Mexico, and there the vegetation is specially adapted to tolerate proximity to the sea.

The coastal prairie changes from north to south, most noticeably at the mouth of the Guadalupe River just north of the Aransas Refuge. Here the curve of the coastline alters the angle at which the prevailing southeasterly winds strike the landmass. This affects the pattern of rainfall. North of the Guadalupe the coastal prairie is wetter and it is less prone to summer drought, so it supports a sward of tall grasses and luxuriant salt marshes. South of the river the prairie is drier and summers are often rainless, so it can support only short grasses and the salt marshes give way to muddy tidal flats studded with mats of low herbs and shrubs. With sparser vegetation, the southern sector is also subject to more severe wind erosion. The refuge lies directly in the transition zone.

The major bodies of water surrounding the Aransas Refuge are San Antonio, Aransas, and St. Charles bays (Figure 4). All contribute to the well-being of the fringing tidal flats, and their associated marine life works its way into every important food chain on Blackjack Peninsula. St. Charles Bay has tidal access into Burgentine and Goose lakes and into both Big Devil and Little Devil bayous on the west side of the refuge. San Antonio Bay routinely inundates Heron Flats, and on exceptionally high tides it floods the area beneath the boardwalk at the observation tower. Mustang Lake is directly connected to San Antonio Bay. Aransas Bay borders the southern tip of Blackjack Peninsula and frequently washes across the broad tidal flats on Blackjack and Dunham points. Along the southeastern margin of the refuge, between San Antonio Bay and Aransas Bay, a series of oystershell reefs has cordoned off several minor bodies of water: Ayers, Mesquite, and San Carlos bays. The Gulf Intracoastal Waterway, a channel for commercial water transport dredged 12 feet deep and 125 feet wide, brushes the eastern edge of Blackjack Peninsula as it passes between Aransas and San Antonio bays.

Because these bays are shallow, their fine sediments are easily roiled by the wind, keeping them too turbid and unstable to support much rooted vegetation. Diatoms, dinoflagellates, widgeon grass, shoalgrass, and detritus form the basis for the marine food chains. Salinity in the

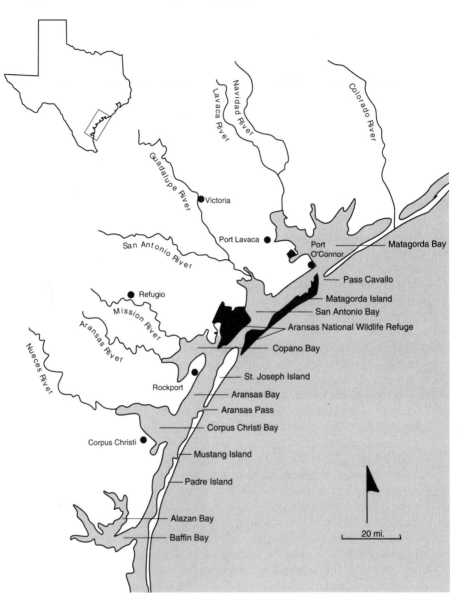

Figure 7. Geography of the Texas Coastal Bend.

bays fluctuates from virtually fresh to hypersaline but averages about 22 parts per thousand (ppt), lower than the open Gulf's nearly constant salinity of about 33 ppt. At the height of a drought in 1956, the lower part of San Antonio Bay registered a devastating 50 ppt. When the drought broke in 1957, the salinity of the bays plunged to less than 1 ppt—fresh enough for human consumption but lethal for most marine organisms. Water temperature in the bays is equally changeable and occasionally extreme. Sometimes the shallows are hot enough to drive out nearly all dissolved oxygen; now and then they freeze. To escape these extremes, marine creatures swim into deeper channels or move through the passes into the Gulf, or they sink into the mud. All vicissitudes in the bays eventually affect the well-being of the surrounding communities of life on land.

The presence of Matagorda and nearby St. Joseph islands about 5 miles at sea renders the bays a sequestered, somewhat independent marine system. Salt water flushes in through Pass Cavallo 30 miles up the coast at the north end of Matagorda Island and at Aransas Pass 25 miles down the coast at the south end of St. Joseph. Cedar Bayou, a narrow cut between the two islands directly opposite the refuge, can be an important exchange point, but it is commonly filled with sand. This natural pass was purposely plugged in 1979 to protect the bays from the Ixtoc oil spill in Mexico. Hurricane Allen partly opened the waterway the following year, but by 1985 it had filled with sand. In 1988, Cedar Bayou was dredged clear, and it has remained open to date. When this small pass is open, the abundance of marine life in the adjacent bays increases and more birds enjoy nesting success on the nearby oystershell reefs.

As far as the Aransas Refuge is concerned, the principal freshwater input into the bays is from the Guadalupe River, and primarily because of its influence, there is a tendency for water in the local bays to flow southward past the Aransas. There is always a marked salinity drop in the direction of the river mouth. After floods, clumps of uprooted water hyacinths, logs, and other riverine debris are deposited along the east shore of Blackjack Peninsula.

Tides along the Texas coast routinely range only one to two feet; strong winds are often more significant in moving the water in the shallow bays. But tides are important in maintaining the tidal flats and in promoting a flushing of the bays through the passes. At certain times of the year the fickle Texas tides may hold high or low for a week or more. Prolonged high tides cover the mud flats, forcing shorebirds into less favorable foraging areas. Conversely, low tides entice the birds to feast on the exposed marine worms, molluscs, and crustaceans.

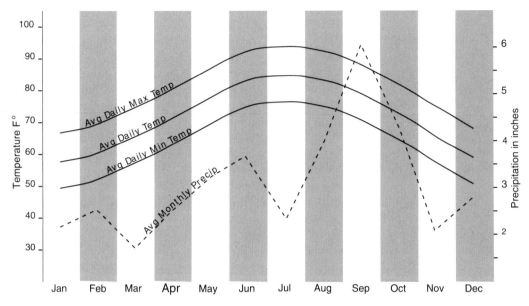

Figure 8. Average monthly temperature and precipitation on the Aransas National Wildlife Refuge. Data are from the national Weather Service and the Bureau of Business Research, University of Texas at Austin.

Climate

The term "weather" refers to short-term meteorological conditions, and "climate" implies long-term trends in weather patterns. Texas weather is notoriously capricious, but the climate of the state can be reliably described. Figure 8 summarizes pertinent climatic data collected on the Aransas over the past four decades. Although the main components of the climate of the Coastal Bend are easy enough to describe, they take on ecological significance only when considered in concert. We have tried to indicate some of this interaction as each component is briefly described.

Precipitation

Rainfall, which makes the difference between a desert and a swamp, between a good year and a disastrous one, is of outstanding importance to the biota of any region. Adequate rainfall affects animals in a multitude of ways, direct and indirect: drinking water, reproductive sites, hunting grounds, soil texture, ease of navigation, incidence of parasites, abundance of prey. Too much rain or untimely rain can drown plants and animals or cancel their reproductive efforts. More fundamentally, both the total amount and the annual distribution of rainfall dictate the type and quantity of vegetation, which in turn determines what animals can find shelter and food in the region.

A routinely dry spring on the Aransas Refuge promotes the nesting success of eastern meadowlarks, dickcissels, bobwhite quail, and Attwater's prairie chickens. However, a dry spring followed by a dry summer rapidly draws down the waterholes. Hatchling mottled ducks and black-bellied whistling-ducks are exposed to excessive predation, young meadowlarks and quail find less cover and fewer insects, and everything from javelinas to alligators is forced into a constant search for fresh water. The stress of dehydration is especially hard on newborn animals, amphibians, land snails, and seedling plants.

Of course, timely rainfall benefits vegetation and animals alike, and good fall rains are vital for the well-being of winter waterfowl. But excessive, prolonged, or unseasonal precipitation can wreak havoc: drowned upland bird nests, flooded rodent runways, poor fawn survival, hoof disease among the deer and swine, reduced acorn crop, poor yield of grass seeds, lowered salinity in the tidal flats, soil erosion, soil waterlogging, nutrient leaching, hordes of voracious mosquitoes.

Average annual rainfall decreases southward down the Texas coast. This decrease takes a noticeable dive in the Coastal Bend. The average annual rainfall on the Aransas is 37.82 inches. In the wettest year on record (1979), 64.23 inches of rain accumulated; in the driest (1950), only 17.36 inches were received. Although Hurricane Beulah (1967) inundated the refuge with a record 20.44-inch rainfall, the heaviest single cloudburst came from an unnamed tropical depression in October 1974, which dropped 14.25 inches in six hours. Notable droughts occurred in 1950–1956, 1962–1965, and 1982–1990. The combination of hurricanes Beulah and Celia left much of the refuge under intermittent standing water during 1967–1970. A string of wet years spanned 1968–1975, and the early nineties seem to be starting another wet cycle.

You can see the annual pattern of rainfall on the refuge in Figure 8. A moderate amount of rain falls each month, with an increase in the spring and a peak in late summer–early fall. But what you cannot see is that even when the Aransas receives its average annual dole of rain, it actually suffers from a chronic deficiency of fresh water.

The tug-of-war between abundant moisture from the Gulf of Mexico and a very porous sandy substrate makes the Aransas Refuge prone to oscillation from extreme dryness to flood and back again, often in only a few months. Figure 9 indicates the sort of wet and dry cycles that have occurred in the area over the last five decades.

Despite the uncomfortably high humidity (an annual average of

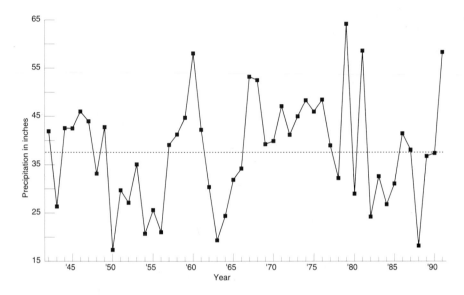

Figure 9. Annual rainfall on the Aransas National Wildlife Refuge, 1942–1991. The 49-year-average, indicated by the dotted line, is 37.82 inches. Data are from the files of the ANWR.

89 percent at dawn decreasing only to 60 percent by noon), the omnipresent wind causes rapid evaporation. The prevailing high air temperature increases the water-drawing capacity of the atmosphere. On the Aransas Refuge an open pan of water would lose twelve inches more fluid to evaporation in a year than it would gain from rainfall.

Finally, the nonabsorbent sand allows rapid percolation of rainwater below the root zone. Because of the sand, even relatively large bodies of water like Jones Lake and Hog Lake are rapidly drawn down when the rains fail. Despite numerous input channels and a restraining dike, Burgentine Lake, the largest inland body of water on the refuge, sometimes goes bone dry.

No wonder, then, that on the Aransas most of the plants and animals have water-conserving adaptations, some of which rival those of desert dwellers.

Temperature

Temperature has as pervasive an impact on a region as rainfall, and the effects of the two work together. We know that cold and wet does not feel the same as cold and dry, nor is hot and dry so uncomfortable as hot and wet. Plants and animals have comparable responses.

The gently sweeping curves in Figure 8 reflect the moderating influence of the Gulf of Mexico on the area's annual temperature. The summertime peak is smoothed by the coastal breeze, and the wintertime trough is constrained by the heat contained in the vast body of water.

The average annual temperature on the refuge is 70.8° F. The coldest month (January) averages 54.9° F; the warmest months (July and August) average 84.0° F. But averages can be deceiving. During a normal year the temperature climbs to 90° F or above on 77 days and drops to 32° F or below on 10 days. The summer of 1983, for instance, was a scorcher, with the temperature reaching or exceeding 90° F for weeks in succession. Then in December of that year the mercury hovered at or below freezing for 10 consecutive days and dipped to a low of 13° F, freezing the bays. In February of 1989 the refuge was closed for 2 days in the midst of an ice storm, yet before the end of March of that same year the temperature shot above 90° F.

The interplay of its subtropical position and the sweep of open country to the north makes the Texas coastal prairie liable to wildly fluctuating winter temperatures. One can easily go from sweating to shivering in a few hours when a howling norther abruptly sweeps out a muggy coastal air mass. Such shifts play havoc with both temperaments and immune systems.

Whereas the average monthly temperatures dictate the well-being of the plants and animals that live on the Aransas, it is the extremes, and especially the duration of extremes, that determine what kinds of creatures can permanently reside in the area. A meaningful expression of the low temperature extreme for plants and for cold-sensitive animals is the average number of frost-free days in a year. This so-called growing season for the Aransas Refuge is a generous 312 days. The average date of the first fall frost is December 16; of the last spring frost, February 7. Freezing temperatures usually occur for only an hour or two before sunrise about ten times a year.

Despite short, mild winters, temperature drops are often rapid and wind chill on the bays can be brutal. Occasionally the bays develop a light crust of ice, and they may cool rapidly enough to cause significant fish kills. On the other hand, the dog days of July can shrivel fruit on the vine and drive oxygen from the water, taking a toll of creatures that lack the appropriate escape behavior. The all-time extreme temperatures recorded on the refuge are 9° F (December 1989) and 103° F (June 1953, August 1955). Extremes of heat or cold exercise a culling effect, eradicating pioneer colonies of less-suited organisms that have entered the region during benign intervals. Ultimately such selective elimination produces what we recognize as the well-adjusted, natural biota.

Wind

To the casual visitor the chief importance of the wind is how efficiently it holds down the mosquitoes. As a matter of fact, many of the animals on the refuge enjoy that benefit. Deer sometimes succumb to what can only be called "mosquito stress"—a chronic malaise and debilitation brought on by continual harassment by clouds of these ravenous insects—and nestling birds can be severely weakened from being drained by mosquitoes. But there is more than that to wind as a coastal climatic factor. Wind (in this case, routine air currents; we consider storms below) has two kinds of major influences on a region.

First, there is its direct mechanical impact. The persistent force of the wind can sculpt a live oak tree, provide lift to a turkey vulture, tumble a grain of sand, misdirect a moth into a spider web, waft a pollen grain, and puff a milkweed seed out of sight. The wind can move water, piling it into waves and streaming it into currents; and the waves and currents will have telling effects of their own.

The wind also has an indirect influence on temperature and moisture by way of evaporative cooling, wind chill, and the passage of weather fronts. The prevailing breeze keeps man and beast from gagging during the sultry coastal summer. If you step into the stagnant air on the lee side of a live oak motte (its wind shadow) on a July afternoon, you will discover the misery of combined heat and humidity without significant air movement. Truly, in this steamy coastal country wind-generated evaporative cooling is the very breath of life.

The Aransas Refuge experiences two annual wind regimes: moderate southeasterlies, persistent from March through November, and brief, gusty northerlies from December through February. The direction and frequency of these winds are suggested by the wind rose in Figure 10, which is actually based on records for Corpus Christi, fifty miles down the coast.

Because of their abrupt arrivals with high energy and low temperatures, the northers have special impact on the coast. Tardy fall migratory birds use the early northers as welcome tail winds, but spring migrants encounter late northers as strong, energy-sapping head winds. Most nonmigratory animals simply hunker down during the worst of the blows. A strong norther drives water in the bays against southern and western shores, where it causes significant bankside erosion. At the same time, on the north shore the water level may drop by as much as

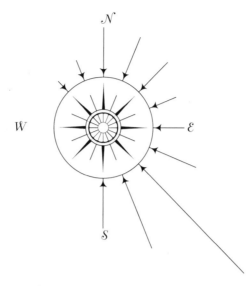

Figure 10. Surface winds at Corpus Christi, Texas. Direction is shown by arrowhead. The length of each line indicates the relative amount of time the wind blows in that direction. Data are from the National Weather Service and the Bureau of Economic Geology, University of Texas at Austin.

two feet, sometimes rapidly enough to expose and kill tidal-flat fauna. The bays churn brown during northers, and much of this sediment is flushed out the passes on high ebb currents. Most northers blow through in 48 to 72 hours, and the cool air often sets off valuable winter rainfall.

Storms

Violent tropical depressions and full-blown hurricanes regularly wheel out of the Gulf of Mexico and slam into the Texas Coast. Historically the sector of the Coastal Bend that includes the Aransas Refuge has experienced a hurricane landfall once every five years. These great cyclones can be expected anytime from late June through early November, with peak frequency in August and September.

A hurricane can wreak more havoc in a few hours than quieter natural forces could effect in years. Direct battering by cyclonic winds, torrential rainfall, and tidal surge are the principal elements of devastation. Much wildlife is killed outright, and much more is displaced.

Plants may be torn asunder or killed by flooding or saltwater incursion. The bays may be fresh for weeks on end from heavy runoff, and the marine fauna suffers and is dislocated. Massive amounts of sand are heaved about. Some areas undergo severe erosion while others experience accretion. Tidal passes are routinely occluded or reopened during storms.

Over the past three decades the Aransas has weathered its share of hurricanes. Carla (1961) sent a ten-foot tidal surge over the barrier islands and across San Antonio Bay, pounding the mainland shoreline and inundating all low-lying areas with salt water. Beulah (1967) brought six-foot tides and torrential rains. The prolonged runoff from Beulah swamped the refuge, washed out roads, and freshened the bays for months. Before the accumulation drained away, tropical storm Candy (1968) dropped a twenty-inch downpour on the soggy refuge. Hurricane Celia (1970) left twelve inches of rain and blew the weather record book away. Paradoxically, behemoth Hurricane Allen (1980) produced only moderate local winds and tides and a much-needed five-inch rainfall. Waves whipped up by Hurricane Gilbert (1988) accelerated shoreline erosion between headquarters and the observation tower and pushed salt water into Cattail Slough on the Heron Flats Trail.

Despite the evident misery and destruction that attend the passage of a hurricane, Nature suffers less lasting damage than do man and his accoutrements. Hurricanes are, after all, natural phenomena to which the coastal biota is adapted. It is indeed an ill wind that blows no good. The rapidly shifting, violent cyclonic air currents whirl across the shallow bays like huge eggbeaters, whipping up sediments and pollutants and eventually heaving them into the Gulf. When conditions settle down, the recently flushed bays put on a fresh surge of marine life, which eventually works into the inland food chains. Resident populations soon resurge, often with renewed vigor.

Many a hurricane has been a boon to the parched Texas coast when it brought life-giving rather than life-threatening rains. Even the manifest death that a severe hurricane levies on vegetation and wildlife has its ecological compensation: storm action culls out weedy and interloping species and thus preserves the natural coastal mix of biota. Several weeks after a hurricane the most evident damage on the refuge, aside from standing water and a scattering of debris, is to the roadways and buildings.

Finally, the awesome tempests add their own inimitable brand of savagery to an already wild landscape of which they are a natural component. Part of the provocative spirit of the coastal country resides in its potential for awe-inspiring, humbling cyclonic cataclysm. To quell that threat would be to tame the land, and that is not what a refuge is all about.

Biota

The assemblage of plants and animals residing on the Aransas Refuge today is the current biotic response to the blend of components that makes up the physical environment.

If we accept the principles of organic evolution, then we admit that each kind of creature gradually diverged from its ancestors over a span of time in a given geographic locality. Since the refuge is too young geologically and too small geographically to have served as the spawning ground for any of its resident species, it follows that all must have come here by their own random wanderings and according to their individual fortunes.

Once here, pioneers of each species had to tolerate the averages and withstand the extremes of the coastal environment. Equally important, they had to establish a thriving population of reproducing individuals that adapted to and finally gained a firm foothold on Blackjack Peninsula and its environs. In addition to becoming attuned to climate and terrain, each newly arrived species faced the difficult task of working its way in among those species already established. Competition, predation, or simply failure to adapt thwarted many would-be colonists; what you see on the refuge today is the ones that managed to survive.

While men have been on the land, beginning with the earliest prehistoric hunters, the biota has also had to contend with the human element and more recently with the host of domestic and feral plants and animals introduced here by people.

Humans have had another significant impact upon the distribution of the local biota. Ancient routes of dispersal have been closed by the clearing of enormous stretches of surrounding land for agriculture and sundry development. The refuge is a biological island isolated in a sterile sea of human activity. Nowadays when a resident population is reduced or extirpated, there is scant chance for natural restocking, and even in the best of times the ills that go with excessive inbreeding become a concern.

Where did the current biota on the Aransas Refuge come from? The best answer is simply from hither and yon, implying that lines of dispersal trace back to many parts of the Western world. But we can be more specific about a few of the larger creatures and some of the plants. For these, the immediate ancestors did not come from very far away; in many cases we know the direction of their homeland.

Many residents on the Aransas have affinities with the moist south-eastern Atlantic seaboard. Both the green treefrog and the squirrel tree-frog find their limit of tolerance to dehydration on the refuge. So does the curious little eastern narrow-mouthed toad. Among the lizards, the ground skink hails from the humus-laden forests of the east, and the slender glass lizard from the sandy land of the deep Southeast. Snakes with eastern ranges that do not continue westward much beyond the Aransas include the mud snake, eastern hognose snake, prairie king-snake, and western cottonmouth. And of course there is the alligator, a creature of the antediluvial swamplands if there ever was one.

Despite their high mobility, some eastern birds show up just of-ten enough to put the refuge at the western limit of their range: blue jays, eastern bluebirds, Carolina chickadees, tufted titmice, red-headed woodpeckers, red-shouldered hawks, American crows. Swainson's war-blers, more at home in the swamplands of deep East Texas, regularly nest on the Aransas. Eastern mammals include the fox squirrel, least shrew, eastern mole, swamp rabbit, and marsh rice rat.

The wave of eastern immigrants is not limited to animals. Red bay, yaupon, tree huckleberry, dwarf palmetto, poison ivy, greenbriar, Span-ish moss, live oak, and even the peninsula's namesake—blackjack oak—all hark to the east.

The biogeographic pursuit takes on added interest when one can find complementary species each reaching range limits in the same area: where one leaves off the other takes over. The Aransas Refuge is a meet-ing ground of many such pairs: southern and Rio Grande leopard frogs, Mississippi and yellow mud turtles, Texas and checkered garter snakes, red-bellied and golden-fronted woodpeckers, great crested and ash-throated flycatchers, northern cardinals and pyrrhuloxias, prickly ash and lime prickly ash, sugar and netleaf hackberry, broomsedge and cane bluestem.

The story is the same for the other cardinal directions: western dia-mondback rattlesnakes, western kingbirds, lark buntings, retama, and tanglewood from the west; Attwater's prairie chickens, short-eared owls, ferruginous hawks, and grama grasses down from the plains to the north; pigmy mice, jaguarundis, golden-silk spiders, groove-billed anis, tropical parulas, pauraques, cayenne ticks, Texas torchwood, and spiny hackberries up from the south; diamondback terrapins, fiddler crabs, clapper rails, bushy sea ox-eye, and marshhay cordgrass in from the Gulf. Those are joined by hundreds of thousands of migrating water-fowl, perching birds, and monarch butterflies as well as seasonal move-ments of marine fishes and crustaceans.

To this wild bustle we must add the introduced species: feral hogs, European starlings and house sparrows, domestic cattle, imported red fire ants, Bermuda and St. Augustine grass, Chinese tallow and petticoat palm trees. And people.

If your interest is piqued by the distributions of wild creatures, you might ponder some biogeographic puzzles associated with the Aransas Refuge. Why are there no kangaroo rats on the peninsula's extensive sandy land when these rodents abound on many of the adjacent barrier islands and the southern mainland? Why have badgers virtually disappeared despite the abundance of pocket gophers, their potential prey? Why are there no earless lizards or indigo snakes? Why did the bald eagles abandon their traditional nesting sites on the refuge? Why have the jackrabbits virtually disappeared and the ground squirrels become locally extinct? Why has the refuge's once vigorous population of Rio Grande turkeys dwindled to near extinction? Why are horned lizards more common on the barrier islands than on the mainland? Is the refuge suffering an ecological malaise, or are such turnovers a normal sequence of events? We can only speculate.

CHAPTER 3

The Land—How It Works

Regardless of their specific interests, most visitors to the Aransas National Wildlife Refuge spend some time on the observation tower. The forty-foot-high deck of the tower is not only a good spot from which to view wildlife, especially birds, but it also offers the best vantage to take in the sweep of the marvelous ecosystem to which the refuge is dedicated.

Climb the ramp to the deck and behold the grand coming-together of sky, wind, water, and land. You can scan the length and breadth of Mustang Lake and work your binoculars along its fringing marshes and tidal flats. Elevate your view across the spoil islands to the southeast; maybe you can make out one of the green channel markers that delimit the busy Gulf Intracoastal Waterway. Turn due east and gaze across San Antonio Bay; with the help of an afternoon sun you should be able to discern the bright strip of oystershell on the lee side of Matagorda Island five miles away.

Turn to the west and you will be looking across the interior of Blackjack Peninsula. Most of the dense tree canopy is composed of the crowns of live oaks. Here and there you might note a grassy opening or a clump of reeds. Can you detect the subtle ridge-and-swale undulation in the tiers of oaks? Certainly you cannot miss the beautiful wind sculpture so evident in the trees along the west bank of Mustang Lake and in those just north of the boardwalk on the edge of the bay. As you gaze out across the unmarred greenery, savor the splendid feeling of pristine isolation.

Finally, turn to the north and look up the paved road. At a break in the trees just to the west of the road and two hundred yards distant, you should see the tops of rattlepods, cattails, reeds, and other bankside vegetation bordering Hog and Jones lakes. Sometimes you can even glimpse the sparkle of the lakes themselves.

Check the sky, especially early and late in the day, to enjoy the shifting pastels and ever-changing shapes of the stupendous Gulf clouds.

Now reflect on your panoramic view. You have looked down on the three major ecological divisions of the Aransas Refuge: marine (saltwater), terrestrial, and freshwater. Doubtless you have observed some birds or other creatures as well as several different kinds of plants. How do they all fit together, know what to do, meet their separate needs, and survive day in and day out and through good seasons and bad? What vital interactions go on in the living fabric all around you that prevent it from unraveling? What makes this wonderful land work?

When you ponder questions like these you are going beyond simple wildlife observation into a quest for ecological understanding. The pursuit will give you a fresh appreciation for nature as well as for the necessity of several management practices intended to ensure the perpetuation of the natural cycles on the refuge.

The essence of ecology is the interrelations between living things. Before deriving a few principles of ecology, let's take a closer look at how creatures interact.

About halfway along the Big Tree Trail you will come to a stand of large, particularly impressive live oak trees with widespread branches. They are probably the oldest living organisms on the Aransas Refuge. The acorns that spawned this magnificent grove of oaks sprouted just about the time that Alvar Núñez Cabeza de Vaca began his odyssey along the Texas coast almost five hundred years ago. Since then these iron trees have taken everything that nature has thrown against them. How do these fine old live oaks interweave with the lives of other creatures in this woods?

Look up. You cannot miss the hollows. Hollows are homes. Homes for raccoons, opossums, and fox squirrels; for daddy longlegs, cobweb spiders, and centipedes; even for an occasional hive of honeybees or a small colony of roosting pipistrelles (bats).

The deep cracks in the bark serve as feeding sites, temporary shelters, and homes for a welter of tiny creatures: beetles, ants, bark lice, springtails, millipedes, spiders, pseudoscorpions, mites. Some of the cracks retain enough moisture and debris to nourish clumps of ball moss and festoons of Spanish moss. Depending on their exposure to wind and sunshine, the intervening bark ridges may support a covering of ash-gray lichen (how many different growth forms can you recognize?) or a green cushion of true moss. If you look closely you may find a tiny hairy caterpillar munching on the lichen. One day it will pupate and turn into—what else?—a small gray lichen moth. Although it will be below your ken, rest assured that the moist interior of the true-moss forest harbors its own menagerie of minuscule fly larvae, rotifers, and nematode worms.

Look among the leafy branches. Can you spot a spider's web? A paper-wasp nest? A ragged wad of dead leaves where a fox squirrel takes its summer nap? A caterpillar-chewed leaf? You may have to use your mind's eye to visualize the aphids, tree crickets, thrips, praying

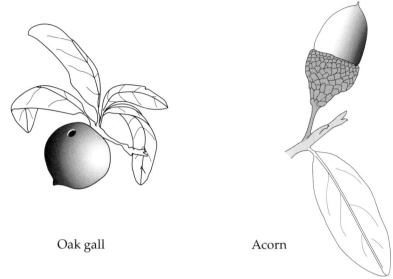

Oak gall   Acorn

mantids, jumping spiders, green anoles, and whatnot that populate the higher foliage.

Sit awhile. Depending on the season, you may see an orange-crowned warbler, a blue-gray gnatcatcher, or a Carolina wren flit through the branches in beady-eyed pursuit of tiny insects. Maybe a ladder-backed woodpecker will hunch along a dead branch, pausing now and then to hammer after beetle grubs beneath the flaking bark. If your visit coincides with spring migration, you may be treated to a warbler fallout, when these live oak branches are alive with colorful, hungry wood warblers of a dozen fidgety species.

Be very still. Perhaps a sharp-shinned hawk or an American kestrel will alight briefly while it scans the surroundings for prey. The hawk can knock an unwary mourning dove from midair; the kestrel will be satisfied with a large grasshopper plucked from the grass. By night a great horned owl will replace the daytime raptors, alert for a white-footed mouse or a cotton rat scurrying across the ground.

Look closely among the tips of the branches for round, marble-sized oak galls, symmetrical swellings produced by the tree in response to the egg-laying habits of tiny wasps. Fresh galls will contain wasp larvae; old ones serve as ready-made domiciles for tiny spiders or colonies of highly specialized carpenter ants.

You can readily recognize another, more familiar kind of object among the branches as acorns. If there are none on the tree, you should be able to find remains of them on the ground. Through the medium of its nutritious acorns the live oak tree works into the lives of a great array of creatures: feral hogs, javelinas, and white-tailed deer; fox squirrels, raccoons, and opossums; coyotes and gray foxes; white-footed mice and pocket gophers; whooping cranes, sandhill cranes, wild turkeys, and bobwhite quail; wood ducks and pintail ducks and Canada and snow geese. Even small birds like Carolina chickadees and tufted titmice eagerly eat up crumbs of acorns that stronger creatures have cracked open. It is little wonder that the live oak acorn is regarded as one of the principal wildlife food resources on the refuge.

We are not done with acorns yet. Pick up a handful of old ones from the ground. Some are sure to be drilled with a neat round hole, the exit portal of an acorn weevil that lived inside the acorn as a larva. A hole clogged with webbing indicates that the caterpillar of an acorn moth has appropriated the acorn to feed on what the weevil missed and to snuggle there until winter is over.

Old, thin-shelled acorns have been partially consumed by fungi. Mites and springtails eat the fungi. In turn, predatory pseudoscorpions stalk those tiny creatures. Finally, bacteria and fungi that produce cellulose-digesting enzymes cause the complete deterioration of the acorn and its contained fecal pellets. The released minerals may return to the live oak through its roots and so begins another round of transformations.

While you have your thoughts on the ground beneath the live oak, visualize the enormous root system with its miles of tiny root hairs sucking up gallons of soil water and absorbing soil minerals by the ounce. Look at the layers of decaying leaves, all leaking growth-inhibiting tannins, which prevent many competing plants from growing directly beneath the oak. Note the patch of shade and its influence on the undergrowth. Move aside a fallen branch. Perhaps you will startle a ground skink or a least shrew from its daytime hiding place. Or maybe you will expose a field cricket, a roach, or one end of an earthworm—all prime victuals for an armadillo or for an eastern mole.

As a final gesture, glance up at the leaves again and think: photosynthesis, oxygen, and carbon dioxide. Have *you* thanked a green plant today?

How many kinds of creatures are mentioned in this brief sketch of live oak ecology? What if we had gone into detail? Extrapolate these sorts of interconnections to every plant and animal that you have observed, and you will begin to grasp both the intricacy and the sheer wonderfulness of the ecology of the Aransas Refuge.

Community Ecology

When living creatures occupy the same area and display such a close-knit set of interactions that they form a single, recognizable interdependent entity, the ecologist refers to that assemblage as a *biotic com-*

munity. The community is the natural base unit of ecology. Before describing the several communities that occur on the refuge, we will briefly mention some of the properties common to them all. You may enjoy trying to discern these for yourself as you trek about.

Within the general confines of a community each of the several or many member species will have its favored *habitat*—the particular setting where it spends most of its time. Sanderling habitat is open shoreline. Fulvous harvest mouse habitat is dense tall grass. Bulrush habitat is shallow water over a muddy bottom. Its habitat is the creature's ecological address.

Many individual animals occupy a well-defined *home range* within their designated habitat. The home range always includes the creature's nesting and resting sites, its main sources of food and water, and all of the trails over which it routinely wanders. Its home range is that part of the habitat with which the individual is most familiar and therefore where it is most secure. The area may be shared, permanently or at least seasonally, with a mate or, in social animals, with a group of kindred individuals. Sizes of home ranges vary with the needs and the mobility of the animal: a square foot for a fiddler crab, less than half an acre for a white-footed mouse, 180 acres for a flock of prairie chickens, eight square miles for a group of coyotes. Generally, carnivores must roam over larger areas in search of prey than herbivores will traverse while foraging. So, the predaceous American kestrel sets up a winter home range on the refuge at least ten times as large as the winter feeding range of a flock of eastern meadowlarks.

Animals frequently mark and defend portions of their home ranges from trespass by members of their own kind. These patrolled areas are called *territories*. Ever watch two mockingbirds in a flutter-fight over a territorial boundary? Or have you seen a bobcat spray a quick jet of urine on a shrub? What about a green anole vigorously pumping his pink dewlap at a rival male? These ritualized behavior patterns are most often engaged in by males, and they serve to protect some concentrated vital resource (food, basking spot, nest site, receptive mate) without necessarily entailing debilitating physical combat.

The out-of-doors is laced with unnoticed posted signs and fencelines; learning to recognize them is both instructive and fun. You can begin by watching the flamboyant visual and acoustical displays of male redwinged blackbirds setting up their springtime nesting territories in the cattails along Thomas Slough. Or try deciphering the silent, semaphore-like gestures of the sand fiddler crabs at the end of the boardwalk. Or catch an acrid whiff emanating from a javelina-rubbed yaupon branch.

If its habitat is a creature's ecological address, then its *niche* (rhymes with "hitch") is its ecological job. The niche describes what the animal does for a living. Since animals spend most of their active lives searching for and consuming food, niches are usually defined by food habits. The niche of an eastern mole is succinctly expressed as fossorial insectivore (a burrowing insect eater). A red-tailed hawk fills the soaring diurnal raptor niche; a snowy egret the wading-and-spearing niche. The adult pipevine swallowtail butterfly is a nectar sipper, and its larva is a leaf chewer. A female saltmarsh mosquito is a flying bloodsucker. And so on.

It is a cardinal precept of ecology that no two species in the same community have precisely the same niche. When niches overlap, competition, especially for food, results. The spontaneous (not conscious) attempt to avoid competition compels each kind of creature to be a specialist in some manner of food-getting. Evolution of unique anatomy and behavior promotes specialization and results in the amazing diversity of life.

Once you know what to look for you can recognize the segregation of niches within any group of similar species in a community, for instance among shorebirds and waterfowl. From the observation tower use your binoculars to watch the birds at work in and around Mustang Lake in the fall and wintertime. First identify them properly, then watch what they are doing. Note the shapes and sizes of their bills, legs, and other parts that work in concert with differences in foraging behavior. Notice also that the several kinds of birds are somewhat separated by favoring different portions of the lake.

The wade-and-spear fishermen are easy to recognize: great blue heron, great and snowy egrets, little blue heron, tricolored heron, and reddish egret. Differences in lengths of neck, bill, and legs and differing hunting strategies bring in different prey. Watch an individual bird. What sort of fishing hole does it choose: shoreline or open water, shallow or deep, mucky or clear, brackish or fresh? How does it go about stalking and striking? Compare, say, the search behavior of a wildly pattering reddish egret with that of a silently advancing little blue heron or the subtle foot-stirring tactic of a snowy egret. How often does it succeed when it strikes? What, precisely, does it catch? Is its prey noticeably limited in size? When birds of two kinds meet, how do they react? Does one dominate, or do they ignore each other? Differences may seem to us to be slight, but they are vital in reducing competition among these spearfishing birds.

Whooping cranes occupy a slosh-and-scrounge niche. Cranes use their heavy bills more as picker-uppers than as spears. They stalk the tidal flats snapping up a variety of crustaceans, molluscs, and insects and also feed on sundry greenery and fruits.

The lakeshore also supports a variety of probers (common snipe, long-billed curlew, willet), pluckers (black-bellied plover, killdeer, greater yellowlegs), peckers (sora and clapper rails), and seedeaters (seaside and savannah sparrows). Other species of probers and pluckers prefer the open mud flats (long-billed dowitchers, dunlin, least and western sandpipers, sanderlings).

Again, watch these birds at work. Length of leg and toe, shape of neck, coloration of plumage, and bill type will mesh with feeding behavior to fit each species to its niche. You can learn a lot of wildlife biology by working out the various adaptive combinations, and you will never get bored just because all of the birds you see are common species.

Most of the ducks in this shallow lake will be dabblers—they upend but do not often dive (gadwall, American wigeon, northern pintail, northern shoveler), and the microarchitecture of their bills allows each species to exploit bottom sediment, floating seeds, and submerged vegetation in its own unique manner.

Pied-billed grebes and double-crested cormorants surface-dive for fish; Caspian and Forster's terns dive-bomb for them; white pelicans scoop them up; ring-billed gulls get them any way they can. You take it from there.

Food connections are so important to the integrity of every biotic community that ecologists have given them special emphasis. Straight-line eat-and-be-eaten sequences like the ones in Figure 11 are called *food chains*. A *food web* results from the intermeshing of the several food chains in a biotic community. Figure 12 shows a small segment of the winter food web that undergirds your view of Mustang Lake from the observation tower. Food webs are appropriately represented with plants at the base and chains extending and interlinking upward. Each

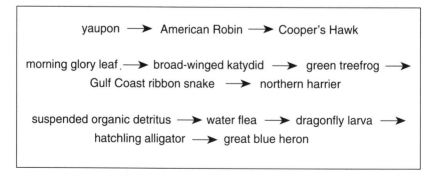

Figure 11. Examples of food chains on the Aransas.

species in the community can then be categorized according to the number of links in its food chain that separate it from the basic plant level. The major categories recognizable in any community are:

- Producers—convert sunlight to energy (green plants such as diatoms, Indian grass, yaupon).
- Herbivores—eat the plants (grasshoppers, white-tailed deer, mourning dove).
- First-level carnivores—eat the herbivores (western diamondback rattlesnake, bobcat, white-tailed hawk).
- Second-level carnivores—eat the first-level carnivores (peregrine falcon, southern leopard frog, alligator).
- Omnivores—eat a variety of plant and animal matter (opportunists such as coyote, raccoon, whooping crane, laughing gull).
- Detritivores—sift organic matter from substrate or water (ghost shrimp, earthworm, fiddler crab).
- Scavengers—specialize in carrion (turkey vulture, carrion beetle, blowfly maggot).
- Decomposers—transform organic material into simpler chemical components (bacteria, fungi).
- Parasites—draw nourishment from living hosts (deer liver fluke, Gulf Coast tick, saltmarsh mosquito).
- Saprophytes—absorb organic matter from sediment and soil (soil bacteria, puffballs, earthstars, mushrooms).

Can you place the creatures that you have seen on the refuge into one of these feeding categories?

When an animal consumes food it never gets out all of the potential calories. Some parts are rejected as inedible or unpalatable. Others are indigestible and so are expelled as feces or regurgitated as pellets. A significant fraction is simply dropped and scattered. Most of the food calories that are absorbed are expended in routine metabolism keeping the animal alive; relatively little is left over to go into growth and reproduction.

This dissipation of calories occurs at every link in a food chain, so there is a dwindling supply of energy as food chains lengthen. A useful geometrical analog to describe a community is a pyramid, with most of the biomass at the bottom and progressively less toward the top. Reflect on the many pounds of mouse and gopher meat there must be on the Aransas Refuge compared to the few pounds of great horned owl and bobcat meat. Many blue crabs, far fewer whooping cranes; many grasshoppers, not so many American kestrels; lots of deer, perhaps only one cougar. The relationship is inviolable: top-level creatures are always

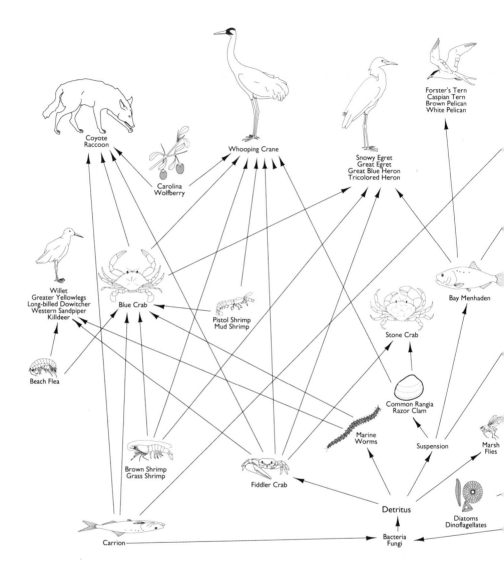

the least abundant in any biotic community. Things just cannot work otherwise.

A community has, at any given time, a *carrying capacity* for each of its component species. Every creature needs food and water to survive, and all have other vital needs as well: shelter, roaming ground, resting and nesting sites, access to members of the opposite sex. Clearly, any community has finite resources, and carrying capacity specifies the

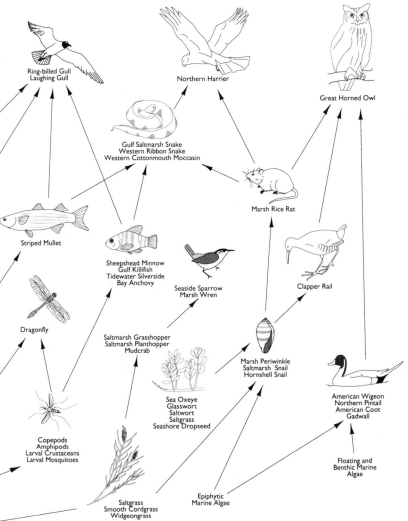

Figure 12. A small portion of the tangled winter food web at Mustang Lake. Arrowheads indicate the direction of consumption.

population level that can be adequately supported under current conditions. If the number of individuals gets too high, vigorous competition for dwindling resources degrades the environment and exhausts creatures in struggles to satisfy their needs. The actual number is not fixed: in a good year life gets easier and numbers rise; in a bad year carrying capacity drops, life gets harder, and populations die back. No matter the conditions, when a population exceeds the community's current carrying capacity, both the organisms and the environment suffer.

Generally, Mother Nature moves quickly to bring things back into balance, with grimly efficient tactics that are harsh by human standards. During such times, disease and predators take heavy tolls of debilitated populations. In 1968–1969, there was a tragic crash of the white-tailed deer population when the number of animals soared beyond the carrying capacity of the refuge. There is even concern that the population of whooping cranes is beginning to feel growing pains. Lately some birds have been establishing their territories outside the traditional wintering area on Blackjack Peninsula. It is nice to have more cranes, but there must be adequate protected tidal-flat habitat to support them. Acquisition of the Lamar and Matagorda units was motivated by this need.

And what about people? The Aransas Refuge has a definite carrying capacity for us too, a physical limit to how much touching, tromping, ogling, shouting, dust-raising, insect-spraying, and automobile exhaust the area can absorb without suffering lasting deterioration. There is also a social limit to how many people can simultaneously enjoy a quality experience in nature without interfering with each other.

What do you think the human carrying capacity is for the Heron Flats Trail, the observation tower, or the Tour Loop on a Sunday afternoon? With an annual visitation rate of about 65,000 and with certain months outstandingly popular (the peak usually comes during the four-day Thanksgiving holiday, when some 1,500 people sign the register), you may be sure that refuge personnel have given these questions considerable thought.

Stratification refers to the layering in a community. When we mentioned the living things associated with various levels in the live oak trees on the Big Tree Trail we were discussing vertical stratification. You can experience the shift directly if you observe the changes in the surrounding branches, foliage, insects, and birds as you climb the ramp to the observation tower. Even a grassland can exhibit vertical stratification on a small but vital scale. On a cold day with a biting north wind, a slender glass lizard can be quite comfortable snuggled in the depths of a clump of broomsedge bluestem.

Horizontal stratification in a community is always correlated with a horizontal gradient in some important environmental factor. From the end of the pier at Jones Lake, notice the concentric rings of vegetation bordering the water: lily pads floating waist deep, Egyptian panic grass and cattails emerging from shallower water; then a band of bushy bluestem grass around the edge; behind that a zone of rattlepod sprinkled with groundsel; finally live oak and yaupon.

Or traverse the boardwalk from the observation tower to the edge of San Antonio Bay and watch the changes as you progress along the gradients of salinity and moisture. Vegetation goes from large clumps of Gulf cordgrass on the inland edge through zones of bushy sea ox-eye, glasswort, and shoregrass to saltgrass, marsh elder, and marshhay cordgrass near the end of the boardwalk and finally to smooth cordgrass growing directly in the bay.

Although they are less clean-cut, there are zones of animal life associated with the plant zones.

Biotic communities develop and mature over time. The sequence of changes through which a maturing community passes is called *succession*. Each stage of succession in a community has a different constellation of species.

When a virgin area such as a fresh sand dune, a newly graded roadside, or a recently abandoned agricultural field is first exploited by living things, only the hardiest species can survive there. Candidates for this pioneer stage must be able to withstand direct sunlight, soil with a low organic content, open ground with few cubbyholes to dodge into, and the brunt of whatever bad weather comes along.

Gradually as the pioneers gain a foothold, their very presence and activities change the area. Shade and a veneer of topsoil appear; there are more places to hide and more things to eat. As the site becomes more favorable, less hardy species can successfully invade it. Slowly the pioneers, which thrive only on adversity, are pushed out and a new complex of species reigns. This second group continues to alter the environment simply by living in it, contributing to deeper soil, more diverse vegetation (including woody species), a more complex food web. A third and perhaps a fourth and a fifth stage follow, all with the same progressive trend.

Finally the community achieves climax: an equilibrium at which it supports the maximum diversity and abundance of creatures possible at that time and place. Until the climate changes or some natural or man-induced catastrophe occurs, the climax community bears pretty witness to the balance of Nature.

Even the Aransas Refuge is not pristine. The floral climax on Blackjack Peninsula was probably a chest-high mixed stand of seacoast bluestem and Indian grass with small mottes of live oaks on the hillocks and a dense growth of switch grass and sedges in the swales. Years of overgrazing by livestock and suppression of natural grass fires have shifted the vegetation in favor of the live oaks.

Certainly the best place to observe community succession on the refuge is on the constantly shifting sands of Matagorda Island. There you can actually walk backward in time by trekking from the beach inland across the progressively more vegetated dunes. We mentioned a much older example of the same phenomenon while discussing the Ingleside

Barrier and the ridge-and-swale topography on Blackjack Peninsula. Comparison of the vegetation on the three shell ridges along the Heron Flats Trail provides another good exercise in discerning succession; again, the younger terrain is closer to the bay.

You can see community succession on a recent time scale by observing the burned areas while you drive the Tour Loop. These deliberate burns are attempts by refuge personnel to return the interior of Blackjack Peninsula to its original savannahlike condition. Compare not just the regrowth of greenery but also the species composition between a burned and an unburned section. Can you age several burns by their degree of succession? Ask at the WIC to confirm your judgment.

Biotic Communities

Using round figures, we can begin the ecological organization of the mainland portion of the Aransas Refuge: The 8,500 acres of wetland includes 1,500 freshwater acres: and 7,000 saltwater acres. The 50,000 acres of upland is split between grassland (26,000 acres) and brushland (24,000 acres). We have recognized twelve biotic communities as indicated on the accompanying map (Figure 13). Six of these communities, representing a major component of the Aransas ecosystem and readily accessible to visitors, are presented first and in some detail. The others are relatively minor and occur on portions of the refuge that are not open to the public.

The plants and animals mentioned in the brief descriptions are characterized in later chapters and described fully in appropriate field guides. Once you know your creatures, you should gain an appreciation of the assemblage of living things that composes each community.

Shell Ridge Community

This is at once one of the smallest, most distinctive, most diverse, and most commonly visited communities on the refuge. To see it, trek the Heron Flats Trail. A brochure with a map, illustrations, and commentary keyed to numbered posts along the trail is available at the WIC.

The key feature of this community is the high lime content of the substrate, a result of its oystershell base. A unique assemblage of woody plants flourishes on the alkaline soil along the more mature inner ridge (the first half of the trail): Texas persimmon, tanglewood, Mexican buckeye, spiny and netleaf hackberries. The ubiquitous live oak dominates this stretch, and yaupon is a common understory shrub.

This community supports the greatest diversity of vines on the refuge: greenbriar, trumpet creeper, mustang grape, peppervine, Alamo

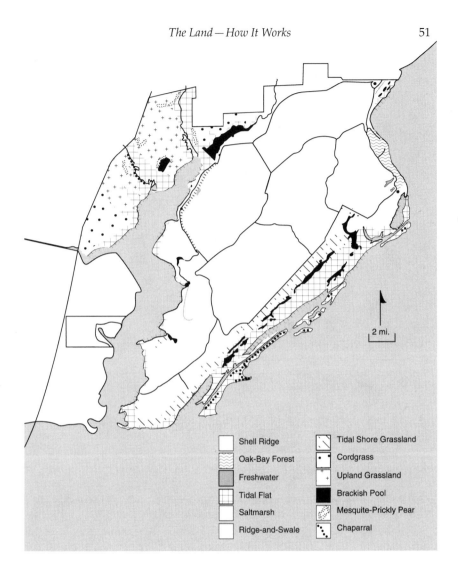

Figure 13. The major biotic communities on the mainland portion of the Aransas National Wildlife Refuge.

vine, poison ivy, milkweed vine, pearl milkweed, and more. Look for good growths of epiphytes (plants that grow on other plants): Spanish and ball moss, true mosses, fungi, and lichens. Deep shade limits understory plants, but watch for the shadow-loving Turk's cap and frostweed. The sunlit portions of the trail will yield a seasonal sampling of refuge wildflowers.

Signs of animal life are mostly limited to cryptic rustles. Ground skinks, wolf spiders, and white-footed mice skitter through the leaf litter. You might see northern fence lizards on the ground and tree trunks and green anoles, rough green snakes, and praying mantids in the branches. Perching birds such as cardinals and white-eyed vireos flit through the dense growth, but these will be difficult to observe. Most nocturnal creatures will be curled up in their daytime retreats: raccoons, opossums, striped skunks. You may run across a foraging armadillo.

After crossing the bridge over Cattail Slough (where you may be scolded by the dry chatter of wintering sedge wrens) you get onto the less fertile, brushy middle ridge. Here the trail courses through a dense stand of lime prickly ash, brasil, torchwood, and tanglewood punctuated with an occasional agarito, mesquite, and prickly pear.

When you gain the more geologically recent outer shell ridge there is less woody vegetation. Gulf cordgrass and marshhay cordgrass creep up from the tidal flat community that borders the bay. Groundsel, marsh elder, mesquite trees, and an occasional retama are scattered through the diversity of grass species along the trail. Watch for the pretty lilac flowers of snapdragon vine among the tangle of grasses and low branches. You cannot miss the impressive Spanish daggers that rise from the middle and outer ridges, and you should notice the leaning profile imparted to the vegetation by the prevailing onshore wind.

More than 150 species of plants have been identified in the shell ridge community, and even this list is not exhaustive. (See Appendix C for a seasonal summary of the flowering plants along the Heron Flats Trail.)

Oak-Bay Forest Community

Although no plant species is unique to this community, the distinctive assemblage of kinds reaches its finest growth on the deep sands that stretch along the bayshore between the Youth Environmental Training Area and the Big Tree Trail. Both the Dagger Point Trail and the Big Tree Trail afford intimate access, and the Wood Duck Pond Trail pushes into the dense midsection of the community. The edge of this forest can also be seen beyond all of the grassy clearings along the east side of the road between the Youth Environmental Training Area and the observation tower.

The oak-bay forest is composed mainly of live oak, red bay, and laurel oak. The branches of these trees are so intermeshed that one cannot enter the thicket without stooping along a game trail. There are a few tall netleaf hackberries along the Big Tree Trail and widely scattered blackjack oaks in the trackless middle reaches of the community. These blackjacks are best picked out in the fall when they take on purple and reddish hues against the green backdrop of evergreen oaks and bays.

Although red bay is scattered across other sandy sites on the peninsula, the finest specimens occur in the oak-bay community.

Yaupon is the principal understory shrub, followed by beautyberry. Greenbriar is the most common vine. Along the Green Route on the Dagger Point Trail the largest stand of tree huckleberry on the refuge occurs. (Because of this species, a high point on the trail is called Blueberry Ridge.) Look for the red flowers of Turk's cap and coral bean along the trailsides in season. The occasional clumps of shin-high grasslike plants are nut rush. With the right combination of warmth and moisture the shaded leaf litter can spawn an amazing diversity of mushrooms.

No large animals are restricted to this community, but it is the best place to observe fox squirrels. Raccoons and opossums den in hollows in the oaks. Armadillos and striped skunks account for most of the burrows in the sand. Deer, javelina, and feral hogs routinely forage through the undergrowth, and you may notice their trails crossing your own. Watch for the little winding ridges of sand thrown up by eastern moles. Although you are not likely to see them, white-footed mice and least shrews are common forest inhabitants.

Except for an occasional roosting great horned owl, birds in this dense forest-thicket are mostly small perching species. It takes an experienced birder to identify them from the brief glimpses they afford, but anyone who is fortunate enough to be along the Big Tree Trail at warbler time (April–May) can anticipate trees full of twitching colors. The evening gloom beneath the trees at the Youth Environmental Training Area is the best place to hear the peculiar call of the pauraque.

Keep your eyes open in this forest for everything from the huge orbs of golden-silk spiders to the harmless defensive antics of an eastern hognose snake.

Freshwater Community

Here we are concerned only with what you can see without actually entering or dipping into the water. You can walk along the shoreline of extensive freshwater sloughs on the Rail Trail and the Heron Flats Trail. Jones Lake has a pier overlook, and Hog Lake has a pier as well as a perimeter trail. There is a temporary pond just north of the large live oaks on the Big Tree Trail and another at the end of the Wood Duck Pond Trail. You will also encounter occasional temporary roadside ponds along the Tour Loop. During wet years every swale on the refuge is brimming full for weeks.

The vegetation will depend on the permanence of the water. Thomas Slough (on the Rail Trail) almost always has water. Look there for submerged plants like hornwort and southern naiad as well as floating ones such as duckweed, pondweed, and pond silk. Emergent plants along the shoreline include cattails, California and American bulrushes, burhead, arrowleaf, and common reed. The pretty little water hyssop usually sprawls on muddy margins. The main bankside trees are black willows. Beneath and between the willows look for both rattlepods and coffee beans as well as dense stands of saltmarsh and spiny asters. The groundsel will also be there, along with an occasional dwarf palmetto and buttonbush.

The edges of temporary pools are almost always marked by a thick stand of bushy bluestem grass and a variety of rushes, especially spike rushes, and sedges. When the pools dry up other species rapidly invade the exposed mud.

The most spectacular denizen of this community is the alligator. The commonest snake is the Gulf Coast ribbon snake, and cottonmouth moccasins are also abundant. If you spot a basking turtle it will most likely be a red-eared slider. Southern leopard frogs leap into the water when startled on the bank, and green treefrogs are frequently seen huddling on the cattails and bulrushes. The chug of bullfrogs often resounds from secluded pools.

The dense bankside vegetation is the special haunt of several species of secretive rails. All of the wading birds as well as roseate spoonbills and wood storks occasionally use the ponds. Watch also for dabbling ducks, American coots, common moorhens, common snipe, belted kingfishers, marsh and sedge wrens, swamp sparrows, and occasional flocks of red-winged blackbirds and great-tailed grackles. Killdeers patrol the open shorelines. All of the small perching birds visit the pools to drink and bathe.

You can hope to see any of the mammals at poolside when they come to drink or wallow (sunrise and sunset are the best times), but those most commonly seen are raccoon, deer, javelina, and feral hog. Check for tracks to see what else has been there. During droughts the drying waterholes take on added significance, and all types of wildlife concentrate nearby to take advantage of the water and of each other.

Tidal Flat Community

This is an extensive and important fringing community on the refuge, and it represents an intricate meeting ground of sea and land. A fine overview of the tidal flats can be gained from the observation tower. The boardwalk between the tower and the bay affords an excellent close-up look without requiring that you sink to your knees in the oozy saline mud. Heron Flats is the name for the extensive tidal flat between the path along the outer shell ridge and the bay on the Heron Flats Trail, and this community continues along the bay side of the paved road as far as the picnic area.

The most distinctive and widespread plant of the tidal flat is the knee-high, semiwoody bushy sea ox-eye. Other plants come in as the salinity and degree of tidal flooding allow: saltgrass and shoregrass; saltwort and glasswort; saltmarsh bulrush and common reed; Carolina wolfberry and marsh elder; golden aster, saline aster, sea lavender, and saltmarsh morning glory. The inland margin of the tidal flat is marked by a zone of marshhay cordgrass and a few clumps of Gulf cordgrass with scattered marsh fleabane and saltmarsh gerardia for color. The tallest woody plants in this community are chest-high groundsels.

Much of the animal life of the tidal flat is hidden from casual observation. Depending upon whether the mud is exposed or flooded, this is the abode of brown shrimp, ghost shrimp, sheepshead killifish, razor clams, blue crabs, fiddler crabs, mud crabs, a variety of marine worms, saltmarsh snails, saltmarsh mosquitoes, saltmarsh grasshoppers, tiger beetles, and wolf spiders. Crayfish burrow along the inland border of the tidal flat.

This community is usually too salty for amphibians (although southern leopard frogs readily invade such sites and even hop directly into the shallow bay if the salinity drops following heavy rains), but the cottonmouth moccasin and Gulf saltmarsh snake are common here. This is also the haunt of the rare Texas diamondback terrapin. All of the wading and mud-probing birds utilize the tidal flat, and clapper rails, seaside sparrows, and sedge wrens are often flushed from the thickets of sea ox-eye. The tidal flat is the special domain of the whooping crane.

Raccoon and feral hog tracks are common throughout this community, and coyotes scrounge along its borders and through its shallows. Even bobcats deign to slog through it. The marsh rice rat reaches its peak density here.

Saltmarsh Community

The term "salt marsh" should be used only sparingly in describing the lower Texas coast. A typical salt marsh on the western shore of the Gulf of Mexico is composed of an extensive zone of smooth cordgrass backed by a broad belt of saltmarsh bulrush and black needlerush. Such salt marshes occur along the upper Texas coast, but because the shoreline is not routinely flushed by significant tides and washed by freshwater drainage, the marshes dwindle rapidly southward. In the Coastal Bend, "salt marsh" usually means what we have described as the tidal flat community.

The mainland refuge does have a thin band of smooth cordgrass along the bayside margin of most tidal flats. You can most easily observe this narrow band of waist-high grass from the observation tower. It can be seen lining the immediate edge of Mustang Lake. From the end of the boardwalk below the tower you can closely scrutinize the patch of smooth cordgrass that grows on the edge of San Antonio Bay. Waves rolling in across the open fetch of bay keep this grass from spreading here.

Smooth cordgrass is one of the few rooted plants that grows well in salt water. It is not more common locally because the bays are usually more brackish than salty. Other brackish water species occasionally grow directly on the bay side: common reed, yellow cowpea, seashore dropseed, beach panic grass, and various sedges. Between Heron Flats and the picnic area there are several swales that support growths of saltmarsh bulrush and black needlerush, but neither of these indicators of a salt marsh is abundant on the refuge.

Because the local salt marsh is only a few feet to a few yards across, it does not support a community of animals distinct from that of the adjacent tidal flat. Where the smooth cordgrass forms occasional patches large enough to afford shelter amid its dense growth, alligators lurk, clapper rails stalk, marsh periwinkles graze, least bitterns nest, and long-jawed orb weavers string their webs.

Ridge-and-Swale Community

This is by far the most widespread community on Blackjack Peninsula. It is a community of the interior, and it owes its occurrence and appearance to both geological and human history.

We discussed the basis for the corrugated ridge-and-swale topography of the peninsula in Chapter 1. The sandy ridges provide the elevation (sometimes only several feet) necessary for woody perennial plants to keep their root systems from being flooded and asphyxiated after heavy downpours and storm-induced tidal surges. So the ridges of sand support trees and shrubs.

The sandy swales are frequently flooded, and some of these troughs may hold standing water for weeks on end. Annuals or water-tolerant perennials grow in the swales. Most of the time these sunny openings are covered with a glorious sward of native grasses the like of which is seldom seen today elsewhere in the Coastal Bend.

In its pristine state the interior of Blackjack Peninsula was a pretty, parklike live oak savannah, with dense mottes of large live oaks crouching on the uplands and a mix of sedges and tall grasses in the depressions. The widespread intermediate ground—the low upland flats—was dominated by a nearly unbroken expanse of waist-high grasses.

Because fire kills or inhibits woody plants while it stimulates rapid regrowth of grasses (which possess protected, subterranean growth tips), it is likely that periodic natural wildfires gave the advantage to the quick-growing perennial grasses in this middle terrain. The result was a sea of grass dotted with wind-sculptured oak islands.

Then came men and livestock. Severe overgrazing and suppression of fires worked against the grasses. Probing lateral roots of the live oaks began to infiltrate the long-disputed upland flats. Soon a veritable thicket of waist-high oak sprouts overtopped the weakened grass sod. The consequence is what you see today—old mottes of large live oak trees, broad stretches of impenetrable chest-high "running" live oak, and occasional low swales still valiantly held by tall grasses, sedges, and rushes.

The vast thickets of live oaks on the refuge have received much attention. In a way they are natural and in a way they are man-induced. They benefit some forms of wildlife (jaguarundis and mockingbirds) and inhibit others (bobwhite quail and white-tailed deer). They provide a bountiful source of natural food (fresh-growth greenery and acorns), but they inhibit the spread of a diverse array of food-producing forbs and grasses. They certainly interfere with human accessibility to wildlife for both enjoyment and management.

What to do about the oak thickets, if anything? Over the years refuge personnel have tried about everything, including inaction and the current vogue of prescribed burning. To date the result is evident: a stalemate. Once entrenched, the running live oak is difficult to eradicate without destroying other elements of the community. Even fire, which is usually so effective at inhibiting woody vegetation and promoting grassland, is inadequate because it does not kill the subterranean rhizomes of live oak thickets. In the long run it seems prudent to wage a low-key, periodic campaign based on carefully planned burns on a rotating schedule with the intent of checking rather than vanquishing the thickets. Currently personnel annually burn about five thousand acres on the refuge; a given parcel of land is fired every two to four years. The strips of cleared ground that are occasionally seen from the road are firebreaks designed to contain prescribed burns.

The ridge-and-swale community can conveniently be subdivided into three units: live oak motte, live oak thicket, and grassland. These might be listed as three separate communities, but they are so fragmented and interwoven that we have combined them for descriptive purposes. The best way to observe the sweep and pattern of this community is from your automobile along the Tour Loop. You can sample it afoot on the several marked walking trails, or you can simply gaze over its extensive canopy from atop the observation tower.

The live oak motte is dominated by large live oak trees with laurel oaks, red bays, and prickly ashes along the edges. The shaded understory supports a dense growth of yaupon, a tangle of greenbriar, and occasional clumps of beautyberry. The oaks are usually laced with mustang grape vines.

None of the larger animals is restricted to these picturesque mottes, but many creatures rest, nest, and feed in them. The mottes are especially valuable as wintertime windbreaks and summertime shade. Unfortunately for many creatures, they also offer sanctuary to mosquitoes and ticks. Drooping branches provide greenery for everything from insects to deer. The acorns work into nearly every food chain on the refuge.

The live oak thickets are incredibly dense (up to fifty sturdy stems per square foot, for acres and acres) stands of scrubby oak shoots that rise waist- to head-high from a ramifying mass of pernicious rhizomes. Low-growing laurel oaks and occasional clumps of shrubby red bays contribute to this brushland. Blackjack oaks are sprinkled thinly through the drier areas, while clumps of wax myrtle occupy moist spots. The entire thicket is laced together with greenbriars to produce a barrier that is nearly impregnable to all except the lowest-slung and most determined of the larger creatures. Deer and even feral hogs generally wend their way through these thickets along game trails worn by generations of their kind.

Many of the most secretive wild creatures on the refuge take advantage of the oak thickets for shelter and foraging grounds. (Despite their stunted size, the oak thickets usually produce an ample crop of easily reached acorns.) This is the place to anticipate a rare glimpse of one of the native cats—a bobcat, cougar, or jaguarundi. Small packs of javelinas wander in and out of the fringes, as do feral hogs, gray foxes, armadillos, and cottontail rabbits. You may be lucky enough to see a long-tailed weasel shoot across the road from one thicket to another.

Then again, you may see none of them. Persistent, occasional sightings by refuge personnel, oilfield workers, and visitors confirm that all of these creatures reside on the Aransas. If you observe them, feel privileged; if not, feel satisfied in the knowledge that they are out there, secure in their natural bailiwicks and probably within earshot of your automobile. Always be alert for something around the next bend.

Look for mockingbirds, loggerhead shrikes, cardinals, mourning doves, long-billed thrashers, American kestrels, and red-tailed hawks in the vicinity. If you have not noticed the sandy mounds of Attwater's pocket gopher elsewhere, they should be conspicuous along the margins of these oak thickets. But there will be scant evidence of the huge population of white-footed mice that resides in this portion of the community.

The interior grasslands are dominated by a wondrous array of tall, mostly perennial bunchgrasses. This is the special domain of bluestems: big bluestem, seacoast bluestem, bushy bluestem, broomsedge bluestem, silver bluestem, splitbeard bluestem, and others. Depending on the local topography, the bluestems are joined by switch grass, dropseeds, paspalums, sprangletops, Indian grass, and Gulf muhly. About 85 species of grasses have been recorded on the refuge, and most of them occur somewhere in these open glades. Late fall is an excellent time to see these grasses, when their foliage has turned a crisp brown and they sport full heads of silver seed fluff.

In areas where fresh water accumulates, stands of saw grass, rattle-pod, cattail, and California bulrush along with occasional dwarf palmettos and sundry sedges and rushes replace the grasses. Where the swags are saline, marshhay and Gulf cordgrasses take over.

You are apt to encounter groups of white-tailed deer feeding in the grassy swales, which are also good spots to see a cotton rat streak across the road or to catch a glimpse of a coyote, a soaring red-tailed hawk, or a skimming northern harrier. Watch also for the explosion of a covey of bobwhite quail and for flocks of eastern meadowlarks and groups of savannah and vesper sparrows.

Although the smaller animals will mostly be out of sight, be aware that the dense grass is alive with crackle-wing grasshoppers, vagabond spiders, slender glass lizards, fulvous harvest mice, and a wonderful array of other wee beasties.

Tidal Shore Grassland Community

This is gently tilted, moist sandy-silty ground densely covered with marshhay cordgrass. Gulf cordgrass rims the community, and several species of bluestem and an array of forbs capture the occasional sandy hillocks. Because of its heavy rodent population and its open aspect, this is good country for observing white-tailed hawks and black-shouldered kites. It is also prime habitat for fast-moving snakes like western coachwhips and yellow-bellied racers. Tidal shore grassland is most extensive outside the area of public access, between East Shore Road and the edge of San Antonio Bay.

Cordgrass Community

Moist, slightly saline clay soil is almost totally captured by Gulf cordgrass. It makes good diamondback rattlesnake habitat and usually harbors high populations of hispid cotton rats, pygmy mice, sedge wrens, sundry sparrows, and a prolific subterranean colony of crayfish. An area north of Burgentine Lake and the southern third of the Tatton Unit support nearly pure cordgrass communities.

Upland Grassland Community

This is a coastal prairie community developed on well-drained, dark soil and composed primarily of seacoast and silver bluestems, fringed windmill grass, knotroot bristle grass, white tridens, Texas wintergrass, and a variety of panic grasses. Both controlled burning and occasional mowing are necessary to counter invasion by shrubby groundsels. It is here that the refuge's small population of Attwater's greater prairie chickens clings to existence. Eastern meadowlarks and bobwhite quail are at home in this community. Dickcissels nest here, and upland sandpipers enjoy stopping in its spaciousness en route to the ends of the earth. The community is best seen on the northern half of the Tatton Unit, where it can be viewed from an automobile traveling on Texas Highway 35.

Brackish Pool Community

This is a community of shallow, usually temporary tidal pools only a few inches deep and surrounded by barren mud flats. Shorebirds frequent these sites to feed on crustaceans, several kinds of killifishes, molluscs, and mudworms. Because the oozy mud and open expanse provide security, many birds spend a significant portion of the day loafing around such sites. They frequently pass the night standing in the saline puddles. The edges of these pools are often black with aggregations of shore flies, which mop up the black detritus and then become the basis for a series of predators, including bright metallic long-legged flies, dive-bombing robber flies, and stalking tiger beetles and shorebugs. Brackish pools occur around the periphery of Blackjack Peninsula, especially along the eastern edge near Sundown Bay and around the southern tip from Dunham Bay to Blackjack Point.

Mesquite–Prickly Pear Community

Mesquite trees, blackbrush, agarito, retama, spiny hackberry, Texas prickly pear, tasajillo, and devil's head cacti have captured clay-loam uplands on the Tatton Unit around the western side of Goose Lake. Birds and mammals typical of the brush country of South Texas occasionally reach this isolated community. Cactus wrens, Bewick's wrens, Bell's vireos, Cassin's sparrows, roadrunners, and wood rats are examples.

Chaparral Community

Dry, somewhat saline clay-loam uplands and low shell ridges favor dense, thorny vegetation: brasil, Carolina and Berlandier's wolfberries, lime prickly ash, mesquite, coma, spiny hackberry, Spanish dagger, Texas prickly pear, and tasajillo. Tanglewood adds its maze of twisted branches to the nearly impenetrable growth. Because this community usually occurs in isolated fragments (sometimes only a few square yards in extent, wherever a favorable hillock of the proper substrate exists), it does not support a distinctive fauna. It is, however, prime diamondback rattler habitat, and many perching birds seek shelter among the numerous branches.

By looking across Heron Flats from the outer shell ridge, you can see one of these brush-covered mounds on the bayshore. The most extensive growths on the mainland refuge occur along Salt Creek on the Tatton Unit.

CHAPTER 4

The Land—What People Have Made of It

No one knows just when the first humans laid eyes on the Coastal Bend. The earliest paleohunters were probably in the region at least twenty thousand years ago. Doubtless they exploited a broad animal and plant food base. They lived among, hunted, and perhaps contributed to the demise of the late Pleistocene megafauna that inhabited the coastal prairie. Although there is no evidence from the Aransas Refuge, archeological finds from elsewhere in Texas reveal that these primitive hunters routinely used both guile and gall to bring down mammoths and that, on occasion, they killed large prehistoric bison wholesale. Surely they were adept at bringing down small game, harvesting local plants, and scrounging after whatever other edibles came their way.

About ten thousand years ago, with the local climate, terrain, and biota becoming what they are today, the resident people adapted their hunting-and-gathering lifestyle to the subtle shifts in natural resources. Eventually they acquired the geographic affinities and the cultural distinctions we associate with historic North American Indians.

Four thousand years ago—about the time the barrier islands were taking shape—local Indians whom we call Karankawas inhabited the littoral margin of the Coastal Bend. The Karankawas were not a consolidated tribe. Each clan of forty or so people had its own territory and hegemony. A half-dozen major clans of these seaside natives haunted the offshore islands, bays, shoreline, and a thin inland strip of the mainland from Galveston Bay to Corpus Christi Bay. Blackjack Peninsula was probably within the domain of the Copanes band.

Most of what we know about the lifestyle of the prehistoric Karankawas comes from inference. Theirs was a culture of simple accoutrements, and the erosive coastal environment has spared only their most durable traces. Shell middens—mounds of discarded oyster and whelk shells—and scattered burial grounds are occasionally uncovered by the wind. Fourteen such sites discovered along the margin of Blackjack Peninsula have yielded a scant assortment of shell ornaments and tools, flint points, and shards of a primitive, distinctive pottery. A small array of these items is on display in the WIC.

By every indication the Karankawa lifestyle was culturally unsophisticated but ecologically finely tuned. They were the aboriginal opportunistic exploiters of the coastline. Habitually nomadic, family groups ranged through the homeground of their respective bands according to the seasons, anticipating natural fruiting times, animal movements, the turns of the tide, and ever ready to take immediate advantage of whatever windfalls came their way. Favored campsites were occupied periodically, not permanently; generations of occasional use produced the middens we discover today.

The Karankawas practiced no agriculture and had no domesticated animals except dogs. They set aside only scanty food stores; theirs was a hand-to-mouth, search-and-glut existence. Their fare was varied and periodically bountiful: the fruits of prickly pear cactus, mustang grape, dewberry, agarito, and mesquite; the roots of cattails, reeds, bulrushes, and sedges; shallow-water fishes, crustaceans, molluscs (especially whelks and oysters), and sea turtles; the myriad waterfowl and their eggs; alligators; every manner of fresh and spoiled wrack cast up by the sea; and from inland hunting sorties, everything from white-tailed deer and javelinas to prairie chickens, box turtles, and beetle grubs.

Despite many exaggerated accounts to the contrary, the Karankawas were no more cannibalistic than the many other North American Indians who occasionally sampled the flesh of relatives or enemies for occult reasons.

The tall, well-proportioned Karankawa men went naked; women wore skirts fashioned from animal skins. Both sexes pierced their lips and nipples with cane splints, and they painted and tattooed their bodies.

These Indians were adept at working flint, shell, bone, and wood into weapons, tools, and ornaments: flint points for their cane arrows, clamshell scrapers, whelkshell hammers, mesquite-wood grubbing sticks, bois d'arc longbows strung with twisted deer sinew, shell-and-tooth tinkler beads. They made use of the natural asphalt thrown up by the sea to affix flint to arrow shaft and to decorate their thin, gray pottery ware. They fashioned fine cord from tough fibers of Spanish dagger leaves. Although they wove cane weirs and poled heavy dugout canoes, they did not use a hook and line and so cannot be regarded as specialized fishermen.

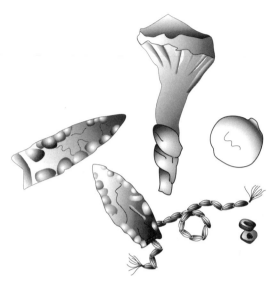

Karankawa artifacts

Although they preferred to camp in the open, these Indians occasionally threw up a flimsy lean-to of branches sparsely covered with vegetation and animal hides. In wet, cold weather and during long humid nights rendered audible by the whine of mosquitoes, the Karankawas substituted stoicism for comfort.

The men hunted, fished, and occasionally bartered or skirmished with neighboring Karankawa bands or with the inland Coahuiltecans. The women and children beachcombed, gathered plant foods, chased down small animals, and did the camp work. Everyone had ample time to loiter, gossip, swim, and play. It was a primitive but by no means a bad life.

When the mood was upon them, the men of a band swilled great quantities of yaupon tea laced with the intoxicating mescal bean, and they chanted and gyrated to euphoric exhaustion. On most evenings, however, the entire group gathered around smoky fires, conversed briefly about the day's events and perhaps of events long past, and then drifted into contented sleep as their kind had done in this wild land for hundreds of generations.

Red man first met white on the Texas coast on November 6, 1528, when Alvar Núñez Cabeza de Vaca and his destitute crewmates were shipwrecked near a Karankawa camp in the vicinity of Galveston Island. For the next five years members of this star-crossed expedition wandered along the Texas coast, and some of them may have trudged over Blackjack Peninsula.

The next significant contact came in 1685, when René-Robert Cavelier, Sieur de La Salle, established Fort St. Louis near the head of Lavaca Bay, about forty miles north of the refuge. Initially as trusting and curious as any aborigines, the Karankawas turned dangerous after exposure to the deceits of civilization. In 1688, they massacred the few remaining inhabitants of the French settlement and in so doing established a merited reputation for haughty and hostile opposition toward all who entered their littoral domain.

During the eighteenth century Spanish priests tried, with indifferent success, to lure the Karankawas into mission life. The Indians preferred their old haunts and old ways, spiced now with persistent guerrilla warfare and nocturnal raids on livestock.

By the dawn of the nineteenth century the inevitable war of attrition was well under way. At the time of the Texas Revolution in 1835, the despised "Kronks" had been hunted and harassed to near extinction. A marauding band of the Indians drew their last white blood when they killed John Kemper on the lower Guadalupe River in 1845. A group of Karankawas was annihilated in a final engagement near Austwell in 1851. After that the Coastal Bend was bereft of one of its most interesting wild elements.

Probably because of simple lack of documentation, there are few specific reports of conflict between Karankawas and early settlers in the vicinity of the Aransas Refuge. Most recorded Indian trouble came somewhat later from raiding parties of displaced Lipan Apache and Penateka Comanche who swept down along the frontier and then retreated to their interior strongholds. Like every pioneer community, the local stretch of the Coastal Bend has its own tense tales of Indian troubles, such as the Thomas kidnapping and the Gilliland massacre, but we must pass these by. By 1875, the local coastal country was secure from Indian attack.

Spanish and Mexican ranchers began moving into the Coastal Bend early in the eighteenth century, and at that time the padres started their missionary effort to save the souls and acculturate the minds of the Indians.

The closest Spanish mission to Blackjack Peninsula is Nuestra Señora del Refugio, which holds the distinction of being the last Spanish mission established in Texas. Originally built of logs in 1793, it was located just north of the mouth of the Guadalupe River. In 1795, the mission was reestablished at a site now on the grounds of Our Lady of Refuge Church on South Alamo Street in present-day Refugio (reh-FURY-o), 25 miles west of the refuge. The old mission is amply commemorated on vicinity maps: Mission Bay, two Mission lakes, the Mission River, and the city and county of Refugio.

Certainly the best nearby place to savor the architecture and aura of the Spanish mission era is the beautifully restored mission and presidio of La Bahía at Goliad, 45 miles northwest of the Aransas Refuge. Missionary work began there in 1749.

One slender thread connecting the Aransas Refuge with Spain lies hidden in the name of Burgentine Lake, the largest reservoir on the refuge. Long years ago, so the story goes, the tidal flood of a fierce storm drove a Spanish brigantine into St. Charles Bay and on up the creek at its head. When the flood receded, the ship was left aground on the open prairie, six miles from the bay. Old-timers commemorated the event by christening the creek with a corruption of "brigantine."

The name "Aransas" is itself an anglicized version of the Spanish "Aranzazu," the name given to an early fort on Live Oak Peninsula that guarded the entrance to Copano Bay just south of Blackjack Peninsula.

While we are reminiscing, we should not ignore the fabled buccaneer Jean Laffite, whose agile corsairs plundered the Spanish caravels and then ducked through Pass Cavallo and Cedar Bayou to the safety of the shallow uncharted bays. Laffite became part of the legend of the Aransas Refuge through the tale of Grandma Frank, a venerable resident of False Live Oak Point and a legend in her own right. In 1821, Laffite was disbanding his crew prior to quitting the region. According to Hobart Huson, Grandma Frank told of observing the pirate leader secrete his ample share of the booty nearby: "Many men went into the woods bearing heavy treasure-chests, but only one man came out." Whether actual fact or senile raving, the story lends a special charm to this already intriguing span of coastline.

When Mexico gained its independence from Spain in 1821, Blackjack Peninsula was removed from the dominion of New Spain to the Mexican state of Coahuila and Texas. Liberal colonization laws brought a flock of prospective Anglo colonists and speculators to the region. In 1828, two Irish immigrants, James Power and James Hewetson, received permission to settle all coastal lands between the Guadalupe and the Nueces rivers. Before their land dealing was done the two men had gained personal possession of nearly 200,000 acres of local real estate, including Live Oak, Lamar, and Blackjack peninsulas as well as Matagorda and St. Joseph islands. In 1836, the land became part of the Republic of Texas. Although the courts generally honored Mexican land statutes, the claims of Power and Hewetson were thrown into extended litigation, which was not finally resolved until 1856. During the hiatus, several squatters and quasi-legal landholders lived on Blackjack Peninsula, and all ran cattle freely on the unfenced range.

Through the days of the republic, into statehood (1845), and until the Civil War, the Coastal Bend saw steady growth and development. Houses and stores appeared on every hillock and within every appealing grove of live oaks. Most buildings had foundations and walls of durable tabby, a product of pioneer ingenuity and marine resources: home-fired oystershell lime mixed with sand and shell aggregate and cast in wooden molds into huge building blocks. (You can find some tabby foundations on Lamar Peninsula near the entrance to Goose Island State Park. Ask for directions at the park headquarters.)

Towns, all associated with shipping interests, sprang up along the mainland: Copano, Aransas City, Lamar, Black Point, St. Mary's. Most of these soon succumbed to the vicissitudes of weather and fortune. Only several old cemeteries still exist to remind us of the names and aspirations of an era gone by.

Both Matagorda and St. Joseph islands were well populated. By 1851, there was even an overland stage route, which began at Saluria on the north end of Matagorda Island, ferried across Cedar Bayou, and continued to the southern tip of St. Joseph. The Civil War brought a complete evacuation of the barrier islands, a blockade on shipping, destruction of many local wharves and warehouses, and several indecisive skirmishes between blue and gray.

Local reconstruction thrived on the teeming herds of longhorn cattle that had built up on the range. From 1865 to 1875, before there was a reliable northern market for beef, the longhorns were slaughtered for their hides, bones, horns, and tallow. The grisly work went on round the clock at large packeries, and the products were shipped out from the local ports.

The bountiful wildlife of the region was also exploited commercially. Sea turtles were netted for their meat and plundered mercilessly for their eggs. Waterfowl and prairie chickens were shot by the hundreds of thousands and sold locally or salted down and shipped out by the barrel, or fed to hogs. The fabulous flocks of tundra swans were so harassed and gunned that they eventually gave up their traditional winter rendezvous in the Coastal Bend. Egrets, herons, roseate spoonbills, and terns were clubbed on their nests for their ornamental plumage. Tern, gull, and pelican nests were raided for their eggs. Fresh oysters and fish were available at every local counter. A great variety of marine fishes was caught, dried, salted, and sent to market. Even the lowly horned lizards were collected and sent off by the crateload to be converted into mummified desktop trivia. In that era of plenty, environmental conservation simply had no calling.

Saltworks dotted the shores of St. Charles and Copano bays, where native salt was scooped from evaporation ponds scraped in the tidal flats. Much of this salt was trundled to the interior by oxcart and wagon, where it was valued as a condiment and even more as a preservative.

With the Indians and Mexicans subdued, the war between the states over, the seaports booming, the economy on the upswing, and good ranching land available for $1 per acre, the countryside began to settle up with the optimistic and dedicated fervor so characteristic of the Anglo pioneer.

Much of Blackjack Peninsula had been declared public domain in 1856, when the courts ruled against the Power and Hewetson estates. By the late 1870's thirty landholders held legal claim to more than 34,000 acres on the St. Charles Peninsula, as the promontory was then called. Many of these people had been displaced from the barrier islands during the Civil War but chose to resettle on the more fertile and accessible peninsula.

Though the last decades of the nineteenth century are not so long ago, they are poorly documented on Blackjack Peninsula. Each resident landowner ranched and tilled small subsistence fields. Most holdings were unfenced so that the peninsula itself served as a commons for the free-ranging livestock. Besides several thousand head of cattle, flocks of sheep and goats, herds of horses and mules, and droves of domestic hogs roamed the country. Under such a system the abuse of overgrazing soon became manifest. The combined impact of the livestock and the habitual burning of winter range left the peninsula much more open and barren than we see today.

Toward the end of the century, there were enough inhabitants on the point of land to merit a community school, a post office, and even a small village, Carlos City, about halfway down the east shore of the peninsula. A few of them left their names on the land: William H. Jones (Jones Lake), Felix B. Webb (Webb's Point), B. L. Bludworth (Bludworth Island), Emile Dietrich (Meile Dietrich Point), Robert McHugh (McHugh Bayou), Don Carlos de la Garza (Carlos City). But most simply lived out their time and faded into oblivion.

You can sample this era on the refuge by pausing in the WIC and looking deep into the eyes of the photograph of George Brundrett, who lived and ranched here in years long gone by. You cannot gaze upon his weathered countenance or at the adjacent picture of an early farmstead without gaining some appreciation and admiration for the grit the land demanded of its early inhabitants. It took more than a little pluck to

Sloop

survive in the worst kind of mosquito country with only a dishpan of burning cow chips in lieu of window screens. In those days a whisk broom was kept beside the front door to brush off clinging mosquitoes before entering. Nights were made tolerable only by mosquito bars— nets draped over beds and cribs; even the chair at the spinning wheel had its special canopy. At our current pampered remove, there is no way we can appreciate the relief these people must have felt when the first dry norther cleared the air of oppressive humidity and voracious mosquitoes.

These were hardworking, self-sufficient people. The men farmed, ranched, hunted, and fished. The women cooked, baked, sewed, washed, churned, gardened, and put up hundreds of jars of tediously home-canned produce. The children worked, played, and ran hog-wild. An occasional risky sailboat trip across St. Charles Bay to Lamar brought back a few store-bought supplies. Mail came by horseback once a week around the head of the bay to the post office at Faulkner on the northwestern side of the peninsula. Intrepid schoolmarms were boated from Rockport to live in for several months while they taught the children at communal schoolhouses.

Life was simple, free, full, and hazardous. Death came in mundane pioneer forms: diseases such as childbirth fever, yellow fever, blackwater fever (malaria), lockjaw, diphtheria, and sundry dysenteries or traumas such as being dragged by a horse, struck by a rattler, drowned at sea, or engulfed in the flames of a kerosene stove explosion. But by and large, the redoubtable mettle paid off and the good times canceled the bad.

If you would pursue the age, visit a public library and peruse a copy of *The History of Refugio County, Texas* or leaf through the definitive two-volume work by Hobart Huson, *Refugio: A Comprehensive History of Refugio County from Aboriginal Times to 1953.*

During the early decades of the twentieth century the Coastal Bend settled into a prepetroleum, pretourism economy based on beef, cotton, and corn. Then as now, most acreage was given over to ranching. Among the many contemporary landowners was a wheeler-dealer named Cyrus B. Lucas, who owned, leased, traded, and sold thousands of acres of rangeland in the vicinity of the budding community of Austwell, seven miles north of the refuge. By 1916, Lucas had managed to acquire nearly all of Blackjack Peninsula, and he ran several thousand head of Hereford and Durham cattle there. At that time the peninsula was referred to variously as the St. Charles Ranch, the Lucas Ranch, or simply the Black Jacks. The original ranch headquarters was located near the center of the estate at a site now called Cow Camp, but it was soon moved to the northwestern part of the peninsula to a spot currently occupied by the headquarters building of the Continental Oil Company. Cyrus Lucas himself never lived at either location.

Between 1919 and 1922, Lucas negotiated mortgages totaling nearly $190,000 against his St. Charles Ranch. When he failed to pay his promissory notes, he lost the ranch by foreclosure to the San Antonio Loan and Trust Company. In 1923, Leroy G. Denman took over the operation of the estate for the company.

Although the property continued to be managed as a working ranch, Denman was also interested in both native and introduced wildlife. In 1924, he sealed off the head of the peninsula with an eight-foot-tall, game-proof fence and proceeded to import an array of animals onto the ranch. The bloodlines of several native and alien species inhabiting the refuge today trace to his early stocking program (see chapters 7 and 8).

The half-century following the Civil War was a critical interval for wildlife in Texas. On the one hand, the destructive tendencies of unfettered market and sport hunting, avid predator eradication, persistent varmint control, and the harvesting of wildlife for hides and plumage were aggravated by a burgeoning population, expanding settlement activities, and a burdensome concentration of domestic livestock. The whole was bound together with the prevailing notions that wildlife resources were inexhaustible and that every individual had an inviolable right to exploit them as he saw fit. On the other hand, there were those who saw that without informed and energetic conservation, many kinds of native plants and animals could not long withstand the pressures being put upon them. The crucial task for the conservationists was to turn the tide of public support in their favor. Unfortunately, they did not succeed with frontier-minded Texans until many wildlife populations were almost beyond recall.

Although commercial hunting was legally banned in Texas in 1903, the establishment of bag limits, the distinction between game and non-game species, and an effective retinue of game wardens to enforce the state laws did not solidify until about 1930. One early glimmer of dawning enlightenment occurred in 1921, when Texas lawmakers agreed to grant a long-term free lease to the National Audubon Society for the custodianship of several small islands along the coast used as nesting sites by waterbirds. The state soon began its system of wildlife management areas, which now totals some quarter of a million acres in about a dozen tracts.

Meanwhile, the federal government was also taking an active role in wildlife conservation. The Migratory Bird Treaty Act of 1918 delegated to the Bureau of Biological Survey (ancestor of the U.S. Fish and Wildlife Service) the responsibility for the conservation of the nation's migratory bird species with an early emphasis on beleaguered waterfowl. As part of its obligation to preserve and manage waterfowl habitat along the Central Flyway, the survey recommended the purchase of the surface rights to the St. Charles Ranch from the San Antonio Loan and Trust Company. When negotiations were completed on December 31, 1937, the Aransas Migratory Waterfowl Refuge was born, the first of its category in Texas.

In the five decades since its inception, the Aransas Refuge has operated under twelve managers, continually upgraded its physical facilities and roadways, more than doubled in size, and survived several profound changes in the philosophy of wildlife management—all in an increasingly complex political environment of relentless industrial and urban development in the Coastal Bend and steadily escalating public demand for wildlife-oriented education and recreation.

The general goal of the refuge has always been to enhance the local wildlife resource, with emphasis on endangered and migratory species, but specific policies have varied with the times. In the formative years before World War II, the first refuge manager, James O. Stevenson, was dedicated to his principal mission of raising the carrying capacity of the area for migratory ducks and geese. To this end an immense amount of ditching and diking work was done to increase the freshwater holding capacity on the refuge. Four major dams, a diversion canal, and many small ponds, scrapes, and windmill outflows that dot the peninsula were constructed. Today they generally benefit all forms of wildlife. The system of roadways, levees, culverts, and firebreaks was also an early priority. Much of this work was carried out under CCC and WPA contract, and most of it was accomplished by mule power and back-breaking pick-and-shovel labor. A superb photograph in the roadside display across from the picnic area shows some of the men who contributed to that energetic era. The waist-high concrete pillar in the grassy area near the bay originally supported the flagpole that stood in the assembly ground for the CCC workers. Their barracks and work area were nearby.

Although Manager Stevenson was well aware that the wintering whooping cranes were not common, neither he nor anyone else fully appreciated the dire plight of the species until about 1940. From that time, maintaining critical winter habitat for the whoopers has been one of the foremost objectives of the Aransas refuge. In 1973, the U.S. Congress passed the Endangered Species Act, and the Aransas Refuge was immediately involved in providing special custodianship for the several endangered or threatened species that live within or pass across its boundary. (See chapters 5 and 6.)

Until well into the sixties it was conventional wisdom to think of wildlife almost exclusively in terms of game species. An unfortunate concomitant of this thinking was that any nongame species that might conceivably inhibit the growth of a favored game population was regarded as intolerable. This attitude ushered in the dark era of predator control, and the Aransas was not exempt from its painful and misguided efforts. For over a quarter-century, bobcats, coyotes, red wolves, gray foxes, raccoons, opossums, and striped skunks were systematically shot, trapped, and baited with cyanide guns. Poisonous snakes—no matter what their role in the natural scheme of things—were destroyed at every opportunity. With grim lessons learned and the encompassing habitat approach accepted, predators now enjoy their place and perform their vital ecological roles among the refuge biota. But for the red wolf, the shift in attitude came too late.

The first public hunt was conducted on the Aransas National Wildlife Refuge in 1966 as a means of reducing the overpopulous herd of white-tailed deer. That hunt was limited to bow-and-arrow hunters, and only bucks could be taken. In 1968, the refuge hosted its first combined deer hunt for both rifle and bow, and does were also fair game. In 1969 feral hogs were added to the huntable list, and in 1970, javelinas. By 1981 a nine-day archery hunt and a five-day rifle hunt had become routine on the Aransas. Beginning in 1991, hunters were required to pay a $15 user fee to participate.

Depending upon the vagaries of weather and the density of game populations, public hunts are still scheduled each autumn on the Aransas Refuge, but the purposes have changed. It quickly became evident that hunters were not able to make significant inroads on the deer and hog populations. (Javelinas are no longer hunted.) The kill rate was simply too low to matter—about a hundred deer and two dozen hogs each year. And hunters had a nettlesome tendency to take the cream of the crop rather than culling the weak and aged animals. But the hunt itself rapidly became one of the most popular events on the refuge, and tradition is difficult to quash.

Recognizing controlled hunting as a legitimate (if suspect) form of wildlife-oriented recreation in concert with the goal of conserving wildlife for the people—and knowing a good public relations tactic when they see one—the Aransas staff has bowed to public pressure and expends a great deal of effort to ensure that the annual hunt is conducted according to strict guidelines.

Yet, the idea of hunting on a wildlife refuge does not sit well with a growing proportion of people. Hunting, many contend, is exploitative, consumptive, and contrary to the spirit of a sanctuary for wild creatures. Even if sport killing is deemed a valid form of recreation, it still has no place on land deliberately set aside for the benefit of beleaguered native biota. Still, much of that land—including Blackjack Peninsula— was purchased with funds obtained from hunters' fees and licenses, and a ban on hunting would quash that lucrative base, which currently finances preservation and expansion of such refuges. (As a matter of fact, the annual Aransas hunt now costs the refuge more dollars in personnel time than accrues from fees, a situation that may soon force the refuge to curtail or cease the hunt.) Could the financial slack be taken up with comparable user fees and licenses levied on nonconsumptive activities like birding and hiking on public lands? Certainly there would be resistance to such a plan, but the ultimate benefit to wildlife might be immeasurable.

All sides have merit, and the resolution lies precisely where it should—with our democratic system. When enough people raise enough political dust in the proper places at the right time, they will get what they want; if they are apathetic, they will get what they deserve. The USFWS is currently reassessing its management policy on wildlife refuges, and it is soliciting public input. In 1991, a tally of public responses to the issue of hunting, trapping, and fishing on refuges yielded 6,820 for and 723 against. Is that a true reflection of public attitude, or is it skewed by organized response from minority interest groups? Whichever, public input will significantly (and justifiably) affect future refuge policy. If you care, make yourself heard.

Refuge 2003, which the USFWS plans to publish to commemorate the hundredth anniversary of the National Refuge System, will test the nation's ability to lay and implement conservation plans, and it will chart the direction of our environmental footsteps into the new century. By then we should know whether our rising environmental awareness can come to grips with the issue of public hunts on public wildlife refuges.

On another front, although there are continual worries about contamination from outside refuge boundaries, it is satisfying to report that the Aransas weathered the decades of indiscriminate use of chemical pesticides and herbicides without indulging in either. Runoff of chemicals from adjacent agricultural fields, which accumulates in Burgentine Lake before flushing into St. Charles Bay, remains a worry, but recent analysis of sediments showed them to be within tolerable limits of known contaminants.

The Gulf Intracoastal Waterway allows heavy commercial boat traffic to navigate along the coastline without entering the rough waters of the open Gulf. Locally it borders twelve miles of prime whooping crane tidal-flat habitat along the eastern edge of Blackjack Peninsula between Mustang Lake and Blackjack Point (see Figure 4). Vessels in the waterway are visible from the observation tower as they pass along the far side of Mustang Lake and follow the green channel markers out across San Antonio Bay.

The conflict between the economic goals of the Gulf Intracoastal Waterway and the conservation goals of the Aransas National Wildlife Refuge exemplifies a problem of our times. Dredged in 1940 and enlarged in 1944, this shipping lane has been a chronic threat to the heart of the area favored by the whoopers for their wintering territories. The initial excavation eradicated many acres of marshland and exposed previously protected areas to erosion by waves wind-driven across the bay. Shoreline erosion is accelerated by the recurrent wakes of cargo vessels, crew work boats, shrimp boats, and recreational craft. The tidal flats are receding at the rate of several feet a year, and the brackish ponds favored by feeding cranes are threatened by incursion of saline bay water.

Although no major cargo spills have occurred, that threat is omnipresent, and the vital marshlands lie within a few scant yards of the channel. There is no reliable technique available to clean up contaminants once they enter vegetated shallows. Over the years, occasional leakage from engines and barges has led to accumulation of toxic chemicals in the soft sediments of the waterway. When routine maintenance dredging stirs these toxins into the water, they are picked up by sundry detritus-eating invertebrates and started on their way up the food chains in the adjacent marsh. Disposal of the huge volumes of muck sucked up during maintenance operations is another problem. At one time it was deposited in a smothering blanket onto the tidal flats, but now it is piled on leveed spoil banks along the bay side of the waterway.

The U.S. Army Corps of Engineers is responsible for maintaining the busy channel at 12 feet deep and 125 feet wide. As a federal agency the corps must conduct its work within the guidelines of the Endangered Species Act, which means that the tidal flats used by the whooping cranes should not be sacrificed. The USFWS is the designated federal custodian of habitat critical to the survival of the whoopers, and refuge personnel are mandated to do whatever they can to promote the well-being of the cranes. Stimulated by the threat of lawsuits from environmental groups, federal agencies began seeking a compromise solution in 1985. Although awareness has been heightened and options clarified, to date little has changed.

Moving the troublesome segment of the waterway away from the shoreline would only put it closer to the marshes along Matagorda Island, where the cranes also occur; rerouting it inland through the Coastal Plain would enter the dwindling domain of the endangered Attwater's prairie chicken. Either alternative would be prohibitively expensive. Since 1989, federal dollars coupled with volunteer laborers and privately donated materials have staked more than 30,000 bags of concrete and interlocking concrete mats along the most vulnerable stretches of tidal flat in a stopgap effort to halt erosion. The Corps of Engineers is considering lining the entire refuge shoreline with a riprap of concrete blocks as a more permanent remedy. Levees atop the spoil banks retain solid fill fairly effectively, although drain pipes from the enclosed vats still allow a potent brew of dissolved and suspended chemicals to return to the water system. In the meantime, both wildlife and mankind coexist in uneasy truce.

The federal government does not own mineral rights on all refuge property. Active drilling sites, storage tanks, roadways, and a maze of underground pipes lace the area. Cooperative agreements between petroleum companies and USFWS have kept spills, disfigurement of terrain, and harassment of wildlife to a minimum. Indeed, the petroleum companies are consistently among the first to answer the call for donation of equipment and personnel for conservation projects on the refuge, and they have built and maintain many of the interior roads on Blackjack Peninsula.

Second only to the well-being of the natural habitat and its biota, the Aransas Refuge is for people. Refuge personnel spend unending hours promoting the observation, interpretation, education, and enjoyment of wildlife by routine visitors, special groups, and professionals. In addition to direct personal involvement at the information desk and in conducting tours and presenting lectures, there has been a continual upgrading of facilities to enhance the quality of visitors' experiences: the sixteen-mile paved Tour Loop was completed in 1970, the Youth Environmental Training Area for educational groups opened in 1971, the Heron Flats Trail was inaugurated in 1972, the current Observation Tower was dedicated in 1973, the Wildlife Interpretation Center opened in 1981, the boardwalk across the tidal flat was completed in 1984, the pier at Hog Lake was constructed in 1985, six interpretive signs were erected along the Tour Loop in 1986, the observation platform on the Heron Flats Trail was constructed in 1990, the observation deck on the Dagger Point Trail was completed in 1991.

But we must beware of how we estimate progress on a wildlife refuge. The improvements mentioned above benefit people, not wild creatures. The Aransas is a federal wildlife sanctuary, not a national park. When visitors occasionally ask for camping grounds, concession stands, and additional tour roads they seldom realize the ecological cost of such facilities. It would seem that in the critical years to come the most enlightened measure of progress on the Aransas Refuge will not be in additional glitter or even in a larger roster of visitors but in the steadfast maintenance of the natural setting. Contrary as it is to American tradition, progress in this case is best gauged not by how much we do but by how much we refrain from doing. The Aransas experience derives from what is already here. Every addition or subtraction puts that irreplaceable legacy at risk.

CHAPTER 5

The Whooping Crane

The whooping crane not only symbolizes the Aransas National Wildlife Refuge but it has also come to stand for wild America in need of care and understanding. In 1952, Robert Porter Allen extolled the wild spirit of the great white bird:

> For the Whooping Crane there is no freedom but that of unbounded wilderness, no life except its own. Without meekness, without a sign of humility, it has refused to accept our idea of what the World should be like. If we succeed in preserving the wild remnant that still survives, it will be no credit to us; the glory will rest on this bird whose stubborn vigor has kept it alive in the face of increasing and seemingly hopeless odds.*

Allen was right to credit the whooper for its tenacity, but he was wrong to belittle our dedicated effort to give the species a boost. A more wholesome view is to regard our precious flock of wild whooping cranes as a triumph of both nature and humanity, a working compromise between the requirements of wilderness and the demands of high-tech civilization. Granted that it takes cranes to propagate cranes, but just as surely it takes visionary people to set aside crane refuges.

Seeing a wild whooper, or simply knowing that they still exist, should instill a feeling of pride in each of us. Every time one of the singular bugle birds spreads its black-tipped wings and, after a half-dozen leaping strides, pushes itself aloft with a powerful downstroke, we can justifiably let our own spirits rise with the majestic creature. The crane, as always, is doing its part, and now we are doing ours. Together we have written a beautiful poem in the sky, prettier verse, perhaps, than either bird or human could have written alone.

The traits of whoopers confirm their inclusion in the family Gruidae (GROO-i-dee), the cranes, and distinguish them from other, similar

---

*R. P. Allen, *The Whooping Crane: Research Report 3* (New York: National Audubon Society, 1952).

groups such as herons and storks. Cranes are large-bodied, long-legged, and long-necked birds that usually fly with steady wing beats, neck and legs fully extended. During routine feeding, cranes walk almost continually with a characteristic aristocratic demeanor.

Cranes are social creatures, but many of them interact more as family groups than as clangorous flocks. They communicate with ritualized head bows, leaping dances, and a variety of vocalizations. Adults usually mate for life (widowed birds readily remate), share duties on the nest, are very solicitous of their young, and defend a familial territory against others of their kind.

Only two kinds of cranes are native to North America—whoopers and sandhills. Both visit the Aransas Refuge in the wintertime, but they do not use the same habitat. Except for regular sorties to burned pastures or to tilled land, whoopers seldom stray from the tidal flats. Sandhills, on the other hand, prefer the open prairies and grain fields of the interior. When the two happen to come together, perhaps foraging on a recently burned upland or a grain field, they ignore each other.

On the Aransas the wary whooping cranes are generally seen only at great distance across the tidal flats. They can be recognized by their large size, telltale curve of the head and long neck, rump bustle, gleaming white plumage, and deliberate, long stride. Their black wing tips show only when they take to the air.

Any good bird guide will depict whooping crane features that are seldom apparent in the field: the red skin on the crown and cheeks; the coarse black feathers at the corners of the mouth; the straight, rather heavy olive-gray bill and fierce yellow eye; the dusky legs and huge feet.

Male and female cranes are distinguishable only by subtle differences in size and behavior. An adult male will stand just short of five feet tall, weigh about sixteen pounds, and spread his wings an impressive seven and a half feet from tip to tip; the adult female weighs about fourteen pounds and has commensurately smaller dimensions. When a pair of cranes is quietly feeding together the alert male looks up more often, scanning his domain for interlopers or any sign of danger. He is invariably the first of the two to bugle an alarm.

On their first visit to the Aransas, whooper chicks are still noticeably smaller than their parents. They lack the red skin on the head, and their body plumage is grayish white heavily suffused with pinkish cinnamon; beside its gleaming parents a juvenile often looks positively orange. Even at a distance, the chick is easily distinguishable in a family group of three. By the time young birds are ready to make their first northbound journey, their body feathers are nearly white but the neck and head are still patched with russet. When they make their second trip south, yearlings are not distinguishable from adults in either size

Whooping crane

or plumage. But they are not mated yet; a crane reaches sexual maturity when it is 3 to 5 years old. A normal life in the wild may span 25 years.

Whooping cranes winter on the Aransas Refuge from mid-October through mid-April. When they begin their northward journey, they do not leave simultaneously as one flock but depart over a period of several weeks as family groups, single birds, and small aggregations. Accommodating to the weather and stopping to rest and feed, the northbound birds traverse the Great Plains of the United States and cross the international border into Saskatchewan, Canada. Paired adults push on with grim determination to Wood Buffalo National Park, an eleven-million-acre wilderness of oxbows, bogs, ponds, and boreal forest in Alberta and the Northwest Territories just south of Great Slave Lake and only 400 miles from the Arctic Circle.

It generally takes the cranes three to four weeks to complete the 2,600-mile trip north from Texas, but some groups make the journey in as few as eleven days, and one speedy family group was only one week en route. Nonbreeding whoopers, which make up about half the population, usually leave the refuge later than the breeding birds, so they arrive later and spend the summer feeding and socializing.

By early May most pairs of adult whooping cranes will be brooding two large, olive-buff eggs sprinkled with purplish brown flecks. The

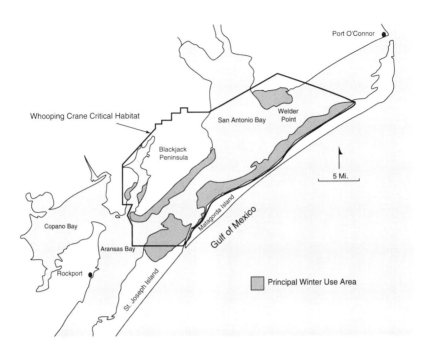

Figure 14. Whooping crane winter range on the Aransas National Wildlife Refuge and vicinity. Critical habitat is that part of an ecosystem
deemed vital to the protection of an endangered species. Map based on
data provided by Tom Stehn, Biologist, ANWR.

eggs are laid atop bulky platforms of rotting marsh vegetation heaped
above the waterline in knee-deep ponds. Despite their vigilance, the
pair sometimes loses a clutch to ravens or foxes. If the season is not too
far gone, they will attempt to renest, but the short Arctic summer often
precludes success. Hatching comes in early June, and the precocious
chicks are ready to quit the nest within a few hours. After several days
the downy, knobby-kneed young cranes are strong enough to stumble
after their parents through the tangled muskeg environment of this
northern wilderness.

Although both parents watch over their charges carefully, and the female broods them at night, chickhood is a hazardous time. Dry years di-
minish the food supply and encourage predation by foxes and wolves.
Prolonged cold or freezing temperatures are always a threat in far
northern latitudes, especially to chicks that have hatched early or late.
One chick, usually the older one, consistently dominates in the severe

early competition for food and attention, and it is normal for only the dominant sibling to survive the first two weeks of life. Young birds can be permanently disabled while learning to manipulate their long wings among the spruce and tamarack snags. But if things go well, by early to mid-September about two dozen of the pairs of whooping cranes will each be accompanied by a single robust, rust-colored juvenile ready for its first flight to Texas. Although the fledgling is physically ready for the journey, it relies on its parents to show it the way.

During September and early October breeding and nonbreeding cranes gather in southern Saskatchewan to fatten on the grain fields and marshes. When their hormones and weather sense tell them that the time is right, groups begin to lift off to cruise south at an altitude of two thousand feet, occasionally soaring on rising thermals to six thousand feet. A typical day begins at midmorning and continues until dusk, rarely even on into the night, and about two hundred miles are covered. Birds set down for food and rest, sometimes at traditional sites but also opportunistically, in remote and open wetlands, preferably within easy distance of grain fields. Strong head winds can ground the cranes for days on end, and they will hold up voluntarily if they discover a rich food source.

The southbound journey is less hurried than the trip in the spring, and the 1,500-mile trip from Saskatchewan to Texas may take more than two weeks, though some complete it in about seven good flight days. It takes six to eight weeks for the entire population to complete the trek, with the last birds arriving on the refuge in early December.

Not all make it. Except for their first weeks of life, the most dangerous period for whooping cranes is the interval of their semiannual migration. Birds are routinely killed or maimed when they strike power lines or fences. Some weaken and simply disappear en route. A few apparently get lost or are untracked by passing flights of sandhill cranes. The juveniles are especially prone to all of these hazards. In 1987, a disoriented crane chick spent its first winter in Oklahoma; it eventually rejoined the main flock. In 1988, another fledgling on its first journey south held up in the Texas Panhandle; the following summer it finally vanished in the Nebraska sandhills.

Fall migration coincides with the waterfowl hunting season, and whoopers still occasionally fall to errant guns. Happily, because of persistent public education and diligent protection, few Aransas cranes have been shot recently. In 1989, one bird was mistaken for a snow goose by a hunter on St. Joseph Island, and in 1991 a northbound crane was wantonly brought down by a camper in Central Texas.

Since records began in 1938, the cranes have managed to bring at least a few chicks south in all but two winters. In more than fifty chronicled

Figure 15. Migration routes of individual whooping cranes bearing radio transmitters, 1981–1983. Data are from the files of the ANWR.

fall trips, all chicks arrived safely eight times; the most recent perfect record was also the all-time bumper crop of 25 in 1988. In 1990, 32 nesting pairs brought 20 chicks to Texas. However, 1991 was a drought year; of 21 chicks hatched, only 12 made it through the Canadian summer. Little wonder, then, that there are anxious eyes watching the sky each

October and on into December on the Aransas Refuge, and sighs of relief or frowns of concern according to how many of the great white birds finally touch down.

Even after they arrive, the cranes face hazards. Overall, however, slightly fewer than one quarter of all recorded whooping crane deaths have occurred on the Aransas wintering grounds. Birds succumb to a variety of natural stresses including occasional predation, though so far the flock has been relatively free of contagious disease. The wet winter of 1990–1991 was a particularly adverse one; eleven birds, including two breeding females, died on the refuge. Ten of these cranes simply disappeared. From the appearance of its mangled carcass, the eleventh was probably killed by a great horned owl. In 1993 five juvenile cranes were lost on the Aransas. At least one was brought down by a bobcat.

While on the Aransas whooping cranes spend most of their time at three activities: maintaining territories, feeding, and, toward spring, getting themselves emotionally prepared for migration.

The territory staked out and defended on the wintering grounds by each pair of adult whoopers is critical to their social organization. A pair of these long-lived birds will occupy the same territory year after year, and when the death of one of the pair creates a vacancy, another individual will move in to carry on the tradition. When young birds form pairs at three to five years of age, they usually try to establish a territory near that of their parents.

This tendency to cluster has led to progressive congestion along the favored east-shore tidal flats of the refuge, where some fifteen adjacent whooper territories are traditionally strung out side by side between Mustang Lake and Blackjack Point. Whoopers also routinely set up home on the lee sides of St. Joseph and Matagorda islands, and since 1971, pairs have established themselves along the shores of St. Charles Bay and at Welder Point on the north shore of San Antonio Bay. In 1990, adult whooping cranes had established 23 territories on the mainland portion of the refuge, 19 on the two adjacent barrier islands, and 4 on Welder Point.

A pair's territory provides the cranes with all of the amenities of life—food, brackish water to drink, shallow water to stand in at night, the security of an open vista by day—so the resident birds spend most of their time within its confines. If the water salinity rises above 23 parts per thousand, the birds are forced to fly inland at least once a day to find fresh water to drink. After their Canadian upbringing, outright cold does not bother them, and they seek the shelter of oak mottes only during severe windy weather.

Territory sizes vary. On prime crane real estate along the east shore of the peninsula, a defended area averages about three hundred acres.

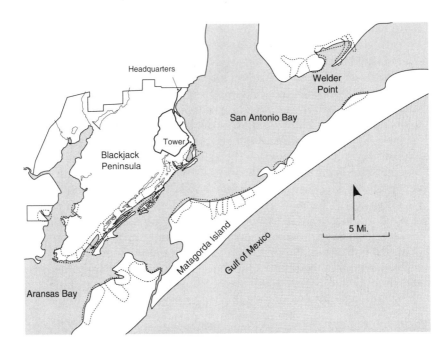

Figure 16. Whooping crane winter territories on and near the Aransas National Wildlife Refuge in 1990. Data provided by Tom Stehn, Biologist, ANWR.

On the less-frequented barrier islands a pair of birds may lay loose claim to more than a thousand acres. Pairs of cranes defend nesting territories of about eight hundred acres in Canada.

Although the birds vary in their tolerance of interlopers, in a whooper's eyes the social boundary of its territory is just as important as the physical resources within it. There is some overlap between adjacent territories, and the cranes seem to rather enjoy squabbling over their self-proclaimed fencelines. Indeed, it appears that considerable suitable habitat goes unused simply because the cranes prefer to be where they can interact with others of their kind.

The male most belligerently defends the territory, although the female joins in on occasion. Both birds are more defensive if they have a juvenile with them, but the young one takes no part in territorial disputes. Subadults usually live together in pairs or small groups, occupying uncontested areas between territorial lines. These uninitiated young birds often inadvertently transgress boundary lines and raise the ire of the resident adults. Juveniles occasionally venture into established territories when the occupants are absent or out of sight, as though testing the determination of the owners.

What defensive tactics do adult whooping cranes engage in? Though they haughtily ignore most other species of birds and other forms of wildlife in general, they watch nearby cranes constantly and closely. (Whoopers will occasionally bugle in response to a passing flock of toodling sandhill cranes, and they sometimes chase white-plumaged ibis and egrets from their territories.) Any invasion of the overlap zone elicits a series of shrill warning bugles from the resident male. He then flies toward the interlopers, often followed by the rest of his family, and all settle near the invaders. The latter ordinarily retreat, thus ending the encounter.

Occasionally feeding cranes of adjacent groups wander relatively close to each other along a common boundary line. Then opposing males walk or fly toward one another. Usually they stop while still well separated, each glaring balefully at his opponent. After this tense staredown the two abruptly break off, perhaps engaging in a brief bout of neck pumping and distractive preening movements. Then each goes off into the heart of his own bailiwick, satisfied that he has defended his territorial line without ever actually trading blows.

So a whooper's territorial defense is mostly bark and no bite, but their bickering is nonetheless critical to the well-being of these very communal creatures. It is also of practical concern to refuge personnel, who now perceive that there is a social as well as a physical carrying capacity for the whoopers. They project that the refuge and its immediate environs should be capable of supporting a wintering population of fifty pairs of contented, quibbling whooping cranes.

Whooping cranes arrive ravenous in the fall, and even in bountiful years they never seem sated. From sunrise to sunset, with scant time out for preening, dawdling, or territorializing, they stalk the tidal flats with giant strides in a never-ending search for food. Both parents feed the young, but the female devotes much more time to the chore, and she is also the youngster's tutor. Although they still beg and never turn down a parental handout, by midwinter most juveniles are capable of catching their own fare.

Because whooping cranes are opportunistic feeders, their diet varies somewhat with the tides, the seasons, and the productivity of each year. In general the refuge provides more animal than vegetable food to their liking. Exceptional years, dry or wet, are often lean ones for the whoopers because these conditions alter the salinity and extent of their favored tidal-flat hunting grounds and thus reduce the abundance of their prey.

What do whooping cranes eat while they are on the Aransas Refuge?

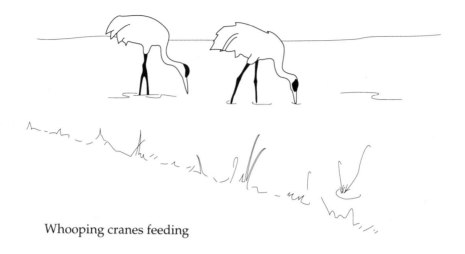

Whooping cranes feeding

Just about any creature they can grasp and swallow, from western cottonmouth moccasins and marsh rice rats to sheepshead killifish and saltmarsh snails, along with a continual nibble at succulent greenery and a sampling of any carrion that presents itself. More pertinent questions are: what do whoopers prefer to eat, and what do they rely on as staples in their diet? In 1952, Robert Porter Allen tabulated the results of an extensive fecal analysis and published a list of 45 known food items for the refuge cranes. More recent investigations have supplemented his results and corroborated his conclusions.

The list of animal prey now includes three kinds of marine worms, two kinds of shrimp and two of crabs, two sorts of crayfish, adults and larvae of an assortment of wetland insects, seven kinds of marine clams, three sorts of marine snails and two of freshwater snails, three species of marine fishes, one kind of frog and two kinds of snakes, one species of rodent, plus a variety of grasshoppers and ground spiders. The plant list is composed of a trace of manatee grass (a shallowly submerged marine plant), the green shoots of three upland grasses, the rootstocks of two shoreline grasses and of three sedges, the bulb of one kind of lily, the green sprouts of two tidal-flat forbs, the fruit of one tidal-flat shrub and the leaves of another, and the acorns of three kinds of oaks.

From that varied menu Allen drew some interesting conclusions. First, the cranes rely more on animal than on plant material. Second, among the animal prey, seven kinds are staples: ghost shrimp, pistol shrimp, blue crab, razor clam, jackknife clam, a marine worm, and a crayfish. All but the crayfish are denizens of the brackish tidal flats. Upshot: if you would save the crane, save the tidal flats.

From the list of prime animal prey the blue crab stands out as the creature taken with greatest frequency and in greatest bulk. A hungry crane in a productive tidal marsh can snatch a blue crab a minute, dismembering larger ones and swallowing small ones entire. Investigators have shown that although the cranes take blue crabs throughout their stay on the refuge, they rely on them most heavily during the winter months, the very season when commercial crabbers set their traps directly beside whooper feeding areas. The impact of commercial harvest on this vital crane food supply line has not been determined, but in lean years it can hardly be anything but detrimental.

During the low tides of springtime the birds shift their attention from blue crabs to worms, ghost shrimp, and razor clams. When warmer weather brings out the fiddler crabs, the cranes, true to their opportunistic nature, begin to gobble up fiddlers. Dictum: to keep the whooping cranes healthy, we must keep the marine crustacean food chains healthy.

It is of interest that although whoopers feed in and around the tidal flats, they are not notable fishermen. They can and do take shallow-water fishes, mostly mullet and killifishes, but they seem more adept at capturing crustaceans and molluscs. Apparently they are unable or unwilling to catch the delectable brown shrimp, which commonly appear in their brackish water haunts.

Captive whooping cranes thrive on a mixture of corn, chicken mash, shrimp, ground horsemeat, hard-boiled egg, and wheat germ oil. Wild whoopers readily eat barley, wheat, grain sorghum, and corn during migration. In earlier years, when their population was critically low, grain was provided for the cranes on the refuge, but the only native plant materials whoopers are reported to take in significant quantity are acorns and wolfberries.

Bright red wolfberries are plucked from the low branches of the plant, which grows abundantly on the tidal flats. Until the chick gets the hang of how to harvest them, mama plucks the fruits and gives them to her offspring. Few observers ever get close enough to hear the appealing squeals that accompany exchanges between mother and chick.

After a burn has opened the foliage, cranes invade oak thickets and avidly pick parched acorns off the ground. In addition, we have seen whoopers on the tidal flats grazing for prolonged periods on the succulent young leaves of maritime saltwort.

By March the cranes' hormones have begun their springtime surge, and one manifestation of it is the birds' dancing behavior. The male is influenced first; the female becomes more enthusiastic as the weeks go by. Juveniles rarely take part and seem totally disinterested in the goings-on. Although frequently referred to as a courtship display, the

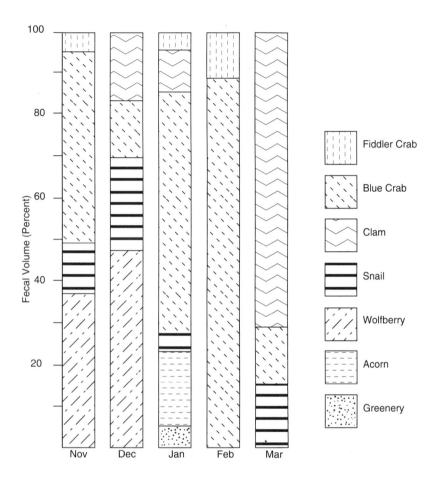

Figure 17. Winter diet of whooping cranes based on an analysis of 171 fecal samples collected on the Aransas by Howard Hunt in 1984–1985. Data are from the files of the ANWR.

dance of the cranes has not been observed to culminate in copulation. On the refuge at least, it seems to be just a release for the rising emotional tension of the coming spring migration and nesting season. Certainly the mutual display serves to strengthen the lifetime bond between partners, and it gives young adults a chance to choose a mate.

A dance begins when the male abruptly starts to pump his neck and crouch low to the ground. He unfurls his pretty white bustle, arches his neck over his back, and points his beak skyward. Sometimes he bugles;

usually he remains silent. As he swings toward the female he engages in a variety of pirouettes and stiff-legged, flapping leaps. The female may appear to ignore all this, but she is eventually enticed to join in. For perhaps a minute or so the two large birds engage in their ancient and mystical *promenade à deux* on the tidal flat, then they suddenly break off and return to their incessant search for food.

In March the staunch territoriality among the cranes weakens, and the birds are obviously restless. Then, when the day length is right, the southeast winds pick up, and all of the environmental cues of springtime are strong, something clicks inside the whoopers and the first group hauls out, climbing high and circling until they catch a good tail wind that jets them on their way. Few by few, the others follow. By mid-April over half of the birds will be gone; the last ones may linger into early May. When they have all departed they leave an evident vacuum behind, and we can only wish Godspeed to these great white birds of passage.

Occasionally one or two subadult birds remain on the refuge for the summer. They take up the migratory habit in their second spring. Rarely an adult oversummers. In 1950, a pair of caged cranes—Josephine and Crip—even nested and produced the first whooper chick ever hatched in captivity and the only one ever to hatch on the Aransas Refuge. Unfortunately, little Rusty survived only a few days.

How are the whooping cranes faring? The best answer is, precariously, but with the same determination of both man and beast that has seen them slowly increase over the past half-century. From their all-time recorded low of 16 individuals in 1941, it took the protected flock less than a decade to double its size. It was another tedious quarter-century before the population doubled again, but only twelve more years until it redoubled. So the Wood Buffalo flock has lately been gaining reproductive steam. In December 1986, cranes arriving on the Aransas Refuge finally topped the long hoped-for 100 mark. The record high was 146 birds in both 1990 and 1991.

Going into the nesting season of 1993, there were 231 known individual *Grus americana* alive on earth. Of those, 152 were wild birds and 136 belonged to the Wood Buffalo flock that winters on the Aransas Refuge. The remaining wild whoopers occurred in two separate managed flocks of 8 birds each: one group summers on the Grays Lake National Wildlife Refuge in Idaho and the other is resident in Florida. Most of the captive birds are housed at the Patuxent Wildlife Research Center in Laurel, Maryland, and at the International Crane Foundation in Baraboo, Wisconsin. Recently brood stock was sent to Calgary, Alberta, to begin a third captive flock.

But we must put these crane numbers in perspective. The whooping crane population enjoyed its heyday ten thousand years ago when the breakup of the last Pleistocene glaciers created vast expanses of open wetlands in North America. The birds then ranged from the high Canadian latitudes to central Mexico and from the Rocky Mountains to the Atlantic. With the glaciers finally gone, their favored moist habitat began to shrink and so did the population of birds. Early on, the whooping crane became a relict species—not necessarily marked for immediate extinction but destined to cling perilously to a withering habitat. By act of Nature, then, the cranes were already past their prime before Europeans appeared on the scene.

In early historical times whooping cranes still numbered in the thousands. The principal nesting area spread from the pothole prairies of Iowa north through similar habitat in Canada. Each fall the birds streamed south along several traditional flyways to winter on the Atlantic and Gulf coasts, especially in Louisiana, and on down into Mexico. There was also a nonmigratory population that nested in Louisiana.

From the beginning, wherever men and cranes met, the cranes lost out. Allen dryly observed, "As the human population curve goes up, the Whooping Crane curve goes down." Hunting for food and for sport, shooting in the grain fields to protect the crop, draining of wetlands, grazing and tilling of prairies, collecting of eggs and skins, plus every form of pioneer thoughtlessness and wantonness—all contributed to the rapid annihilation of the whoopers. Allen reckoned that between 1850 and 1920, over 90 percent of the whooping crane population was unceremoniously wiped out. Certainly the chronology is grim:

1850—Crane eggs go for 50 cents each and skins for $2.

1877—Cranes are common winter migrants from Houston to Brownsville and inland onto the prairies and into the grasslands of the Texas Panhandle, and are popular winter game birds.

1894—Wintering cranes are reduced throughout their Texas range, entire population probably about 1,000. Last migratory whooper nest is recorded in the United States, in Iowa.

1912—About 200 whooping cranes remain in the world.

1916—Passage of Migratory Bird Treaty Act confers protection to whooping cranes and other migratory birds; although shooting cranes is now illegal and hunting attrition has declined, losses continue.

1918—About 50 whoopers are left. Louisiana migrants are shot out; only wintering sites are at King Ranch and Blackjack Peninsula; nonmigrant Louisiana population is much reduced.

1922—About 35 migrant whooping cranes are left; last known migrant crane nest is in Saskatchewan, Canada. Wood Buffalo National Park is established in Northwest Territories, Canada, where, by happy coincidence not realized until 1954, the last of the migratory whooping cranes are nesting.

1924—Last whoopers are seen in the Rio Grande Valley of Texas.

1936—Last whoopers are seen on upper Texas coast.

1937—King Ranch migrants are gone; Blackjack population is down to 18; nonmigrant Louisiana group probably no more than a dozen—about 30 whooping cranes left in the world.

1939—Resident Louisiana population nests for the last time.

It should now be evident that for the whooping cranes, the founding of the Aransas National Wildlife Refuge in 1937 came during the waning minutes of their eleventh hour. It is also worth noting that Blackjack Peninsula is not even prime whooper habitat; the cranes prefer a wetter, more heavily vegetated sea-rim terrain. But the area did have the one thing the cranes needed most—a respite from human harassment. That coveted isolation gave them their chance.

Still the birds faded. A hurricane in 1940 was the beginning of the end for the small Louisiana flock. The Texas population dipped to an all-time low of sixteen birds in the winter of 1941. The whooping crane was indeed teetering on the brink of extinction. In 1945, the USFWS and the National Audubon Society began the concerted effort to save the whooping crane that continues today. The consequence of this effort on the Aransas wintering flock is plotted on the graph in Figure 18.

We return to the guarded term "precarious" to describe the current whooper population. Fewer than 250 individuals is hardly a safe margin for a bird that is large, migratory, social, tradition-bound, space-demanding, and relatively slow to reproduce. It does not help that the living remnant must survive on a dangerously inbred bloodline. Yet, the wild Wood Buffalo flock seems healthy and able to rebuild.

Annual success at getting chicks to the wintering grounds has varied from 0 to 25, and yearly mortality rates have oscillated widely. In the turnaround year of 1941, the 12 birds that disappeared represented 46 percent of the migrant population. Over a third of the flock was lost in the drought year of 1951; nearly a quarter died in 1972; 13 percent was lost in 1990. Since the fifties, the population has shown a ten-year cycle of slight decline followed by modest recuperation.

Migrating cranes have managed to bring an average of about six young per year to the Aransas, an annual population recruitment of 13.7 percent. In the meantime, an average yearly loss of about four year-

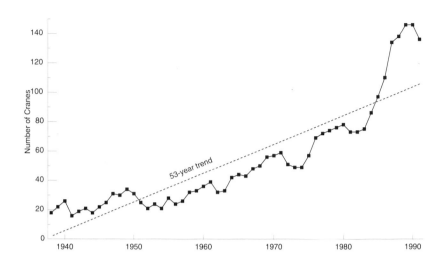

Figure 18. Through good years and bad, over the past half-century the population of whooping cranes wintering on the Aransas National Wildlife Refuge shows an increasing trend. Census data are from the files of the ANWR.

lings or adults gives an annual mortality rate of 10.1 percent. Bringing these vital statistics together yields a healthy 3.6 percent annual growth rate.

So, despite severe inbreeding and the multiple hazards of surviving in the modern world, the wild cranes still have what it takes for a comeback. Their natural survival strategy is based on low but steady recruitment balanced by low mortality among the cadre of experienced, mated adults that make up, in any given year, only about half the population. Fortune went well enough for the whoopers until humans lowered their recruitment rate and sharply raised their death rate at the same time. Now, with people on the cranes' side, things are looking up again.

Humans are indeed trying to make amends. Whooping cranes are charter members of the Endangered Species Act of 1973, which accords them full protection from exploitation and harassment. Penalties for violators have been swift and severe. For the individual who wantonly shot the crane in 1991, that meant two months of jail time, four years and ten months of probation, a $10,000 federal fine, a demand for payment of $8,100 restitution to the State of Texas, and 200 hours of community service.

The designated critical habitat for the Wood Buffalo flock encompasses its wintering and nesting sites as well as traditional stopover points along the narrow migration corridor. Thirteen state wildlife agencies, three USFWS regional districts, and the Canadian Wildlife Service cooperate in managing the migrant birds, and the National Audubon Society assists in keeping tabs on the population. The practice of banding juveniles was terminated in 1988, but many adult cranes still wear colored leg bands that help investigators keep track of movements and mortality. Some birds have carried radio transmitters along their flyway. These monitoring tactics have yielded a wealth of information that is now being applied to whooping crane management.

Of course, there is no guarantee that the Wood Buffalo flock is beyond decimation or annihilation. A contagious disease, a storm, a toxic spill, or just a series of inclement years could wreak ultimate tragedy. As insurance against severe setback or total loss, the USFWS maintains a small captive colony of whooping cranes in Maryland. In 1975, an effort was begun to establish a second wild flock by inducing sandhill cranes in ancestral habitat at the Grays Lake National Wildlife Refuge in Idaho to hatch and rear whooper chicks. Although the first part of the scheme was successful—there were eventually more than thirty fostered whoopers—the second part failed because the birds did not pair and nest, so the program is being phased out. Now officials are attempting to establish a wild flock of whooping cranes in south central Florida, in the hope that the birds will develop a nonmigratory nesting population. (The migratory habit is learned rather than innate, so captive-reared birds should remain at the release site.) Fourteen juveniles were freed in Florida in January 1993. Predators quickly trimmed the group to eight. The project goal is to establish a self-sustaining population by releasing twenty birds annually for ten years. Released offspring from the captive cranes at Calgary are destined to generate another migratory wild flock.

What of goals? The first one is to improve the whoopers' situation enough to move them from the endangered category to threatened. For this, the USFWS recommends a population of 40 pairs of breeding birds in the Wood Buffalo (Aransas) flock and 25 pairs in each of two other wild flocks. The Wood Buffalo group achieved its quota in the 1992 nesting season; for the others, only time will tell. On a more wishful projection, a wild whooper population of 500 to 700 birds by the middle of the twenty-first century would imply enough security to drop the cranes from the threatened category—a crowning achievement for both whoopers and people.

We have learned much and come far in our attempt to save the whooping cranes. Despite our high-tech programs, the keys to the continued survival of wild cranes—cranes possessed of wild survival knowledge, wild genes, and wild, imperious behavior, the only kinds of cranes worth seeing and hearing—are precisely those that Robert Porter Allen stressed forty years ago: adequate habitat and public education. As it always has been, the choice is ours.

Certainly you will want to see a whooping crane while you are on the Aransas Refuge. Everyone does, and many people come great distances for no other purpose. How can you promote your chance of success?

First, plan to be here when the cranes are here: between November and March to be sure, extended from mid-October to mid-April if you are willing to gamble. Second, bring a good pair of binoculars or, better yet, a birding scope.

There is a small chance that you will spot a family of whoopers in the fallow fields along FM 2040 about three miles outside the refuge gate. Watch for two or three (not a flock) of large, long-legged white birds. Pull well off the pavement to ogle the cranes with your binoculars or spotting scope. Stay in your car; they see quite well and don't like company.

As you register at the WIC, ask about the current locations of whoopers. You will likely be directed to the observation tower, or perhaps

Bugling whooper

you'll be told about special guided tours to other observation points. Be sure to look at the many whooping crane displays and listen to the excellent recordings of crane calls to get the birds' appearance, size, and sound firmly in mind.

En route to the tower, be skeptical of any white birds you may see; whooping cranes seldom use this portion of the shoreline. However, since 1986, perhaps in response to mounting congestion in the wintering population, a family of whoopers has appeared at close range on Heron Flats and (more rarely) cranes have visited Jones Lake. The observation deck on the Heron Flats Trail has a public telescope and affords an excellent vantage for observing birds if they visit the adjacent tidal flat. Check a bird book to rule out great and snowy egrets, white pelicans, white ibis, and snow geese.

From atop the observation tower scan the tidal flats with binoculars or telescope for anything white out in the vegetation. Remember, whoopers demand privacy, so look way off. If you do not initially mistake one of the white refuge boundary signs for a whooping crane, you are probably not looking far enough. Once you spot a possibility, work by elimination: it isn't a whooper unless it is large (compare with something of known size), all white, with a rump bustle, long legs, straight or gently curved neck (never folded), deliberate movements, and usually paired or with an orange-tinted juvenile (never in a flock). If you see something in flight (not often), check for the combination of extended neck and legs and black wing tips. Unless the birds are aroused, do not count on hearing their distinctive bugle.

Most commercial tour boats offer a money-back guarantee of seeing a whooping crane, generally at close range. Tour operators are experienced and do not alarm the birds. Although the four-hour cruises are not sponsored by the Aransas National Wildlife Refuge, you can get scheduling information, prices, and directions at the WIC or by contacting the Rockport/Fulton Area Chamber of Commerce, P.O. Box 1055, Rockport, TX 78382; 800-242-0071 in Texas and 800-826-6441 elsewhere.

CHAPTER 6

The Endangered Ones

An endangered species is one judged to be so rare that it is in imminent danger of extinction. A threatened species, although it may still be moderately abundant, is one that is experiencing a rapid decline in numbers in some parts of its range. Already in deep trouble or only headed that way, they both need special consideration, and the national refuge system plays a clear and vital role in the sustaining effort.

Diminished species vary in their ability to recoup, but the one salient remedy is ample habitat combined with freedom from harassment. A wildlife refuge provides sanctuary; protective legislation and public education can significantly reduce human disturbance. Given such an even break, most beleaguered species begin to recover.

All of the accounts that follow are necessarily concerned with population numbers—always too few, occasionally perilously few. For some species, as far as the local area is concerned, final extirpation has left only a wistful memory.

The Aransas National Wildlife Refuge is implicated with nearly three dozen animal species on the current federal endangered and threatened lists. The whooping crane was treated separately in Chapter 5; several other cases are of historical significance only.

Brown Pelican

In the early decades of this century Texas supported a healthy population of about five thousand brown pelicans, which nested in 24 colonies on islets in bays along the coastline. By the midthirties that number was reduced to approximately a thousand through wanton shooting and nest destruction by hunters and fishermen who were mistakenly convinced that the pelicans were serious competitors for game fish.

In the late fifties the remnant Texas population of brown pelicans went into catastrophic decline. By the midsixties, only some fifty individuals remained, and most of those experienced nesting failure or did not even try to nest. Their last-ditch reproductive effort occurred on the Second Chain of Islands, a series of oyster reefs strung across the southern end of San Antonio Bay between Blackjack Peninsula and Matagorda Island.

The trouble was poisoning by organochlorine pesticides, mainly DDT and endrin, washed and blown into the bays from surrounding agricultural fields. DDT became concentrated in Gulf menhaden, a favorite food fish of pelicans. The toxin upset the hormones governing the birds' normal breeding cycle and caused them to lay thin-shelled eggs. When a brooding pelican lifted off the nest, it inadvertently crushed its fragile clutch. Endrin either poisoned pelicans directly or permeated their body fat; a stressed or underfed bird died after calling on its contaminated fat reserves.

By 1970, the brown pelican was in such dire straits that it was listed as endangered throughout its U.S. range. In 1972, only a single brown pelican chick was raised on the entire Texas coast. But in that same dismal year the Environmental Protection Agency banned DDT and curtailed the use of endrin, giving the birds the help they so desperately needed. During the seventies pelicans moving up the coast from Mexico began to repopulate some of their old Texas haunts. In 1974, 35 brown pelicans were seen in Texas. Everyone was elated to see the droll symbol of the local coastline staging a comeback.

By 1983, two nesting colonies of brown pelicans had reestablished: one on the Second Chain of Islands and the other on a bank of waste dredge material, appropriately named Pelican Island, 35 miles south of the refuge in Corpus Christi Bay. A grand total of 96 nests produced 170 young in that year.

In 1984, all nesting birds had moved to Pelican Island, where they fledged 230 young. By 1987, 300 pairs of brown pelicans in Texas fledged nearly 500 young, and a new nesting colony had taken over Sundown Island in Matagorda Bay just inside Pass Cavallo.

In 1989, the Texas Colonial Waterbird Census recorded 679 brown pelicans, 85 percent of them in the Coastal Bend between Matagorda and Baffin bays. These birds nested in five locations and collectively fledged more than 900 young. This reproductive effort was partly countered by the loss of about 40 adult pelicans during the freeze in December of that year. Although still deserving of its endangered status, going into the last decade of the twentieth century the Texas population of brown pelicans is on the upswing.

One of the real delights of birding is watching a brown pelican feed. The bird flaps along with a slow, measured wing beat while watching the shallow bay fifty feet below. When it spots a school of its favorite

Brown pelican

Brown pelicans feeding

prey—menhaden, striped mullet, or bay anchovies—the pelican goes
into an abrupt half-roll, partly folds its wings, and hurtles down like a
banking dive-bomber, smacking into the water bill-first and briefly disappearing from view in a cascade of foam. As soon as its head is submerged, the pelican opens its bill, drawing over two gallons of water

and, if the strike is successful, prey fish as well into the gular pouch. A special layer of air sacs beneath the skin buffers the bird from the impact of the dive and then rapidly bobs it back to the surface.

Riding the waves like a cork, the bird presses the full pouch to its breast to drain the water out through the gaped bill. Then, with an adroit backward toss of its head, it swallows the fish. Although the gular pouch appears to be a handy basket for storing and transporting the catch, it is in fact never so used. Indeed, a pelican with a loaded pouch would be too nose-heavy to fly.

Facing into the wind, the pelican labors to get airborne again. If it is finished hunting it may set out for a favorite perch on a piling, skimming along with wing tips barely clearing the water. Otherwise it will gain altitude and begin another foraging sortie.

In February brown pelicans begin to congregate on their nesting islands, where they crowd their nests to within pecking distance of each other. The nest is a large, ragged basin of dead twigs and branches laid atop scant, shin-high vegetation of bushy sea ox-eye and clumps of prickly pear cactus.

The uncommonly ugly, leathery-skinned hatchlings appear in late April and May. They grow rapidly on gullet loads of semidigested fish, and they fledge in July and August. As with all birds, nestlings lead a hazardous existence, plagued by everything from tidal surges and infestation by ticks or fire ants to dehydration, reef erosion, and lethal encounters with cactus spines.

Both nests and young are utterly defenseless, so the pelicans use offshore islets to escape predation by coyotes, raccoons, and skunks, but they remain vulnerable to human disturbance, whether malicious or inadvertent. The National Audubon Society guards the islands against trespass during the breeding season, but few people realize that even a close pass by a boat can flush the tending adults and leave the entire budding generation open to one of the most dangerous elements in its environment—the direct rays of the broiling Texas sun.

A brown pelican chick fortunate enough to fledge still faces a formidable challenge, for its parents abruptly abandon the youngster. Relying on its reserve of body fat and reckoning on pure instinct, the forsaken fledgling must master the tricky art of dive-bombing for a living. Learning to take advantage of the wind, reading the waves, cruising at the right altitude, recognizing appropriate prey fish, banking, accelerating, striking the water in proper form—none of it comes easily. Young pelicans plunge repeatedly and often come up empty. They must perfect their skills before their body reserves are exhausted or they starve; nearly 70 percent do not survive this harsh test.

Numbers of brown pelicans on the Aransas Refuge are usually highest in late summer and lowest when they retire to their nesting islands in the spring. From your vantage on the observation tower, work the pilings, channel markers, and oystershell bars with binoculars in search of perching individuals. Also check any exposed oyster reefs in San Antonio Bay. Stop at the picnic area and the bay overlook to scan the broad expanse of sky for fishing birds.

Many birds drift southward in the winter, but more than fifty brown pelicans have been counted during recent Christmas censuses on the refuge. You can reasonably anticipate seeing a brown pelican at any time of the year, but if you visit Matagorda Island in the summertime, you will surely see them loafing on the beach and diving in the surf.

Attwater's Greater Prairie Chicken

This southernmost grouse once ranged across seven million acres of Gulf coastal prairie from southwestern Louisiana to the Nueces River in Texas. In a peak year a million birds occupied the unbroken mid- and tall-grass habitat, with the greatest concentration on the upper and central Texas coast. Their troubles began with the arrival of the earliest white settlers. Prairie chickens were great sport to flush and shoot, and during the springtime mating season, males were pathetically easy to approach on their courtship grounds. They made delicious tablefare; during the latter half of the nineteenth century the plump birds were shot by the wagonload for the restaurant trade.

Attwater's prairie chicken became extinct in Louisiana in 1919. In 1937, a census along the Texas coast showed the population reduced to 8,700 birds in several widely scattered colonies. Hunting them was forbidden, but by that time the more formidable danger of habitat destruction was stalking the chickens. Row cropping (wetland rice farming was especially destructive), overstocked range, introduction of exotic grasses, altered drainage patterns, brush invasion, broadcast of pesticides and herbicides, indiscriminate burning, roadways, utility rights-of-way, and—most recently and most relentlessly—residential and industrial development all uprooted and overlaid the native grasses and shattered forever the splendid isolation of the prairie habitat.

Along with the chickens, other less noticed denizens of the prairie rapidly began to draw back: Woodhouse's toads, ornate box turtles, Texas horned lizards, slender glass lizards, bullsnakes, western coachwhips, massasaugas, black-shouldered kites, white-tailed hawks, eastern meadowlarks, dickcissels, lark sparrows, horned larks, harvest mice, ground squirrels, black-tailed jackrabbits, spotted skunks, badgers, red wolves, and an extensive menagerie of grasshoppers, ground spiders, butterflies, beetles, and ants. The very fabric of the land was unraveling as it lost its once continuous sweeps of little and big blue-stems, yellow Indian grass, switch grass, tanglehead, crinkleawn, eastern gamagrass, paspalums, and great diversity of sedges, rushes, and forbs. The prairie chickens were only bellwethers heralding the demise of the entire coastal prairie ecosystem. It is ironic that we can be concerned about tropical rain forests while the wonderful prairie at our doorstep is being driven to extinction.

Hemmed in and harassed at every turn, the Attwater population went into a tailspin; there were only about two thousand birds left in 1967 when the species was placed on the endangered list. Through 1985, the Attwater count hovered around fifteen hundred birds scattered in woefully vulnerable flocks in eight coastal counties in Texas. But in 1986 the population dropped below a thousand, and the chickens began to display the ominous signs of a species in the last throes of extinction: widely isolated breeding groups, dwindling and subject to being wiped out by local drought, storm, disease, or skilled predators and susceptible to the debilitating consequences of inbreeding; maladapted individuals; a skewed sex ratio and infertile adults. For such highly social birds as prairie chickens, the severe drop in numbers also brought on a social malaise that inhibited their appearance on the courting grounds. The dispirited creatures seemed to be losing their will to survive.

By 1991, fewer than five hundred Attwater's prairie chickens clustered into four breeding flocks were all of their kind left on earth. Wet weather during the nesting period in 1993 wiped out two-thirds of the struggling population, leaving only 158 birds. Most of the survivors reside on private ranchland in Refugio County near the Aransas Refuge. Unless the chickens can effect a turnaround, the gloomy prediction is extinction in the wild by the turn of the century. All agree that the Attwater is the most critically endangered bird species in the state; even the numerically inferior whooping cranes have brighter prospects.

Technically, Attwater's prairie chicken (*Tympanuchus cupido attwateri*) is a subspecies of the greater prairie chicken. It was named after Henry P. Attwater, a pioneer conservationist in Texas in the late nineteenth century. A second subspecies, the northern greater prairie chicken (*T. c. pinnatus*), once occurred in northeast Texas and still ranges through the central prairie states, although its numbers too are declining. A third subspecies, the heath hen (*T. c. cupido*), once abundant on the eastern seaboard, went through the same sporadic decimation before it became extinct in 1932.

Efforts are now being made to save Attwater's prairie chicken. In 1972, the 8,000-acre Attwater's Prairie Chicken National Wildlife Refuge was established in Colorado County, fifty miles west of Houston.

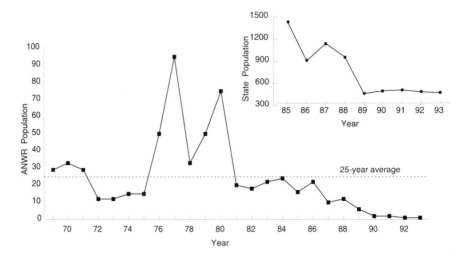

Figure 19. Population estimates of adult Attwater's greater prairie chickens show that the birds are almost gone from the Tatton Unit of the Aransas National Wildlife Refuge. The state trend (inset) emphasizes the precarious status of this endangered species. Census data are from the files of the ANWR and the TPWD.

Here the native prairie is intensively managed for a resident population of only about twenty birds, and the refuge coordinates plans for managing chickens on private lands, for acquiring or leasing additional acreage, for initiating a captive breeding-and-release program, and for publicizing the plight of the species. In 1993, the first captive-laid Attwater eggs hatched at Fossil Rim Wildlife Center south of Fort Worth, thus giving hope for a release program. The U.S. Fish and Wildlife recovery plan calls for a population of five thousand birds in two or more groups on 30,000 acres of suitable habitat. Clearly, the chickens have a long way to go to attain security.

In 1967 the Tatton Unit was donated to the Aransas National Wildlife Refuge, and with it came an endowment of about thirty prairie chickens. Though the poorly drained area, mostly covered with Gulf cordgrass and groundsel trees, is not prime habitat for the chickens, it is managed exclusively for their benefit. The harrowing roller-coaster, fortunes and near demise of the Tatton colony can be traced on the accompanying graph (Figure 19). The few birds remaining in 1992 were probably immigrants from adjacent ranchland, birds still making sorties into terrain where once their kind was common. The last confirmed nest on the refuge was in 1982. But as long as a few chickens remain, there is always the chance that good times will return for the Attwater on this 7,500-acre tract.

It is in the courtship behavior of the males that the Attwater displays its most grouselike and most fascinating attribute. There are few sounds more enthralling than the prairie chickens' haunting moans drifting through the cold mists of a dark and boundless prairie. The ritual begins in the cold February predawn when several cocks silently materialize in a fog-wrapped short-grass clearing. This same hallowed spot may have been the stage for the coming drama for untold generations of these shy, tradition-bound social birds. If the site is destroyed, the demoralized colony may scatter and never regroup.

Each male selects his own small patch of ground. Then, as his mood begins to build, he stretches his neck out rigidly, displays his fleshy yellow eyebrow combs, erects the twin horns of stiff feathers behind his head, and spreads his tail in a rich brown fan over his rump. Leaning stiffly forward, he extends his wings to the ground and suddenly sprints ahead several feet while maintaining his comical, humped posture. Then he stops abruptly and commences to dance in place, the primary feathers of his wings scraping the ground and his rapidly stamping feet making an audible staccato.

At the height of this energetic shuffle the cock bows low until his chin brushes the grass stubble. With a few quick pumping motions, he inflates his gular air sac into a pair of huge orange-yellow blisters on the sides of his neck. Then he brings his act to an eerie crescendo when he emits a melodious, melancholy, and rather ventriloquial "whooo-LOO-wooo." This is the so-called booming, a sound aptly likened to that produced by blowing across the top of a large jug. Like a jug, the gular sac acts as a resonating chamber that amplifies and modulates the call.

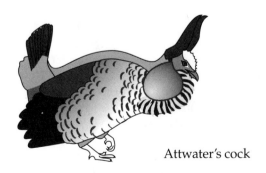

Attwater's cock

Attwater's hen

The routine is over in fifteen seconds, but it will be repeated many times before the rising sun drives the birds to cover. When the frenzy is full upon them, adjacent cocks square off and flap and spar, or chase each other about while producing a variety of cackling sounds. This is all ritualized bluff; no blood is drawn, but a great deal of pent-up energy is released and ages-old social patterns are relived.

In time a hen or two appears on the edge of the arena, feigning disinterest in the goings-on but in fact watching intently. Eventually each hen copulates with one or several of the most dynamic cocks. Then she quits the field.

The booming activity peaks in March and tapers off in April. The hens hide their nests in clumps of tall grass and brood their clutches of twelve to fourteen olive-colored eggs alone. Hatching occurs in April and May in the half of the nests that escape predation by skunks, raccoons, armadillos, coyotes, and snakes. The precocious chicks begin to follow the hen almost immediately. In six weeks or so the survivors, usually less than half the brood, set out on their own. High egg and chick mortality plus an annual death rate of about half the adults make for risky population statistics.

For most of the year prairie chickens lead cryptic lives, only occasionally bursting above the grass clumps on whirring wings before they level off in a smooth glide and abruptly drop back into the safety of their grassy retreat. Because the birds are difficult to observe directly, population estimates on the Tatton are based on the number of males heard on the booming grounds. Assuming a balanced sex ratio, doubling the male count yields a reasonable measure of the adult population. The 1991 estimate of two chickens derived from hearing one lone cock valiantly reenacting the primal tradition of his kind for one hypothetical female. In 1992 a pair of birds was flushed. It appears that only spillover from good reproductive success among the prairie chickens on the surrounding ranchlands can prevent the impending and lasting silence of cold spring dawns across the Tatton.

You almost certainly will not see an Attwater's prairie chicken on the Aransas Wildlife Refuge; the few resident birds stay well concealed in their Tatton sanctuary. For a chance to see the prairie chickens, contact the Attwater's Prairie Chicken National Wildlife Refuge, P.O. Box 519, Eagle Lake, TX 77434; 409-234-3021. Although it is no substitute for the real thing, you might pause to read the population-that-once-was sign just inside the refuge fence at the rest area bordering the Tatton Unit on Texas Highway 35.

At this low point in their history, it should be reward enough to simply gaze at chicken habitat and know that there are still a few of the birds resolutely hanging on there. This you can do by driving along Highway 35 between its junction with FM 774 and Salt Creek. The Tatton Unit borders the highway on the east; private ranchland stretches to the west. Look out your car window, muse about the way things used to be and the way they have become, and feel privileged to share in the secret that this is still, for a while at least, Attwater country.

Southern Bald Eagle

The 35,000 bald eagles in the United States today, most of them in Alaska, are only a fragment of the population of colonial times. Despite being chosen as our national symbol, the bald eagle was accorded neither respect nor protection in the field. It was commonly shot on sight, not to satisfy any particular grudge but simply because it was a large and showy member of the generally maligned birds of prey. In the early part of the century there was even a bounty on the bald eagle's silver-white head.

Besides guns, the eagles faced other problems. When favored nest trees were felled, the tradition-bound birds often quit an area rather than choose an alternate site. Nesting eagles demand not just security but isolation as well; if disturbed during incubation they abandon their eggs. Waterfront development, recreational boating, and a tangle of high-voltage power lines despoiled the eagles' hunting grounds, so early on the big birds began to quietly fade away.

The DDT decades were dark ones for all American wildlife, and the poison hit hardest at the top of the food web, where final consumers, in relatively small populations, fed upon prey loaded with concentrated quantities of toxic chemicals. Bald eagles, at the highest trophic echelon, paid the price for their lofty status. Only those birds that nested in the unsullied wilderness of Alaska and Canada escaped the decimation. In addition to suffering from pesticide contamination, eagles that scavenged waterfowl wounded or killed by lead shot were weakened by lead poisoning.

In 1967, the bald eagle was listed as endangered in 43 of the conterminous states of the United States (including Texas) and threatened in the remaining 5.

There are two races of bald eagles and Texas hosts both. The northern race nests in the far north and moves south sporadically during the wintertime. The southern race scatters northward to feed during the summertime and returns south to nest in the fall. From September through December about a thousand bald eagles move into Texas, some as winter visitors and others as winter breeders. A few of the southern birds are resident all year.

In 1971, the Texas Parks and Wildlife Department began keeping a close watch on all known nests of southern bald eagles in the state. For a decade they could find only half a dozen active aeries each year. The number went up to 15 in 1981 and to 29 in 1990, when a record 29 eaglets were fledged between Corpus Christi and Houston. Most nests were in towering trees located in strips of dense forest along the lower reaches of rivers in the central coastal prairie. There are more than a dozen active nests within fifty miles of the Aransas Wildlife Refuge, all sequestered on private property.

Between 1971 and 1985, Texas bald eagles fledged 130 known young, and a banding program has revealed that some of those birds have now matured and returned to breed in the Lone Star State. So the southern bald eagles are doing their part in a comeback effort, but they are still so sparse as to merit their endangered listing. The northern race is recovering rapidly enough that it may soon be downlisted to threatened status.

Bald eagles are long-lived birds that mate for life and frequently reuse traditional nest sites. Since the Aransas Refuge was established, 26 nesting attempts at six different sites on the refuge have been recorded. During the forties there were 13 attempts, including the record of 3 nests in 1944. There were 7 tries during the fifties, 5 in the sixties, and 1 in the seventies. The last documented nesting was in 1971. These records probably cover the activity of a small and dwindling number of adults. When they died, there was no ready recruitment from the devastated local population. The persistent current nesting vacancy may be a consequence of increased human activity on and around the refuge. Favored nest sites have been atop tall live oak trees where the accumulating platforms of sticks are routinely refurbished and lined with shredded grass in December. Locations of the aerie sites on the Aransas

Figure 20. Nest sites of the southern bald eagle on the Aransas National Wildlife Refuge. Eagles have not nested on the refuge since 1971. Data are from the files of the ANWR.

are indicated on Figure 20, but no remains can be seen today. Eagles have never tried to use the artificial nesting poles that were erected for them at three sites.

Eaglets are in the nest during the coldest months of January and February, and they finally fledge in early April. Food items found in the nests on the Aransas generally confirm the eagles' diet of fish and waterfowl: flounder, mullet, red drum; a white pelican, many American coots, pintails, scaups, and numerous grebes; swamp rabbits and cottontails, and one armadillo that may have been picked up as carrion. One adult eagle was seen in flight carrying a struggling scaup duck in its talons. Another was observed over Dunham Bay dive-bombing an osprey in an apparent attempt to make it drop its fish.

The records from annual narrative reports of the refuge clearly reveal the hazards with which nesting eagles must contend. On two occasions tree limbs broke beneath heavy accumulations of sticks, destroying the nesting sites. In 1940, a pair of eagles abandoned their nest when an oil well blew up in flames nearby. There are several observations of eggs and no subsequent hatchlings, and many of hatchlings that never fledged. The causes of such failures could only be vaguely ascribed to predation. In one instance a half-eaten eaglet had apparently been attacked by its two nestmates.

In January 1941, an unknown predator ate the eggs in an eagle nest and precipitated the only refuge record of a renesting attempt. The same pair of adults had week-old eaglets in another nest at the end of March.

You can most reasonably aspire to see a bald eagle on the Aransas Refuge during fall migration. Although the birds are never common, if one is in residence it often has a favored perch and hunting ground. Ask at the WIC. Otherwise, keep an eye peeled throughout your visit. Even a glimpse of a fast-flying bald eagle is a thrill, and if you see a pair engaged in aerial courtship or an individual deftly plucking a mullet out of Mustang Lake, you have a lifetime memory to cherish.

The adults are easy to identify, but check your bird book so that you can distinguish young birds, which lack the distinctive white head and neck until their fourth year. Northern and southern bald eagles both may visit the refuge, but they cannot be distinguished in the field except by the nesting activity of the more common southern race.

Winter visitors who are eager to see a bald eagle might try Lake Texana State Park fifty miles north of the refuge near Edna. Seventy-five miles northwest of Austin a cruise boat plies Lake Buchanan looking for bald eagles; for information and reservations call 512-756-6986. If you have sharp eyes, you can spot a bulky eagle nest against the skyline in tall trees on the north side of FM 239, eight miles west of Tivoli. Ask at the WIC for specifics.

Peregrine Falcon

Two races of peregrines, the American and the Arctic (or tundra), occur in Texas. The American peregrine is a partial migrant that occupies a few mountain ranges in far West Texas and occasionally moves coastward in the wintertime. Although it was never especially abundant, this is the bird that originally ranged the entire continent until it was extirpated east of the Mississippi River and severely reduced in the

West during the DDT era. In 1970, its plight finally earned it endangered status and nationwide attention. An intensive captive breeding-and-release program has been highly successful in helping the American peregrine reclaim lost terrain, and there is hope that the subspecies can soon be removed from the endangered list.

The Arctic peregrine is a migratory form that nests in Greenland and the high North American tundra and winters in South America. The relative isolation of its nesting and wintering grounds buffered this race from the brunt of the pesticide onslaught, although migrating birds encountered contaminated prey. Originally put on the endangered list in 1970, this race was reclassified as threatened in 1984. Now that the population seems secure, the USFWS has removed the birds from the threatened list entirely.

It is the Arctic peregrine that passes across the Aransas Wildlife Refuge twice each year and occasionally drops off a wintering individual or two. Fall migrants generally appear from September through October and spring migrants from March through April. Because the peregrines prey on waterfowl and shorebirds, they prefer to sweep along the open barrier islands.

The Texas barriers are an important staging area for tundra peregrines—a spot where the birds traditionally pause to rest and fatten before shoving off on the remainder of their 5,000-mile trek between the high Arctic and the Andes in Peru. Over the past decade more than three thousand of these falcons have been trapped and banded by researchers on Padre Island. The blood of these peregrines is routinely sampled both to monitor pesticide levels and to reckon the birds' points of origin.

Seeing a peregrine falcon stoop (dive on its prey) ranks as one of the most thrilling of wildlife observations. The drama may begin on Matagorda Island with a small flight of green-winged teal batting steadily upwind against a brisk October norther. En route to a freshwater depression on the central part of the island, they do not see the speck in the sky above them, but the speck sees the teal.

The peregrine begins its long slanting descent on folded wing. It picks up speed rapidly, pumping its wings now and then for added thrust. By the time the speck has transformed into a feathered dive-bomber it is moving at an incredible 150 miles per hour and accelerating.

Finally the teal spot it, and they immediately scatter and plunge for cover. But one of them is already marked for doom. The peregrine strikes the hapless teal hard in the neck and back with widespread raking talons. The duck crumples in midair amid an explosion of feathers. The falcon pulls out of its dive in a graceful arc, wheels, and lightly touches down beside its shattered prey.

Peregrine stooping

Migrating peregrines are seen now and then as they cruise and perch along the margins of San Antonio and St. Charles bays, but most refuge sightings occur along the beach on Matagorda Island. Prime time is October; for the past several years about twenty birds have been seen in a routine sunrise survey during the first three weeks of that month. Occasional individuals linger through the winter. Migrating falcons can also be observed along the Gulf beach south of Port Aransas, at Mustang Island State Park, and they are especially numerous at Padre Island National Seashore.

Aplomado Falcon

"Aplomado" (ap-lo-MAH-doh), from Spanish, refers to the bird's steel-gray head, back, and wings. According to early accounts this trim, medium-sized falcon was rather common in the virgin brush-studded grasslands of South and West Texas. However, by the thirties its numbers had declined drastically, and it has not been known to nest in the state for fifty years. It was a noteworthy event in the winter of 1992 when a transient individual edged across the Rio Grande and spent several months in far West Texas.

No single factor stands out to account for the disappearance of the state's aplomado falcons. Deterioration of habitat certainly contributed. Brush encroachment into their favored arid savannah probably interfered with the falcons' swift pursuit and midair capture of passerine birds and grasshoppers. (The birds often hunt in cooperative pairs.) The reduced crop of grass seeds and loss of ground cover surely caused a change in the abundance and diversity of favored prey species. "Improving" pastures by the introduction of a monoculture of exotic buffel grass certainly did not enhance the falcons' food chain.

Because aplomado falcons prefer to rear their young in the abandoned nests of other raptors, available nesting sites became scarce as all birds of prey fell before the multifarious inroads of advancing civilization. For a change, we cannot incriminate DDT, for the simple reason that the aplomado falcons were already virtually gone before the pesticide era began. Today they range through suitable habitat in Mexico and into South America.

The Aransas Refuge lies on the northern periphery of scattered recent reports of this species. There were several sightings on the Tour Loop in the early seventies, but none was well verified. The most recent creditable observation was of a single bird in the winter of 1991.

Using expertise developed in rearing and releasing peregrine falcons, researchers freed two dozen fledgling aplomados in deep South Texas from 1985 to 1989. Three more birds were set free there in 1993 to begin a fifteen-year program of introductions. The Tatton Unit is prime aplomado habitat, and it was considered as a release site, but putting an avian predator into the endangered Attwater's prairie chicken range set programs at cross-purposes. So the center of release activity has been the Laguna Atascosa National Wildlife Refuge 150 miles down the coast from the Aransas. It is still too early to determine if the species can reestablish a wild population in South Texas.

If you think you have spotted an aplomado falcon on the Aransas, try to get witnesses with birding experience to corroborate your identification; take a photograph of the bird if you can and alert a refuge ranger.

Piping Plover

These uncommon little shorebirds with sandy plumage and pale orange legs do not stand out from the several other kinds of plovers that run in stop-and-go fashion along the bay margin and the mud flats. Their one unfortunate distinction is their determination to nest only on clean sandy beaches, precisely the sort of places that lure sunbathers, beachcombers, fishermen, dune buggies, automobiles, and waterfront developers and that eventually support marauding dogs and an increased population of predatory raccoons and skunks.

Even though they rallied from merciless turn-of-the-century market hunting, piping plovers have declined drastically in the past decade, mainly because of disturbance on their nesting grounds. In 1985, they were listed as endangered in Canada and in a principal nesting area around the Great Lakes, and the next year they were given threatened status throughout the remainder of their range. A 1991 census recorded about four thousand piping plovers in North America. The Texas coastline is a favored wintering ground for the species, which seldom goes farther south than Yucatan.

Piping plovers are regular but uncommon winter residents on the Aransas from September through February. Even when the birds are present they are easily overlooked, though a few individuals are routinely recorded during the annual Christmas bird count. During the 1991 census 44 birds were tallied on the mainland refuge, 20 of them on the bay side at the end of the boardwalk.

Consult your bird guide and work out the proper combination of back, leg, and bill colors and the degree of breast banding, all appropriately adjusted for drab winter plumage. Then find a mud flat or sand barren alive with tiny scrambling birds, most of them probably too far away to tell front from rear, and enter the delightfully frustrating world of the birder on the Texas coast. Your chance of success is much higher on the beach and tidal flats on Matagorda Island, but piping plovers are often forced to the mainland shore during stormy weather.

Eskimo Curlew

This slim and delicate species was once as abundant as any inland plover, but by 1900 it was almost extinct, and today it remains one of the rarest birds in the world.

Eskimo curlews bred in the Canadian tundra and wintered in the Argentine pampas. Each fall they congregated in Newfoundland and Labrador before launching on a nonstop flight down the Atlantic seaboard. In the spring the birds followed a more leisurely inland route that took them over Texas and up the Central Flyway back to Canada.

Because their plump breasts were regarded as epicurean fare and the gregarious, twittering flocks were easy to shoot, curlews were forced to run a deadly gauntlet of recreational and commercial gunfire throughout their migration route, and they were further hunted on their wintering grounds. Immense flocks of "prairie pigeons" were eagerly an-

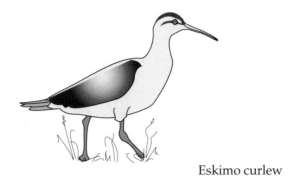

Eskimo curlew

ticipated across Texas each April during the 1880's, until the wanton shooting so decimated their numbers that the species, in a scant two decades, was brought to the brink of extinction.

Today, long protected by law and even more so by absolute scarcity, the few remaining curlews seem unable to rally their kind. They were gentle birds that reveled in the midst of their own joyous, dithering congregations, a contentment the furtive stragglers can no longer enjoy. The dispirited few cling to life, but without their accustomed enthusiasm. The fault is certainly not theirs.

Three Eskimo curlews were seen in 1905, and when there were no more sightings for forty years, the species was thought to be extinct. Then two individuals were spotted on Galveston Island in 1945. (Imagine the stir in the birding world!) During subsequent years just enough confirmed sightings have been made to justify the hope that the Eskimo curlew is indeed hanging on.

Between 1946 and 1968, there were nine more reports involving a total of 12 birds. All of these were in the Texas Coastal Bend, and the one seen on April 27, 1950, was the first verified observation of an Eskimo curlew on the Aransas Refuge. In 1981, a pair of experienced birders reported a flock of 23 of the rare birds at Galveston. There were four creditable sightings in the spring of 1987: a single bird in Nebraska, a pair in Canada, 1 on the Texas-Louisiana border, and 3 individuals on Blackjack Point at the tip of the Aransas National Wildlife Refuge.

Other than a continued watch for migrants and an annual check of protected ancestral nesting grounds in Canada's Northwest Territories, where the last nest was found while the Civil War raged, there is no active conservation program for the Eskimo curlew. Wildlife biologists are practicing at raising a related species of curlew in captivity so they can apply their experience to Eskimo curlews if the happy circumstance should arise. But at the moment, hope is our only real prerogative.

Clearly you cannot anticipate seeing an Eskimo curlew on the Aransas, but you can realistically aspire to do so if you are prepared. During March and April, pick meticulously through the flocks of shorebirds, especially those that wander across moist glades well away from the water's edge. Check your bird book carefully to distinguish the relatively common long-billed curlew and the less common whimbrel, both much larger birds than the rare quarry you seek.

If you should become convinced that you have spotted an Eskimo curlew, do not disturb it. If possible, get other birders to confirm your suspicion; snap a photograph of the bird if you can. Highball to the WIC and alert a member of the staff who can verify your observation.

Wood Stork

Standing 3½ feet tall and with a wingspan of 5½ feet, the wood stork is the largest long-legged wading bird native to the United States. The unfeathered head and neck with its wrinkled dusky skin lends the stork a vulturine aspect. Its bright white body plumage is trimmed with glossy black flight feathers and a stubby black tail. The bird's trademark is its massive black bill, curved down near the tip. Wood storks perch in a characteristically gloomy, humped posture on dead tree limbs or on open banks, and they soar and flap with outstretched necks slightly declined. Silent but social, wood storks usually feed, roost, and nest in flocks.

Although many eager visitors mistake them for whooping cranes, whether in the air or on the ground, it should take only a quick second glance to recognize an ungainly wood stork. High-gliding storks might be taken for white pelicans, but neck and bill conformation, dark tail, and the storks' long trailing legs should clinch their identification.

Wood storks range from South America through Central America and Mexico and into the southern United States. On the northern edge of their distribution, they historically nested from the swamplands of East Texas around the rim of the Gulf of Mexico and up the Atlantic coast to South Carolina. Today their rookeries north of Mexico are restricted mostly to Florida, with some in Georgia and South Carolina. The birds that visit the Aransas each summer are thought to come up the coast from undetermined nesting sites in northeastern Mexico.

Because wood storks do not sport filigreed plumage and are not regarded as tasty, they avoided the decimation of the plume trade and the market-hunting decades. As far as is known, they also escaped the deadly impact of the DDT era. However, as soon as accurate population estimates began, decline in nesting pairs of wood storks in the United States became evident. The breeding population of about twenty thousand pairs in the thirties had dropped to half of that by 1960 and has been halved again, to about five thousand pairs today. In 1984, the breeding population of wood storks in the United States was listed as endangered. Because birds summering in Texas probably come from Mexico, they are not part of the listed population.

The wood stork's massive bill and long, stout legs suggest its lifestyle: a wader specializing in relatively large prey in shallow fresh and brackish ponds, bayous, and marshes. Storks customarily forage in flocks, walking along in loose aggregations, each bird sweeping the muddy shallows with partly open bill. Although they snap up anything they encounter, including insect larvae, crustaceans, amphibians, and small reptiles, their staple prey is fish.

It takes considerable biomass to stoke their large bodies and to feed their ravenous young. To get this bulk, wood storks prefer to feed where fish are concentrated: in freshwater pools that are drying up. Therein lies the birds' current ecological trouble. The marginal wetland habitat upon which the wood storks depend is precisely the type of terrain that lends itself to draining for agriculture and for industrial and residential development.

Investigation shows that the durable wood storks, which had avoided gunfire and pesticides and withstood the inroads of cypress loggers, are succumbing to a more insidious and insistent threat—starvation. There are simply too few good feeding sites left. Also, the storks' breeding cycle is geared to take advantage of normal summer drawdown of natural waterways, so that nestling demand is highest when fish are most easily obtained. Water control projects upset this seasonal progression, resulting in nestling starvation. The key to maintaining breeding wood storks in the United States (and along with them, a whole community of beleaguered wildlife and plants) is to protect their vital wetland foraging grounds.

Wood storks begin arriving on the Aransas in June, and they linger into September. Their favorite roosting and feeding site is at Burgentine Lake, which is not routinely open to visitors. Throughout the hot Texas summer, Burgentine progressively dwindles in size, and it sometimes goes completely dry. Nothing could suit the hungry wood storks better. They glut on teeming thousands of trapped grass shrimp and sheepshead killifish. At peak periods several hundred storks populate the lake area. When the mud flats are exposed at low tide, you might find storks working the edge of San Antonio Bay off the bay overlook and the end of the boardwalk, and they are occasionally seen from the observation tower loafing on mud spits in Mustang Lake. Wood storks also frequent the bay side of Matagorda Island.

Least Tern

A dainty tern with a black cap, white forehead, bright yellow bill, and deeply forked tail, the least tern adroitly hovers over the water and suddenly plunges for a small fish. Two races occur in Texas (and a third in California); both winter in Central and South America and pass across the refuge in migration, but they cannot be distinguished except by nesting site.

Coastal least terns, which live near and nest on sandy beaches or expanses of crushed shell, range around the rim of the Gulf of Mexico and up the Atlantic seaboard. Encroachment by people and their free-ranging pets onto favored nesting grounds has caused a severe decline in the number of coastal least terns. A few local birds have found sufficient sanctuary to nest on the tip of Blackjack Peninsula and on Matagorda Island. This sparse population seems to be maintaining itself.

Inland least terns nest on sandbars and gravelly or sandy islets along large rivers and reservoirs. They are suffering from destruction of their nesting habitat as a result of channelization and damming of streams. In 1985, when the population of the interior race was estimated to total about 1,500 individuals, it was put on the endangered list. Largely because of loss of nesting habitat and degradation of feeding sites, all three races of least terns are now listed as endangered in the United States.

We are fortunate to still have least terns at all; these petite "sea swallows" were almost exterminated by plume hunters in the early decades of this century.

Gray Wolf

As far as Texas is concerned, the designation of the gray wolf as an endangered species in the lower 48 states (threatened in Minnesota) in 1976 came much too late. Guns, traps, poisons, hunting from airplanes, incessant pursuit by professional wolfers, bounty hunters, and "sportsmen"—all driven by near maniacal prejudice—had finally harried the animal beyond even its legendary endurance. The last documented gray wolf kill in Texas occurred in 1970.

Although an occasional wolf still wanders across the Rio Grande into far West Texas, there has been no breeding population in the state since the early twenties, and now the Mexican gray wolf population is feared to be nearly extinct in the wild. Most of the estimated 40,000 wild gray wolves left in North America occur in Canada and Alaska. The USFWS is planning to reintroduce animals in several western states.

It is uncertain whether gray wolves ever traversed Blackjack Peninsula in historical times. Certainly packs occasionally coursed across the coastal prairie, but their favored range was the open and broken country of West and Central Texas and across the endless North Texas plains. There they were the top-level predator on hooved game, especially on the southern herd of American bison. Abundant local pioneer references to wolves are notably untrustworthy, since they commonly confuse the state's two native species of wolves with coyotes.

Red Wolf

There are no more wild red wolves in Texas, and it is unlikely that those in captivity can ever be manipulated to alter that situation. The fact is lamentable because with the gray wolf gone, the state is now destitute of wolves. There can be no more telling testimony that Texas is no longer the wild and open country it is often portrayed as.

Red wolves were exquisite, rangy beasts, smaller than a gray wolf but larger than a coyote. A large male went to sixty pounds. They were more tawny than red, heavily suffused with gray and darkening to blackish over the shoulders and back. Their heads were distinctively wolfish: slanted, almond-shaped eyes rimmed with pale eyebrow spots, broad pale muzzle, and heavy jaws. They held their long ears cocked out at an angle rather than vertically like gray wolves and coyotes, giving the face a triangular outline. When cornered a coyote gapes widely, squalls, arches its back, and tucks its tail between its legs; gray and red wolves raise their hackles and snarl wickedly. But a mere glimpse in the wild was seldom enough to distinguish the animals accurately.

Ancestral red wolf range spanned the moist Southeast and struck up the Mississippi Valley to southern Illinois. As late as 1900 there were scattered groups of three to five individuals across the wooded eastern half of Texas. They were primarily small-game predators: swamp rabbits, cottontails, muskrats, beaver, marsh rice rats, cotton rats, bobwhite quail, greater prairie chickens, coots, rails, insects, fish. They also took sheep and poultry when they had a chance.

But such petty stock pilferage was not the main reason that people turned against red wolves. Rather, it was the simple fact that they were predators, meat-eaters, killers. Worse, they were *wolves*, steeped in all the venomous legend that Old World tales conveyed with that epithet. Backed by such popular prejudice, humans set themselves upon a relentless campaign of extermination, which probably has no parallel for sheer determination and viciousness. Wolves were shot, trapped, poi-

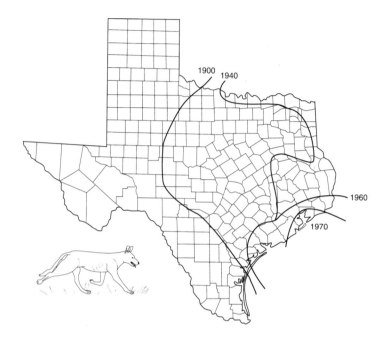

Figure 21. Historic range of the red wolf in Texas. Data are from the files of the TPWD.

soned, clubbed, maimed, trailed with dogs, spotted from airplanes, lured with chemicals and electronic devices, gassed in their dens, scalped for bounty money, and skewered on barbed wire fences for show. Professional wolfers were respected members of society.

In 1915, the federal government launched its predator control program with the avowed intent of protecting livestock and game animals. Wolves were near the top of the wanted list, and government trappers were the best in the grim trade. In the mid-forties they began to use the potent poison called 1080 and the devilishly effective cyanide gun. By 1964, they had driven the red wolf into a small corner of its former range, and there a new, more insidious menace was poised to finish off the harried animal.

Years of deforestation and overgrazing worked against the red wolf and in favor of the coyote, so that by the forties coyotes were moving eastward across the Blackland Prairie and into the cleared land beyond. The more adaptable and elusive coyote was on the increase; the less adaptable and more gullible red wolf was on the decline. Wherever the two met in the zone of ecological disruption they interbred, and abundant coyote genes swamped rare wolf genes. By the seventies there were only a few recognizably pure red wolves left in deep southeastern Texas.

Blood analysis suggests that these animals—and perhaps the entire original population of red wolves—may have been stable hybrids between gray wolves and coyotes. It is not uncommon for such natural mongrelization to give rise to a new species, but it takes some time in isolation. In this case the process was being undone by habitat destruction and the resultant breakdown of behavioral barriers that had prevented excessive backcrossing between coyotes and red wolves.

Finally, public sentiment did an about-face, and in 1965, only a year after government trappers were taken off their trail, red wolves were recognized as being worth saving. They went on the endangered list in 1967.

For several years in the mid-seventies a concerted effort was made to save the wild remnant holed up deep in the coastal marshes of Chambers and Jefferson counties in the southeastern corner of Texas. The problem of scant numbers crowded into a parasite-infested swampland was greatly worsened by the need to protect those precious few from a heavy infusion of coyote blood. It could not be done. In desperation captive stock was collected in 1976. Then, in 1980, everyone conceded that there was no point in going on with the field work. Sixty years of determined attack had won out; the red wolf in the wild was gone.

Of the 40 animals in captivity, only 17 were judged pure enough to use in a breeding program. Despite its restricted gene pool, by 1991, the captive project had spawned 159 red wolves, and a few individuals had been successfully returned to the wild on wildlife refuges and barrier islands in the Southeast. However, it is likely that coastal Texas has no areas remote enough from either humans or coyotes to sustain reintroductions.

Red wolves were still moderately abundant on the central coast in 1937 when the Aransas Refuge was established, but this was during the heyday of the notion that predator control (that is, predator eradication) was an important means of conserving wild game species. The first red wolf of record on Blackjack Peninsula was trapped in 1939. From then on, the onslaught was waged with customary zeal. For the next quarter-century the resident trapper often drove over forty miles to check his line of fifty steel traps and seventy cyanide "getters."

These trappers were skillful and meticulous men who worked long hours in the field, who grunted their satisfaction when they caught a pregnant wolf or a nursing female, who did their paperwork, weighed their catch, and dutifully sent off skulls, hides, and stomach contents to Washington. They had no reason whatsoever for not sleeping well after a good day's work. In hindsight, they did their job too well.

By 1960, there was a growing awareness of the vital role predators play in maintaining prey species—including game species—in harmony with their resource base. Mercifully and astutely, the predator control program was halted on the Aransas Refuge in 1963. Unfortunately, it was too late to save the red wolf.

In 1956, the skulls of six canids trapped on the refuge were sent to Washington. Five were confirmed to be red wolves. The sixth was a large coyote. Between 1956 and 1963, 86 more canids were taken. All looked more like coyotes than wolves. In 1971, 17 canids were tranquilized, checked, and released. All were large coyotes. The narrative report for 1972 provides the epitaph for the red wolf on the refuge: "A dismal fact looms larger than ever . . . the red wolf is gone from the Aransas."

So, the red wolf, with its phantom voice and its long, tireless stride, is gone forever from the Coastal Bend. We can redeem ourselves only if we have learned a lesson by its passing.

The Texas Zoo in Victoria, sixty miles from the Aransas Refuge, participates in the red wolf captive breeding program and usually has animals on display.

Jaguar

El tigre, largest cat of the Americas, is known from the Texas Gulf Coast both as Pleistocene fossils and from scattered early historical records. There is no documentation of this species from the Aransas Refuge, although one late nineteenth-century reference mentions its occurrence in Aransas County.

Jaguars definitely used to thread their way through the dense brush of the Rio Grande Valley and the thick woods along watercourses up the coast and on into the tangled vegetation of Southeast Texas, but they were always scarce. Even in earliest times, every encounter with one of the great blotched cats was worthy of mention, so pioneer tales of jaguars reflect the animal's sporadic occurrence rather than its abundance. It is doubtful that there has been a breeding population of jaguars in Texas in historical times. Displaced or restless old males set to wandering far from their normal haunts in Mexico probably account for most sightings in the state. There have been only two verified kills in Texas since 1900: one in 1903 and the other in 1946.

Jaguars have everything going against them: they are large predators, stock killers, isolationists, thrilling and even dangerous adversaries, and the owners of beautiful spotted coats. They are in trouble even in the depths of their tropical strongholds and well deserve the endangered status conferred upon them in 1972.

It is both impractical and imprudent to consider releasing wide-ranging jaguars into the modern Texas landscape. Both time and place have irrevocably passed the big spotted cats by. If we would tingle from hearing their hoarse cough quicken the gathering dusk in a tangled ravine, we must go elsewhere while there is yet time.

Ocelot

Many people regard *el tigre chiquito* as the most appealing and beautiful of the native cats of Texas. It is about the size of a bobcat but with a better-proportioned, lithe feline body and long tail. The tawny yellow coat is overlaid with a soft pearl-gray opalescence, and it is profusely ornamented with black spots, streaks, bars, and blotches; the tail is marked with broken black rings. No two ocelots bear the same pattern. Unfortunately, humans covet the pretty pelts.

These little tiger cats were once moderately common in the dense brush of South Texas and the rugged portions of the southern Edwards Plateau, and they ranged up the coast into East Texas and beyond. Always, they drew back from civilization. The last time they were regarded as occasional over most of their Texas range was about 1900.

Today ocelots are considered to be very rare in the nearly vanished brushlands of South Texas. These are creatures of the densest undergrowth and the dead of night. Because of their secretive habits and rarity, their presence is seldom suspicioned and sightings are few. One animal was trapped on the Santa Ana National Wildlife Refuge in 1967. Another was shot near Falcon Dam in 1971. A population of perhaps twenty animals was discovered on and near the Laguna Atascosa National Wildlife Refuge (150 miles south of the Aransas) in the seventies. Two dozen sightings were made in deep South Texas between 1978 and 1980. How many of those animals were residents and how many were immigrants from Mexico is not known. Workers in the Feline Research Program at the Caesar Kleberg Wildlife Research Institute in Kingsville estimate a state population of about one hundred.

Although ocelots live southward through Central America to Paraguay, by the seventies it was recognized that the species was declining throughout its range. Habitat destruction and hunting and trapping for pelts are the main reasons. In 1973, some of the pressure on tropical spotted cats was eased with an international agreement to curtail trafficking in both the animals and their hides. Nonetheless, the species went on the endangered list in the United States in 1982.

Ocelots absolutely require the seclusion of thick undergrowth and its attendant prey fauna of rodents, cottontails, and low-flying birds. In Texas, pastureland, citrus orchards, cropland, and urban sprawl have usurped all but isolated remnants of the native brush thickets. When their cover goes the ocelots move, leading to the second greatest hazard: they get run over on highways while trying to shift from one isolated patch of brush to another. Little wonder that ocelots and an entire fascinating semitropical ecosystem have all but vanished from the state.

Current conservation efforts include field studies to learn more about the animals' ecological requirements and tolerances, and the acquisition of patches of native brush. These clumps of native chaparral, connected by vegetated corridors, will compose the Lower Rio Grande Valley National Wildlife Refuge. Hopefully, the cats can hold on until their refuge becomes reality.

Are there ocelots on the Aransas? No one knows for sure. There is no question that ocelots occurred in Aransas County in historical times, and researchers include the region within the northeastern margin of the animal's probable current range. In its original savannah aspect Blackjack Peninsula would not have been especially attractive, but the dense live oak thickets of today should be prime ocelot habitat. The refuge, however, is not extensive enough to harbor more than a few pairs of these territorial creatures.

The interesting questions are whether ocelots can live permanently and breed here, and whether occasional individuals can bring fresh blood across the gauntlet of civilization that surrounds this island refugium. The situation is tenuous at best. Despite many hours in the field and a recent live-trapping effort, refuge personnel have never confirmed the presence of an ocelot on the Aransas. However, in March 1979, a pair of visitors gave a good description of such an animal, which they saw while driving the Tour Loop.

So we can all hope. It is part of the mystique of the Aransas that any time we clear a bend in a trail we just might find ourselves—for a fleeting instant—face to face with a shy spotted cat with huge brown eyes and twitching tail tip. Then it will vanish, and we will never be the same again.

Jaguarundi

This is the rarest and surely the most enigmatic of the native cats of Texas. Indeed, it does not even look much like a cat.

A jaguarundi (yah-gah-RUN-dee) is a little larger than a big tomcat. It is a slab-sided, short-legged, long-tailed creature with an unusually small head, flattened forehead, small rounded ears widely separated, and a snub nose bordered by inconspicuous whiskers. The yellow eyes are rather small, and their uncatlike round pupils give the animal a somewhat treacherous expression. The sinister aura is enhanced by the beast's nervous, slinking demeanor and uncatlike inchworming lope.

In a departure from the feline mold, young jaguarundis are born with adult coloration, not passing through the spotted pattern usual in young cats. Both of two color phases, salt-and-pepper gray and a grizzled rusty brown, may occur in the same litter.

The low-slung, weasellike body of *el leoncillo* is well adapted to threading its favored habitat of thick thorn brush. Here the animal creeps and glides with ease, moving by day and by night in the perpetual gloom, stalking everything from packrats to chachalacas. The creature is so secretive that it is seen only by chance. Most reported sightings are made by deer hunters sitting quietly in their stands or by travelers who happen to see an animal crossing the road. It is uncommonly difficult to trap and can be flushed from its impenetrable haunts only by specially trained dogs.

The jaguarundi ranges from the proximity of the Rio Grande in Texas southward to Argentina. Except for a thin coastal extension, it apparently never occurred more widely in the state. (There are recent reports of the cats in Florida, where they have probably escaped from captivity.) The last verified jaguarundi in Texas was a road-killed animal near Brownsville. If there is a significant breeding population in the state, it is most probably in the remaining brushlands of deep South Texas.

In both Texas and Mexico this retiring little cat is in trouble for one main reason—the opening up of its brushy habitat for agriculture and development. (The jaguarundi's rather drab pelt has exempted it from commercial hide hunting.) When fields, citrus orchards, pastures, and shopping malls replace natural chaparral the entire native community disintegrates, and the shy jaguarundi is among the first members to vanish. Then we lose something unique that we were hardly even aware we possessed. Such wholesale environmental disruption has transformed all but small isolated patches of the original brushland in South Texas, so the jaguarundi well deserved the endangered status conferred upon it in 1976.

Do jaguarundis occur on the Aransas Refuge? Happily, the consensus is that they do. How many individuals are present and whether they constitute a viable resident population is not known. Efforts to live-trap them have failed, as have trip wires attached to flash cameras, but every year since 1978, jaguarundis have been glimpsed by both visitors and staff (see Figure 22). Although some of these sightings have been made in good light by trained wildlife biologists, the fact remains that the cat has yet to be reliably documented on the refuge in recent times by either photograph or specimen in hand. There is one tantalizing photograph

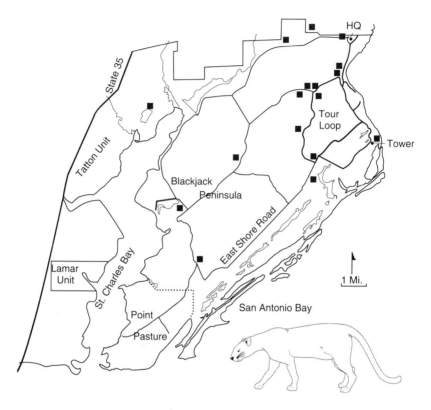

Figure 22. Reported sightings of jaguarundi on the Aransas National Wildlife Refuge through 1990. Data are from the files of the ANWR.

in the 1940 narrative report labeled "jaguarundi kitten pet in CCC camp" but without further details.

Keep your eyes open, especially at dusk, for a slinking, long-tailed phantom darting from one live oak thicket to the next. You may become one of the privileged few to glimpse one of the rarest mammals in the state in its native haunts. You can see captives in the Texas Zoo in Victoria.

West Indian Manatee

Although in years long gone by these large marine mammals surely came up from the Bay of Campeche to summer in the lush submarine pastures in local bays, there are no verified historic or recent sightings in the Coastal Bend. In U.S. waters a population of about 1,500 animals is resident along the Gulf and Atlantic coasts of Florida. Manatees have been on the endangered list since 1970.

American Alligator

On any balmy afternoon two hundred years ago, hundreds of thousands of alligators of all sizes would have been lying crisscrossed and heaped like so much driftwood along rivers, sloughs, and estuaries from North Carolina to South Texas. Basking contentedly in the sunshine, these great reptiles were carrying on a lethargic tradition handed down unchanged among their stolid kind for more than 200 million years. That carefree habit was to change abruptly over the span of a few decades when the slaughter of these vulnerable beasts began.

Alligators were shot for meat, for the domestic use of their belly skins, even for idle sport from the days of the earliest white explorers and settlers. In the 1850's, when alligator leather became fashionable, the pace of the killing stepped up. By the 1870's commercial buyers and tanneries had made market hunting of alligators a profitable business, and the era of the professional gator hunter was ushered in. It was a grisly, deadly efficient enterprise. Even though the beasts rapidly became wary, they were relatively easy to shoot at night by the orange-red glow of their eyes in a light beam; many were dragged from their lairs on hooks attached to poles; others were snagged on baited hooks and then dispatched with shotgun or ax; young animals were methodically collected and sold as pets or stuffed as curios. There was even a market for alligator eggs.

By the 1960's continued unregulated hunting had woefully reduced the American alligator in all portions of its range, and the creatures were further suffering a loss of habitat to waterfront development and the drainage of wetlands. In 1967, the reptile went onto the federal endangered species list.

Relieved of persecution, the alligator made a spectacular recovery, and by the mid-seventies the wild population had rebounded so well that it was reclassified as threatened. Within a few years gators had become so numerous in several states that limited and carefully regulated hunting was allowed. Texas held its first regulated alligator hunt in selected counties in September 1984. Annual hunts have continued to date, with a projected sustained harvest of two thousand animals a year. Despite its recovered numbers, the alligator remains on the threatened list because it superficially resembles the endangered Florida crocodile. Tight regulations on the threatened alligator allow for closer regulation of commerce in their hides and make it less likely that Florida hunters will mistakenly kill a crocodile.

Alligator

The alligator is one of the most popular species on the Aransas Refuge. It is a rare daylight hour when there are not at least a few visitors observing and photographing the several large gators that loaf at the edge of Thomas Slough beside the WIC. Indeed, a fence had to be erected there to keep reptile and admirer safely separated. Other popular observation spots include the pier overlooking Jones Lake, the observation deck on Hog Lake, and the several pools in Muskgrass Slough bordering the outer ridge on the Heron Flats Trail. The human fascination with the alligator seems inexhaustible. This survivor from an alien, antediluvian time exudes an aura of awesome power even when it lies unmoving on a sunlit mud bank. Somehow, alligators always manage to generate a thrill in children of all ages.

Questions about alligators are countless.

How big do alligators get? The accepted record is a monster of nineteen feet two inches taken by the father of alligator researchers, Edward A. McIlhenny, in Louisiana in 1890. The largest Texas gator was a sixteen-footer shot in Powderhorn Lake at Indianola, just twenty miles up the coast from the refuge. Several individuals over thirteen feet long have been taken in recent Texas hunts.

These days any alligator over twelve feet long is regarded as unusually large. One of the individuals that haunts Thomas Slough has been estimated to be a thirteen-footer, and another in Jones Lake must be at least that large. The skeleton of an alligator found in Tule Lake on the refuge in 1988 was judged to be that of a fourteen-footer. Most wild ones are in the range of four to ten feet.

Hatchlings are eight inches long. They grow about a foot per year for the first five years. Then the rate slows, but these reptiles continue to grow throughout life. An alligator matures when it is six feet long.

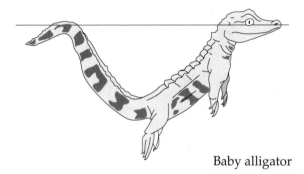

Baby alligator

Males grow faster than females: at an age of ten years males are about eight and a half feet long, females only seven feet. A twelve-foot bull alligator may be twenty years old and weigh 400 pounds; one massive wild-caught thirteen-footer tipped the scale at 850 pounds.

For idle amusement try this. From a safe distance, estimate the span in inches between a gator's nostril and eye. This will be approximately equivalent to the animal's total length in feet. By using this handy ratio you can judge an alligator's size even when you can see only its head above the surface of the water.

How many alligators are there on the refuge? Counts during the annual June census yield an estimate of 225.

How do alligators reproduce? They lay eggs. Mating on the refuge occurs from April to June, nesting in June and July, and hatching in August and September. The female alligator spends several days dragging bankside vegetation into a flat-topped mound about six feet across and two feet high in the center. With her hind legs she digs a cavity into the mound in which she deposits several dozen leathery, three-inch-long eggs. When she covers these with mud and rotting vegetation the mound becomes a natural incubator. Interestingly, if the nest temperature averages 86°F or below, the young will all develop into females; if 93°F or above, all hatchlings become males. Most nest temperatures fall in the intermediate range that yields both sexes.

Although the female attempts to guard her nest, raccoons and feral hogs manage to filch many alligator eggs. Hatchlings, even though they stay near Mama for several months, face a world of hungry predators, ranging from raccoons and great blue herons to alligator gars and larger alligators.

Alligator nests have been found near most bodies of fresh water on the refuge. It is not uncommon to see freshly hatched babies in Thomas Slough across the road from the WIC and from the pier on Hog Lake.

What do alligators do in the wintertime? Very little. Being cold-blooded creatures, they become quite torpid. Although they do not actually hibernate on the Aransas, they cease to feed and their sluggish metabolism grinds to a near standstill. They still enjoy soaking up the sunshine even on quite cool days. In really cold weather alligators remain submerged except to surface at infrequent intervals for a breath of air. Valves in their nostrils, throats, and ears and membranes over their eyes make it easy to stay under, and large individuals can stay submerged more than 24 hours.

Alligators can survive being frozen in ice for brief periods, but the resultant stress often causes them to succumb to respiratory disease weeks later. After a December freeze in 1989, eight dead alligators, including one ten-footer, were found at Burgentine Lake.

Do alligators make any sounds? They certainly do, and they have acute hearing to make their sounds useful. All gators produce a wicked hiss when provoked, and during the mating season the bull gator makes a loud rumbling roar, which, it is thought, challenges other males and also attracts females. The female utters a less intimidating groaning call in response to the male, and she also has a gruntlike sound to call her hatchlings. Baby alligators produce appealing burping and chirruping sounds.

What do alligators do if the water dries up? Actually, this happens rather frequently on the Aransas Refuge, and the alligators have some options. They may simply lie up in the surrounding vegetation and await a rain. Alternatively, they may retreat to a depression or den they have excavated deeply enough to retain some stagnant water, and simply wait for better times. These gator holes are important for the survival of other denizens of the refuge during droughts; everything from killifish and leopard frogs to cottonmouth moccasins and aquatic insects seek refuge in them.

Finally, alligators are quite capable of lumbering overland for a mile or so in search of water. Although the animals on the refuge are not marked for positive identification, it is felt that individuals do move from pond to pond according to the vagaries of the weather and the dictates of their own social fraternity. Sometimes they show up in odd places. Occasionally an alligator chooses the center of a refuge road to bask in the sun; once a nine-footer decided to take a nap in the center of the parking lot at the observation tower.

Can alligators live in salt water? They can, for a while at least, but they definitely prefer brackish or fresh water. They are occasionally seen cruising along the bayshore, and in 1965 a gator became entangled in a shrimper's trawl well out in San Antonio Bay.

What do alligators eat? Any live animal they can catch and swallow, and carrion, too. Alligators do not chew their food but gulp it down whole or tear off and wolf down large chunks, leaving their powerful digestive juices to do the rest. They feed when they have the chance, but because of their low metabolic rate they do not need to eat frequently. A large adult can gain weight on fifty pounds of prey a year, and if necessary it can survive for over a year without a meal at all.

Alligator diet varies with the season and the size of the individual. Young ones, up to about five feet long, consume a smorgasbord of invertebrate fare: crayfish, blue crabs, fiddler crabs, adult and larval aquatic insects, surface-walking spiders, errant grasshoppers. They also eat frogs and whatever fishes they can catch. Larger alligators take a greater proportion of vertebrate prey, especially fish; when fishes are trapped in drying pools alligators will gorge on them. In the summer of 1984, when Jones Lake was reduced to a muddy puddle, 56 alligators were congregated there feasting on alligator gar and carp. One alligator taken by a hunter in the Coastal Bend had the stinger from a large sting-ray lodged in the roof of its mouth.

Reptiles also loom large on the adult's menu: nonvenomous water snakes, cottonmouth moccasins, all kinds of turtles, and small alligators. Birds are taken readily; alligators wait beneath rookeries to snap up fallen nestlings. They also snatch occasional adults of most waterfowl, but during the heavy winter concentrations of ducks and geese the alligators are usually dormant and not feeding. Any mammal that comes within range may be taken by an alligator: nutria, swamp rabbit, raccoon, marsh rice rat, feral hogs, and white-tailed deer.

In the refuge files there is a record of a 150-pound feral hog being killed and totally consumed by an alligator and another of an adult great blue heron removed from the stomach of a six-foot gator. And then there was the contented alligator found in a duck trap along with the remains of at least nine ducks.

How long do alligators live? It varies, of course, but they are not quite the Methuselahs they are renowned to be. Researchers estimate that less than 10 per cent of the young live to be two years old. If they make it that far, their survival rate improves. An average life span for an alligator in the wild is thought to be about fifty years.

Are alligators dangerous? Generally not, but they should never be trusted; individuals that have frequent contact with people, like those on the refuge, are less prone to retreat. In the summer of 1992 a youth swimming in Hynes Bay (just north of the refuge) was briefly mauled by an alligator. Such attacks are very rare; undoubtedly the gator mistook the boy for natural prey.

Generally a provoked gator will announce its disposition by inflating with air and hissing menacingly. A female guarding her nest or young will advance on an intruder, and she can move with unexpected speed. Beware of both ends: jaws chomp and tails swipe with leg-breaking force. So admire alligators from a prudent distance—no touching, close-up photography, molesting, or feeding. Of course, keep the kids in hand and pets on a leash.

Sea Turtles

Of the five species of sea turtles native to the Gulf of Mexico, all are widely distributed in the warmer portions of the Atlantic Ocean, and most range throughout the warm seas of the world. However, all of these marine reptiles are so continually harassed and so reduced in numbers that each is currently listed as either threatened or endangered. The only significant nesting sites of sea turtles in U.S. waters are along the Atlantic coast from North Carolina to central Florida.

The several species of sea turtles share a common life history. Adults live singly at sea, mostly over the shallow continental shelf. In the springtime the sexes meet in offshore aggregations, and then the females come onto traditional sandy beaches to lay their eggs. When the hatchlings dig out they immediately return to the sea, where they spend a perilous several years before taking up the adult lifestyle. Females do not mature until they are about twenty years old, but once they begin to lay, they may do so several times a season for the next thirty years or so.

Although pelagic and littoral adults are routinely harpooned and

Sea turtle

netted in tropical parts of their range, it is the vulnerability of their beach-side nesting grounds that has brought the sea turtles to dire straits. Persistent overexploitation of the nesting females for meat, shell, skin, and oil and the wholesale collection of their eggs for food and an imagined aphrodisiac quality account for most human depredation. Seaside resort development and recreational activity have usurped or disrupted many of the favored nesting sites of these tradition-bound reptiles. Bright lights disorient the emerging hatchlings. Natural predation on the eggs by raccoons, coyotes, and crabs has been augmented by the activities of domestic and feral dogs and hogs. In U.S. waters, the principal threats to sea turtles are unintentional, but significant. Injury or drowning of turtles in shrimp trawls is the single most important destructive activity. Entanglement in or ingestion of cast-off plastic materials, contact with toxic chemicals, and disruption of marine food chains are also implicated.

Protection of the eggs and young is important, but modern effort is focused on the rapidly dwindling stock of maturing and breeding turtles. Conservation programs have been hampered by the lack of a unified effort among the many maritime countries that are involved in the life histories and welfare of the wide-ranging sea turtles.

Both the leatherback and the Atlantic hawksbill sea turtles, each endangered, are rare vagrants along the Texas coast, but there is no documentation of either ever nesting on the local barrier islands. Two hawksbills have been stranded on the Gulf beach of Matagorda Island, and two dead leatherbacks have been found there.

The green sea turtle is the most economically important reptile in the world, and it briefly supported a local industry in the last decades of the nineteenth century. When the cattle drives and then the railroads began to move longhorns northward, the dockside beef canneries were put out of business and they turned to green turtles. One of the busiest of these new enterprises was located at Fulton, on Live Oak Peninsula half a dozen miles south of Blackjack Peninsula. Special nets for green turtles were first set in Aransas Bay in 1881. In 1890, the local industry processed a quarter of a million pounds of turtle meat (more than nine hundred turtles). Many of the animals were trussed up and sold alive for a penny a pound, but most were processed into canned meat and soup at the bustling Fulton plant.

By 1895, the local turtle industry had exhausted its resource base, and it closed down in 1900. But the area's green turtle population never recovered. Hunted and harried throughout its range, the Gulf population has continued to decline. Today it is endangered in Florida and threatened elsewhere.

It is quite likely that green turtles once nested on the surf side of the

Texas barrier islands, but there are no historical or recent records for the Coastal Bend. Individuals still appear in Texas waters, accounting for about 4 percent of the annual sightings of sea turtles. They are probably animals that come up from the Caribbean or from nesting grounds in Florida.

The Atlantic loggerhead sea turtle is a rather hardy species that ranges from tropical into temperate seas around the world. It is the most common species in Gulf waters and makes up about 80 percent of the annual sea turtle sightings in Texas. Because its flesh is less esteemed than that of the green turtle, the loggerhead has suffered less from commercial exploitation. Yet these turtles are hunted and their nests are robbed in a multitude of small-scale operations, so they well deserve their current threatened status.

This species probably nested on the local barrier beaches in early historical times, but the only recent documentation occurred in 1977 and in 1979 on South Padre Island.

Although individual Atlantic ridley sea turtles (also called Kemp's ridley) are frequently swept into the North Atlantic by the Gulf Stream, this species is more narrowly restricted to the Gulf of Mexico than any of its kin. The ridley is also the most critically endangered, the result of gross overexploitation of its egg clutches on the single known nesting beach. In 1966, the Mexican government began protecting this beach, a fourteen-mile stretch on the coast of Tamaulipas between Tampico, Mexico, and Brownsville, Texas.

In 1978, a consortium of U.S. governmental agencies initiated an effort to establish a nesting colony of Atlantic ridleys on South Padre Island. Eggs collected in Tamaulipas were briefly exposed to Padre sand, and the hatchlings were given a dip in Padre surf in an attempt to imprint the little turtles to their foster locale. Then the young turtles were nurtured in facilities at Galveston until they were a year old and had grown to the diameter of a salad plate.

The first batch of manipulated ridleys was released off Padre Island in 1979. About two thousand were set free there annually through 1992. The turn of the century is the earliest these ridleys can be expected to return to nest. In 1991, a single female did lay on Padre, but it could not be determined whether she was one of the headstart progeny. Nonetheless, the historic event raised hopes. Despite all, the expensive hatchling program was discontinued in 1993, and effort will now be focused on watching for marked turtles, protecting the Mexican nesting beach, and enforcing legislation designed to protect free-roaming ridleys. Only time will tell whether the rehabilitation effort will reinstate this sea turtle on a portion of its ancestral range.

The principal feeding grounds of Atlantic ridleys lie off the Mississippi delta and in the Bay of Campeche, where the turtles forage for crabs. This species once nested from the vicinity of Corpus Christi south to Vera Cruz; a few nested on South Padre Island in the late seventies.

Intensive patrols on the surf side of Matagorda Island have yielded only sea turtle carcasses washed up on the beach. During the five-year period from 1978 to 1982, 108 dead turtles were discovered: 94 loggerheads, 13 Atlantic ridleys, and 1 green sea turtle. Most of them had been killed or maimed when they were entangled in shrimp trawls. In 1990, special trapdoors called turtle excluder devices (TEDs) were being tried by many members of the Texas shrimp fleet. In that year the count of stranded sea turtles on Matagorda Island dropped to 15. TEDs became mandatory for the shrimpers in 1991.

Your chances of seeing a live sea turtle on the Aransas are slim. You might try walking the beach on the Matagorda Unit during the spring or fall. If you see a beached turtle—live or dead—do not disturb it, but report your observation to refuge personnel.

The Texas Parks and Wildlife Department maintains its own lists of threatened and endangered species. Criteria generally follow federal guidelines, but the scope is limited to the confines of the state. All species on the federal lists that occur in Texas are also on the state lists.

There are some creatures that while they maintain healthy populations elsewhere, are rare and declining in Texas. As of January 1991, the following animals, which have been recorded from the Aransas National Wildlife Refuge, appeared on the threatened or endangered list of the state of Texas but not the federal list.

Endangered mammals
    coati
Threatened birds
    reddish egret
    white-faced ibis
    sooty tern
    American swallow-tailed kite
    white-tailed hawk
    zone-tailed hawk
    tropical parula
    Botteri's sparrow
Threatened reptiles
    Texas horned lizard
    Texas scarlet snake

None of the native plants on either the federal or the state lists is known to occur on the Aransas National Wildlife Refuge.

CHAPTER 7

Game Animals

In this chapter we include all those forms of wildlife on the Aransas National Wildlife Refuge that are regarded as game animals by the state of Texas. Of these, only the white-tailed deer is actually hunted on the refuge.

White-tailed Deer

Without question, this animal provides more enjoyment to more visitors than any other resident species on the Aransas Refuge, from the half-tame individuals that wander around the lawns at headquarters to magnificent, thick-necked bucks and large feeding groups that are routine Aransas sights. The tame deer allow close observation and photography, while the more nervous ones that frequent the roadsides and glades provide a genuine opportunity to observe whitetails in their native habitat. Wherever seen, there can be few wild creatures more appealing than an innocent-eyed, floppy-eared, wobbly-legged fawn.

You can appreciate the deer better if you are familiar with their annual life cycle.

In early spring (late March to early April) all of the adult does and most of the female yearlings are heavy with young, and the bucks have nubbin antlers covered with soft fuzzy skin. By late April to May the fast-growing antlers have branched into rounded tines, and because they are still covered with skin and hair, the deer are said to be "in velvet."

Early fawns may be born during the first week in April, and late ones appear throughout the summer, but most appear from mid-April through the first half of May. (On June 9, 1983, Ginger, a friendly doe, had twins in the refuge manager's back yard. The following year, on May 9, she bore a single fawn in the same place. In 1989 Ginger dropped twins at headquarters again, this time on April 26.) The fawns at first are inactive and remain hidden, but they are soon seen following their mothers.

During early summer (June and July) the bucks, in the final stages of antler growth, are still in velvet. Successful does are accompanied by single or twin offspring. The youngsters can forage for themselves by this time, but they nurse as long as the does will put up with them.

In late summer the rapidly growing offspring are still at their mothers' sides, but by this time nearly three-quarters of the year's progeny will have succumbed to various natural hazards. By August the bucks have rubbed the dried skin from their antlers, and each now carries a fully grown and polished rack.

Autumn (late September through early December) is the season of rut, the time that deer are most active. Now the impassioned bucks clash with each other, pursue the does endlessly, and finally mate with as many of them as they can. This vigorous interval peaks from late October to mid-November. By this time of the year, the young have lost their spots, and all of the deer begin to shed cinnamon-brown summer coats and acquire a darker, shaggier winter pelage.

As winter comes on (late December), the exhausted bucks wind down, start to shed their antlers, and settle in to feed and survive the brief winter months. The bucks roam singly or in twos and threes, while the does with their young cluster in feeding groups under the influence of a dominant matriarch. You may see a lopsided buck with one antler still clinging to the knob on its skull, but by the end of February all antlers have been dropped.

Aside from bucks' antagonism during the rut, the social nature of white-tailed deer allows for broad overlap of home ranges; rather than defending its chosen turf, a deer prefers the company of its own kind. The home range is made up of several interconnected activity centers where the animal spends most of its time. During a year a given whitetail in good habitat may roam over no more than 150 acres. Use of such localized sites varies with forage conditions, the season, and even with the time of day (deer routinely venture into the open at night and seek cover by day). All deer, and especially bucks, make occasional short exploratory excursions outside their home range, and a few "floaters" are prone to wanderlust.

As with most wildlife, the brunt of the mortality among white-tailed deer falls upon the very young. Only six out of ten fawns live for two weeks; by the end of their first summer another three will have succumbed, leaving just three fawns out of ten for recruitment into the population.

What strikes down the fawns? A dry summer saps the does and leaves the fawns undernourished and weak. Parasites—ticks, deer flies, mosquitoes, liver flukes, and roundworms—further wear down the young animals. In unusually wet years the fawns are prone to salmonellosis, a fatal bacterial disease of the lower intestine.

Whitetail buck in velvet

When deer occur at high densities, as they sometimes do on the Aransas, social stress can interfere with the mother-young bond. Does seek out a secluded spot to give birth, and for the first week the fawn moves about very little. If favored sites are already occupied, or if other deer wander past, the doe may get upset and abandon or lose her offspring; the fawn may be frightened into the open or try to follow the wrong doe. What appear to us to be mere annoyances may easily prove fatal for the delicate fawns.

There are always predators ready to take advantage of a succulent fawn whose only defense is its camouflaged coat and absence of body odor. Predation is difficult to study, but at the Welder Wildlife Refuge, 25 miles southwest of the Aransas, newborn fawns were fitted with radio transmitters. Predators eventually got half of these free-ranging animals. In all but one case coyotes were implicated. The exception involved a bobcat. It is quite likely that the same two species are the principal predators on Aransas deer.

Three-quarters of all the deaths in the Aransas herd each year are young. A deer that makes it through its first summer stands a good chance of living several years, and it may reach the relatively ripe old age of ten to twelve years. Death of aged adults usually results from poor nutrition brought on by severely worn teeth and reduced resistance to parasites and disease.

How does a deer herd stand such heavy attrition? Actually, it could not make ecological and adaptive ends meet without it. Behind the grim deaths of the fawns lies the natural mechanism that keeps the deer population genetically tuned up and in balance with the resources in its habitat.

The Aransas herd has one recorded experience with a breach of the universal dictum called carrying capacity. In 1938, soon after the refuge was established, there were about 3,000 deer on Blackjack Peninsula. An intensive 25-year predator control program allowed a sustained, exceptionally high fawn survival rate. The deer did so well that between 1940 and 1966 the Texas Parks and Wildlife Department live-trapped more than 13,000 animals on the refuge and used them to restock areas in the state where whitetails had been hunted out. The booming Aransas herd easily took in stride this imposed deletion of 500 deer a year.

In the early sixties the predator control effort was phased out, but by that time Aransas deer numbers were spiraling out of control. By 1965 the herd had doubled to some 6,000 animals. Browse lines developed where hungry deer snipped off leaves and twigs as high as they could reach on the mustang grape vines and prickly ash trees. Favored sedges disappeared from the moist banks of ponds. The range looked bad and so did the deer, but still the herd rocketed on.

Driven to desperate measures, the USFWS arranged the first public hunt ever held on the Aransas. For the entire month of October 1966, more than three thousand archers tried their luck and skill. They got 185 bucks, far too few to affect the population trend. In 1968, a survey indicated an all-time high of more than 13,000 deer on Blackjack Peninsula, a staggering density of one animal for every three acres of deer range. The annual public hunt was opened to firearms, but still with no significant impact on the herd.

At last, Mother Nature stepped in to right things. Two hurricanes in as many years turned the refuge into a vast lake, reducing deer habitat by 80 percent and crowding the remaining animals into an impossible density of nearly two per acre. Many deer migrated inland, while salmonellosis and hoof rot ran through the congested population. Fawn production was almost nil, and adult deer began to die from malnutrition. Hunters sloshing about in the first combined archery and rifle hunt managed to bag 908 of the starved and overcrowded animals.

Finally, the size of the deer herd began to drop, neatly and subtly, without even telltale carcasses lying about; dense oak brush teeming with scavengers and a climate that fosters rapid decomposition do not leave lingering evidence of death. The population plunged to 5,400 in 1969, to 1,800 by 1970, and has since stabilized at about 2,000 healthy animals.

What do the deer eat? White-tailed deer are highly selective browsers; they forage by moving along continuously, gingerly snipping desired vegetation as they go. They are known to use more than 160 species of plants in the Coastal Bend, but only about a dozen of these make up the bulk of their diet. On the refuge over half their annual food mass comes from the most common tree—the live oak. Deer browse its grow-

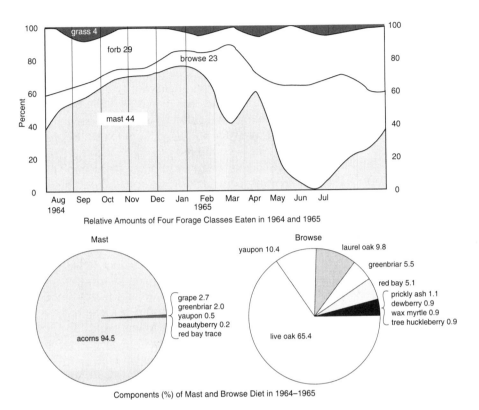

Relative Amounts of Four Forage Classes Eaten in 1964 and 1965

Mast

acorns 94.5

grape 2.7
greenbriar 2.0
yaupon 0.5
beautyberry 0.2
red bay trace

Browse

yaupon 10.4
laurel oak 9.8
greenbriar 5.5
red bay 5.1
prickly ash 1.1
dewberry 0.9
wax myrtle 0.9
tree huckleberry 0.9
live oak 65.4

Components (%) of Mast and Browse Diet in 1964–1965

Figure 23. Annual diet of the white-tailed deer on the Aransas National Wildlife Refuge. Mast is the fruits of woody plants; browse is foliage of woody plants; forbs are nonwoody plants other than grasses. Figure modified from M. White, *Texas Journal of Science* 30(4):457–489.

ing leaves and twig tips and eat its pendulous flower clusters. Whenever its acorns are available, whitetails consume them (as well as acorns of other oak species) in great quantity. Acorns are the hands-down staple for Aransas deer, especially during fall and winter.

Besides acorns, deer consume the fruits of greenbriar, beautyberry, yaupon, red bay, and mustang grape. They browse the greenery of these plants as well as that of prickly ash, wax myrtle, and tree huckleberry and a wide variety of herbs (even including poison ivy) and sedges. They also nibble on lichens and mushrooms. Although deer avidly graze tender grass sprouts, which emerge in the spring and after burning or mowing, grass makes up less than 10 per cent of their yearly diet.

Early and late in the day are the best times to enjoy the Aransas deer.

Watch them from your car window or from the observation tower. A startled deer may let out a whistling snort as it wheels and takes off, always showing the white underside of the tail for which it is named. You can learn a lot about deer behavior by watching the tame animals that frequent the lawn at headquarters. When you can read their body language you can eavesdrop on whitetails communicating with each other.

Watch during the rut for male interactions. When a buck shakes his head slightly and drops the angle of his ears, he is telling a second buck to move on. If this gesture is ignored he will flatten his ears, stretch out his neck and glare fiercely. If he gets a mean look in return, the first buck may tuck his chin on his chest, raise the hair on his neck and take several prancing side steps toward his adversary.

If this display does not send the object of his threats into retreat, then the angered buck will drop his head and make several wicked mock thrusts with his antlers. Finally, if all these attempts at intimidation are met by similar behavior, then the two will close on each other with a loud crackle of antlers. A bone-rattling shoving match may go on for a quarter-hour, until one of the combatants has had enough and breaks for the nearest oak thicket.

Body gestures of does are like those of the bucks, but in their scuffles over social rank, lacking antlers, the does substitute their sharp fore-hooves, sometimes rearing up on their hind legs to flail at an opponent.

You can see rudimentary versions of most of their body movements by watching young deer at play.

A nine-day archery hunt and a five-day gun hunt for white-tailed deer are scheduled on the Aransas Refuge each fall. (For economic reasons, the refuge manager is considering suspension of the gun hunt.) These activities are held in areas outside the zone of routine public access. Between 1980 and 1990 participants managed to kill an average of 40 deer with bow and arrow and an average of 73 deer with a rifle. Those numbers are not significant for population control, so the hunts must be viewed as recreational sport—a dubious activity on a wildlife refuge.

Javelina

Javelinas (hava-LEEN-ahs), with a refuge population of 250 to 300, are moderately common, and many occur in the area of public access. If you see a family group of these peculiar little native pigs snuffling along the roadside, by all means stop and enjoy them. Do not confuse your Spanish and call them, as some visitors do, "jalapeños."

Be sure to distinguish these native animals from the introduced feral hogs. From the side javelinas have a humped and smoothly rounded profile; their snouts are relatively short and their rounded ears never flop down. When seen from fore or aft, javelinas are narrowly slab-sided, which allows them to thread their way through dense brush with ease. Adult javelinas are much smaller than adult hogs: about 22 inches at the shoulder and weighing about sixty pounds. But the best field mark is the tail; if you see a tail it is a feral hog. Javelinas have a tail, but it is very short and kept tucked against the body.

Although feral hogs come in a variety of colors, javelinas are always grizzled gray-black with a silver-gray band across the shoulders and around the neck. The collar is the basis for an alternate name, "collared peccary," seldom used locally but often seen in books. Javelina pelage is bristly, especially along the neck and back, and the animals readily raise these stiff hairs when they are suspicious or disturbed.

When agitated, these pigs release a musky, pungent odor from a scent gland that can be seen, on an animal with its hackles up, as a hairless area high on the rump. (Early explorers reported that the animal's navel was misplaced!) It is thought that group members maintain contact in dense brush by this rather skunklike scent. They also mark their herd territories by rubbing the gland against tree trunks and shrubs. Such odorous signposts may be stained brown from repeated applications.

You may even witness javelinas confirming social relations by exchanging chemical signals. Two pigs stand side by side, each with its chin on the other's rump; then each animal, by several vigorous sideways tosses of the head, rubs its jowls across the partner's scent gland. This brief interchange is usually accompanied by soft grunts and snuffles of satisfaction.

Peccaries usually move about in small groups, each group maintaining a territory several hundred acres in extent. In the heat of summer they are mostly nocturnal, but during the winter or in overcast or rainy weather, they may be seen abroad any time of the day. Young have been recorded at all times of the year on the Aransas, but most are born in spring or fall. The little brownish piglet (only one or two at a time) stays adeptly at its mother's ankle; not even a shadow could stick closer.

Although javelinas will chomp up what insects they come across, they are basically herbivores, feeding on the fallen fruits of persimmon, mesquite, yaupon, and greenbriar and, like so much of the local wildlife, stuffing themselves on acorns in season. In South and West Texas, prickly pear cactus is a staple, but the widely scattered plants on the refuge are not heavily used. Acorns very likely take their place.

Javelina tracks

Javelina

Unlike the feral hogs, javelinas do not root deeply, but they do nose along the top of the soil for tender greenery, rhizomes, tubers, and fungi. Occasionally they grub up such delectables as the subterranean stalks of young Spanish dagger plants.

These relatively innocuous creatures have an unjustified reputation for being aggressive and dangerous toward people. In fact, they will beat a hasty retreat on contact. But they are nearsighted, and when a group scatters, one or more may inadvertently blunder toward rather than away from an intruder. Members of a dispersed and frightened group usually mill about in the brush, fouling the air with their scent glands, uttering alarming woofing sounds, and chopping their teeth ominously. This is all bluff, however, and if you stand quietly the entire group will melt away until only their peculiar essence lingers in your nostrils.

Javelinas are notoriously erratic. When they deign to make an abrupt appearance from the oak thickets, you cannot miss them; but if they choose to remain hidden, there is no way to find or follow them in their impenetrable domain. Watch for them along all the refuge roads, and observe them with binoculars from your car window; they are less disturbed by automobiles than by people afoot. If a troop shows up while you are picnicking, resist the temptation to feed them.

Fox Squirrel

You can expect to see fox squirrels hurrying through the branches along the Big Tree and the Dagger Point trails, and they are occasionally seen scampering across the roads. Most of the larger live oak mottes on the

Fox squirrel

refuge are included in the home range of one or more squirrels, but in this dense twiggy environment they are not readily visible. Those living at the picnic area and around headquarters are less shy than others.

One of the most noticeable signs of squirrels is their bulky summer nests. These unkempt globular masses of dead leaves and twigs lodged high in the trees are used during the warmer months. Each animal also maintains a permanent den site in a hollow tree limb. Young are born in the dens in February and again in September.

Fox squirrels are most active at sunrise, when they are busy feeding. Acorns are their staple on the Aransas Refuge, picked directly from the trees and gleaned off the ground. Squirrels bury many acorns for emergency use. They also consume a variety of leaf and flower buds, hackberries, beautyberries, and yaupon fruits, and they spend considerable time foraging on the ground for mushrooms and insects. Fox squirrels have been observed feasting on swarms of queen Texas leaf-cutter ants emerging after spring rains.

If you surprise a fox squirrel in a tree it will probably flip to the opposite side of the limb. Sit or stand quietly; squirrels are curious, and they are one of the few forms of wildlife with less patience than humans. Soon an ear, then an eye will appear over the edge of the limb. Eventually the squirrel will be in full view. If it is sufficiently piqued by your presence, it may switch its tail and harangue you with its scolding chatter.

Wild Turkey

Like white-tailed deer, a wild turkey captivates observers with its streamlined beauty, its air of resourcefulness, and its alert, genuinely wild demeanor. Aransas birds belong to the variety called the Rio Grande turkey. A flock of these vigilant, high-stepping birds provides an extra thrill because they are not so common as deer and they do not stay in view for long. If you are fortunate enough to spot wild turkeys, get your lenses up in a hurry and enjoy the privilege.

If you have the opportunity, eavesdrop on a little turkey talk. You are most apt to hear the choppy "pit-pit" of suspicious discovery followed by a liquid "putt-putt" of alarm, but these social birds have quite a vocabulary. If a group of birds has startled and gotten separated, listen for the plaintive, singsong "yip-yip, yarp-yarp-yarp" as they regroup.

Male and female turkeys spend the winter months foraging in separate flocks. About February, the toms' hormones begin to bubble, and they separate, each seeking out an open area for his courtship display.

A twenty-pound dominant gobbler in peak performance is a regal spectacle. Puffed up to his fullest, he fluffs his breast and back feathers until they shimmer like molten copper with iridescent flashes of purple and greenish bronze. His huge black-barred, brown tail with its chestnut-cream trim is fanned vertically above his back. The skin of his naked head is gleaming turquoise, and his brilliant carmine wattles spill out over his breast above a unique beard of bristly black feathers. Thrumming the ground with the tips of his stiffened wings, the gobbler slowly pivots to take best advantage of the early morning light. Now and then he stretches out his neck and, with every ounce of vigor, proclaims his own magnificence: "Obble-obble, gobble-gobble-gobble."

The call is both a challenge and a lure. Rival males gobble back and forth, sometimes closing on each other flapping, spurring, and pecking. Upstart young toms brash enough to get in the way are quickly put in their place. At the height of display, in late February and early March, the hens are drawn in, and a few dominant gobblers lay claim to almost all of them.

By April the toms will have toned down, and the hens will be brooding their ten to fourteen eggs in nests concealed in the tall grass. Predators usually destroy at least half the nests, but the young that do hatch are ready to follow the hen and begin feeding on insects as soon as their down feathers are dry.

Through their first summer turkey poults lead a hazardous existence. Predators, accident, disease, a dry year with few insects and scant ground cover, a wet year with chilling nights and saturated feeding grounds—all take a toll. Those that make it to their first autumn, when they will be eating a variety of plant material and relying heavily on acorns, may survive as adults for another half-dozen years.

Ground-living turkeys spend the day foraging along at a steady walk, pausing occasionally to scratch at the leaf litter. They do eagerly flap up into trees to feast on high-climbing mustang grapes. Sharp eyes and ears miss little, and if alarmed the birds walk or run for cover. If pressed, they crouch a moment and then explode into the air like enormous pheasants, then quickly level off and flap-glide over the treetops for several hundred yards before setting down and slinking into the undergrowth.

Because the hatch and survival of ground-nesting birds is heavily influenced by weather and range conditions, the size of the Aransas flock of turkeys varies greatly from year to year. It has historically oscillated between one hundred and four hundred adults, but a downward trend begun in the late seventies has continued to near extirpation today. The census of 1985 tallied fewer than fifty birds. In 1987, only fifteen adult turkeys were counted, and the one hen with poults marked the last known nesting on the refuge. By 1990, only one pair of hens was seen around headquarters and foraging along the roadside to the observation tower. Now the once vigorous flock may be reduced to occasional immigrant birds. Who would have believed that the Aransas Refuge would one day support more whooping cranes than wild turkeys?

What happened to the Aransas turkeys? Probably a combination of misfortunes. A sequence of dry years in the late seventies decreased

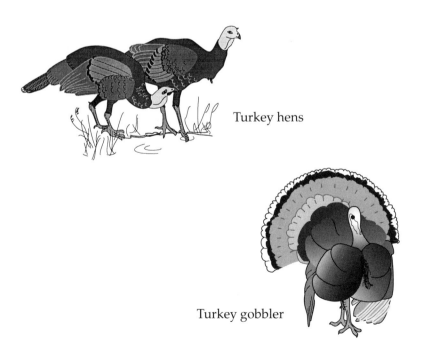

Turkey hens

Turkey gobbler

herbaceous plant cover, curtailed the production of fruits, seeds, and greenery, and reduced insect fare. Undernourished hens may not even attempt to lay, and the few that do nest are forced to use inferior sites where both the brooding hen and her clutch of eggs are discovered by predators. Any poults that hatch soon succumb to malnutrition or they are taken by predators. Raptors easily spot young turkeys in sparse vegetation; great horned owls are particularly destructive.

Wild turkeys need a secure night roost. Though preferring tall stream-side trees, on the Aransas they settle for the larger live oaks near a reliable windmill. Since cattle were removed from the refuge, many of the windmills are no longer maintained, so turkeys have fewer watering sites.

Despite prescribed burns to inhibit woody growth, the progressive encroachment of running live oak thickets on the refuge has surely worked against the turkeys. The dense knee-high oak canopy inhibits the birds' movements, crowds out favored forbs, and allows the close approach of bobcats, coyotes, gray foxes, and jaguarundis. Once reduced to the critical level of a few lingering individuals, these very social birds seem unable to muster a comeback, and the expanse of open agricultural land bordering the refuge reduces the likelihood of significant immigration from the sparse outlying population. Although there are no immediate plans for restocking wild turkeys on the Aransas, it would not be the first time (see Chapter 8), and it may be necessary to revive the local flock.

Unless their fortunes rise, you may not see wild turkeys on the refuge. Ask at the WIC about your chances.

Bobwhite Quail

Of the four species of quail native to Texas, the bobwhite is by far the most widespread, and it is the only one found on the Aransas Refuge. Although Blackjack Peninsula supports a moderate population, bobwhites are not often seen along the public access routes. Preferring relatively open ground without dense stands of tall grass and extensive live oak thickets, quail are more common on the Tatton and Matagorda units.

Along the Tour Loop in April you will hear unmated males pouring out their distinctive "bob-bob-WHITE." During autumn and winter the quail are silent, and if you encounter them at all it may be in a startling explosion of whirring wings as a covey of a dozen birds takes off from the grass at your feet. Stand your ground, let your nerves settle, and listen for their pretty little aggregation whistles.

Mourning dove

Bobwhite

Bobwhite chicks depend on insects, and the adults snap up an assortment of invertebrates as they forage, but these birds are mainly herbivorous. Fruits of greenbriar, yaupon, mustang grape, prickly ash, hackberry, bumelia, brasil, and mesquite are readily consumed, but the seeds of sundry forbs are their staples: doveweed, partridge pea, broomweed, ragweed, sunflower. Quail eat grass seeds, but they do not push into dense growths of tall grass where they are vulnerable to predators.

Would you believe that a bobwhite can swallow an acorn whole? They can and will, although they prefer smaller morsels. In the spring bobwhites pluck much tender greenery, and to do so they readily enter fresh regrowth in prescribed burns.

Doves and Pigeons

Texas boasts five native species of doves. Four of them have been recorded from the Aransas Refuge, and two of these are regarded as game birds.

The mourning dove is a common year-round resident and very nearly a year-round nester. The soft cooing of the males can be expected at any season. The mourning dove population increases perceptibly in the autumn and winter as a weak progression of northern birds arrives in the Coastal Bend.

White-winged doves are larger than mourning doves, and the white slash on the wing margin is usually easy to spot; their melodious series of cooing calls is distinctive. These birds are customarily associated with the Lower Rio Grande Valley of Texas, where they nest and feed from March through November before migrating deep into Mexico for the winter. Recently the species has begun to expand its range northward; scattered resident breeding colonies are now established up the coast as far as Galveston, inland to San Antonio, and as far north as Waco. Small groups of birds appear sporadically on the refuge, but to date no nests have been found.

On December 18, 1971, a solitary band-tailed pigeon was seen near the observation tower. This bird, which is at home in the mountains of far West Texas, was evidently lost. Although the species is accorded game status, it has been protected with a closed season for decades.

Sandhill Crane

Sandhills begin arriving in the Coastal Bend on the early northers of mid-October. Their numbers increase erratically, and by mid-December in a good year the refuge population peaks at several thousand birds. The record count was 6,300 in 1968. Just how long the cranes stay depends on their success at foraging on open ranchland and the availability of waste grain in local fields. In any case, they begin to get restless by early spring, and by mid-March they have spiraled up to mere specks in the sky and caught a brisk southeasterly airstream. The wind pushes them north to that great sandhill rendezvous on the sandbars

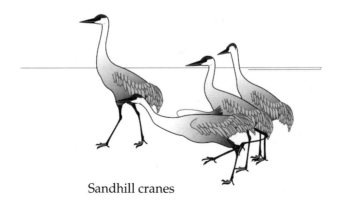

Sandhill cranes

and braided shallows of the Platte River in Nebraska. From there it is off to nesting grounds in Alaska and the Canadian Arctic, perhaps even across the Bering Sea to Siberia.

The refuge is primarily a roosting and resting site for the cranes. They stand at night in the shallows of Goose and Burgentine lakes or on the boggy tidal flats near Sundown Bay. Occasionally they settle on Heron Flats, but the proximity to people makes them uneasy there.

At first light low lines and ragged V's of sandhills begin to move out, trumpeting their distinctive, throaty yodel that can be heard for a mile. This melodious, rolling trill is a quickly recognizable element of the avian clamor that enlivens wintertime on the Texas coast; do not mistake it for the sharper, more explosive bugle of whoopers.

Morning flights of cranes are off to feeding grounds, which by late winter may be as much as forty miles away. They drop down on unplowed prairie or into barren-looking winter fields that yet harbor waste grain, scattered greenery, sundry rhizomes, tubers, earthworms, and insect larvae that can be easily extracted from the loose soil. Locally cranes are dependent on sorghum, corn, and rice left over from fall harvests. The flocks may move out of the area when these resources are depleted.

Sandhills forage across grassy uplands, frequently probing in moist areas but not ordinarily feeding in water or marsh. They probe the ground for bulbs of false garlic, purple pleat leaf, water penny, and alophia, and they relish the rootstocks of nutgrass and the fruits of ground cherry. On the Aransas, small groups of cranes readily stride across recently burned tracts, pulling at fresh greenery, gobbling up parched acorns, and waylaying careless crayfish at the entrances to their burrows. Caterpillars, snails, grasshoppers, crickets, beetles, ribbon snakes, harvest mice, and cotton rats are all snapped up as they are encountered, but overall, the cranes' diet in the Coastal Bend is composed of about 85 percent plant material, mostly agricultural grain, and 15 percent small invertebrates.

Late in the day the sky again resounds with the rattling calls of the sandhills as wave after wave come home to roost. With long necks outstretched, each arriving group circles warily while birds already on the ground call reassuringly to them. Finally the birds aloft make a last turn, extend their long legs, and parachute down on cupped wings; touchdown is greeted by a ripple of tootles from the entire flock. The cranes jockey about and converse softly in muffled cats' purrs until well after dark, but finally the gray mass stands silently in the muddy shallows, ever alert for approach of the occasional coyote or a bobcat that does not mind getting its feet wet.

During a fall or winter visit to the refuge, you are likely to hear sand-hills and to see them in flight, but your best chance to observe them will be in the extensive tilled fields and open pasturelands on the surround-ing coastal prairie. Watch for groups of several dozen typical cranelike birds standing alertly on open ground a hundred yards or more from the roadway. Look sharp; even though they stand four feet tall, immo-bile sandhills blend into plowed furrows and winter grassland. Pull over and use your binoculars from the car window. Do not mistake soft gray sandhills for whooping cranes as many eager observers do. White whoopers are virtually never seen in such inland terrain, and they do not ordinarily occur in flocks.

Waterfowl

The Central Flyway is one of four great aerial freeways that funnel mil-lions of migrant waterfowl, shorebirds, raptors, and passerines on their biannual journey across North America. This corridor, invisible to our eyes, is a 600-mile-wide, north-south, midcontinental conduit floored by the Great Plains; arched over by star patterns and wind currents; permeated with odors of shifting latitudes; shot through with gradients of magnetism, polarized light, and day length; and seeped deep into the hereditary maps of the birds that hark to its irresistible call and fol-low its ages-old contours.

The Central Flyway begins on insect-rich nesting grounds in the high Arctic and northern prairie pothole country, sweeps down across the vast central grasslands with their checkerboard of grain fields and vital mid-journey staging areas, and finally spreads out into the wet prairies and marshlands of the Gulf Coast. Waterfowl comprise a significant fraction of the avian avalanche along the flyway, and fully two-thirds of them—nearly seven million—come to Texas. About 10 percent of these birds move on south; the remainder hold over as winter residents, and their gabbles, rafts, and high-flying V's are as characteristic of the season as the northers themselves.

Whooping cranes were not even mentioned in the presidential proc-lamation that established the Aransas Migratory Waterfowl Refuge. The area was set aside specifically as a sanctuary for the multitudes of migrant geese and ducks that pause in or pass through the region. This remains one of the preeminent roles of the refuge, rendered even more critical now, in an age of disappearing natural habitat. Each year thou-sands of waterbirds of some 25 species descend upon the Aransas to rest, roost, and feed.

The arrival and departure of migratory waterbirds on the Aransas follows a fairly predictable schedule, though actual numbers and species composition vary from year to year. Winter numbers are determined basically by the degree of success on the northern nesting grounds, but each year's migration bears its own peculiarities. Severe cold may push migrants south of the Coastal Bend, whereas mild weather persuades them to hold up farther north. Birds will delay their journey for days or weeks if they encounter exceptional natural or artificial food sources en route. Many flocks of waterfowl await favorable northwesterly tail winds before moving south, and they abruptly vanish northward on strong southeasterlies. A wet winter fills more inland waterways, allowing the birds to scatter more widely so fewer of them are seen at traditional rendezvous. Drought makes the bays hypersaline and fresh water for drinking becomes scarce, forcing the birds to move on. Waterbirds compelled to congregate in drying ponds may be decimated by fowl cholera or avian botulism.

Goose numbers are quite dependent on the status of local grain fields; if weather conditions have permitted complete tillage, there will be less scattered grain and the geese may haul out. Both geese and ducks quickly detect the sudden cessation of shotgun pressure in January, and their numbers dwindle on the refuge as they move into the now relatively secure fields and prairie watercourses.

Still, there is a discernible pattern in waterfowl use of the Aransas. Geese begin arriving during the last half of October, mostly Canadas and snows. The Canada geese that winter on the refuge belong to the Tallgrass Prairie population, which nests along tundra streams north of Hudson Bay and skims down the eastern edge of the Central Flyway, some 150,000 strong, to the rice fields and coastal marshes of Texas to spend the winter. Raucous waves of lesser snow geese totaling about half a million birds come to Texas from nesting grounds on high tundra within the Arctic Circle. Most of these birds are white with black wing tips, but in a common color variant called "blue goose" the body is brown. In 1989, a snow goose shot in Manitoba had a leg band that showed it had been tagged on the Aransas nineteen years earlier.

Several thousand white-fronted geese are among the early October arrivals, but most of these birds soon move on into Mexico. Any Ross's geese that appear will be rare individuals displaced from their usual route along the Pacific Flyway.

The numbers of Canadas and snows increase through November and peak in December or January, when most of them, as many as 40,000 birds, roost in the shallows of Goose Lake and Burgentine Lake, with lesser concentrations in the protected bay shallows bordering Blackjack Peninsula.

By day the birds fly off to feed in surrounding fields where they glean

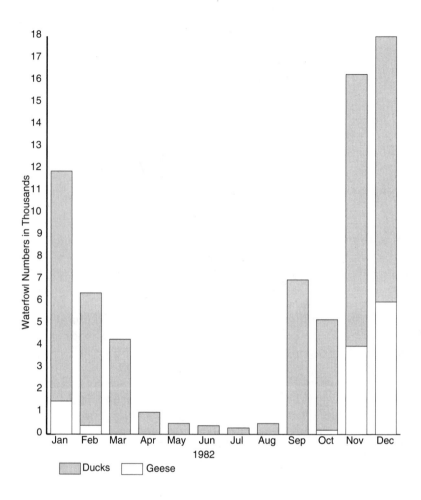

Figure 24. Peak numbers of waterfowl determined by aerial census on the Aransas National Wildlife Refuge in 1982. Although the number of birds varies each year, the data show the typical annual pattern of abundance. Data are from the files of the ANWR.

waste sorghum, corn, rice, and soybeans. They also settle in grassy pastures across the coastal prairie, and they frequent marshes to graze on saltgrass, seashore paspalum, and marshhay cordgrass. Flights of both species can usually be heard or spotted, early and late in the day, from any vantage on the refuge. Canadas frequently rest in San Antonio Bay

Canada goose

opposite the picnic area and at the observation tower. Snows often settle on Heron Flats. If you get the chance to observe these geese feeding, see if you can detect why Canada geese are referred to as grazers while snow geese are called grubbers. Their mannerisms and food preferences are quite distinctive.

Although goose numbers may remain high through February, in early March the birds abruptly begin to haul out, and the last ones will have deserted the refuge by the end of the month.

The eighties saw a serious decline in the populations of most species of ducks due to loss in both the extent and the quality of their nesting habitat in the prairie pothole region in the northern Great Plains. A series of drought years dried up many ponds where the ducks traditionally feed and rear their young; drainage for agriculture eradicated many more. Crowded into the diminished wetlands that remained, the beleaguered ducks encountered agricultural pesticides, acidified waters, and epidemic avian diseases. A change in land-use policy allowed haying operations on favored upland nesting sites. The combination of natural and human-induced misfortunes reduced the 1985 fall flight of ducks in North America to a record low of 62 million birds, less than two-thirds the number that characterized flights in the seventies. A peak of more than 80,000 ducks was recorded on the Aransas in November 1984, but a comparable census in 1991 revealed fewer than 3,000 birds. Going into the nineties, despite conservation efforts, populations have not rallied, but public and private organizations cooperating in the current Waterfowl Management Plan feel that a fall flight of 100 million birds by the turn of the century is a realistic goal.

Duck season makes an unlikely beginning in the crackling heat of mid-August when the first blue-winged teal splash down on the Aran-

Pintail

sas. Considerable numbers of these small ducks will be on the area throughout the winter, but most move on southward.

The first northern pintails arrive in early September; other ducks begin to appear according to the frequency and severity of the northers. By the end of October at least a few representatives of all the commoner kinds will be on the refuge: gadwall, American wigeon, green-winged teal, and northern shoveler.

Numbers and diversity of ducks continue to rise through November and December. Many of these birds settle on the huge freshwater lake on the Whitmire Unit. Even in a year when waterfowl numbers are not exceptional on the Texas coast, more than seventy thousand ducks might be tallied on aerial surveys of the refuge. A sudden influx of redheads, lesser scaups, or ruddy ducks may dramatically, but briefly, increase the count. One December morning in 1987, the sun rose on an immense raft of more than twenty thousand lesser scaups riding the quiet water in San Antonio Bay off the bay overlook. The next morning every bird had vanished, presumably headed south down the coast. The species composition will be augmented by variable numbers of buffleheads and, more rarely, by ring-necked ducks and canvasbacks.

Participants in the Audubon Christmas Count usually spot more than fifteen species of ducks on the Aransas in their one-day survey. This generally includes some of the less common species: mallard, cinnamon teal, wood duck, greater scaup, common goldeneye, and hooded and red-breasted mergansers.

From November through January ducks can be expected in all aquatic habitats on the refuge. Some of the best spots for viewing birds in San Antonio Bay are at the picnic area and the bay overlook, near the end of the boardwalk at the observation tower, and from the tower itself.

Table 1. *Waterbirds Seen during Audubon Christmas Counts on ANWR, 1980–1990*

	Total Seen	Average Seen	Times Seen
Common loon	34	3	9
Least grebe	2	<1	1
Pied-billed grebe	326	30	11
Horned grebe	14	1	6
Eared grebe	367	33	11
White pelican	3,633	330	11
Brown pelican	415	38	11
Double-crested cormorant	21,174	1,925	11
Neotropic cormorant	9	1	4
Anhinga	20	2	7
Canada goose	13,478	1,225	11
White-fronted goose	642	58	8
Snow goose	17,703	1,609	11
White-winged scoter	2	<1	1
Black-bellied whistling-duck	8	1	2
Fulvous whistling-duck	9	1	3
Mallard	111	10	8
Black duck	1	<1	1
Mottled duck	606	55	11
Gadwall	5,709	519	11
Northern pintail	17,825	1,620	11
Green-winged teal	1,652	150	11
Blue-winged teal	260	24	10
Cinnamon teal	11	1	3
American wigeon	5,151	468	11
Northern shoveler	1,291	117	11
Wood duck	20	2	6
Redhead	3,011	274	11
Ring-necked duck	185	17	6
Canvasback	565	51	11
Greater scaup	1	<1	11
Lesser scaup	4,633	421	11
Common goldeneye	201	18	11
Bufflehead	1,238	113	11
Ruddy duck	1,919	174	11
Hooded merganser	118	11	11
Red-breasted merganser	442	40	11

Data are from the files of the ANWR.

Table 2. *Midwinter Aerial Waterfowl Survey, Middle Texas Coast (Galveston Bay to Corpus Christi Bay), January 1990*

Dabbling Ducks	Number Seen	%	Diving Ducks	Number Seen	%
Green-winged teal	62,235	43.0	Canvasback	22,638	67.1
Northern pintail	45,297	31.3	Lesser scaup	8,333	24.7
Gadwall	18,991	13.1	Redhead	2,053	6.1
Mottled duck	7,186	5.0	Ring-necked duck	320	1.0
Mallard	6,224	4.3	Mergansers	192	0.6
Northern shoveler	2,823	2.0	Bufflehead	128	0.4
American wigeon	1,770	1.2	Common goldeneye	64	0.2
Blued-winged teal	257	0.2	Ruddy duck	37	0.1
Total	144,783		Total	33,765	

Grand total: 178,548—81% dabblers, 19% divers

Data are from the files of the TPWD.

Take advantage of a morning sun to watch a variety of species at close range from the pier on Jones Lake; shift to an afternoon sun to scan Heron Flats from the observation platform on the Heron Flats Trail.

There are differences between dabbling ducks and diving ducks. Dabblers frequent bay margins and freshwater ponds. They upend when they feed and spring directly off the water when they take to the air. Gadwall and pintail are dabblers. Divers, on the other hand, prefer deeper waters of the open bay. They disappear from view while they search for submerged vegetation or clams and typically patter across the surface before getting airborne. Redheads and scaups are divers.

Most of these ducks are herbivorous. In freshwater ponds they feed on a variety of bankside, floating, and submerged plants. The most important food plants in the bays are widgeon grass and shoalgrass and their attached streamers of algae. Some species, like northern pintail and blue-winged teal, efficiently pluck seeds directly from plants or they sieve fallen seeds from the water. The shoveler uses its outsized bill to scoop up surface algae. Dabblers upend for submerged vegetable matter in the shallows, and divers plunge for it farther out. American wigeon, which are dabblers, often swim out to pilfer plant fragments that have floated to the surface before hardworking divers can rise to claim them. Goldeneyes and buffleheads stay well out in the bays, where they dive for clams and crustaceans. Beside them flotillas of red-breasted mergansers plunge after schools of mullet and anchovies.

There are usually several thousand ducks still on the Aransas through

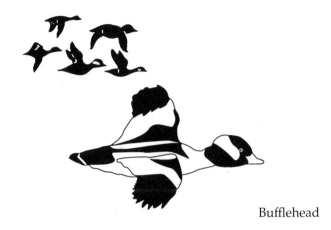

Bufflehead

February, but numbers decline rapidly in March despite the influx of northbound blue-winged teal. By the first of April the only migratory ducks left are a few lingering gadwall, wigeon, shovelers, and teal. Most of these are gone by early May.

After serving as duck heaven for the five cooler months, it may seem strange that the Aransas can boast only one resident nesting species. The mottled duck is a common year-round dabbler in the coastal marshes and wet prairies. Adults pair up in early March and establish nesting territories, which the males defend with vigorous aerial pursuit of any other mottled ducks that happen to fly overhead. Hatchlings from the first clutches appear in late March and April. Predation is heavy; raccoons and Texas rat snakes eat the eggs, and the bite-sized ducklings attract a host of hungry mouths: alligators, alligator gars, blue crabs, cottonmouth moccasins, snapping turtles, and great horned owls. Because of all this, females attempting to renest may be found throughout the summer. But as the weather gets hot and dry, ponds deteriorate into expanses of cracked mud, and mottled duck broods are more exposed to predation and suffer from malnutrition. Few survive late nesting in a dry year.

Although research suggests that three of every four mottled duck nests fail to fledge young for natural reasons, this is not the main cause of the current persistent decline in their numbers. The pitifully small reserve left must combat the inroads of modern civilization—the all-too-familiar relentless destruction of their coastal habitat by urban and industrial development and agriculture.

Neither fulvous whistling-ducks nor black-bellied whistling-ducks, which visit the Aransas in small numbers, fit the pattern set by the northern migratory species. These are Mexican birds, some of which move northward to nest along the Gulf Coast in the springtime. Fulvous whistling-ducks mostly bypass the Aransas Refuge and continue to the rice belt along the upper central coast. Small flocks of about a dozen birds sometimes pause in Mustang, Jones, and Burgentine lakes.

Originally restricted to the southern tip of the state, the black-bellied whistling-duck began to expand its range northward in the fifties. The species was added to the refuge checklist in 1972, when a pair of adults with a brood of eleven young was observed near Patrol Station Pond. Today, when migratory flocks arrive from Mexico in April, they push up the entire Texas coast and occupy suitable wetland habitat around reservoirs and river drainages 150 miles inland. They fly south again in late October, although a few laggards are still seen during Christmas counts on the Aransas.

Black-bellied whistling-ducks are easily distinguished by their chestnut plumage, lustrous black breasts, and coral-red bills and legs. They live up to their name by uttering high-pitched squeals in flight. These birds forage mostly at night, striding gooselike on land, harvesting seeds and grazing on greenery or both dabbling and diving. They prefer to nest in tree cavities, but they also weave well-formed baskets in

Blue-winged teal

dense clumps of grass. On the refuge, perhaps because of predation by raccoons, most clutches have been hidden on the ground, but in 1981 one brood hatched from a nest box.

By July or August you can anticipate seeing a pair of black-bellied whistling-ducks on Jones Lake carefully tending a train of windup-toy ducklings decked out in downy convict-striped suits of yellow and black.

Refuge personnel are justifiably proud of their lone sighting, in 1980, of the rare and erratic little masked duck in a drainage canal near McHugh Bayou. This tropical species is rare in Texas even in the Rio Grande Valley. A pair reported at Jones Lake in 1990 vanished before the observation could be verified.

You can greatly enhance your enjoyment of waterfowl if you learn the field marks that distinguish the various species of ducks. Although many of these birds will be observed only at great distance and in unfavorable light, a good bird book, a pair of binoculars, and determination can often resolve them. Recognizing the glitter of male buffleheads amid the distant whitecaps, the startlingly white bellies of tippling gadwall, or the resplendent colors of a male green-winged teal caught in full sunlight is a delight worth working for.

Rails

All nine American species of rails have been recorded from the Aransas. The American coot (locally also called mudhen or pull-do) is by far the commonest and most visible. In peak years the margins of San Antonio Bay are darkened with flocks of more than thirty thousand birds.

During the winter months, rafts of coots are almost always evident somewhere in the shallows of San Antonio Bay, and scattered individuals can often be seen at close range in Thomas Slough and Jones Lake. If you observe a group of coots for a while, you will note that these rather comical birds are continually communicating. Clucks, cackles, and pops; neck arching; wing flapping; feather fluffing; tail erection; swim-chasing; and even pecking-and-clawing combat are all parts of their repertoire.

Most visitors regard a coot as one more kind of duck. They do have ducklike habits, but notice the white, chickenlike bill, the relatively small head, and the pumping motion of the neck when they swim, traits that mark them as rails. Coots dabble, dive, and surface feed, and they patter extensively before takeoff.

Because coots have difficulty getting airborne, they swim away from threat and many dive when startled. A wily coyote may know this, and one has been observed purposefully splashing along the margin of

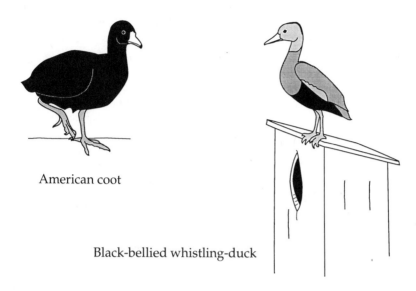

American coot

Black-bellied whistling-duck

Black-bellied plovers

Mustang Lake to frighten the coots and then pouncing on those that submerged in the clear shallows. Within five minutes this skilled predator had cached three feathered bodies in the reeds.

Also watch in Thomas Slough and Jones Lake for common moorhens and purple gallinules, both resplendent birds, especially when seen through binoculars in full sunlight. Distinguish adults by the scarlet forehead of the moorhen or the blue-violet forehead of the gallinule. The moorhen also has a white streak along the lower side, which helps differentiate juveniles that have not developed the colorful head plumage. Like coots, moorhens continually socialize. A winter visit to the refuge is not complete without a pause at Jones Lake to hear the maniacal cackling and bursts of eerie pops and hoots issuing mysteriously from the cattails—social intercourse among the moorhens. After an aggressive encounter, two birds will often splash apart and raise their wings and tails to reveal a pair of bright white rear patches that resemble car headlights.

Clapper rails (one of several rail species called marsh hens) are common enough in the tidal-flat community, but they are secretive birds. Look from the observation tower; if you are lucky, you may spot one slinking along after mud fiddlers at the fringe of cordgrass bordering Mustang Lake. An afternoon sun helps. Their presence is more reliably indicated by their clattering call.

There are indeed rails along the Rail Trail—king, Virginia, sora, black, and yellow—but your chance of flushing one is slim. If you know their weird calls you will do better by ear than by eye.

Shorebirds

Although all species of shorebirds are accorded game status by the state of Texas, the hunting season is closed semipermanently for all but common snipe and American woodcock. You might spot a snipe moving mouselike along the edge of any slough or pond, but you are most likely to experience it as an explosive burst of whistling wings when it erupts vertically from an unseen frozen crouch. The Aransas Refuge does not have the mesic woodland favored by woodcocks, but this species is seen rarely along Burgentine Creek on the western side of the peninsula, and in 1988 two were flushed on the Heron Flats Trail.

CHAPTER 8

Introduced Species

In this chapter we consider those animals and plants that have been deliberately introduced onto Blackjack Peninsula.

In 1924, the last private owner of Blackjack Peninsula, Leroy G. Denman, Sr., attorney for the San Antonio Loan and Trust Company, had a game-proof fence built across the neck of the peninsula. He prohibited public hunting and commenced to introduce native and exotic wildlife to the area. Although the records are not complete, it appears that between 1925 and 1936, some 1,200 individual animals of seven species were released, five of which were exotic. Three of those releases have persisted, two native and one exotic.

Ring-necked Pheasant

Between 1933 and 1934, 400 adults and cage-hatched fledglings of this adaptable Asian pheasant were released. Some of these birds nested, but no young were raised. The last individual that might reasonably be traced to these introductions was collected in January 1939.

In 1963, the Texas Parks and Wildlife Department began an intensive effort to establish ring-necked pheasants on the Gulf Coast. By 1977, carefully selected hybrid stock had produced a huntable population. To date these birds have spread from the central coast eastward. The closest feral population to the Aransas is just across the Lavaca River, 45 miles up the coast.

No pheasants were seen on the refuge for more than forty years until, in 1981, a pair was observed in Point Pasture. Solitary cocks were seen in 1982 and 1983. These recent sightings are probably of escapees from nearby private landholders.

The refuge can well do without exotic ground-living birds, which can only compete with the native species, including the endangered Attwater's prairie chicken.

California Quail

Records show the release of 252 adults, and perhaps some cage-hatched fledglings, between 1933 and 1935. Most of the birds disappeared quickly, probably falling to predators and maladaptation to the coastal environment. None was seen during extensive surveys when the refuge was established.

Wild Turkey

This is, of course, a bird native to the area (see Chapter 7), but it was apparently extirpated from Blackjack Peninsula by the time Leroy Denman took over the St. Charles Ranch.

From 1933 to 1935, approximately six hundred turkeys were released on the ranch. About half of these birds turned out to be indistinguishable from the domestic variety. They did not disperse into the wild and were finally destroyed to prevent hybridization with wild stock.

The other three hundred turkeys all derived from a wild population in Kenedy County, one hundred miles south of Blackjack Peninsula. These native Rio Grande wild turkeys are presumed to be ancestral to the current refuge population, which is once again in danger of extinction on the mainland refuge.

Fallow Deer

Between 1930 and 1936, the San Antonio Loan and Trust Company spent $2,639 for 73 of these European deer and released them on Blackjack Peninsula. Twenty-two animals were in the area when it became a federal refuge; 14 were live-trapped and removed. A group of three fallow deer was seen occasionally through the forties, and a solitary animal was observed near the site of the current picnic area in December 1949. The last sighting was of a single individual on the Tatton Unit in 1988, but it probably strayed from a local ranch and was not part of the original Denman introduction.

Fallow deer are popular with novelty-minded landowners, but they are known to compete with native whitetails and certainly have no place on a wildlife refuge.

Axis Deer

This pretty, spotted Indian deer is a popular import and breeds prolifically in Texas. Although it was never deliberately introduced onto the refuge, eleven animals were seen in the early seventies. Apparently they had drifted onto the Aransas from surrounding ranchland.

Mule Deer

Records on this species are incomplete, but apparently about fifty individuals were liberated on the St. Charles Ranch from 1931 to 1935. These animals were purchased from a dealer in Salt Lake City, Utah, so they were presumably not even the variety native to West Texas. Little wonder, then, that they failed to adapt to the Texas Gulf Coast. None was alive at the time of a survey in 1939.

White-tailed Deer

Native whitetails were scarce and seldom seen on Blackjack Peninsula when the game fence was built in 1924. The relatively open, overgrazed condition of the area as well as heavy hunting pressure probably accounted for the rarity of the animals.

Once the fence was in place, the native remnant began to proliferate. In addition, between 1925 and 1936, approximately fifty whitetails were released on the peninsula. Almost all of them were of Texas origin. By 1937, there was a healthy and growing herd of about four thousand white-tailed deer on the refuge (see Chapter 7). This almost purely native bloodline gave rise to the deer that occupy the Aransas today.

Feral Hog

This is the only exotic animal that has established a viable breeding population on the Aransas National Wildlife Refuge. Feral hogs are at once stirring creatures to observe and the most destructive animals in residence. Whatever statement is made regarding them, their presence cannot be ignored.

Domestic hogs came into the Coastal Bend with the earliest settlers. These animals were mostly allowed to roam freely and to forage off the land. Hogs were baited and shot, trapped, or penned as needed. Many went wild. This loose sort of pioneer swine management was practiced on Blackjack Peninsula into the early decades of the twentieth century. Consequently, there was a population of semiwild hogs in the area when Leroy Denman closed it off with his game fence.

Between 1930 and 1933, Denman released eleven yearling and adult European boar on the St. Charles Ranch. All were purchased from American zoos, and although their ancestry is uncertain, it is likely that all derived from wild stock direct from Europe or Asia.

Feral hog

The domestic hog is merely a selected variety of the European boar, so it is not surprising that the two began to interbreed immediately on the Aransas. Despite being far outnumbered, the several boar managed to influence the appearance of the hogs on the peninsula. A study of skull characteristics conducted in 1978 revealed that about half the population shows intermediate traits, a quarter favors the boar, and the remaining quarter is nearly identical with domestic hogs.

Although there is much variation, most hogs on the refuge do show some of the distinctive traits of the European boar: long guard hairs with grizzled tips; a scraggly mane of coarse, black hairs extending down the spine from neck to tail; a straight tail with a tuft of coarse hairs on the tip (one of the best field traits to distinguish hogs from javelinas); floppy ears covered with long hairs; a long, narrow muzzle with bristly whiskers; curved tusks in both upper and lower jaws; and a long-legged and rangy build. A large boar will stand nearly thirty-six inches at the shoulder and may weigh in excess of four hundred pounds. All in all, a feral hog is a formidable-looking creature.

Traditional boar coloration is brown or black, and the piglets are reddish brown with distinctive dark brown longitudinal stripes. Aransas hogs come in a variety of colors, some showing the white shoulder stripe characteristic of the domestic Hampshire breed. Among a sample of 64 fetuses, half had the watermelon-striped longitudinal color pattern.

Regardless of their appearance, the mixed stock of feral hogs adapted well to Blackjack Peninsula. Females mature at eight months and have litters all year long, with at least half a dozen piglets in a brood. They eat almost anything, are not prone to debilitating disease, have few predators, and in their early years at least, they were neither hunted nor harvested by man, and so they multiplied in hog heaven.

When the refuge was established the feral hogs were recognized as both a nuisance and a competitive threat to native wildlife. In an intensive campaign waged from October 1936 through July 1939, an astounding total of 3,301 hogs were removed from Blackjack Peninsula. With the population diminished, control efforts were reduced to incidental trapping and shooting on sight. The narrative report for 1945 optimistically anticipates the imminent eradication of feral hogs from the Aransas.

The hogs, however, were far from finished, and the casual control efforts served only to make them more elusive. Beginning in 1955, refuge personnel stepped up the program of attrition, which has continued to date, still based on trapping and especially on nighttime baiting and shooting. The annual removal rate is about 250 animals, which translates into approximately 7,500 hogs over the past thirty years. That this approach does nothing more than crop the surplus is evidenced by the size of the current population of feral hogs on the Aransas Refuge, conservatively estimated at more than 500 animals.

An important reason there has been no more determined effort to rid the refuge of feral hogs is that their presence confers a definite political advantage. There is no question that most visitors are genuinely thrilled at the sight of one of these bristle-backed beasts with the ominous aura of power and viciousness. Indeed, the "big old federal hogs" have become somewhat of a legend on the Aransas. They are not only exciting to see, but they also offer a big-game experience to stalk and shoot. The taking of more than two hundred hogs a year definitely breaks the tedium of routine refuge duty.

In 1969, the general public got its first opportunity to hunt hogs on the Aransas when a special archery season was allowed. The public hunt was eventually extended to include firearms, and it is now conducted concurrently with the Texas white-tailed deer hunting season. Although the thirty or so hogs taken each year is insignificant for control purposes, the public hunt has become the single most popular event on the Aransas, and the feral hogs are an important part of it.

Finally, it has long been the policy of the Aransas Refuge to make freshly butchered wild pork available free to selected local charitable organizations and sundry VIPs. On occasion, outdoor barbecues are conducted for such gatherings at special group sites on the refuge itself. Needless to say, the tradition has proved to be of immense public relations value. As one narrative report comments, "After chomping down on a juicy bit of hog, everyone agrees that Aransas and wild hog is a winning combination." There are, however, some serious attendant losses.

Consider a lanky feral hog weighing 125 pounds. Day in and day out such an animal puts a heavy drain on the resources of a natural community: food; water; cover; deposition of body wastes; dispersion of parasites; extensive uprooting of the topsoil along trails, at foraging sites, and in favored resting places; wallowing in waterholes; the outright disturbance generated by the passage of a large body. Multiply the individual impact by five hundred or more. Exacerbate the result to account for sows with piglets. Aggravate the situation with a drought or a hurricane. You can begin to appreciate the unremitting burden that feral hogs place on the delicate natural cycles that oscillate on Blackjack Peninsula.

It is easiest to grasp the competitive nature of feral hogs by considering their food. They disrupt the natural food web in three important ways: by eating foodstuffs that might otherwise succor native animals, by disrupting soil and vegetation while foraging, and by acting as predators.

Hogs are not only arch omnivores but also alert opportunists. When the acorns drop the hogs consume them by the peck for as long as they last. When the mustang grapes ripen, the hogs feast on this choice wildlife food almost exclusively, often rearing up to drag the fruit-laden vines to the ground. When the yaupon and greenbriar fruits fall, the hogs are there to nuzzle them up. When grass covers a recent burn, the hogs turn their heads sideways to drag in mouthfuls of the fresh verdure.

All bankside and shallowly submerged freshwater vegetation is hog fodder—both the greenery and the rhizomes. Apparently oblivious to nearby alligators, hogs commonly wade shoulder-deep into freshwater ponds and plow along with head submerged to grub up the tender bases of cattail stalks. They are also inveterate beachcombers, consuming everything from crabs to masses of marine algae. They wade out into the shallow bays to dig up razor clams and swim the Intracoastal Canal to forage on nearby spoil islands. Many upland sprouts, forbs, and bulbs are hog delicacies, and they chomp up all fungi with equal gusto. Earthworms, insect larvae, stranded fish, meadow frogs, ribbon snakes, marsh rice rats, carrion—all go into their maws. Hogs will even eat mud if it contains a significant portion of decomposed fishes or algae.

One worker recorded 32 species of plants used by feral hogs in South Texas. On the Aransas the animals are especially fond of yellow nutgrass, longtom, burhead, cattail, spadeleaf, western ragweed, frogfruit, spiderwort, ground cherry, water clover, and they even relish stinging nettle.

There is no more relentless and destructive predator on ground-nesting birds than the feral hog. The nests of lizards, turtles, alligators, and rodents are in equal jeopardy. The predatory nature of the hogs

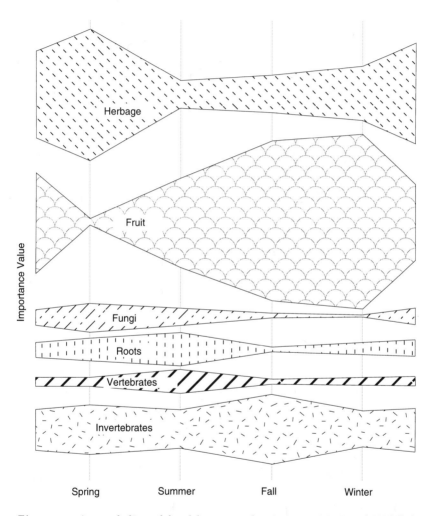

Figure 25. Annual diet of feral hogs on the Aransas National Wildlife Refuge. Importance value incorporates both volume and frequency of occurrence of food items in hog stomachs. Figure modified from M. D. Springer, master's thesis, Texas A&M University, 1975.

takes on a particularly savage twist when they occasionally kill and consume newborn whitetail fawns.

The activities of feral hogs touch virtually all other life-forms on the refuge. They are in direct and total competition with javelinas all year long. In the early spring they beat the geese to the fresh Bermuda grass sprouts. No attempt to rehabilitate the Attwater's prairie chicken population can succeed with hogs on the Tatton. There will never be an undisturbed freshwater community so long as there are hogs on the peninsula. No tidal flat is free of hog rooting and trampling. When times are hard, they will always be harder with aggressive hogs on the scene.

What to do? Perhaps hog-proof crossfencing with traps set at critical gaps would be effective. It is possible that the introduction of a swine-specific disease could achieve in a few years what half a century of cropping has failed to do. There are other options. Prudent control is a more realistic goal than outright eradication. A testimonial to the tenacity of these creatures is that although they may be hunted by any means at any time of the year without bag limit, feral hogs occupy much of Texas and are expanding their range westward.

If you desire to see a feral hog, be alert early and late in the day. Foraging animals may be glimpsed in grassy clearings, and groups are frequently seen hustling across the road anywhere along the Tour Loop. Individuals are commonly spotted on the tidal flat at the observation tower. Look carefully as you approach the end of the pier at Jones Lake; hogs are often seen at the water's edge directly across from the pier. As you drive and walk around the refuge you cannot fail to notice the extensive areas of plowed-up soil. This is all hog work. Ponder its ecological ramifications.

Domestic Cattle

Cattle have been on Blackjack Peninsula and Matagorda Island in significant numbers since before the Civil War. On the mainland the small holdings were gradually consolidated, and by 1919 the entire peninsula was being ranched essentially as a unit. From that date to the establishment of the Aransas Refuge about six thousand head of cattle plus sundry horses, mules, goats, sheep, and hogs roamed the area. The cumulative impact was far beyond carrying capacity.

The San Antonio Loan and Trust Company maintained grazing rights on the newly formed refuge. Through the forties, the severe drought of the fifties, and until 1964, from 3,500 to 4,000 head of cattle foraged virtually unfettered across Blackjack Peninsula. In 1965, because of severe overgrazing, the number of cattle was mercifully reduced to 2,500 head. In 1967, cattle were finally fenced away from the bayshore between headquarters and Mustang Lake. In that same year the Tatton Unit was acquired and a grazing permit was granted on the tract. A systematic grazing rotation program was begun in 1971, and cattle were fenced away from the tidal flats used by whooping cranes. The overall number of cattle was reduced to less than 1,000 head. In that same year the Aransas inherited the negligently liberal grazing policy on the Matagorda Unit.

From 1973 to 1982—for the first time in well over a century—there were no cattle on Blackjack Peninsula. Everyone professed amazement at the phenomenal growth of the native grasses.

By 1986, cattle were again grazing in three sections of the refuge, each under a carefully scrutinized rotation schedule. The 7,500-acre Tatton Unit supported 350 head. The 6,000-acre Point Pasture (the southern tip of Blackjack Peninsula) had 300 cattle. The 19,000-acre Matagorda Unit was grazed by 1,100 head of stock. The cattle were intended to help keep the Tatton open for the prairie chickens. The animals in Point Pasture were a dubious part of an attempt to entice whooping cranes to inland forage. The presence of livestock on Matagorda was an admitted ecological blunder seemingly irremediably bogged down in politics.

Regardless of the stocking rate, cattle have many negative influences on sandy coastal terrain subject to frequent summer stress. Grazing manifestly changes the composition of native vegetation, with selective removal of the more palatable grasses. Overgrazing degrades the range, and on the Aransas it promotes sand erosion and the spread of running live oak. Cattle feed on acorns and browse and graze on greenery in direct competition with wildlife. One study in South Texas found cattle feeding on 22 kinds of grasses, 30 forbs, and 5 woody plants. Cow hooves cut deep eroding trails across the land, muck the waterholes, and severely degrade the tidal flats. Wherever cattle roam they spread several species of ticks and attract numerous kinds of flies. Cow droppings alter the chemical composition of the soil and succor unnatural communities of insects.

The presence of cattle also demands other sorts of attendant interference in what should be an undisturbed environment: fencing, corrals, roadways, salt blocks, water troughs, plants escaped from imported feed, rats and mice at outbuildings, blackbirds and cowbirds at feedlots, the periodic rattle of vehicles, and intrusion of people.

In a region that has always been cattle country, it is difficult to break entirely with a hallowed tradition. Yet, it finally happened on the Aransas National Wildlife Refuge. In 1989, cattle were removed from the Tatton; the next year they came off Point Pasture; and in 1991, after heated public debate and heroic persistence on the part of the refuge manager, the last cattle were barged off Matagorda Island. In

1992, only the newly negotiated Whitmire Unit still supported a grazing program.

The option to reintroduce domestic grazing stock to control vegetation remains. If cattle are returned to the Aransas in the near future, it may well be to help keep the Tatton Unit free of rank growth that reduces its attractiveness to prairie chickens. In the meantime, prescribed burning is the management tool of choice.

Exotic Plants

Although it is more buffered from intrusion than most areas, the Aransas Refuge harbors many species of herbs, weeds, and grasses that have been imported incidental to human activities. You might reflect upon what seeds dropped from the tire treads, radiator grille, and undersides of the fenders and bumpers of your vehicle while you visited the refuge. Here we consider only those species that were deliberately introduced.

Over the years plantings have been attempted on the refuge for a variety of reasons. Some were meant to supplement native wildlife food resources. Others were intended to lure wildlife into public view. Plants are also used for ornamental landscaping around headquarters and for windbreaks and control of soil erosion. In a few cases, especially in the early years, sundry seeds and cuttings were broadcast randomly without any clear objective other than to add variety to the monotonous coastal vegetation. Fortunately, most of these endeavors were self-limiting. Either the introduced plants failed to survive, or they remained highly localized. Yet, anyone with an eye for native vegetation will notice some alien plants.

Thousands of tubers and hundreds of pounds of seeds have been sown in the freshwater lakes, ponds, and scrapes to make them more attractive to waterfowl and to entice the birds into view for visitors. These include wild celery, duck potato, sago pondweed, coontail, American lotus, smartweed, wild millet, spike rush, southern naiad, muskgrass, chufa, giant bristlegrass, and California, American, and three-square bulrushes.

Bahia grass was sown along rights-of-way. Bermuda grass has been extensively spread for erosion control, lawn cover, and as springtime goose fodder. Blue panic, rye grass, King Ranch bluestem, sand lovegrass, and weeping lovegrass, were broadcast across the interior uplands. St. Augustine grass is planted at headquarters, and patches of this hardy species can be found near old house sites all over the refuge.

Indiscriminate introductions include three cubic yards of mud hauled from a fish hatchery in Uvalde and heaved into ponds on the Aransas in the hope that some sort of duck food might result. In an attempt to start phlox and bluebonnets, several pickup loads of soil were brought in from outside the refuge and spread along the roadside. In one instance more than two hundred pounds of assorted grass seeds were broadcast over the interior of the peninsula from an airplane.

Many trees still linger to mark the vicinity of the St. Charles Ranch headquarters and the patrol station on the west side of the refuge: Chinese arbor vitae, Chinese tallow, Russian olive, chinaberry, cottonwood, athel, petticoat palm. Some of these are entwined with Japanese honeysuckle and bougainvillea. There is one small patch of oleander.

Various ornamentals have been planted at headquarters and around public use sites. A large slash pine struggles to survive near one residence. Three small sago palms grow on the slope at the WIC, and a large one occurs in a residential yard. There is a fine large sycamore in the clearing between the picnic area and the bay overlook and a young one in the parking lot at the visitors center.

None of the above can eclipse the ambitions of the refuge's first manager. Taking advantage of CCC and WPA labor in 1938–1939, he directed the planting of 30,250 white mulberry and 7,350 American plum seedlings all over the peninsula and of 125 cenizos around the parking lots. At headquarters he started 500 Arizona cypress and 300 Kentucky coffee trees for later transplantation. He had his men scatter fifty pounds of Russian olive seed and another fifty of elderberry seed at Jones and Big Tree lakes. For better or worse, only an occasional white mulberry exists today to testify to this spirited enterprise.

CHAPTER 9

Mammals

 Thirty-nine species of native mammals have been recorded from the Aransas National Wildlife Refuge. If you are unfamiliar with the mammals of the state, you might get a copy of *The Mammals of Texas,* by W. B. Davis. If you know your mammals but want to learn more about them, we recommend *Texas Mammals East of the Balcones Escarpment,* by D. J. Schmidly.

Opossum

Because opossums are almost exclusively nocturnal, visitors seldom see them unless an early-rising animal decides to visit the garbage cans at the picnic area. Yet these creatures are one of the commonest medium-sized mammals on the refuge. Six live traps set in the vicinity of the Youth Environmental Training Area caught five possums in one April night, two with litters of young in their pouches. These marsupials are probably more common around the public access area than in the interior of the refuge, because near man they find more varied fare and more nooks for their daytime retreats, and predators are kept at a greater distance.

Even if you have never seen an opossum, you will recognize one at first glance. An animal with a long, naked semiprehensile tail; soft, tangled gray fur with long white guard hairs; bulging black button eyes; papery black ears; a drooling, toothy pink grin; and a comical, shambling gait can be nothing but an opossum.

When roughly handled, these animals often feign death—"play possum." But there is also truth in the ditty "If you want your finger bit, poke it at a possum." They will snap wickedly in self-defense, so refrain from feeding or provoking them.

Opossums are consummate omnivores and scavengers. One was observed near the boardwalk contentedly munching mouthfuls of mud filled with the partly decomposed remains of sheepshead killifishes. Presumably the animal's iron gut would absorb the fish remains and pass the mud.

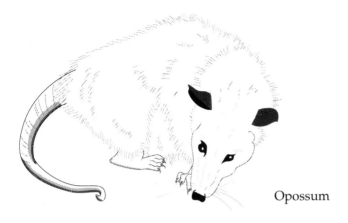

Opossum

Being relatively immune to pit viper venom, possums readily kill and consume small rattlesnakes and cottonmouth moccasins. Because they are adept raiders of birds' nests, they are generally relegated to the varmint category, and they were much persecuted on the refuge during the predator-control days. However, today they are allowed their place in the natural food web, and possums and birds seem to have struck a tolerable balance with each other.

These marsupials run at a lower body temperature and have smaller brains than equal-sized, nonpouched mammals, but rather surprisingly for so slow-paced a creature, they have a shorter life span; even well-tended captive animals seldom live more than four years.

Short on gumption but long on perseverance, the opossum has been content to let the higher-strung world pass it by for fifty million years. To call it a living fossil is to pay it life's highest compliment.

Insectivores

These mammals feed primarily on insects. The Aransas has three terrestrial species—two shrews and a mole—and at least four kinds of bats.

Shrews are small, secretive, quick-moving predators with long snouts, a wicked set of sharp teeth, tiny eyes, and ears hidden in fur. They live in shallow subterranean tunnels and surface runways amid dense grass and leaf litter, where they stalk and consume all manner of insect larvae, grasshoppers, crickets, centipedes, spiders, and pillbugs. If they discover the nest of a mouse or small bird, they will kill and eat the young. Shrews are in turn preyed upon by hawks, owls, skunks, bob-

Shrew

cats, gray foxes, coyotes, and rat snakes. They are important links in the food web.

You are very unlikely to see a shrew, but it is satisfying to appreciate that the little creatures must be all around you as you tour the refuge. The least shrew, the tiniest mammal on the Aransas, is the more common of the two resident species. From snout to tail tip, an adult spans three inches and weighs about as much as a dozen aspirin tablets. It certainly merits its name.

The southwestern short-tailed shrew is only slightly larger. When first discovered on the refuge in 1941, it was described as a unique variety; its closest relatives occur in deep East Texas. This species is apparently rare, or at least it is difficult to come across. Only ten specimens have been taken on the refuge, and a trapping survey in 1989 failed to catch additional individuals. However, in 1991, a collection of regurgitation pellets cast by barn owls on the refuge contained the remains of ten least shrews and three southwestern shorttails.

How and when did the southwestern short-tailed shrew make the 250-mile leap from the southeast to its isolated location on the Aransas? Actually, it never did. Fossil evidence shows that two million years ago, when the Coastal Plain was more moist and forested, short-tailed shrews ranged completely across it, and they pushed westward onto the Edwards Plateau. As the region dried out, shrews followed the retreating forests eastward—except for Aransas' own variety, which got left behind in the dense oak-bay thickets that cap the Pleistocene sand dunes. Recently the same subspecies that occurs on the refuge has been found living alongside its eastern counterpart in sandy land beneath pine trees in Bastrop State Park, a site about 135 miles north of the Aransas and midway between the refuge and the East Texas forest.

Although you are also unlikely to see an eastern mole, the Big Tree Trail winds through favored mole habitat, and there you can occasionally see evidence of their presence—low meandering ridges of earth snaking across trails through the oak mottes. One of these ripples is the roof of a shallow feeding tunnel; do not confuse it with the much more common sandy mounds made by pocket gophers.

The rat-sized mole swims through the sandy soil with breaststrokes of its powerful forelegs, searching for insect larvae, wolf spiders, earthworms, and ground snakes. Moles' feeding ridges have also been seen in moist sand on the tidal flats, where they may be in search of fiddler crabs.

Moles are moderately common on the refuge, but they are restricted to sand with enough moisture to support their tunnel walls. After rain showers they are particularly active in their subsurface passageways, but during the dry months they burrow more deeply. Despite their subterranean lifestyle, moles routinely fall prey to owls, foxes, and skunks, which have ears and noses keen enough to detect feeding moles.

Only four species of bats have been documented on the refuge, but at least four other kinds are likely to roost and feed here, especially during the spring and fall migration seasons. Bats use their sonar mechanism to seek and catch a variety of night-flying insects on the wing, and the aggregate biomass consumed per night makes these little mammals important members of the food web.

The Mexican free-tailed bat stops over on the Aransas en route between its wintering grounds in Mexico and its summer haunts on the Edwards Plateau in Central Texas. In April 1983, about a hundred Mexican freetails were found roosting on the ceiling of a shop building at headquarters. You are most likely to see these relatively large bats at

Bats

dusk during March and April or October and November. They typi-cally fly high and fast with frequent changes of direction but little al-teration in altitude. Their favorite types of prey are moths and flying beetles.

The big free-tailed bat is similar to the Mexican free-tailed, but it is considerably larger and has relatively longer ears. This bat usually oc-curs in West Texas, but on two occasions individuals have been found roosting in a shop building at refuge headquarters; likely they were off course en route to their South American wintering grounds.

Bats are not noted for their beauty, but the red bat, with its bright brick-red fur, is one exception. The red hairs on the female are tipped with white, giving her an appealing frosted appearance. This is also a migratory species, but individuals are doubtless on the refuge through-out the summer. Refuge narrative reports mention one red bat roosting on a window screen at headquarters and another dangling from a grapevine in a live oak tree. Watch at dusk for habitually solitary red bats flying close to the ground or fluttering along beneath the canopy in a live oak motte.

The silver-haired bat surely stops over on the Aransas during its spring and fall migration flights, which apparently take it directly across a portion of the Gulf of Mexico. One, found roosting in a build-ing at headquarters in September 1978, is the refuge's only record.

Judging from known distributions, at least four other species of bats should migrate across and perhaps spend the summer months on the Aransas Refuge: eastern pipistrelle, hoary bat, northern yellow bat, and evening bat.

Rodents

For the most part these are nonmigratory animals, small, secretive, fid-gety, and numerous. At any given moment there are certainly more in-dividual rodents on the Aransas Refuge than individuals of all other mammal species combined. This is partly because tiny creatures, de-manding fewer resources, can live at higher densities. It is also a con-sequence of living in the ecological fast lane. In the Coastal Bend ro-dents are not only active year-round but also breed all year. With large litters and short life spans, populations wax and wane with the times.

Rodents play an immensely important ecological role in all of the ter-restrial communities on the refuge. Primarily herbivorous, rats and mice, along with insects and crustaceans, are the principal means by which plant material is converted into tempting packets of meat of ap-propriate size and sufficient abundance to support the first-level carnivores. Rodents are the staple in the diets of many raptors (hawks and owls) and snakes, and they are an important supplement for most carnivorous mammals. Without rodents, the diversity and abundance of other wildlife on the Aransas would be greatly reduced.

Widely diverse, rodents are also interesting in their own right. Most live on the ground, but some live underground, others live in trees, and a few live near the water and voluntarily swim. They eat mostly seeds, and all take some greenery and fungi, but most also eat a surprisingly large number of insects when these are available. Rodents have their own social arrangements, territories, home ranges, competitive struggles, and courtship patterns.

Although you may not see a single rodent during your visit to the Aransas, you certainly should appreciate the pivotal contribution of this often-maligned group to the natural cycles that so delight the eye.

Since the establishment of the Aransas National Wildlife Refuge, thirteen resident species of rodents have been documented. One is probably now extirpated. Three are introduced species. It is likely that at least one and perhaps as many as four more kinds may occur on the Aransas and have so far escaped verification.

Mice and Rats

Every grassy acre of the Aransas Refuge supports the principal triumvirate of rodent species: pigmy mouse, fulvous harvest mouse, and hispid cotton rat. Their peak densities are in the luxuriant grasses of the ridge-and-swale, tidal shore grassland, cordgrass, and upland grassland communities. Collectively these three rodents are staples in the diets of all hawks and owls on the refuge. They are heavily utilized by rat snakes, kingsnakes, racers, and rattlesnakes, and coyotes, gray foxes, bobcats, and striped skunks routinely prey on them.

Pigmy mice are Mexican rodents that have worked their way northward through the eastern half of Texas in recent historical times. These gray mites, the tiniest and cutest rodents on the refuge, hustle along appropriately minuscule runways amid the jungle of grass stems, where they feed on grass seeds and assorted greenery and on snails, beetles, and grasshoppers.

The fulvous harvest mouse has a long tail, a golden-brown back, and a soft wash of orange on its sides. This pretty little mouse sometimes constructs globular nests of shredded grass in low shrubs.

The hispid cotton rat is a plump, fist-sized rodent with coarse brown fur. Its presence is revealed by a maze of clipped and trampled trailways ramifying beneath the canopy of grass. Cotton rats have an excep-

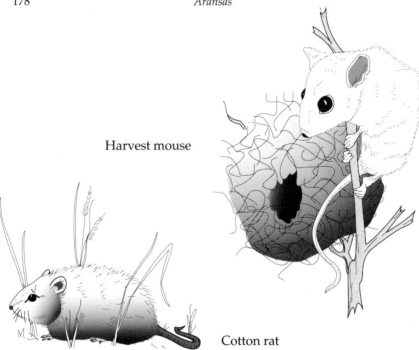

Harvest mouse

Cotton rat

tionally high reproductive rate, even for rodents, and in favorable years their populations increase dramatically. Several narrative reports mention cotton-rat plagues on the refuge. Because they are aggressive competitors, the density of neighboring kinds of rodents drops when the cotton rats are riding a high. At such times the predators feast, rendering service to man and nature alike.

The white-footed mouse occurs throughout the upland portion of Blackjack Peninsula. It lives in any grassy habitat but prefers access to woody plants, logs, and a diversity of herbs. This big-eared, beady-eyed species is the commonest rodent in the oak-bay forest community, and it is responsible for most of the nibble marks you may notice on acorns beside the walking trails. Personnel will testify that white-footed mice frequently invade residences on the refuge, especially in the wintertime.

The marsh rice rat, resembling a medium-sized house rat, is most at home in the moist grassy swales, cordgrass tussocks, and tidal flats. It readily moves over boggy ground and through shallow water in search of grass and sedge greenery, saltmarsh snails, and birds' eggs and nestlings. If pressed by a predator, these rats sometimes dive, and they can swim rapidly underwater for short distances. As you scan the tidal flats and the fringe of smooth cordgrass from the observation tower, you are looking down on prime marsh rice rat habitat.

The large, slate-gray south plains wood rat is at home in the dry mesquite and prickly pear country of South and West Texas; the Aransas Refuge lies on the northern edge of its range. Apparently it was once common on Blackjack Peninsula when the area was open and overgrazed. Although old wood-rat middens (mounds of sticks, cow chips, and oystershells that the rats pile up for their dens) can still be found, these rodents are apparently rare on the peninsula today. One was trapped beneath mesquites on the Heron Flats Trail in 1981. Wood rats are currently common only in the mesquite and prickly pear community on the Tatton, and fresh den sites have been seen on the Lamar Unit. They do not occur on Matagorda Island.

The hispid pocket mouse is a medium-sized, rather slow-moving rodent that prefers open, weedy habitat. Its rather coarse pelage is yellowish brown above, white below, with a clear buff stripe along the sides where the colors meet. It moves about on the surface by night, stuffing its fur-lined cheek pouches with seeds to carry to its underground food store. This hoard sometimes contains a pint of assorted seeds of Indian blanket, evening primrose, winecup, grassbur, and panic grasses. After plugging the entrance to its vertical burrow with sand, the hispid pocket mouse sleeps the day away.

One rodent is seldom seen but leaves evidence of its subterranean existence all over Blackjack Peninsula. You cannot help noticing the mounds of sand left by Attwater's pocket gopher, named in honor of Henry P. Attwater, the same early-day Texas naturalist for whom the local subspecies of prairie chicken is named. The bright heaps of sand, which these animals pile up while excavating their extensive system of underground tunnels, are especially noticeable in recently burned tracts. Each individual gopher turns over more than five tons of soil annually, significantly influencing the soil texture and vegetation of many sections of the refuge. Drummond's phlox and several species of grasses grow especially well on old gopher diggings. The Aransas Refuge, with its sandy substrate and dense cover of vegetation, is a regular pocket gopher heaven, but since the mounds persist for months, their abundance probably exaggerates the standing population of the rodents themselves.

An interpretive sign on the Tour Loop points out a pimple mound, one of many large rounded hillocks of sand scattered throughout the ridge-and-swale community. It has been suggested that localized digging activity of generations of gophers actually created pimple mounds, but it is at least as likely that windblown sand captured by vegetation was then invaded by the gophers. Because they lie several feet above the shallow water table, these ready-made sand piles are rapidly colonized by live oaks, yaupon, Gulf Coast toads, ground skinks, hognose snakes, and pocket gophers. Regardless of the sequence of events leading to their formation, pimple mounds harbor a diverse and rather distinctive array of life.

A pocket gopher is about the size of a rat but not at all rat-shaped. The blunt head, with tiny eyes and ears and a spray of long whiskers, joins the compact, cylindrical body without a noticeable neck. The short brown pelage is dense and grainless. A stubby, naked tail serves as a handy touch-and-temperature sensor in the burrow. Muscular forelegs, armed with stout curved claws, and large incisors are the gopher's digging tools. It works like a jerky, animated bulldozer, using its chest and forelegs to push sand out of its burrow into the characteristic surface mound.

Pocket gophers are solitary, seemingly ill-humored creatures that spend most of their time underground, either hustling along their passageways or energetically digging fresh ones in search of roots, tubers, and succulent greenery to eat. They will also venture warily onto the surface to harvest fallen acorns and berries.

Pocket gopher

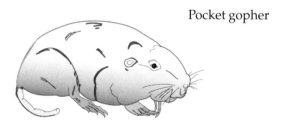

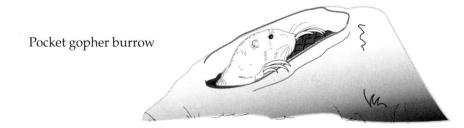

Pocket gopher burrow

Gophers assiduously keep their burrow systems plugged, but the animals frequently expose themselves as they push out a fresh mound of sand. Many predators—coyotes, bobcats, foxes, hawks, and owls— are alert to the slight movements and the odor of moist sand at a new mound, and they routinely snatch up working gophers. Snakes and weasels can go into the burrow system, and badgers and striped skunks are equipped to dig into them. In addition, many small creatures such as crickets, wolf spiders, ground snakes, spadefoot toads, and narrow-mouthed toads enjoy the damp gloom of active and abandoned gopher burrows.

Other Rodents

The fox squirrel is considered among the game animals in Chapter 7.

There are early references to Mexican ground squirrels on Blackjack Peninsula, but since these diurnal and easily observed animals have not been seen in recent years (the last sighting was in 1968), they are surely extirpated. The advancing live oak thickets likely made the area uninhabitable for the open-ground rodents. The soil and topography on portions of the Tatton Unit are of the sort that ground squirrels prefer, but no evidence of these animals has been found there. The spotted ground squirrel occurs on the deep sands of Padre and Mustang islands, but it is curiously absent from Matagorda Island as well as from the local mainland.

Three introduced rodents are known to occur on the Aransas. The black rat is confined to the residential area. House mice are likewise limited, but small groups of individuals occasionally move into adjacent weedy and grassy habitats.

The large, aquatic nutria is a South American rodent that has been feral on the Gulf Coast for more than forty years. They were first sighted on the refuge in 1962 and were moderately common during the wet years following Hurricane Beulah, but it is likely that in routine years the Aransas' alligators snap up nutria about as fast as they arrive. The few recent sightings have been in Thomas Slough.

The Aransas Refuge is on the extreme eastern edge of the distributions of the silky pocket mouse, the deer mouse, and the northern grasshopper mouse. None has been documented since the refuge was established, but as all three prefer more open and sparse vegetation than now exists in the area, they might be expected, if anywhere, on the Tatton and Whitmire units.

Finally, though there is no specific record from the refuge of the Norway rat (the large brown house rat), it is hard to believe that this universal immigrant does not occasionally appear in the residential area.

Rabbits

Like rodents, rabbits are herbivores and therefore ecologically important for transforming vegetation into meat. They are preyed upon by coyotes, foxes, bobcats, owls, hawks, rat snakes, and rattlesnakes. Although rabbits, too, may reach high densities, they are larger than rodents and so are never as numerous.

Historically the Aransas has supported populations of three species of rabbits: black-tailed jackrabbit, eastern cottontail, and swamp rabbit. Technically, the jackrabbit is a hare, distinguished from rabbits not only by anatomy but also by bearing its young fully furred with eyes open and ready to follow their mother almost immediately.

Jackrabbit and cottontail traditionally have been the common species on the Aransas, but their fortunes have varied with the times. For the first two decades after the refuge was established, both were abundant. But that was in the days of heavy grazing pressure, the drought of the fifties, and less thicketized live oak. Blackjack Peninsula was much more open than it is today, and jackrabbits outnumbered cottontails by about five to one.

In 1961 Hurricane Carla wracked the area and, according to the narrative report for that year, the jackrabbits and cottontails "vanished." Populations of both were still low in 1967 when Hurricane Beulah put all but the highest ground under water. Not until 1972 were a few jackrabbits and an occasional cottontail seen on night surveys.

Between 1973 and 1982 cattle were removed from Blackjack Peninsula, and the grasses resurged phenomenally. Jackrabbits demand sparsely vegetated, open ground. Cottontails prefer brambles and short grass studded with forbs. The lush grass and barren islands of running live oak suited neither.

Jackrabbit

Going into the eighties both jackrabbits and cottontails were at a low ebb on the Aransas. Although the reasons for it have never been worked out, the number of jackrabbits in the entire Coastal Bend has recently plummeted. With the predominance of dense woody cover and scant recruitment from outside, it is not surprising that jackrabbits have not been seen at all on Blackjack Peninsula for the past several years. The latest sighting, of a lone animal, was on the Tatton Unit in 1987.

Cottontails are currently present in low numbers. Being creatures of community edges, they live along the border between ridge and swale, where they utilize the greenery in freshly burned tracts and feed on the roadsides at night. You might see one at dawn or dusk on any of the refuge drives, but they will quickly dive into their favorite briar patch.

The case of the swamp rabbit is different. This close relative of the cottontail is at home in the wetlands of East Texas. On the Aransas, at the southwestern edge of its range, it ekes out a living among the common reeds and sedges at the edge of the tidal flat and freshwater communities. Probably because of frequent droughts and the population of hungry alligators, swamp rabbits have never been common on the refuge. Look for these secretive creatures while you walk around Thomas Slough and Hog Lake. Individuals have recently been seen late in the afternoon on the roadside at the bay overlook.

Swamp rabbits are larger, darker, and stockier than cottontails, and they tend to skulk along under the protection of bankside vegetation. If you startle one you may hear it thump the ground with a hindfoot and utter a piercing alarm squeal before it bounds away.

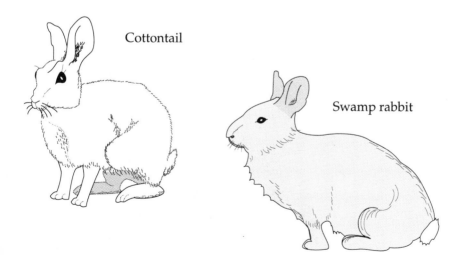

Cottontail

Swamp rabbit

Armadillo

Though most natives of Texas and the Gulf Coast take the armadillo for granted, many visitors consider it the most curious denizen of the Aransas National Wildlife Refuge.

The armadillo was probably the last mammal to establish itself on the Aransas without the direct intervention of man. Only one species of this South American mammal has extended its range into the United States. As it moved north, the armadillo pushed through the Coastal Bend about 1880, and it may now have reached its northern limit in Kansas and Missouri. Neither the Indians nor the earliest pioneers on Blackjack Peninsula ever saw armadillos.

Armadillos are unmistakable. They are the only native mammals with bony plates fused into their skin. An adult is a little larger than a football and weighs about twelve to fifteen pounds. A solid mosaic of plates over the shoulders and rump is broken by a set of nine accordionlike bands around the middle. The forehead is heavily armored, but the large ears are membranous and the muzzle tapers to a naked piglike snout. All four stocky limbs, though less heavily sheathed, are armed with stout claws, and the belly is merely clothed with a tangle of long hairs. The long tapering tail is encased in bony rings.

Armadillos have exceptionally poor eyesight. They navigate and forage primarily by smell and count on their keen sense of hearing both to help locate prey and to detect the approach of potential predators. These animals feed mostly on small creatures from the ground litter and the top several inches of soil: insect larvae, earthworms, crickets, millipedes, pillbugs, ground spiders, small lizards, and snakes. Occasionally they dig into fire-ant nests and lap up both adults and larvae

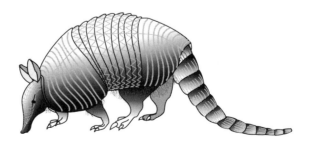

Armadillo

with their sticky tongues. Armadillos also relish the pulpy fruits of persimmon, dewberry, and yaupon, but they are one of the few resident creatures that do not eat acorns; their tiny peg teeth cannot manage a tough acorn.

Home for an armadillo is a series of burrows among which it rotates as the mood strikes it. Each burrow has an entrance about eight inches wide, and in the easily dug sandy soil of the Aransas, the sloping, unbranched tunnel may be over ten feet long. In addition to serving their makers, armadillo holes are used as dodge-in escape sites by everything from fence lizards to cottontails. A large array of insects and arachnids retreat into the cool, dank interiors, and rattlesnakes commonly pass the day there. An abandoned armadillo den is soon taken over by a raccoon, opossum, or skunk, and even a coyote will sometimes enlarge one for her own use at whelping time.

Young armadillos, always born in identical quadruplets, are tender, miniaturized versions of the adults. They fall prey to coyotes, bobcats, raccoons, feral hogs, and horned owls. Adults are less susceptible to attack, but any coyote, if he catches one in the open, can flip and kill an armadillo.

Regardless of popular myth and even of photographs in reputable field books, when startled or attacked the one thing no live armadillo ever does is roll into a ball. Instead, it sets off at a hopping gallop directly for the nearest burrow. The armored body pays for itself when the racing animal barges through the thickest undergrowth on its way to safety. No man and few other mammals can close on a wheezing, fear-struck armadillo running hell-bent through the brush.

Armadillos are common enough on Blackjack Peninsula, but it is difficult to locate one on purpose. They are active year-round, but in the summer they are mainly nocturnal, and in very cold weather they remain in their dens. On a hot day, they generally emerge from their burrows late in the afternoon; on cloudy days or sunny winter days they are abroad earlier. There is nothing like a shower of rain to bring the armadillos out in force to forage in the moist soil.

The best way to see an armadillo is to scan the roadsides and clearings as you tour the refuge in your vehicle. If you spot one snuffling along, watch it from your window or quietly approach it from downwind for a photograph. Sometimes you can locate an armadillo by the heedless commotion it makes while searching for food.

Cloven-hooved Mammals

The two native species, javelina and white-tailed deer, are considered in Chapter 7. The several introduced species are included in Chapter 8.

Raccoon and Its Kin

It is a tribute to the adaptability of raccoons that they are abundant on the Aransas to the point of being pestiferous. They prefer to forage along the margins of freshwater ponds, tidal pools, and the edges of the bays, but omnivorous raccoons range through all of the local biotic communities. They also raid camp stores at the Youth Environmental Training Area, scavenge in the refuge dump ground, rummage through the garbage cans at the picnic area, and skulk around the residences. An occasional individual will even beg openly at the picnic area. Please refrain from feeding them. Hand-fed animals get more insistent and ultimately become dependent on handouts. They are also the ones most likely to have an opportunity to nip proffering fingers.

Because they are such adept and persevering predators of birds' nests, there has never been any love lost between raccoons and refuge personnel. During the predator-control days the conflict took on a particularly grim aspect. In the late forties a big concern was to build up the wild turkey population. In 1948, to that end, more than five hundred raccoons were live-trapped and removed. The turkeys did not increase, and the raccoon population appeared undiminished.

In 1950, the only whooping crane chick ever hatched on the Aransas Refuge was housed in a special enclosure on the tidal flats opposite headquarters. When the precious chick was only three days old it was killed by a predator; a raccoon was suspected. When another whooper egg was laid in 1951, the raccoons paid the price for their nefarious reputation. Dog food mixed with warfarin was set out in hoppers, and shrimp and prunes laced with strychnine were scattered up and down the East Shore. Several hundred raccoons—and no telling what else—took the bait and died. The whooper egg never even hatched.

Raccoon control continued in high gear until such tactics were finally abolished in 1963. It is conservatively estimated that nearly four thousand of the animals were dealt with before the modern notion of ecosystem management took hold.

Raccoons are mainly nocturnal, but you might well see one abroad in the daytime. Watch for them grabbling in the shallows of any roadside ditch or pond as you drive the roadways. In early summer you might even see a mama accompanied by several cute little coons busily learning their versatile trade. Sometimes you can spot a raccoon poking around on the tidal flats below the observation tower. Any place you find a muddy spot you should be able to locate a set of the raccoon's distinctive handprints.

The secretive and strictly nocturnal ringtail is an agile, rather catlike

Raccoon tracks

Raccoon

relative of the raccoon. It prefers more broken terrain than the Aransas affords, and the only one ever seen on the refuge was flushed from a lumber pile at headquarters in 1954.

The coati (ko-AHT-ee), also related to the raccoon, is a larger animal with an elongate body, a tapered snout, and a long, indistinctly banded tail held in an erect curve over its back. Coatis range from northern South America through Mexico, and though a few individuals occasionally cross the Rio Grande into Texas, it is doubtful if a breeding population occurs anywhere in the state.

One coati was seen several times near Mustang Lake in 1938. Another was seen near the Big Tree Trail in April 1974. No more were observed until 1984, when a maintenance worker managed to coax a semitame coati into his pickup truck and another animal was reported from the west side of Blackjack Peninsula. At least the first of those surely was an escaped or released pet. It is unlikely that a coati could work its way to the Aransas from the Rio Grande across today's fragmented landscape.

Skunks and Their Kin

Skunks are all nocturnal, so they are seldom observed by visitors, but three species of these omnivores have been recorded on the Aransas. The three kinds can be distinguished by their patterns of white markings on black bodies. The striped skunk has two white stripes on the back that join at the neck to continue atop the head. The spotted skunk has four thin white stripes that break into a series of dashes and spots on its rump. The Gulf Coast hog-nosed skunk has a single narrow white band from head to rump. All three species can emit the well-known odorous defensive spray.

The striped skunk, the commonest of the three, emerges early in the evening to forage along ditches and around poolsides for insects, spiders, birds and their eggs, unwary rodents, and whatever pulpy fruits it happens upon. You may see an individual that has learned to scrounge for scraps at the picnic area; just give it the right-of-way. It spends the day curled up in a den of its own making or in a remodeled armadillo burrow.

The spotted skunk is less common and much more secretive. It is prone to climb into trees and shrubs in search of prey but is also known to occur on the nearly treeless Tatton Unit. When provoked, this little skunk has the peculiar habit of doing a handstand on its forelegs before reluctantly releasing its foul-smelling anal secretion.

The Gulf Coast hog-nosed skunk, largest and rarest of the three, has exceptionally long foreclaws and an enlarged snout to go along with its habit of rooting and digging industriously for insect larvae, ground spiders, earthworms, and small reptiles. The two reported sightings on the refuge in the seventies are suspect; no specimens of the Gulf Coast hog-nosed skunk have been verified from the Coastal Bend since the first decade of this century. There may still be a population of this southern skunk in the remote sandy uplands on the King Ranch in South Texas.

Badgers lead solitary lives and are not abundant anywhere in their

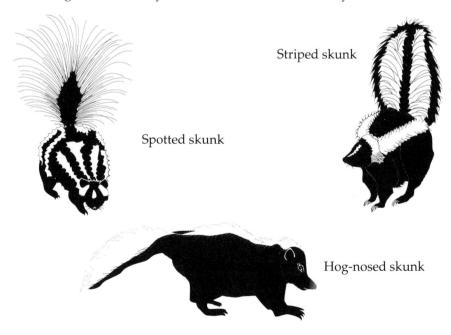

Striped skunk

Spotted skunk

Hog-nosed skunk

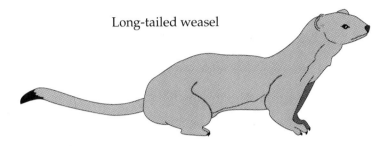

Long-tailed weasel

extensive range across the western three-quarters of Texas. Although they may have been more common when the local area was open enough to support ground squirrels (a favorite prey species), badgers have been very rare on Blackjack Peninsula since the establishment of the refuge. Two were seen in the early forties, one in 1958, and another in 1970. On Matagorda Island, however, badgers are routinely observed.

The broad-backed, low-slung badger uses its long foreclaws and muscular shoulders to rake the sandy coastal soil in search of pocket gophers and cotton rats. It supplements those staples with any other small animals it encounters: fiddler crabs, insects, arachnids, lizards and snakes, ground-nesting birds and their eggs, nests of rodents or cottontail rabbits.

The virtual disappearance of the badger from Blackjack Peninsula is puzzling, since the abundance of pocket gophers should provide an ample food source and the deep sand should be to the badger's liking. The few originally present may have been incidentally wiped out during early predator-control campaigns. (Both of the individuals seen in the forties were "collected," the polite term for killed.) Hurricanes may have taken their toll, and badgers were probably inhibited by the progressive overgrowth of woody and herbaceous plants. Once they were gone from the peninsula, recruitment by natural immigration across the surrounding blackland fields was unlikely. The reintroduction of badgers into their native haunts on Blackjack Peninsula might have ecological merit.

Long-tailed weasels seem to be uncommon throughout their range; only two have been seen on Blackjack Peninsula, the latest in 1985. But these slender, quick-moving little carnivores may be more abundant and simply avoid detection. They prey almost exclusively on rodents; pocket gophers are among their favorites, so they should find good hunting on the Aransas.

The mink is at the southern border of its range on the Aransas Refuge. This semiaquatic weasel tolerates either fresh or brackish water and prefers waterways choked with debris and vegetation. The only two mink ever observed on the refuge were both seen at the one site best suited for them—Thomas Slough.

Carnivores

The status of the gray wolf and the extirpation of the red wolf are recounted in Chapter 6. Two more wild canines occur on the Aransas: the coyote and the gray fox.

The reputation of the coyote (kye-YO-tee, or in many parts of Texas, KYE-oat) is well established in art, literature, and legend. This is the archetypal wild dog: slender build trimmed for endurance running, long legs, erect ears, narrow muzzle, bushy tail, sharp and clear yellow eyes, acute hearing, keen nose. Coyotes display intricate social behavior, including distinctive mannerisms as well as chemical and vocal cues, and an overall alertness, which is often better referred to as cunning or even as downright cleverness.

Adaptable to almost any habitat, coyotes occur statewide, but they definitely prefer open terrain. Although common on Blackjack Peninsula, they are not abundant; the dense inland vegetation and the coyotes' own social interactions probably limit the population to an estimated forty adults. There are surely many vagrant animals, since coyotes can easily move back and forth from the adjacent coastal prairie. A thriving population of coyotes also exists on Matagorda Island.

One of the coyote's most adaptive features is opportunistic feeding behavior; it will consume anything from carrion to feathers to keep going. On Blackjack Peninsula coyotes probably subsist largely on cotton rats and pocket gophers. If the cottontail rabbit population rises, the coyotes turn to them as a major prey species. On Matagorda Island, jackrabbits are an important food item. In the springtime coyotes eat a surprising amount of fresh grass; in the summertime they consume large numbers of grasshoppers and beetles. In season they enjoy persimmons, ground cherries, mustang grapes, yaupon fruits, acorns, mesquite beans, dewberries, prickly pears, and wolfberries, and they even eat a variety of mushrooms. Sometimes their feces is crammed with the fruits of the dwarf palmetto. They snap up any frog, crayfish, fiddler

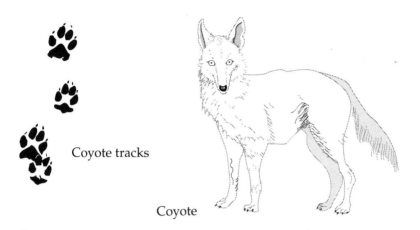

Coyote tracks

Coyote

crab, or small snake they run across, and they routinely patrol the beaches and tidal flats for marine offal.

Coyotes can be devastating predators on birds, and they surely find many nesting bobwhite quail, eastern meadowlarks, and—when the birds were more common—wild turkey and Attwater's prairie chickens. Defense from coyotes is the main reason that the winter waterfowl spend their nights standing or floating in the water or roosting on islets and oyster reefs. Despite these evasive tactics, piles of feathers around roosting sites testify that coyotes and bobcats routinely slog through the shallows to reach the birds. The same threat forces resident wading birds to nest on isolated islands and spoil banks.

The coyote is justifiably regarded as the principal predator on white-tailed deer, and virtually all of its toll is levied in the springtime on freshly dropped fawns. A coyote can apparently recognize a doe that is about to give birth and will follow the deer in anticipation of an easy meal.

Your best chance to see a coyote is to keep a sharp eye out as you drive the refuge roads, especially early and late in the day. Watch for them crossing the road or hustling across clearings on their way to cover. The creatures are wary, so expect no more than a glimpse. Sometimes, however, if a coyote does not feel especially threatened, it will pause at the edge of the brush and gaze curiously at human observers. Then it affords a good view if you have your binoculars on the animal. You can usually find the doglike tracks of coyotes in the moist sand along the edge of San Antonio Bay and beside the boardwalk.

If you are lucky, you may be treated to the haunting, mournful howl that coyotes produce on occasion. Midwinter at sundown is a good time to listen. Usually one animal will be answered by others, and these may eventually build into a brief and ecstatic chorus, which trails off into a series of feisty yip-yaps. Listen to the full repertory. You will not hear a more sincere expression of wildness on the refuge.

The gray fox, not much larger than a house cat, glides along the game trails on dainty ghost feet. These are pretty animals—a grizzled steel gray with bright chestnut trim. The ample gray tail is tipped and striped along the upper side with black.

Gray foxes are at home in the dense interior of Blackjack Peninsula and also hunt the grassy swales. They eat mainly rodents, shrews, moles, and birds, supplemented with an array of insects and arachnids as well as most available pulpy fruits; of all the wild canines, they most readily take to the trees to forage. Foxes do not howl like coyotes, but when curious or provoked they often make a startlingly loud, hoarse bark.

Watch for a shadow-animal melting into the brush anywhere along the Tour Loop. If you glimpse its large, trailing tail, you may have seen about as much as a gray fox ever reveals of itself.

Wild cats are remarkably like domestic cats in both appearance and behavior. They have supple bodies, keen eyes with vertical pupils, exceptionally sensitive hearing, retractile claws, and a twitching tail. They bury their feces and scent-mark their territories against feline interlopers. Silent tread and lightning reflexes make them masters of both the stealthy stalk and the patient ambush. And as with domestic cats, you can never be quite sure what they are going to do next.

Wild cats are notorious for avoiding observation until—for no apparent reason—one will perversely break cover and stroll insouciantly along the roadside in broad daylight or stare quietly into the beam of an oncoming headlight.

At least intermittently, the Aransas harbors three, possibly four, native species of cats. The jaguarundi and the questionable status of the ocelot are considered in Chapter 6. That leaves the bobcat and the cougar.

The bobcat is by far the commonest native cat in Texas and on the refuge. It is most frequently seen on night patrols by refuge personnel, but visitor sightings, incidental glimpses from vehicles or at drying waterholes, are not unusual.

Back in the predator-control days of 1956, 52 bobcats were trapped on the refuge in one four-month interval, which indicates a very high density for a top-level carnivore. The population was exceptionally high on the Aransas in 1983, and sightings have continued to be numerous going into the nineties. Mamas with two or three cubs have been seen on the Heron Flats Trail and occasionally crossing roads

Bobcat

around headquarters in August. Now and then a solitary adult is sighted slogging across the open mud flats and shallows of Mustang Lake, completely oblivious to the exclamations of those visitors on the observation tower fortunate enough to observe it.

Bobcats are unmistakably feline in general anatomy, but they are distinctive. They are the only local cat with a short tail. The hindquarters are higher than the powerful forequarters, giving a characteristic rump-to-shoulders slope to the profile. The beige pelage is washed with russet and dappled with dusky smudges and bars. Amid grass clumps or in sun-flecked undergrowth a bobcat is virtually invisible.

These cats feed mainly on mammals and birds; all of the local rodents and rabbits are prime game, and cotton rats and cottontails are staples. They know how to waylay a pocket gopher busy ejecting sand from its burrow, and they also take whitetail fawns and piglets of javelinas and feral hogs when they can. An adult cat can kill a grown deer if it catches the animal at a disadvantage. Because the nocturnal bobcat climbs with ease, it claims birds and their nestlings and is even agile enough to make a calculated leap from the ground and snatch a low-flying dove or quail from midair.

Like most carnivores, bobcats will take anything they can get: an occasional snake, a stranded fish, a fat grasshopper, a fly-blown deer carcass. They have the uncatlike habit of readily sloshing through shallow water and are among the many creatures that stalk the tidal flats and beaches at night in search of blue crabs, fiddlers, crayfish, roosting birds, and whatever else presents itself.

Probably more so than any other local species, the cougar—also called mountain lion, puma, and panther—symbolizes nature at its wildest and most menacing. In addition to being at the top of the mammalian food chain, these big cats embody the multiple intrigues of silent beauty, brooding temperament, and ominous power. This is the stuff of which legends are spun, and cougars are attended by their share of yarns.

Because every sighting of this impressive animal on the refuge is both thrilling and noteworthy, there is a need to confirm each occurrence. Observations are typically brief, totally without warning, and in bad light. Add inherent excitement, uncertainty about field marks, a dole of wishful thinking, and a touch of anxiety. Especially if the observer does not have much outdoor experience, it is astoundingly easy to mistake a yearling deer or a wind-whipped clump of bushy bluestem grass for a hurrying cougar. Even professionals are led astray.

The Texas Parks and Wildlife Department estimates a state population of about six hundred cougars, with most animals on large private ranches in South and West Texas and a local concentration in the oak

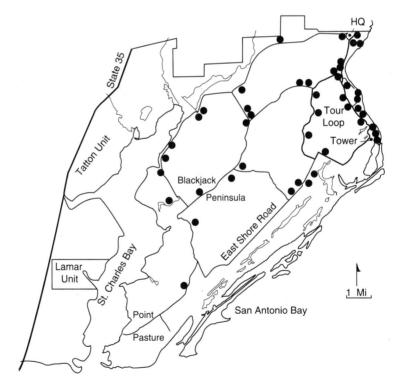

Figure 26. Reported sightings of cougars on the Aransas National Wildlife Refuge through 1990. Data are from the files of the ANWR.

thickets and chaparral in the Coastal Bend. Since the refuge's establishment in 1937 through 1992, there have been approximately 75 reported sightings of cougars on the Aransas. The first was in 1948, the most recent in 1991. Nineteen sightings were by refuge employees; the rest were reported by hunters, petroleum company employees, cowhands, and routine visitors. Six sightings were confirmed (that is, made by experienced wildlife personnel). The greatest number of annual sightings, 8, was made in 1978 and in 1984. Several sightings have been made by visitors from the observation tower and include reports of an unusually dark individual—a "black panther." Occasionally people have reported seeing a pair of cougars together. One of the confirmed sightings was of a cougar stalking a deer. In March 1981, a freshly killed deer was discovered near the Youth Environmental Training Area with all the marks of having just been pulled down by a big cat.

There definitely are, at least now and then, cougars on the Aransas. They lie up in the dense brush by day and stalk the abundant white-tailed deer, javelina, and feral hogs by night, but they are just fickle enough to be occasionally abroad most anytime. These solitary, retiring animals are mobile and highly territorial. Maybe one, a pair, or several routinely include the Aransas in their extensive home ranges.

If you see a cougar, you can count yourself among the privileged few. Simply appreciating that you are in good cougar habitat and knowing that one of the great cats may well be dozing securely nearby, perhaps turning an ear slightly at the sound of your automobile passing by, is a thrill in itself. That fact and your appreciation of it constitute a major part of what wildlife refuges are all about.

CHAPTER 10

Birds

Because of its position along the Central Flyway, its proximity to both the Gulf of Mexico and the tropics, and its interdigitated variety of protected estuarine and terrestrial habitats, the Aransas hosts a tremendous diversity of birds. As of 1991, a total of 390 species had been recorded, the highest count in the entire national wildlife refuge system. Annual Christmas bird counts routinely tally about 150 species. Little wonder, then, that the ANWR is high on the list of birding hot spots in North America.

Of course, not all these kinds of birds are on the refuge simultaneously. Only a minority are year-round residents; the rest are seasonal visitors or hurrying migrants. Many of the tallied species are rare, some are clearly displaced waifs, and several have been observed only once since documentation began. Since a solitary verified observation puts a species permanently on an area list, you must look beyond simple occurrence and learn about annual and seasonal abundance to evaluate the status of a species on the refuge. For instance, the Aransas list includes the Chihuahuan raven, a bird at home in South and West Texas and not characteristic of the Coastal Bend. Two ravens were seen on Matagorda Island in 1937, nine months before the Aransas Refuge was established; there has been no local sighting since. That makes the raven a bona fide member of the ANWR list, but you can hardly expect to see one there.

Day in and day out, however, there are enough kinds of birds on the Aransas, and some of them in staggering numbers in certain seasons, to satisfy both professional and amateur birders and to stimulate anyone interested in the outdoors. The presence of the birds and the ease with which most of them can be viewed in the open coastal habitat promise a rewarding experience for any visitor at any time.

The endangered forms and the game birds are treated in Chapters 5, 6, and 7. It is beyond the scope of this guidebook to do more than briefly mention some of the common members of the many other groups of birds that reside on or routinely pass across the refuge. If you are interested in serious bird study, ask at the desk in the WIC for a free copy of the birding checklist that includes the kinds of birds known from the refuge and indicates their seasonal abundance, favored habitat, and nesting status.

There are many books to help you learn to identify birds. The single best one for the Coastal Bend is Roger Tory Peterson's *Field Guide to the Birds of Texas and Adjacent States*. You can browse the bookshelves in the WIC for other field guides. If you can already recognize the coastal birds and want supplementary information, consult J. H. Rappole and G. W. Blacklock's *Birds of the Texas Coastal Bend*, which includes directions to additional birding sites along the local coast. Finally, *A Birder's Guide to Aransas National Wildlife Refuge*, by Barry Jones, provides an excellent annotated list of the birds of the Aransas.

Proper identification is just the first step in getting to know a bird. Can you recognize it by call notes? In spring plumage and in winter plumage? In which of the communities listed in Chapter 3 is the bird usually found? At what season of the year is it on the Aransas? If it leaves, where does it go? Does it nest here? If so, in what sort of site? If not here, then where does it nest? What is the bird's niche—what does it eat and what eats the bird? How is its anatomy—feet, legs, wings, bill, coloration—correlated with its niche? By what sorts of sounds and gestures do individuals of the same species communicate with each other?

Consider the last question—bird body language—in terms of the least sandpiper, the lowly "mud peep" that is relatively common along the edges of the tidal flats during spring and fall migration. Most visitors seldom bother to distinguish these unassuming little birds from the look-alike semipalmated and western sandpipers and several other small skittering species that also probe for polychaete worms and chase amphipods during the same migratory periods. But let's say that you have taken the time to recognize a mud peep when you see one: the sparrow-sized, unmistakably sandpipery body; the dappled brown back; the brown-streaked breast; the yellow-green legs; the short, thin bill, ever so slightly down-curved at the tip; and so on. Now that you can identify a mud peep, you are ready to watch them converse.

Find a flock busily feeding on the edge of the tidal flat at the end of the boardwalk. (You almost never see a solitary mud peep—another field trait.) The individuals will be rather evenly spaced, each with its own traveling square foot of mud to probe. Observe what happens when two birds drift too close together. Up go their tails, exposing the white undersides. You can see these bright little semaphores flickering continually across the flat as the birds try to maintain their shifting feeding territories. Any least sandpiper that fails to heed the tail-warning signal usually gets chased to the edge of the flock. Sometimes two adjacent birds come to a standoff in a boundary dispute. Then each one freezes in a rigid forward-tilt position, sometimes with wings slightly raised and bill pointed directly at its neighbor. After a few seconds of ritualized staring, the two antagonists abruptly break off and proceed to feed again, presumably each one better aware of the limits of the other's feeding space. Suddenly the entire flock explodes in tight-knit, zigzag flight.

What other fragments of mud-peep talk can you pick up? You will know that you have become an apt translator when you can correctly anticipate a bird's response to a particular signal. Here is a whole new dimension to birding—getting better acquainted with old feathered friends as a welcome supplement to searching ceaselessly for more and more new ones.

However, there is no denying the pleasure and satisfaction that derive from observing a large number of different kinds of birds on a single outing. A long and varied trip list, perhaps enhanced by an addition to one's life list, is the record of an enjoyable excursion. For such a venture, the Aransas Refuge is made to order.

For boosting your success in searching for birds, nothing can compare with dumb luck, but careful planning is what most consistently puts you in the right place at the right time. You must learn to read the signs to anticipate the birds. Everyone knows that most birds are hyperactive (and therefore more readily observed) early in the day; try to be on the Aransas at sunrise, for the birds and the rest of the wildlife as well as for a spectacular sky. A cool day beats a stifling one for both birds and birders. Rain and high winds suppress birds, but in the aftermath—just after a shower or following the passage of a storm or a norther—avian activity is stimulated.

Like all wild creatures, birds are driven by the seasons: they come and go, wax and wane, get bright or turn drab, skulk or sing, court and nest, according to the march of subtle cues in their environment. Generally speaking, springtime on the Aransas is March through May, summertime is June through mid-August, fall is from late August through mid-November, and wintertime spans late November through February. The slowest birding is during the summer; at all other seasons the pace is just short of frenetic.

The Aransas offers three exceptional callings for birders: whooping cranes, spring-fall transients, and winter residents. To see whoopers, visit the refuge from late October through early April. A better guarantee is November through March. For further comments, see Chapter 5.

Spring migrants pass across the Aransas from March through May,

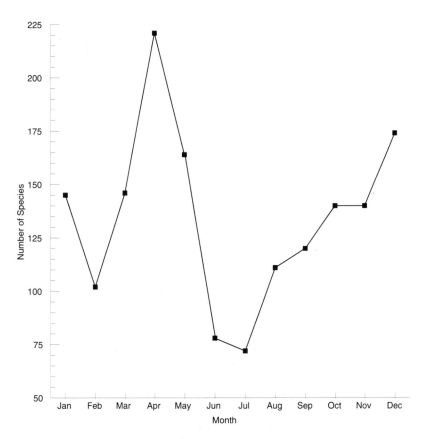

Figure 27. Number of species of birds seen each month on the Aransas National Wildlife Refuge during 1987. Although the documented number of species varies each year, the data show the typical annual pattern of abundance and the effect of spring and fall migration. Data were compiled by Barry Jones from the files of the ANWR.

with peak numbers from mid-April through mid-May. Shorebirds and waterfowl usually move early in this interval. The spectacular kettles of soaring raptors and the frenzy of northbound warblers soon follow. The passage of miscellaneous songbirds is often heralded by the appearance of blue-gray gnatcatchers in the trees and darting groups of barn swallows in the sky.

Fall migration begins with the soul-lifting sky calls of upland sandpipers and the arrival of the first blue-winged teal in late August. Fall migration is more relaxed than spring migration; the birds are merely

moving down to comfortable latitudes rather than hurrying to synchro-
nize nesting with the brief favorable season in the high north. Southbound bird movement is in high gear from mid-September through
mid-October. While shorebirds and raptors capture the attention,
warblers usually either wing across the open Gulf or slip by in scattered
nocturnal flights.

The great array of winter residents is ordinarily on the refuge from
November through February. The observation tower is the most popular site for casual birding on the refuge at that time. Heron Flats, San
Antonio Bay off the picnic area and bay overlook, and the boardwalk
are all excellent with a low tide and an afternoon sun. Portions of the
Dagger Flat Trail also offer a good vantage for scanning the bay. For
prolonged close-up viewing, nothing can beat a good birding telescope
or binoculars used at the pier on Jones Lake early in the morning.

Herons and Egrets

This is one of the most evident and easily recognized groups of birds
on the refuge. All species are large, and the adults are distinctively colored. Most of them stalk the shallows on long legs, ready to stab after
prey with long, supple neck and rapier bill. In flight these birds fold
their necks onto their chests and trail their outstretched legs. They are
either silent or utter hoarse squawks and croaks. Most prefer to nest in
crowded colonies called rookeries. Part of the refuge population moves
inland to build skimpy twig nests in willows and swamp privets in
flooded sloughs along creeks and rivers. The rest use the many islets
of dredge spoil and low oystershell reefs in the adjacent bays. (See
Table 3.) Here, fully exposed to the elements but protected from terrestrial predators, hundreds of herons, egrets, terns, gulls, and other local
waterbirds gather for two months of ceaseless squabbling, brooding,
hatching, feeding, much dying, and some fledging. After the ecstasy
and mayhem are done, they filter back to their normal haunts, leaving
their few gangly offspring to learn what they can about survival.

Twelve species of herons and egrets occur in North America, and the
Aransas Refuge hosts them all. Ten are permanent residents.

Watch for great blue herons at all seasons around all brackish and
freshwater sites. Several of these birds can usually be spotted standing
in the shallows off the picnic area and more around the edge of Mustang Lake. These are the largest of their clan, and they seem to have the
grumpiest temperament. When they are not feeding, these herons commonly stand in a sullen hump; if disturbed they laboriously flap off,
uttering a guttural protest. Great blues are proficient fishermen. The
abundant striped mullet is their staple food fish, but they will thrust

Table 3. *Waterbird Nesting Colonies on Second Chain of Islands, 1986–1990*

Species	Estimated Number of Breeding Pairs					Avg.	% of Average Total Colony
	1986	1987	1988	1989	1990		
Great egret	236	300	208	413	400	311.4	12.81
Snowy egret	132	200	285	279	30	185.2	7.62
Reddish egret	68	150	56	64	75	82.6	3.40
Cattle egret	31	150	110	28	25	68.8	2.83
Great blue heron	37	50	37	82	65	54.2	2.23
Tricolored heron	416	440	560	845	32	458.6	18.86
Black-crowned night-heron	36	100	89	41	10	55.2	2.27
Roseate spoonbill	42	100	65	148	50	81.0	3.33
Total waders	**998**	**1,490**	**1,410**	**1,900**	**687**		
Laughing gull	316	1,500	515	925	320	715.2	29.41
Forster's tern	75	100	173	90	20	91.6	3.77
Gull-billed tern	19	150	30	138	40	75.4	3.10
Common tern	113	210	137	126	75	132.2	5.44
Total gull tern	**523**	**1,960**	**855**	**1,279**	**455**		
Brown pelican	0	0	0	10	0	2.0	0.08
Black skimmer	69	150	87	135	150	118.2	4.86
Total other	**69**	**150**	**87**	**145**	**150**		
Grand total	**1,590**	**3,600**	**2,352**	**3,324**	**1,292**	**2,431.6**	

Data are from the files of the TPWD and the Texas Coastal Waterbird Survey.

after everything from cottonmouth moccasins and young alligators to blue crabs and marsh rice rats. You will be astounded at the large size of some of the fish these birds can manhandle and slide down their expandable gullets.

The little blue heron is seen occasionally on the margins of freshwater ponds and sloughs and brackish tidal flats until it moves to inland swamps to nest in the spring. The pretty slate-blue adults are distinctive. Yearlings are white, and second-year birds are white with blue-gray splotches. Check bill and leg traits to distinguish them from egrets.

Tricolored herons are quite common on the refuge all year. They can almost always be seen from the observation tower as they quietly stalk the margin of Mustang Lake. Their white underparts and a thin white line down the front of the neck contrast with dark upper plumage.

The crow-sized green-backed heron generally prefers more densely vegetated swampland than the Aransas offers, but you might spot one crouched on a snag at Thomas Slough or Hog Lake.

Snowy egret

Great blue heron

   Egrets are actually herons with plumes, and they paid dearly for that distinction during the grim days of the feather trade in the early 1900's. Local populations were decimated because the birds were shot during the reproductive season, when their plumes were best developed. The two commonest egrets are the great and the snowy. The great egret is the most noticeable large white wader on the tidal flats. It is the bird most often mistaken for a whooping crane by visitors. The smaller snowy egret has a black bill (yellow bill in the great egret) and sports cadmium-yellow feet on black legs. Both birds are expert fishermen, specializing in small to moderate-sized prey like killifishes, silversides, and menhaden.
   Reddish egrets are on the state list of threatened species; a 1990 cen-

sus projected only about 1,400 pairs along the entire Texas coast. They are not common birds, but there is a healthy population on the refuge. More than other egrets, this one is closely limited to the coastal habitat, and its population has suffered from degradation of shallow-water marine food chains and scarcity of secure offshore rookeries.

The lively feeding behavior of reddish egrets makes them stand out in any crowd of brackish-water waders. Watch one of these birds prance and whirl in a drunken, lopsided gait and with wings partly spread as it tries to scare up small fishes along the edge of San Antonio Bay.

Most reddish egrets display dark-phase plumage—smoke-gray bodies with shaggy violet-cinnamon head and neck—but about 10 percent are pure white and might be confused with snowy egrets or immature little blue herons. If in doubt, note the relative size of the bird (the reddish egret is larger) and check the bill. In adult reddish egrets, both dark phase and white phase, the basal two-thirds of the relatively heavy bill is soft peach-pink while the tip is dusky or black.

Originally from Africa, the cattle egret came to Texas in 1954 by way of South and Central America. The first birds were recorded on the Aransas Refuge in 1959; twenty years later their Texas population had exploded to over a quarter million. Happily, the birds seemed to fill a vacant niche and did not compete or interbreed with their New World kin. Although it has since become the most abundant kind of egret in the Coastal Bend (nearly thirteen thousand breeding pairs in 1990, over a dozen times more than any native heron), it is not frequently seen in the area of public access on Blackjack Peninsula. Cattle egrets are not wetland feeders. They eat insects, especially grasshoppers and crickets, and are prone to follow grazing animals to snatch prey stirred up by the moving feet and heads. They have also learned to follow tractors to glean insect larvae from freshly turned earth.

General tolerance of humans and an ability to turn artificial environmental changes to their advantage have contributed to the rapid expansion of cattle egrets throughout the United States and into southern Canada. In Texas the population may have peaked because of saturation of available nesting sites. Although cattle egrets do not nest on Blackjack Peninsula, pairs are common in rookeries in the surrounding bays. You may occasionally see cattle egrets resting on Heron Flats, but you are most likely to spot flocks of these white birds in pastures and fields and along roadsides inland of the refuge.

The stocky black-crowned night-heron is rather common on the Aransas, but it is seldom observed because it spends the day humped in dense stands of reeds or willows. At night these birds sally forth to fish and to stalk crayfish and crabs and gobble down marsh rice rats and any unprotected nestling birds they happen across. If you disturb a group of roosting black-crowns, they will flap off in confusion, uttering a series of popping "quoks." Yellow-crowned night-herons are less common on the refuge, and they do not nest locally. Check your bird book to learn how to recognize juvenile night-herons.

Bitterns are secretive herons that seldom stray outside the confines of thick growths of tall reeds, cattails, and bulrushes. It takes sharp eyes to discern an occasional American bittern in Thomas Slough or at Jones Lake. The smallest of our herons—the least bittern—may be there as well, but it is even more elusive unless it flushes. The least bittern is more easily detected by its gentle "coo-coo-coo-coo," which adds to the symphony of intriguing sounds that rise from the bankside vegetation along Thomas Slough at dusk.

Other Large Waders

Both white and white-faced ibis are resident on the Aransas. Look for them on Heron Flats. The less abundant white ibis also use the brackish

Table 4. *Large Waders Seen during Audubon Christmas Counts on ANWR, 1980–1990*

	Total Seen	Average Seen	Times Seen
Great blue heron	1,277	116	11
Green-backed heron	7	1	6
Little blue heron	155	14	11
Cattle egret	46	4	7
Reddish egret	149	14	11
Great egret	769	70	11
Snowy egret	405	37	11
Tricolored heron	214	19	11
Black-crowned night-heron	193	18	11
Yellow-crowned night-heron	13	1	1
Least bittern	2	<1	2
American bittern	16	1	7
White-faced ibis	396	36	11
White ibis	626	57	11
Roseate spoonbill	314	29	11
Whooping crane	466	42	11
Sandhill crane	6,154	559	11

Data are from the files of the ANWR.

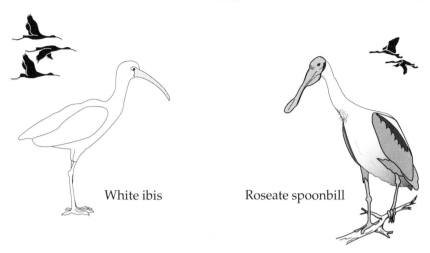

White ibis   Roseate spoonbill

flats at Mustang Lake, where they sometimes form into ranks and sweep the shallows for grass shrimp and schools of fresh-hatched killifishes. Adult white ibis are indeed white. White-faced ibis will appear to be black until they wheel in the sun; then they present a brilliant display of iridescent bronze-green on their backs and flashes of violet-chestnut on their necks. Both species fly with neck outstretched and decurved bill well exposed. White ibis nest on the offshore islets; white-faced ibis nest in swamps on the adjacent mainland.

The wood stork is discussed among the endangered species in Chapter 6.

By 1890, plume hunters had wiped out all breeding colonies of roseate spoonbills along the Texas coast. Largely because of the efforts of the budding Audubon Society, protective legislation for nongame birds was finally enacted in 1903. In 1923, breeding spoonbills were again seen in Texas, just north of the Aransas in the delta of the Guadalupe River and on oystershell islets between Blackjack Peninsula and Matagorda Island. The species mounted a slow recovery and, in 1990, numbered nearly 2,500 breeding pairs (more than 800 in the Coastal Bend) in scattered colonies along the coast.

Roseate spoonbills can be seen year-round on the refuge, but they are more abundant in the summer and fall. Watch for small groups winging rapidly high across the tidal flats. If one crosses your horizon, you will not miss its unmatchable pink plumage, even more radiant when the sun is low. The observation tower is the best vantage for observing the strange sidewise feeding movements of spoonbills. The partly opened spatulate bill, richly supplied with sensory receptors, allows the birds to feel small fishes and crustaceans in the murky water and then deftly snap them up. While watching spoonbills, do not join the crowd who claim to be viewing flamingos!

Gulls and Terns

Watch for gulls winging over San Antonio Bay and for terns hovering and diving into the bay. Both kinds of birds rest on pilings, exposed reefs, and the bayshore. The bay overlook, Dagger Point, the observation tower, and the adjacent boardwalk all offer excellent viewing sites.

In the wintertime the ring-billed gull is the most frequent large white gull on the refuge. Even larger white adult herring gulls and their brown juveniles are occasional.

The resident laughing gull is the commonest local species of its medium-sized group. Juveniles and wintering adults do not sport the distinctive black-marked head that is characteristic during the remainder of the year. Beginning in late March, one is seldom out of earshot of the maniacal calls of the laughing gulls. You might spot flocks feeding in the wakes of boats on the Gulf Intracoastal Waterway or see a screaming horde following a shrimp boat in the bay. These birds nest on the fringe of the heron rookeries on islets in San Antonio Bay. Use your field

Laughing gulls

Table 5. *Gulls and Terns Seen during Audubon Christmas Counts on ANWR, 1980–1990*

	Total Seen	Average Seen	Times Seen
Herring gull	347	32	11
Ring-billed gull	2,086	190	11
Laughing gull	1,330	121	11
Bonaparte's gull	58	5	9
Gull-billed tern	17	2	6
Forster's tern	1,562	142	11
Common tern	4	<1	3
Royal tern	140	13	11
Sandwich tern	25	2	4
Caspian tern	710	65	11
Black skimmer	375	34	8

Data are from the files of the ANWR.

Forster's tern

guide to distinguish the similar Franklin's gulls that pass across the refuge in spring and fall.

From the observation tower you can regularly see large, red-billed Caspian terns fly by in ones and twos, often uttering rasping nasal calls. Be sure to distinguish them from the less common royal terns. Caspians have blood-red bills; royals' bills are pale orange. The most abundant terns plummeting into Mustang Lake are Forster's terns, perhaps in company with a few common and gull-billed terns. You should see dainty least terns during the spring and summer all along San Antonio Bay. These little terns nest on isolated sandy bayshores as well as on offshore islets and on the old runways on Matagorda Island. The interior race of the least tern is mentioned among the endangered birds in Chapter 6.

Black terns are beautiful birds with a jet-black head and breast and soft, silvery wings and back. There are usually at least a few of them on the refuge at all seasons except midwinter. Watch for these graceful fliers as they swoop swallowlike to pluck insects from the tips of tidal-flat plants.

Shorebirds

The endangered eskimo curlew and piping plover are considered in Chapter 6; the common snipe and American woodcock, with open hunting seasons, in Chapter 7.

This large and diverse group of birds encompasses a shifting mix of species according to the seasons. The greatest variety is on the refuge in the spring and fall, but there is a large array of winter residents. Summer is the slack season for shorebirds on the Aransas.

Most species are small to moderate-sized and thin-legged, and they make their living by probing and plucking along the shorelines and mud flats of both brackish and fresh water. Their foraging activity is strongly influenced by the tidal cycle, and most tend to feed, rest, and fly in flocks. The two largest groups are sandpipers and plovers. Learn to distinguish the slender, long-legged sandpiper build from that of the plump, short-legged plover. Sandpipers skitter about, but the plover gait is characteristically run-and-stop. Shorebirds make excellent subjects for prolonged telescopic study of feeding behavior and social interaction.

Six kinds of shorebirds nest locally, though not all do so every year: snowy plover, Wilson's plover, killdeer, willet, American avocet, and black-necked stilt. Some, such as the killdeer, willet, greater and lesser yellowlegs, western sandpiper, black-bellied plover, long-billed dowitcher, and sanderling, are among the most frequently seen birds on the refuge during all seasons except summer. Other shorebirds, like semipalmated, pectoral, solitary, and stilt sandpipers, pause only briefly in the spring and fall; yet others, like lesser golden plovers, are seen only in the spring (in the fall they stream south directly across the Gulf of Mexico). Marbled godwits are most common stalking the mud flats in spring and fall, but a few birds linger through the winter. Dunlin and western sandpipers are winter residents.

Table 6. *Shorebirds Seen during Audubon Christmas Counts on ANWR, 1980–1990*

	Total Seen	Average Seen	Times Seen
King rail	13	1	7
Clapper rail	9	1	5
Virginia rail	3	<1	2
Sora	30	3	9
Yellow rail	2	<1	2
Common moorhen	114	10	11
Purple gallinule	1	<1	1
American coot	8,542	777	11
American oystercatcher	71	6	11
Semipalmated plover	146	13	6
Piping plover	19	2	6
Snowy plover	181	16	5
Wilson's plover	7	1	2
Killdeer	749	68	11
Black-bellied plover	604	55	11
Ruddy turnstone	77	7	8
American woodcock	9	1	2
Common snipe	126	11	11
Long-billed curlew	286	26	11
Spotted sandpiper	33	3	11
Willet	519	47	11
Greater yellowlegs	444	40	11
Lesser yellowlegs	106	10	11
Baird's sandpiper	5	<1	1
Least sandpiper	382	35	9
Dunlin	1,941	176	11
Short-billed dowitcher	88	8	3
Long-billed dowitcher	1,358	123	11
Semipalmated sandpiper	3	<1	1
Western sandpiper	2,176	198	10
Marbled godwit	50	5	7
Sanderling	433	39	11
American avocet	1,077	98	11
Black-necked stilt	4	<1	2
Wilson's phalarope	2	<1	1

Data are from the files of the ANWR.

Long-billed curlew

The long-billed curlew is also a prominent member of this coterie. Watch for this bird at the water's edge along San Antonio Bay and on the mud flat in Mustang Lake. Individuals frequently stalk across interior grasslands and mowed areas, including the lawns at headquarters, in search of insects. You cannot miss the namesake seven-inch-long, downcurved bill that gives the bird an advantage in probing for marine worms and snagging mud shrimp and fiddler crabs from their burrows. If you flush curlews, watch for their cinnamon wing linings and learn their melodious, two-note alarm call.

The upland sandpiper nests in the northern United States and Canada and winters on the pampas of Argentina. It passes over the Aransas in August–September and in March–April, and small flocks occasionally set down on the open grasslands of the Tatton and Matagorda units and in Point Pasture on Blackjack Peninsula. You may see them on the coastal prairie en route to the refuge. Even if you do not spot this thimble-headed bird, listen for its sweetly whistled sky call. The urgent notes are unfailing harbingers of the thousands of birds that will soon be funneling along the Central Flyway.

Nonbreeding individuals of shorebird species that routinely nest in the north occasionally hold over on the refuge, so you may see a few of these oddballs almost any time of the year.

Although not notable for their songs, many shorebirds have distinctive alarm notes and sky calls, and flocks of peeps continually twitter and squeal. The rapidly repeated "pill-will-willet" of breeding willets can be heard all across the tidal flats in late March and April. In June the endlessly repeated, nervous "keck" of a nesting black-necked stilt can drive you to distraction.

All of these birds can be observed along the edge of San Antonio Bay, especially at low tide. Although the observation tower is the single best spot, the smaller species are better viewed from the end of the board-walk, at Dagger Point and opposite the picnic area. Heron Flats is often very productive, and an afternoon sun there makes for excellent viewing.

We have included two separate sets of data to give you an idea of what shorebirds you can expect to see on the Aransas. The tower count in Figure 28 reveals the species of birds seen from the observation tower during a thirty-minute interval each month throughout the year. This includes more than shorebirds, and it suggests what an unskilled but informed individual can anticipate. The Audubon Christmas count in Table 6 reveals the numbers of each species of shorebird seen on the refuge by a group of skilled birders during one twelve-hour period near the end of the year. The results from 1980–1990 indicate annual trends and variation, and the composite list encompasses the winter resident species.

Other Waterbirds

Anytime during the winter look for pairs and small groups of sleek common loons well out from shore in San Antonio Bay, riding low among the waves and diving deeply for fish. If you happen to be on the refuge early on a calm, foggy morning, listen to the stillness that encompasses the bay. You just might hear the muffled yodel of a loon. If so, you have shared in one of the choicest secrets of the Aransas, for winter loons are usually silent.

Six species of grebes (pronounced "greebs") are on the refuge list, and three of them are commonly observed. All dive for small fish, crustaceans, and molluscs and swim energetically while underwater. Distinguish them from ducks by their stubbier bodies and more chicken-like bills. Watch one of these birds when it becomes suspicious or feels threatened. Without appearing to move a muscle, it will slowly sink vertically in the water until only its head is visible. Then it will disappear entirely, straight down. How do you suppose it manages to submerge so subtly?

Pied-billed grebes can almost always be found in the brackish shallows near the observation tower and along Thomas Slough; their rolling social chatter is a common sound in Jones and Hog lakes that you will want to learn to recognize. In the summertime they move to inland waters to nest. One pied-billed grebe brooded on her floating nest in plain view of the pier on Jones Lake in 1990.

The Aransas Refuge is on the northern edge of the range of the least grebe, but these little slate-gray, red-eyed divers are occasional in the

Figure 28. Bird species seen by the authors during a monthly thirty-minute interval on the observation tower at the Aransas National Wildlife Refuge, 1985–1986.

Gulls and Terns

	Jan	Feb	Mar	Apr	May	Jun	Jul	Aug	Sep	Oct	Nov	Dec
Caspian Tern												
Black Tern												
Forster's Tern												
Gull-billed Tern												
Laughing Gull												
Least Tern												
Ring-billed Gull												
Royal Tern												

Shorebirds

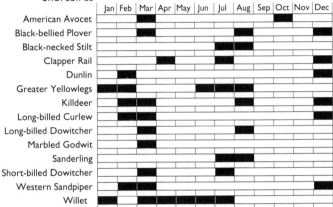

	Jan	Feb	Mar	Apr	May	Jun	Jul	Aug	Sep	Oct	Nov	Dec
American Avocet												
Black-bellied Plover												
Black-necked Stilt												
Clapper Rail												
Dunlin												
Greater Yellowlegs												
Killdeer												
Long-billed Curlew												
Long-billed Dowitcher												
Marbled Godwit												
Sanderling												
Short-billed Dowitcher												
Western Sandpiper												
Willet												

Passerines and Others

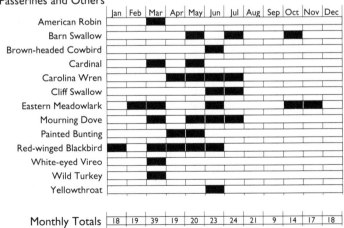

	Jan	Feb	Mar	Apr	May	Jun	Jul	Aug	Sep	Oct	Nov	Dec
American Robin												
Barn Swallow												
Brown-headed Cowbird												
Cardinal												
Carolina Wren												
Cliff Swallow												
Eastern Meadowlark												
Mourning Dove												
Painted Bunting												
Red-winged Blackbird												
White-eyed Vireo												
Wild Turkey												
Yellowthroat												

Monthly Totals	18	19	39	19	20	23	24	21	9	14	17	18

wintertime, and they seem to be getting more common. They were first seen on the Aransas in 1942, and their first nest was found in 1988. Females with hatchlings were seen in both Jones and Hog lakes in 1989. Look for them in pairs in any freshwater pond or slough.

Small flocks of eared grebes can be expected in the open expanse of San Antonio Bay during the winter. If you set up a telescope at the picnic area, you may be able to spot the large upright profile of an occasional western grebe or a small flock of horned grebes riding the waves far out in San Antonio Bay. Both species are sporadic wintertime visitors on the Aransas.

White pelicans can usually be seen in small fishing flotillas on San Antonio Bay and Mustang Lake. The exposed oyster reefs offshore from the picnic area and the edge of False Live Oak Point are favored resting sites. If you spot a flock of these birds flap-gliding through the air, marvel at their effortless grace. Do not mistake these white birds with black-tipped wings for whoopers. Note their folded necks, distinctive bills, and the absence of long trailing legs. On the water, watch the pelicans' rhythmic head movements as they seine for fish, drain their pouches, and gobble down their catch—so different from the feeding habits of brown pelicans. (The latter species is endangered and is discussed in Chapter 6.) White pelicans are most common on the refuge during the winter, when up to ten thousand birds populate the Coastal Bend. A few leave in the spring to join a nesting colony of about three hundred pairs on an island near Corpus Christi, while most migrate to lakes in the northern Great Plains.

Wintering double-crested cormorants can sometimes be seen by the hundreds from the observation tower as they feed and loaf near False Live Oak Point. They abruptly haul out for their nesting grounds in the spring. Although they breed locally, neotropic cormorants are less commonly seen on the refuge. These birds prefer inland freshwater sites. If you see a cormorant on the Aransas in the summertime, it is probably a neotropic.

High-soaring kettles of anhingas pass over the refuge during their spring and fall migrations. A few birds nest in local freshwater sites, so you might find one at any season. One of the real delights of an idle walk along Thomas Slough is seeing the keen-billed profile of one of these "water turkeys" suddenly break the surface. The birds swim completely submerged or with their heads and long necks exposed. They frequently perch on overhanging willow branches while they preen and dry their feathers.

The black skimmer is a unique and highly specialized waterbird. Since it is a resident and nests on shell islets and sand bars in the local bays, you can expect to see it year-round. Skimmers are seen at their

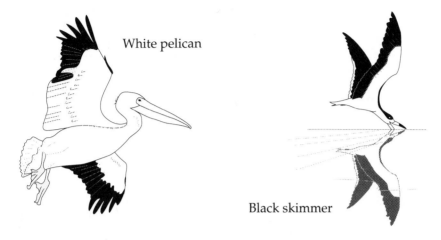

White pelican

Black skimmer

best when feeding. The peculiar bill (the lower half is longer than the upper) and exceptionally long wings make good adaptive sense only when you watch the birds expertly cleaving the water's surface with the tip of the lower mandible. When they encounter a morsel, they snap the upper mandible closed with a quick downward jerk of the head. Skimmers prefer quiet bayside water and are frequently active at dusk and into the night when small fishes and crustaceans are near the surface. You might be lucky enough to hear a pair of skimmers in flight making soft doglike woofs to each other.

Can you imagine slipping the blade of an oyster knife into a feeding oyster and severing its adductor muscle before the creature can clamp its shells closed? The American oystercatcher uses its flattened red bill to turn that trick. Some individuals use their stout bills to hammer their prey apart. They also feed on mussels, crustaceans, and marine worms. The birds are not common locally. Watch for them in pairs on exposed oyster reefs and shell banks at low tide. Their black-and-white plumage, bright bill, and rapidly repeated piercing squeals make them instantly recognizable.

Do not be surprised to hear the dry rattle of a belted kingfisher from any freshwater site or at Mustang Lake, especially during the wintertime. Probably because of the lack of earthen banks to serve as suitable nesting sites, kingfishers are scarce on the refuge in spring and summer.

Raptors

On the Aransas Refuge, the birds of prey constitute a large group with a varying set of component species. All have a hooked beak designed for grasping, tearing, and snipping meat, and except for vultures and

Table 7. *Raptors Seen during Audubon Christmas Counts on ANWR,*
1980–1990

	Total Seen	Average Seen	Times Seen
Turkey vulture	2,531	230	11
Black vulture	1,269	115	11
Black-shouldered kite	121	11	11
Sharp-shinned hawk	20	2	11
Cooper's hawk	7	1	6
Red-tailed hawk	245	22	11
Red-shouldered hawk	40	4	11
Broad-winged hawk	1	<1	1
White-tailed hawk	63	6	10
Harris' hawk	1	<1	1
Bald eagle	2	<1	2
Northern harrier	393	36	11
Osprey	9	1	4
Crested caracara	56	5	11
Merlin	17	2	8
American kestrel	783	71	11
Peregrine	4	<1	3

Data are from the files of the ANWR.

the caracara, each is equipped with sharp talons and a sure grip for
seizing and holding live prey. Keen eyesight, dive-bombing attack, and
an alert, wary nature also characterize the group. Because they exist at
the top of the food web, raptors are usually not abundant, but the few
individuals serve critical roles in maintaining the balance between producers and consumers.

To see raptors, you need to keep a sharp eye out; scan potential perching sites as well as the sky as far ahead as your binoculars will allow.
Your best bet is a slow, alert drive around the Tour Loop.

Large, silent swirls of migrant hawks and kites move across the Aransas in spring and fall. In early April, for instance, as many as fifty thousand raptors may sail northward across Blackjack Peninsula. The bulk
of these are usually broad-winged hawks, with a scattering of Swainson's and sharp-shinned hawks and Mississippi kites. Wintertime is the
best season to see birds perching and hunting.

The American kestrel is probably the most commonly observed of the
overwintering raptors. You might detect them first by their excited
"killy-killy-killy" warning call, but these colorful little falcons can be

found perching, hovering, or winging swiftly along the roadsides. You may see a kestrel drop on a grasshopper. They also take mice, and they are agile enough to knock small passerine birds from the air. Kestrels are even quick enough to include dragonflies in their routine fare, and that means very quick indeed.

Migrating merlins occasionally stop over but are never numerous. Check your field guide to distinguish them from kestrels. The other falcons—the endangered peregrine and aplomado—are considered in Chapter 6.

A step up in size from the small falcons are two crow-sized accipiters (ack-SIPPY-ters), Cooper's hawk and the sharp-shinned hawk. Expect both species in the winter and during migration, although neither is common. These broad-winged, long-tailed raptors are adept at navigating amid the tangle of oak thickets, where, with a quick maneuver and a burst of speed, they are deadly in the pursuit of small birds. They usually offer a startled observer only a blurred silhouette.

The red-tailed hawk is the commonest of the buteos (beauty-ohs), large broad-winged, fan-tailed hawks. You are apt to see them perching on a dead branch or soaring aloft on a winter afternoon. Watch for the brick-red tail, which is its hallmark, and listen for its hissing squeal of disapproval at your presence. The redtail, an arch predator on rodents, nests infrequently on the refuge.

The white-tailed hawk, another buteo, but less abundant and less versatile than the redtail, is seen only over open grassland. These hawks not only cruise freshly burned tracts but also actively work the line of flames, swooping down on fleeing cotton rats and grabbing grasshop-

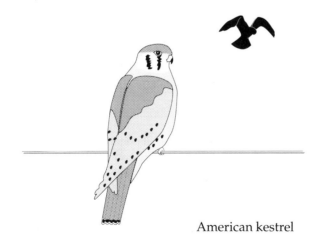

American kestrel

pers in midair to eat on the wing. They are usually seen in ones or twos, but one burn on the Aransas attracted 14 and another lured 28. White-tails occasionally nest on Blackjack Peninsula but, like the coyote and the jackrabbit, were apparently more abundant when the peninsula was more open.

The Aransas Refuge lies on the northeastern edge of the range of Harris hawks, but individuals have been seen on the Tatton Unit and the western side of Blackjack Peninsula in recent years. If you spot one of these brushland raptors, enjoy its rich chocolate plumage, handsome chestnut shoulders, and bright white rump band. If you see one Harris hawk, look for another; they usually hunt in small family groups.

Most of the thousands of hawks that pass across the Coastal Bend in long streams or towering gyres during spring and fall are broad-winged hawks. The larger Swainson's hawks migrate at the same time and sometimes also in large, hushed flocks. Peak spring numbers on the Aransas occur in early to mid-April. During their passage, the broad-wings usually settle for the night in the live oaks, while the Swainson's roost on the ground in open fields. Early in the day, you might find aggregations of these hawks still abed, waiting for the sun to generate the rising air they need to soar aloft.

Kites are the most graceful of raptors. Watch for an occasional black-shouldered kite hovering buoyantly over open areas along the Tour Loop in the wintertime. They also occur on the Tatton and Matagorda units, and you may expect to see them over pastures and roadsides inland of the refuge. Black-shouldered kites, originally rare in Texas and restricted to the vicinity of the Rio Grande River, are one of the few raptors to benefit from brush eradication. Replacing brush with grass makes rodents and grasshoppers more accessible to the hovering tactic of kites. Black-shouldered kites began to expand their range northward in the sixties, and now they routinely nest on the Aransas.

Mississippi kites are mostly seen as high-flying migrants. American swallow-tailed kites appear only as rare spring visitors. The best year ever for refuge sightings was in 1981, when for a three-week span in March, the acrobatic swallow-tailed kites were seen almost daily.

The northern harrier can usually be spotted from the observation tower or along the Tour Loop at all seasons except summer. Of all the birds of prey, this long-winged, long-tailed "marsh hawk" is the best adapted for gliding at grasstop level regardless of coastal wind or blustery norther. One reason for its low-level flight is that this raptor hunts by ear as well as by eye.

The osprey is another long-limbed raptor. Individuals stop over during the spring and fall migrations, and an occasional bird winters on the refuge. Watch for one from the observation tower or the bay over-

Northern harrier

look. If you are lucky, you may see an osprey plunge feetfirst into San Antonio Bay and then labor into the air with a striped mullet clutched in its ice-tong talons. The bird may feed on the wing or seek out a high perch to devour its prey. In 1978, in an attempt to attract nesting ospreys, eight tall poles surmounted by open platforms were erected at various sites on the refuge. One is visible on the bayshore opposite the Heron Flats Trail. To date the birds have spurned these offers.

The endangered southern bald eagle is discussed in Chapter 6. Since the first golden eagle sighting on the refuge in December 1964, there have been half a dozen more, the most reliable recent one in 1972. All of the birds have been immature.

While en route to the Aransas, you may have flushed a crested caracara from a road kill. These handsome "Mexican eagles," with cream-and-black plumage and red facial skin, may be seen along the Tour Loop at any season, winging swiftly overland on flat wings. They consort with vultures on carrion, but they can bring down birds, reptiles, and small mammals. Caracaras are residents but prefer the more open, mesquite-studded terrain on the Tatton and Matagorda units for nesting.

Turkey vultures outnumber black vultures by about five to one, but both are numerous enough on the refuge to border on being pestiferous. Both species roost in the live oaks at the picnic area and near the Big Tree Trail, and scattered individuals can be found resting on dead limbs along the Tour Loop, where they enjoy spreading their wings to the morning sunshine. Vultures prefer to soar on rising parcels of warm air, but they will zoom along on buffeting north winds if they must. Their infallible scavenger service meshes well with the natural food web.

Turkey vulture

Six species of owls have been recorded on the Aransas Refuge. Two, the eastern screech owl and the barred owl, prefer riparian woodlands and visit Blackjack Peninsula only occasionally. Two others, the burrowing owl and the short-eared owl, are uncommon winter visitors to open terrain on the Tatton and Matagorda units. The barn owl is rarely seen on the peninsula, probably because of the scarcity of secluded roosting and nesting sites, but it is the common owl on Matagorda Island, where it occupies outbuildings. Wherever it occurs along the Coastal Bend, the barn owl is a significant predator on cotton rats and marsh rice rats.

The great horned owl is without question the commonest nocturnal raptor on the Aransas, and except for the scavenging vultures, it is the commonest resident bird of prey everywhere except on the treeless Matagorda Unit. Indeed, great horned owls rank among the most important predators on the refuge.

Great horned owls are implacable and insatiable hunters, taking a heavy nightly toll among cotton rats, gophers, cottontails, roosting waterbirds, skunks, young opossums and raccoons, snakes, and even stranded fish. There is even suspicion that in 1991 a great horned owl brought down a whooping crane.

Eggs are laid in January in abandoned hawk nests, and remains of pied-billed grebes, American coots, purple gallinules, black-crowned night-herons, snowy egrets, cattle egrets, and bobwhite quail have been recovered from nests on the refuge. For the past several years a pair has nested near the headquarters.

Watch at dusk for the distinctive silhouettes of great horned owls in trees along the Tour Loop. Their beguilingly gentle, six-part hooting is most often heard in January and February. They begin at dusk, and almost invariably the call of one member of a pair will be answered by its partner.

Table 7 enumerates raptor sightings from the Christmas bird counts held on the Aransas Refuge between 1980 and 1990.

Wood Warblers

Forty-one of the 48 species of these colorful passerines that routinely occur in Texas are on the current refuge checklist. The newest addition was the tropical parula in 1988. In that same year the most recent of the few nesting species was confirmed when singing males led to the discovery of a breeding population of Swainson's warblers in the live oak thickets around headquarters and down the main road to the observation tower.

Only three wood warblers—the orange-crowned and yellow-rumped warblers and the common yellowthroat—are reliable winter residents. Two species, the common yellowthroat and Swainson's warbler, stay to nest. Singing males in July suggest that hooded warblers may also nest on the Aransas.

Northbound warblers begin to move across the Aransas Refuge in late March, when the first yellow-throated warblers, black-and-white warblers, and northern parulas arrive. Soon thereafter the refuge will ring with the "witchity-witchity-witch" of common yellowthroats. In a routine year some twenty other warbler species pass through, sometimes in brief, noticeable waves, sometimes in prolonged cryptic trickles. The intermittent flurry continues through mid-May. The passage of wood warblers is usually attended by other passerine species, which add

Great horned owl

Yellowthroat

Table 8. *Birdlist for May 7, 1972*

Species	Number of Individuals Seen	Species	Number of Individuals Seen
Mourning dove	1	Black-and-white warbler	50–100
Inca dove	1	Worm-eating warbler	2
Roadrunner	1	Golden-winged warbler	3
Pauraque	3	Tennessee warbler	4
Common nighthawk	5	Yellow warbler	50–100
Ruby-throated hummingbird	1	Magnolia warbler	50–100
Eastern kingbird	50–100	Black-throated green warbler	10
Western kingbird	1	Blackburnian warbler	50–100
Scissor-tailed flycatcher	4	Chestnut-sided warbler	50–100
Brown-crested flycatcher	2	Bay-breasted warbler	50–100
Eastern wood pewee	12	Ovenbird	6
Tree swallow	100–200	Northern waterthrush	5
Bank swallow	100–200	Kentucky warbler	5
Rough-winged swallow	100–200	Yellowthroat	3
Barn swallow	200+	American redstart	50–100
Cliff swallow	50–100	Eastern meadowlark	50–100
Purple martin	100–200	Red-winged blackbird	50–100
Black-crested titmouse	1	Boat-tailed grackle	50–100
House wren	1	Brown-headed cowbird	3
Mockingbird	1	Scarlet tanager	6
Catbird	50–100	Summer tanager	50–100
Brown thrasher	4	Cardinal	50–100
Wood thrush	1	Rose-breasted grosbeak	1
Swainson's thrush	50–100	Blue grosbeak	2
Gray-cheeked thrush	3	Indigo bunting	50–100
White-eyed vireo	3	Painted bunting	3
Red-eyed vireo	3	Savannah sparrow	1
Philadelphia vireo	6	Lark sparrow	4

Data are from the files of the ANWR.

to the ongoing color, song, and nervous movement across the Coastal Bend: indigo and painted buntings, summer and scarlet tanagers, orchard and northern orioles, blue and rose-breasted grosbeaks, great and brown-crested flycatchers, eastern and western kingbirds, ruby-crowned and golden-crowned kinglets, as well as a host of thrushes and vireos.

When a cell of bad weather sweeps across the Coastal Bend and collides with peak waves of migrating warblers moving north over the open Gulf, the birds are hard put to make landfall. Many cannot with-stand the buffeting head winds and rain squalls, and windrows of pretty bodies wash up on the beaches of the barrier islands. Those birds that make it are exhausted, ravenous, and confused. They spend several days feeding and regrouping. During that brief interval of revitalization the Coastal Bend experiences a warbler fallout, when all of the trees are abustle and all of the birders are afield.

To see spring warblers on the Aransas, come in mid-April. To expe-rience a fallout you must simply be lucky. In any case, the large live oaks along the Big Tree Trail, at the picnic area, and around headquar-ters as well as the mixed forest enclosed by the ramp at the observation tower are the best places to search. Have your field guide handy, be-cause this ephemeral, colorful ecstasy of small birds is notorious for offering only quick, neck-wrenching glimpses high among the boughs.

Although the fall migration of wood warblers is usually less spec-tacular than the spring movement, there is a steady stream of these dauntless little birds passing southward across the Aransas from mid-August through late October. Peak numbers usually pass during the last two weeks of September.

To give you an idea of the frenzied bird action on the Aransas in a good warbler year, we have included one staff member's list for May 7, 1972 (Table 8). The peak diversity of birds on the refuge occurs in April, when there are routinely 20 to 25 kinds of migrating wood warblers moving through.

Cuckoos

Yellow-billed cuckoos arrive in the spring and remain through the sum-mer to nest. Unlike their European relatives, the females occasionally lay their eggs in the nests of other kinds of birds, but they mostly make their own nests and tend their own broods. Watch for these slender, long-tailed birds methodically searching in the live oaks for hairy cat-erpillars, and learn their melodious bell-like call. Black-billed cuckoos are spotted rarely as they pass through headed north.

Grooved-billed anis (AH-nees) are Mexican birds at the northern limit of their range in the Coastal Bend. They appear irregularly on the refuge, mostly in the wintertime, but sightings have been getting more common in recent years. Look for them in small, loose flocks in the brush on the middle ridge of the Heron Flats Trail. Do not mistake these long-tailed black birds for grackles; their peculiar bulbous beaks quickly distinguish them.

The greater roadrunner is a resident throughout Texas, and during the forties and the droughty fifties, when Blackjack Peninsula was much more open, paisanos (pie-SAHN-ohs), as they are often called locally, were common here. But the spread of live oak thickets and tall bunchgrasses has apparently forced an exodus of this species, and it is currently notably rare on the Aransas Refuge. The birds occur routinely in the mesquite and prickly pear community of the Tatton Unit, and they probably nest there. Their distinctive cooing has been heard on the Lamar Unit, and isolated sightings are still made along the northern and western boundaries of the peninsula.

Goatsuckers

Six species of these weird, night-flying birds have been recorded on the refuge. (We leave it to your own research to discover why they are called goatsuckers.) You may startle up a resting individual from the leaf litter along a trail through the oak mottes. While leaving the refuge at dusk, watch for the glowing red eyes of a nighthawk in the beam of your headlights and listen for their variety of distinctive calls, which contribute to the semitropical aura of the Coastal Bend.

The common nighthawk is the most frequently observed member of the group. The birds arrive in April, nest on bare open ground (and, in most years, on the flat pebble roof of the WIC), and remain until fall. During the heat of the day you might see resting individuals, with eyes closed to slits, hunkered on dead branches and atop posts and snags. Late in the afternoon they take to the air and fly a high, erratic course, hawking for insects and continually uttering their nasal "peent." Most Texans call these birds "bullbats."

The pauraque (pav-RAH-key), the giant of the clan, is another Mexi-

Common nighthawk

can bird that reaches its northern limit on the Aransas Refuge. These nighthawks are residents, although nesting is yet to be documented. They haunt the live oak mottes and are most frequently observed around the picnic area and the Youth Environmental Training Area. Watch for them on the road at dusk and listen for their rasping "pic-pic-p'YEER."

The chuck-will's-widow and whip-poor-will pause only long enough to punctuate early spring evenings with their easily recognizable calls; lesser nighthawks are more at home in the brushland southwest of the refuge, so they are rare spring and summer stragglers.

Swifts and Swallows

These are birds of the open sky. The joyous chittering of chimney swifts verifies that spring migration is in full swing. They are common in the Coastal Bend throughout the summer, but a scarcity of nesting sites may account for their relative rarity on the Aransas. White-throated swifts are western birds; the few spring sightings over headquarters are surely of displaced transients.

Three of the seven recorded species of swallows hurry across the refuge in spring and fall: the tree, bank, and rough-winged swallows. Three more—the barn and cliff swallows and the purple martin—linger through the summer, but the absence of adequate nest sites probably accounts for the erratic occurrence of these birds on the Aransas. The seventh species, the cave swallow, is on the refuge list because a few birds nested in an outbuilding on Matagorda Island in 1989. Cave swallows have not been documented on Blackjack Peninsula, but this traditionally southwestern species is becoming more common in the Coastal Bend and is to be watched for. Be sure you can distinguish them from the similar and more common cliff swallows.

The most common swallow species on the Aransas, the barn swallow, is often seen hawking low over the tidal flats. You may have noticed an occasional whirling group of cliff swallows while you were en route to the refuge. These birds commonly nest under highway bridges, and a small colony uses a culvert at Burgentine Lake. Although the purple martins that occasionally utilize the houses erected for them around headquarters feed heavily on mosquitoes, even they cannot keep outbreaks of the vigorous Aransas bloodsuckers in check.

Hummingbirds

The ruby-throated hummingbird is the only species that makes a reliable appearance on the refuge each spring and fall. Since 1978, buff-bellied hummingbirds have apparently extended their range into the Coastal Bend. Both species may be seen occasionally through the summer, but the withering coastal heat forces most of them to inland riparian forests to nest.

Always check the bright red flowers of Turk's cap for hummers. The thicket at the parking site beside the bay overlook seems to be a favored spot. Also scan the trumpet creeper flowers on the Heron Flats Trail. The watered area around headquarters may also yield some hummers, and a feeder there lures in migrants. Hummingbirds frequently pause to refuel on the Aransas before starting south in the fall. Besides the two kinds just mentioned, occasional black-chinned, rufous, and even a broad-tailed hummingbird have been seen. Doubtless others zip through undetected.

Woodpeckers

Despite all of its oaks, the Aransas Refuge does not have the diverse and abundant standing crop of dead branches that attract woodpeckers. If you spot a small woodpecker in the live oaks it will likely be the resident ladder-backed. Red-bellied woodpeckers drift in from the local riverbottom forests to the north, and golden-fronted woodpeckers invade from the brushland to the southwest. Although neither species stays on Blackjack Peninsula for long, there is a small resident population of golden-fronted woodpeckers in the mesquite and prickly pear community on the Tatton Unit.

In the wintertime, northern flickers come and go, and rarely, a displaced red-headed woodpecker will put in a brief appearance, as will an occasional yellow-bellied sapsucker and downy woodpecker.

In 1987 and again in 1988, Aransas personnel were astounded to host a solitary pileated woodpecker. This large species is common enough in nearby riparian forests, but this one (presumed to be the same individual both years) took a liking to the oaks around headquarters.

Miscellaneous Common Perching Birds

The northern cardinal, the commonest resident songbird on the Aransas Refuge, occurs wherever woody cover is at hand. The bright red plumage of the males makes them an easy target to identify; the dark females have waxy-red beaks. During the winter, cardinals often forage in flocks for seeds and berries. Pyrrhuloxias look like off-color cardinals but can be easily distinguished by their heavy, yellow-white beak. They sporadically invade the Tatton and Blackjack Peninsula from the brush country to the southwest.

Cardinal

Scissor-tailed flycatcher

Northern mockingbirds are much at home in the vast brushy interior of Blackjack Peninsula. A slow drive around the Tour Loop in the springtime should make you aware of their cheek-by-jowl nesting territories. During the winter months, watch the mockers work themselves into a frenzy trying to defend a favorite yaupon thicket against an invasion of American robins.

During most winters the live oak thickets along the Tour Loop harbor enough long-billed and brown thrashers to enliven dawn and dusk with their low, churring calls and repertory of liquid notes. Look carefully to distinguish the subtle differences in coloration between these two species. In most years the long-billed is the more common kind on the refuge. Curve-billed thrashers are inhabitants of the brush country southwest of the Aransas; they have been seen on the Tatton Unit and on Matagorda Island.

The matchless scissor-tailed flycatcher is one of the most eye-catching summer residents on the refuge. The arrival of the cheerful, twittering scissortails, on or about March 15, sets the mood for springtime on the Aransas. The birds nest here and stay until mid-November.

The loggerhead shrike is a permanent resident, but it is most often observed in the fall and winter. Watch for this soft-gray bird with a black mask perched on dead branches along the Tour Loop. Despite its small size, the shrike is an energetic predator on insects, frogs, lizards, small snakes, mice, and birds. Shrikes have been seen with freshly killed horned larks, mockingbirds, warblers, and sparrows. The species earns the name "butcher bird" by impaling the bodies of lizards and grasshoppers on mesquite thorns, the tips of Spanish daggers, or barbed-wire fences. On the refuge they also frequently skewer green treefrogs. This grisly habit is practiced mostly by males, and although they do occasionally consume a morsel, it appears to be primarily a display of hunting prowess to entice a female into the territory.

Most of the meadowlarks on the tidal flats, roadsides, and recently burned tracts are resident eastern meadowlarks. Their lilting songs can be heard on sunny mornings throughout the spring and early summer. Western meadowlarks move into the Tatton Unit during most dry winters, and a few invade Blackjack Peninsula. If you are a birder, you know that the ear is better than the eye for distinguishing the two, but in the wintertime the birds seldom sing.

Watch for horned larks, almost always in pairs, on open ground on the roadside and in sandy or silty clearings on the tidal flats, where they walk along nibbling the fresh tips of glasswort. The feathery horns for which the bird is named are seldom evident, and because the sparrow-sized birds have a black breast badge and a yellow throat, they are sometimes confused with meadowlarks.

Dickcissels (be sure you give them all their sibilants: DICK-sis-sels) arrive in April, and in most years there is a heavy nesting population of these cheery birds on the open portion of Blackjack Peninsula and all over the Tatton Unit. From atop weed stalks in their nesting territories, the males repeatedly utter a raspy version of their epithet.

You may see red-winged blackbirds and both boat-tailed and great-tailed grackles in the reeds and trees around most permanent fresh water. If the redwings are nesting, be sure to watch the males declaring their nesting boundaries by singing and displaying their colorful epaulets. Occasionally, in the wintertime, flocks of common grackles appear briefly on the refuge. Winter is also the season for swirling flocks of Brewer's blackbirds to descend on the Aransas and into the adjacent fields and feedlots. Both brown-headed and bronzed cowbirds occur in the Coastal Bend. The impact of these confirmed nest parasites on resident nesting birds has not been systematically studied on the refuge.

The commonest of the eight species of wrens recorded on the refuge is the resident Carolina wren. You can locate it in most thickets and oak mottes around headquarters and on the Big Tree and Dagger Point trails. It is most easily detected by its loud musical song. These friendly little birds frequently lodge their wad of nesting material in odd nooks and containers around headquarters.

Sedge wrens and an occasional marsh wren will scold you with their dry chatter during the wintertime along Thomas and Cattail sloughs and from the vegetation bordering Hog and Jones lakes. Most birders know how to squeak in return to get these curious little birds to show themselves briefly. Marsh wrens occasionally nest in the Coastal Bend, but they have not been confirmed to do so on the Aransas.

House wrens take up the task of winter chiding from the thickets

Carolina wren

around the Tour Loop, where their staccato has been likened to the rapid clack of typewriter keys. Both Bewick's (pronounced like the automobile, Buick) and cactus wrens are uncommon residents limited to the mesquite and prickly pear and the chaparral communities on the Tatton Unit. The tiny winter wren is probably more common on the Aransas than the few sightings indicate. The lone rock wren seen on Matagorda Island was surely displaced from its western range.

White-eyed vireos are common residents on Blackjack Peninsula. The presence of nesting Bell's vireos and of verdins on the Tatton is more reason to regard that unit as an eastern margin for the ranges of southwestern species.

Most of the twenty species of sparrows recorded from the Aransas are transient or occasional winter residents. The absence of extensive open, short-grass savannah probably limits winter sparrow numbers; expanses of tall bunchgrasses make the observation of some species difficult.

The savannah sparrow is the common winter resident in grassy clearings and on the roadsides. Vesper, chipping, grasshopper, and field sparrows show up wherever mesquites dot the grassland. Lincoln's sparrows skulk in the greenbriar thickets in the wintertime, and swamp sparrows do likewise in dense bankside vegetation. Song, white-throated, and white-crowned sparrows make sporadic winter appearances. The resident lark sparrows become more evident in spring and summer, the same season when Cassin's sparrows sing and skylark on the Tatton Unit. Watch for seaside sparrows amid the sea ox-eye on the tidal flats at any time of the year. In the spring and early summer the males repeatedly produce their raspy calls from perches atop knee-high tidal-flat vegetation. The Christmas bird count in 1990 was an excep-

Table 9. *Breeding Bird Survey, ANWR*

Species	Number of Individuals			
	1983	1984	1985	Average
Laughing gull	416	37	6	153
Cardinal	159	69	121	116
Red-winged blackbird	114	42	49	68
Mourning dove	99	53	30	61
Eastern meadowlark	60	48	43	50
Carolina wren	38	65	11	38
White-faced ibis	14	7	86	36
Dickcissel	25	38	31	31
Mottled duck	13	3	47	21
Bobwhite	22	16	25	21
Common nighthawk	30	20	11	20
White-eyed vireo	20	5	33	19
Snowy egret	17	37	0	18
Painted bunting	12	4	37	18
Turkey vulture	30	13	9	17
Black-necked stilt	20	13	11	15
Killdeer	10	15	11	12
White ibis	0	0	34	11
Great-tailed grackle	24	0	9	11
Great blue heron	17	5	9	10
Common moorhen	15	8	7	10
Yellowthroat	1	6	15	7
Scissor-tailed flycatcher	8	4	8	7
Roseate spoonbill	2	13	2	6
Caspian tern	6	6	5	6

Data are from the files of the ANWR.

tional one for sparrows; fourteen kinds were seen, including the elusive Le Conte's sparrow.

Despite the refuge's reputation as a mecca for birds, some species that are generally regarded as quite common are only occasionally noted on the Aransas, because of its lack of tall trees and the predominance of oak thickets and windswept coastal topography: Carolina chickadees, tufted titmice, eastern bluebirds, red-bellied woodpeckers, and even American crows, for instance. Blue jays are sometimes common in winter flocks, but they usually pass on when the acorns are harvested. Urban birds like European starlings, house sparrows, and rock doves (domestic pigeons) seem to feel out of place in the natural setting.

Breeding Birds

The Aransas biologist conducts a survey of breeding birds on the refuge during the first week in June. Table 9 presents data for the 25 most common species recorded. Such a summer survey tallies several hundred individuals of about 45 species. In contrast, a one-day Christmas count may document thousands of birds of about 150 species.

Incidentals

Just for birders, here are a few refuge entries calculated to set you on edge.

Red-throated loon—two in breeding plumage in Aransas Bay, April 1976.

Red-necked grebe—sighting in San Antonio Bay, November 1953.

Magnificent frigatebird—regularly seen in summer on Matagorda Island; sightings occasional over Blackjack Peninsula.

Tundra swan—one seen December 1946; two seen 1957; four in February 1970 and two in December 1970; one immature in November 1986.

Oldsquaw—one sighting, pond near headquarters, December 1948; one in St. Charles Bay, November 1977; one in Intracoastal Canal, February 1989.

White-winged scoter—scattered sightings in 1970s; latest sighting January 1986.

Zone-tailed hawk—one sighting, associated with vultures, November 1972.

Rough-legged hawk—first seen 1952, irregularly since; latest sighting on Tatton, February 1975.

Ferruginous hawk—first seen 1940, irregularly since; latest sighting April 1977.

Aplomado falcon—one seen at East Shore Road and Tour Loop, November 1972; one at Alamo Mill, February 1973; two seen at East Shore Road and Tour Loop, March 1973.

Hudsonian godwit—scattered early records; eight on St. Charles Bay, May 1986; one sighting June 1988; four at Burgentine Lake, April 1990.

Green kingfisher—one seen at Tule Lake, February 1973.

Great kiskadee—pair throughout summer, 1948; one on North Boundary Road, October 1972; latest sighting on Heron Flats, December 1985.

Dusky-capped flycatcher—one sighting at headquarters, June 1972.

Red-breasted nuthatch—first record October 1941; one at headquarters, November 1974; latest sighting 1980 CBC.

Clay-colored robin—lone record, Heron Flats Trail, February 1988.

Phainopepla—one sighting January 1973.

Golden-winged warbler—two on Big Tree Trail, April 1972; one on Big Tree Trail, May 1973.

Tropical parula—one at Youth Environmental Training Area, January 1988; singing male at headquarters, June 1989.

Western tanager—seen in 1970's; latest sighting on Rail Trail, February 1987.

Black-headed grosbeak—first seen 1956; several at headquarters and on Big Tree Trail, April 1972.

Crimson-collared grosbeak—one at headquarters, February 1988.

Botteri's sparrow—singing individuals on Tatton Unit, May 1989.

Olive sparrow—one on Bludworth Island, May 1986; three on Heron Flats, March 1988; one on Lamar Tract, June 1989.

Green-tailed towhee—several early sightings; recent ones at headquarters, January 1990, and at observation tower, November 1991.

Clay-colored sparrow—six seen on Tour Loop, May 1972; several at Burgentine Lake, April 1987.

Golden-crowned sparrow—one sighting on Tour Loop, February 1973.

Yellow-headed blackbird—scattered sightings, latest in April 1989.

House finch—one at headquarters, April 1989.

Pine siskin—scattered sightings; latest at headquarters, May 1988.

CHAPTER 11

Herptiles

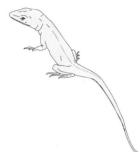

Herpetology is the formal study of amphibians and reptiles, so the two groups collectively are referred to as herptiles. The single best manual for the identification of local representatives is *A Field Guide to Reptiles and Amphibians of Eastern and Central North America*, by Roger Conant.

Herptiles have backbones, but they lack the ability to regulate their internal body temperature, so we call them cold-blooded. On cool days herptiles bask in the sun, and on hot days they conduct their business early or late, or they go abroad at night. Because of the moderate climate in the Coastal Bend, at least a few species of these cold-blooded creatures can be found astir in every month of the year, but most become semidormant during cold spells, and their low metabolic rate allows them to survive through the cool season without eating.

Herptiles are mostly carnivores, and they are ecologically important not only as predators but also because they are themselves prey for a great number of higher-order meat-eaters. They are important links in almost all of the major food chains on the Aransas.

Amphibians

Amphibians are easily distinguished from reptiles by their moist, scaleless skin. Also, they must lay their eggs in water and pass through an aquatic larval stage before metamorphosing into an adult. Because of their delicate skin, amphibians cannot tolerate brackish water, and they are apt to dehydrate in dry air. That is why they concentrate in moist swales and around fresh water and are most active during warm, rainy weather. It is not unusual to see a leopard frog hop from the shoreline into San Antonio Bay. This is not a contradiction of the statement that amphibians cannot withstand brackish water; rather it is evidence that the bay is sometimes nearly fresh.

Amphibian populations follow a boom-or-bust pattern: great abundance and reproductive success in wet years; a low-profile, nonbreeding status in dry years. After a rainy winter and spring, it may be difficult to dodge the hundreds of juvenile leopard frogs hopping across the Tour Loop, and evenings ring with choruses of green treefrogs. On the other hand, some species of amphibians may not be seen on the refuge for a decade or more if conditions remain unfavorable for them. With its searing summers, periodic droughts, and occasional overwashes of salt water, the Aransas does not always present an easy environment for the three kinds of salamanders and thirteen species of frogs and toads known to reside here.

Salamanders

None of these creatures is likely to be seen by the casual visitor. Two kinds—the eastern tiger salamander and the small-mouthed salamander—breed during late winter or early spring while the water is still quite cool, and they spend practically all of their adult lives beneath surface debris or underground. The former species is not common, and the latter has been collected only once, in 1981. Larvae of tiger salamanders are most likely to be seined up from freshwater ponds, which do not have large populations of predatory fish. In 1967, the extensive flooding caused by Hurricane Beulah, which allowed fish to enter every freshwater system in the Coastal Bend, may have caused a reduction of this species. By the eighties, however, tiger salamander larvae again appeared in seine hauls on the refuge.

Although seldom discovered without a special effort with dipnet or seine, the permanently aquatic lesser siren is the most abundant salamander on the refuge. This twenty-inch-long, eellike creature has external gills and only one pair of legs—the tiny forelegs. Sirens spend the day nestled in burrows in the bottom muck, and they emerge to swim-and-slide about at night foraging for crayfish, aquatic worms, and insect larvae. Occasionally they briefly surface for a gulp of air. This is the only kind of salamander known to communicate vocally. Individuals produce a series of sharp clicks, especially when they encounter another siren. Although these creatures can emit a sharp bleat if caught by a snake, look to Greek myth, not to fire trucks, for the derivation of "siren."

Sirens live in the nearly permanent water in Thomas Slough, but they also manage to survive in freshwater ponds and ditches that dry up completely by burrowing into the wet mud and secreting a cocoonlike mass of mucus around their bodies. There they lie entombed, sometimes for months, awaiting the return of life-giving rains.

The Aransas lies directly in the overlap area between the ranges of the southern black-spotted newt (a state endangered species) and the

Lesser siren

eastern red-spotted newt, but neither of these small salamanders has been found on the refuge.

Frogs

The semiaquatic frogs and the more terrestrial toads lead similar lives. All are mainly nocturnal insectivores that use their extensible tongues to capture prey. They have enlarged hind legs with which they attempt to leap away from their numerous predators. Toads are also somewhat protected by poison glands in their skin. On warm moist nights in the spring and early summer the males congregate in noisy choruses to coax the females to the breeding pools. The eggs hatch into tadpoles, which feed on aquatic vegetation and detritus until they metamorphose.

Many snakes, birds, and mammals feed on the adults and larvae. Tadpoles trapped in drying puddles and waves of emerging froglets provide windfall feasts for sirens, water snakes, ribbon snakes, cottonmouths, herons, egrets, grackles, raccoons, and feral hogs. Sometimes tadpoles are even killed and consumed by predaceous water bugs and dragonfly larvae. Alligators snap up all the adults and tadpoles they come upon. The piercing shriek of a predator-caught frog is a common sound on the Aransas.

One of the most frequently observed and certainly the most appealing frogs on the refuge is the green treefrog. This is the clay-smooth, leaf-green frog often found hunkered on the shady side of a bulrush stem or a palmetto leaf with its legs tucked beneath its body. Sometimes a cluster of individuals waits out the day on the moist concrete walls at the observation tower, on buildings at headquarters, or on the protected side of refuge signs. By using your binoculars at the pier on Jones Lake, you might spot as many as two dozen individuals clinging tightly to the waving stalks of cattails.

Each evening from late spring throughout summer the musical, bell-like calls of green treefrogs ring from well-vegetated freshwater sites. In warm, wet weather their huge nighttime choruses sound from a distance like the clangor of a busy factory.

You should be able to spot a green treefrog hugging a bulrush or cattail stem along the margin of Thomas Slough or Hog Lake. Also listen for the occasional individual that gets inspired enough to suddenly peal out a series of ducklike yarps from his daytime perch in the willows.

The squirrel treefrog is also common on the refuge, but it is less prone than the green treefrog to settle for the day in an exposed position. Its call is a series of raspy quacks.

The spotted chorus frog is hardly ever noticed until heavy early spring rains fill the roadside ditches. Then the males produce their tinkling mating calls that sound like a thumb being drawn across the teeth of a comb. Strecker's chorus frog emits a series of clear, high-pitched whistles and is most frequently heard during wet weather in midwinter.

The thumb-sized Blanchard's cricket frog is moderately common on the refuge in wet years, but the population dwindles to near extinction during a series of dry years. Although they were absent through the eighties, a few were heard calling at Jones Lake in 1990. If they are present, cricket frogs will be startled from their resting sites on the banks of freshwater ponds and sloughs. Their calls sound like pebbles being rapidly clicked together.

The Aransas Refuge lies on the junction between the ranges of the Rio Grande leopard frog coming up the coast and the southern leopard frog coming down the coast. Although some local specimens have intermediate traits, most of them are southern leopard frogs. However, the distinctions are esoteric; for most visitors, the very common, medium-sized greenish frog with numerous brown blotches frequently encountered around all freshwater sites is definitely a leopard frog.

Leopard frogs travel widely overland in wet weather and often congregate at windmill overflows. They are often seen on roadways; in the very wet spring of 1992 half-grown leopard frogs were so numerous that it was difficult for drivers on the Tour Loop to avoid running over them. Because of their size and abundance, leopard frogs are important prey for alligators, many kinds of snakes, all wading birds, many raptors, and raccoons. Other birds and mammals will take a leopard frog if they have the opportunity.

Green treefrog

Southern leopard frog

Almost everyone will recognize the deep and resonant "jug-o-rum" of the bullfrog booming out of the thick vegetation in Thomas Slough on a balmy afternoon, but it is quite a feat to spot one of these wary beasts. Stalk the sound. Use your binoculars to scan not only the bank but also the vegetation that emerges from the water. You may finally see only a large green head with a pair of enormous protruding eyes poking up among the bulrush stems.

If you do get a good look at a bullfrog, you can determine its sex by the size of its eardrum: larger than the eye in males, smaller than the eye in females. Of course, if you actually see your frog calling, you have its sex pegged: only males make sounds.

Frogs are basically insectivores, but large bullfrogs frequently snap up bigger prey: crayfish, sunfish, sirens, tadpoles and frogs, water snakes, young turtles, and even mice and shrews. It is likely that on the Aransas bullfrogs occasionally gulp down hatchling alligators as well as displaced nestling and recently fledged birds.

Watch the shallows in the pools along the Heron Flats Trail for bullfrog tadpoles lolling in the sun on submerged vegetation. Older ones (they take more than a year to mature) may be nearly as broad as the palm of your hand. If Jones Lake has held water through the spring and summer, it too will be populated with bullfrogs.

Toads

Narrow-mouthed toads are plump, brown, wet-skinned little creatures with pointed snouts. They are seldom seen unless uncovered by rolling aside the log or board under which they hunt for termites and ants, their favorite prey. Then they dart mouselike for the nearest cover. Both eastern and great plains narrow-mouthed toads occur on the refuge. The latter is more common. The two kinds can be distinguished by looking at their bellies: mottled gray in the eastern, bright white in the great plains.

The great plains narrow-mouthed toad is known to live in association with tarantulas; it purposefully scurries down the spider's burrow when threatened by a predator. Why doesn't the huge arachnid regard the tiny toad as prey? Perhaps its skin secretion, which protects the toad from ants, also deters the tarantula.

When summer rains fill all the depressions, narrow-mouthed toads congregate, and the males, submerged except for their little turret heads, produce buzzing, insectlike calls. The call of the eastern narrow-mouth is deeper and coarser than the clean, humming whine of the great plains species. Most visitors never realize that these peculiar sounds coming from roadside ditches are made by amphibians.

The commonest true toad in the Coastal Bend is the Gulf Coast toad. These medium-sized, warty amphibians, though abundant around Thomas Slough and the watered lawns at headquarters, are not often seen in the daytime. At night they feed on insects beneath lights, and the penetrating trilled calls of the males are heard on most spring evenings. After a successful breeding season, hordes of bug-sized toadlets can be seen scampering across the roads. Many predators shun adult toads because of their toxic skin glands, but eastern hognose snakes seem immune to the poison and specialize in eating these creatures.

After exceptionally heavy summer rains, the rapidly repeated, riveting trills of Texas toads can occasionally be heard on the western side of Blackjack Peninsula and on the Tatton Unit. These toads have been reported from St. Joseph Island and might occur on Matagorda Island as well, but they have not been documented there. When a male toad calls, it inflates a thin-skinned vocal pouch beneath its chin. The pouch of the Gulf Coast toad is spherical; that of the Texas toad is sausage-shaped.

Hurter's spadefoot toad is among the most peculiar and secretive amphibians on the Aransas Refuge. These are fist-sized, plump-bodied, smooth-skinned creatures with a prominent bony bump on the top of the head. Their eyes have vertical pupils, and their skin secretes an irritating mucus. Spadefoots are named for a black shovellike tubercle on their heel, which is used to dig rapidly backward into the sand. Spadefoot toads spend most of their time underground. On the Aransas they have been unearthed from pocket-gopher burrows.

Spadefoots become explosively evident during and immediately following hard summer rains. The males bob buoyantly in rain pools, calling lustily with an agonized, groaning bleat meant to attract a ripe female. Following downpours, their harrowed choruses can be heard day and night from flooded swales in the dense growth along the Tour Loop. It is a wild, haunting sound that befits this reclusive amphibious gnome.

Spadefoot eggs hatch quickly, and the tadpoles develop rapidly, allowing these toads to breed successfully in temporary rain pools. They thus avoid competition with other species that require more permanent water for a longer developmental stage.

At least seven other kinds of frogs and toads could reasonably be expected to occur on the Aransas, but to date none has been reliably documented: gray treefrog, upland chorus frog, southern crawfish frog (one credible visitor sighting in 1992), sheep frog, Woodhouse's toad, eastern green toad, and Couch's spadefoot toad (early reference to specimens on northern half of Blackjack Peninsula).

Reptiles

Reptiles are readily distinguished from amphibians by their dry, scaly skin. Although some kinds live in and around water, many others survive in the driest portions of the refuge. Most deposit eggs in the soil; a few kinds bear live young, but none has a larval stage.

Reptiles are generally carnivorous, although some turtles live principally on plant material. In contrast to amphibians, most reptiles are silent or only hiss when provoked. A few species are venomous. The group contains many important predatory and prey species.

The American alligator and the several kinds of sea turtles are discussed in Chapter 6.

Turtles

The Aransas National Wildlife Refuge, with recurrent drought that reduces or eliminates freshwater sites, presents a rather hostile environment to turtles. The abundant raccoons and feral hogs are adept at digging up turtle eggs, and numerous alligators are ever-ready to chomp up juvenile and adult turtles. Yet, about half a dozen species of turtles manage to beat the odds.

The red-eared slider is certainly the kind that visitors are most likely to see. Look for it basking on the bank, on an emergent log, or out in the water with only its head exposed at Jones Lake, Thomas Slough, and the ponds along the Heron Flats Trail. As its name implies, there is a red slash behind the eye, although this "red ear" becomes obscure in old individuals. These omnivores feed on a variety of aquatic insects, tadpoles, and algae; sometimes they are reduced to gorging on bottom

Red-eared slider

muck. Alligators eat sliders; a large alligator gives a big turtle a single crunch before swallowing it.

Although ornate box turtles are not common on the peninsula, you might see one ambling across the road around headquarters or on the Tour Loop. Be sure you give the slow-moving creature the right-of-way. This terrestrial turtle feeds on dewberries, yaupon and greenbriar fruits, fresh greenery, mushrooms, and whatever insects it can catch. When provoked it can pull in its legs and fold the ends of its bottom shell tightly against its top shell for protection that even a hungry coyote cannot breach. Box turtles are more abundant on the barrier islands and even on some of the offshore spoil islets than they are on the mainland, perhaps because island nests are less often pilfered by feral hogs.

Both the yellow mud turtle and the similar Mississippi mud turtle are rather abundant on the Aransas, although they are not often seen. These little turtles, about five inches long with smooth brown shells, prefer permanent freshwater ponds with emergent vegetation and muddy bottoms, where they forage for aquatic insect larvae, crustaceans, worms, and fish. The more abundant yellow mud turtle is most often noticed when it crosses roads after heavy rains. Mud turtles are favorite prey for medium-sized alligators and raccoons, and young turtles are gobbled down whole by great blue herons and black-crowned night-herons.

Even though the common snapping turtle has not been reliably documented here, the refuge lies well within its known geographic range. Despite their large size—a shell length of more than a foot and a weight of twenty pounds—snapping turtles are habitually wary and shy, and they almost never leave their submarine haunts. Individuals could occur in Thomas Slough and perhaps in other semipermanent bodies of fresh water on Blackjack Peninsula and remain thus far undetected. They are voracious carnivores powerful enough to clamp down on any small or medium-sized vertebrate that wanders within reach of their wicked jaws: fish, frogs, sirens and tadpoles, small alligators, ribbon snakes, and cottonmouth moccasins. They are arch predators of mottled ducklings and young moorhens and clapper rails and also eat aquatic insects, blue crabs, and carrion.

The Texas diamondback terrapin fills the ecological niche between true sea turtles and freshwater turtles. Diamondback terrapins, named for the sculptured scales on their carapace, are most at home in the brackish shallows along the shoreline of the mainland, the lee sides of the barrier islands, and the margins of the islets and oyster reefs scattered throughout the bays. Diamondbacks feed on marine crustaceans, worms, molluscs, and small fish. The species is uncommon locally, or at least it is infrequently observed, probably because of the relatively sparse fringing salt marshes. In earlier days they were abundant enough to be harvested for their tasty flesh; today significant numbers are caught incidentally and drowned in shrimp trawls and crab traps. On Blackjack Peninsula about the best you can hope for is to find a shell or several of the distinctive scutes washed up on the beach along San Antonio Bay. With a telescope, you might spot individuals basking on the oyster reefs off the sandy eminence on the Dagger Point Trail.

Two other turtles bear mention. The Guadalupe spiny softshell turtle is a riverine species that occasionally gets flushed into the brackish environment. It is seen now and then in the local bays and on the refuge around Burgentine Lake. Softshell turtles prefer running water and probably do not remain in residence on the Aransas.

The Aransas Refuge lies on the northern edge of the range of the Texas tortoise, and there are a few vague references to this southern species. The dense vegetation on Blackjack Peninsula would surely not be to their liking, but they would not be out of their element on the more open Tatton Unit. The Texas tortoise is accorded threatened status by the state.

According to their known ranges, two other species of turtles might eventually be found on the refuge: the three-toed box turtle and the Texas slider.

Lizards

The green anole, locally called a chameleon (kah-MEAL-ee-yun) because of its ability to change from green to brown, occurs sparingly in the larger oak mottes and the oak-bay forest on Blackjack Peninsula.

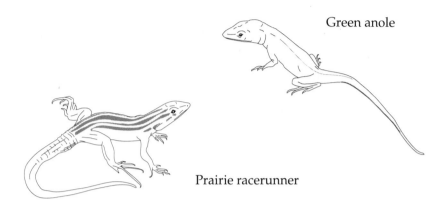

Green anole

Prairie racerunner

The best place to look for an anole is around the residences at head-quarters and amid the tangle of vines and shrubs where the Heron Flats Trail borders Thomas Slough. This arboreal species stalks flies, katy-dids, and spiders, and individuals must be alert to avoid becoming a meal for a western coachwhip or a loggerhead shrike.

If you spot one of these pretty lizards slinking along a branch in the springtime, watch for a male to pause to pump his forequarters and spread the pink bib beneath his throat. That colorful little flag is a no-trespass sign to neighboring males and a lure to females; your own bright clothing might provoke the display.

Two kinds of spiny lizards have been documented on the refuge. The larger Texas spiny lizard is rare; it prefers to live in trees in more open and diversified forests. The northern fence lizard is probably the most abundant and widespread lizard on Blackjack Peninsula, and it is re-sponsible for many of the rustles you hear along the trails. Fence lizards are quite at home in the trees as well as on the ground in oak mottes, and they range through the oak thickets and even onto the treeless tidal flats. You may see them basking on the warm pavement along the Tour Loop or searching for insects on the roadsides. The northern fence liz-ard is well camouflaged in grays and browns, but you may observe an aroused male raising the side of his body to reveal a bright streak of metallic blue. That is his way of attracting a female and of warning other males to keep their distance—the fence lizard equivalent to the anole's throat bib.

The prairie racerunner is the long-tailed, striped lizard that sprints across open ground along the roadsides in the summertime. It is also fairly common in mowed grassy places around the picnic area and at headquarters, and it skitters across sunny stretches of the Heron Flats Trail. Prairie racerunners chase down all sorts of ground-living insects and arachnids, and they are particularly fond of termites and ants. The lizards are, in turn, preyed upon by western coachwhips and red-tailed hawks, and fresh-hatched racerunners are even caught by large ground spiders. These wary lizards are best observed with binoculars. You can recognize a male by his exceptional coloration: besides his pattern of black and pale-yellow stripes, his head is a powder blue and the front third of his body bears a bright chartreuse wash. The closely related but less colorful spotted whiptail occurs on the Tatton Unit.

Skinks are ground-living lizards with such small, shiny scales that they are often mistaken for salamanders. These active little lizards live in the deep leaf litter in live oak mottes and oak-bay forest and are often uncovered when logs or boards are lifted from the ground. They feed on small insects and arachnids.

The Aransas hosts two kinds of skinks. The rare five-lined skink has been seen only in the vicinity of headquarters, where the watered lawn provides the moisture it prefers. The ground skink is most common in leaf litter under trees but ranges through the grassland and onto the inner edge of the tidal flats. These little lizards (with tail they are about four inches long) are coppery brown with a dark stripe down each side. Their tiny legs are weak, and they slither through their habitat like stumpy snakes. As they wriggle through the leaf mold, they can see even with their eyes closed because the lower eyelid has a transparent window. Large wolf spiders are important predators on young ground skinks.

Ground skinks are especially common along the Big Tree Trail and around the base of the ramp to the observation tower, but you are more likely to hear a gentle rustling in the debris than to see one.

The Texas horned lizard is now rare on Blackjack Peninsula, probably because of the spread of running live oak thickets across once open sandy uplands and of nest predation by feral hogs. The numbers of this reptilian symbol of Texas have dropped so alarmingly that it was placed on the state's threatened list in 1967. Although at one time horned lizards were severely overcollected, the main reasons for their continued decline are encroachment into their favored open habitat by agriculture and urban expansion; roadways, with their attendant deadly traffic; and disruption of their specialized ant diet by the widespread use of pesticides.

Horned lizards are occasionally seen on the more open Tatton Unit. However, on the roads of packed shell on the Matagorda Unit, the species is still delightfully common. The best way to find one is to walk along on a sunny afternoon and wait for a patch of ground to suddenly erupt at your feet and go spraddle-legging off ahead. Keep your eye on it until it stops. Then ease up for a close look at this weird prickly pancake.

Slender glass lizards are legless animals often mistaken for snakes, but their less supple body movements and possession of eyelids and ear openings suggest their true nature. They are well adapted to sliding through the dense tangle of stems on the tidal flat and in all grassy areas on the peninsula, and they easily slide over or wriggle through the loose sand on Matagorda Island. An adult glass lizard is about twenty inches long; at least twelve of those inches are tail. When leaped upon by a predator, the glass lizard lives up to its name by readily disjointing its tail into several twitching pieces. While the predator is temporarily distracted by the tail, the eight-inch body slips quietly away to safety. The lizard can regenerate another tail. (Legend has it that when the danger is past, the lizard returns and rejoins its tail segments to its body. What do you think?)

Slender glass lizards are common on Blackjack Peninsula. You may see one on the open stretches of the Heron Flats or the Hog Lake trails, where they prey on all sorts of ground-living insects and arachnids. Also watch the ground along the boardwalk. These lizards frequently move across the paved roads late in the afternoon and often pause on the warm asphalt. When startled, their movement on the pavement is frenetic and much less sinuous than that of a snake.

The Mediterranean gecko is an Old World lizard that has been spread widely to warm seaports because of its habit of tucking into cargoes of lumber and plants. It was first found in South Texas in 1955, and today it is known from 41 counties. Mediterranean geckos seldom stray from human habitations. On the refuge they have been found inside and around buildings at headquarters. These rather appealing, strictly nocturnal animals are pale in color, with huge eyes, prominent toe pads, and warty skins. They frequently appear on walls, screens, and ceilings to harvest insects at lights; several can usually be found snapping at moths beneath the all-night light outside the door of the WIC. When caught, an individual may utter a soft, mouselike "geck."

Two other species of lizards should be mentioned in passing. Although it has not been seen there, the southern prairie skink may occur on the Tatton Unit, where it would occupy a habitat similar to but somewhat drier than that of the ground skink. One of the real biogeographic mysteries of the Aransas is the absence of the keeled earless lizard, a species adapted to coastal sands. Although the species is abundant on Padre and Mustang islands, it has not been seen on Matagorda Island, nor is it known from the extensive sands on Blackjack Peninsula.

Snakes

Thirty-three species of snakes, over 40 percent of those native to Texas, have been documented on the Aransas National Wildlife Refuge. Many are small, secretive, and seldom seen, but several common larger kinds are often noticed crossing the roads, where you can observe them from your car window.

Four small resident snakes spend most of their time underground or beneath surface debris and are seen abroad only at night after summer rain showers. The Texas blind snake is the smallest species on the refuge. Adults are sometimes mistaken for earthworms. These little pinkish brown serpents burrow through the sand in search of termites and ant larvae. Their useless eyes are visible as a pair of dark dots through the scales on the head. Armadillos and moles routinely dig up and eat blind snakes. The flat-headed snake, Texas brown snake, and rough earth snake each attain a length of about ten inches. They live beneath logs and in leaf litter and feed on earthworms, crickets, ground spiders, centipedes, and the like. All of these little snakes are pursued in their subterranean haunts by coral snakes and kingsnakes, and Texas brown snakes move about on the surface frequently enough to be common prey for raccoons, herons, egrets, and hawks.

Two kinds of garter snakes, each a little over two feet long, live on the refuge, but neither is common. The coloration of the eastern garter snake is variable, but it usually includes a wide reddish orange stripe down the middle of the back and a thin straw-colored stripe along each side. Between the stripes the body is olive brown, sometimes with a vague pattern of darker spots. The checkered garter snake has a thin orangish midline and a bold checkerboard of square black spots on a yellow-olive background. Garter snakes are almost always found around fresh water or in damp swales, where they feed on frogs, tadpoles, fishes, and insects. In turn, they are preyed upon by all wading birds, most raptors, and a variety of mammals. Even bullfrogs, alligators, and other snakes enjoy a meal of garter snake.

The most abundant serpent on the Aransas, the Gulf Coast ribbon snake is colored somewhat like its close relation the eastern garter snake, but it is much more slender in all its proportions. Young ribbon snakes (which, like the garter snakes, are born alive) are newly minted, six-inch replicas of the adults. When you see a medium-sized, thin, striped snake slither away from the edge of Jones Lake or hear the shriek of a snake-caught frog in the damp grass, a Gulf Coast ribbon snake is likely the culprit.

Most of the dull-colored, stout-bodied snakes seen basking on banks or emergent snags are water snakes. They stay in or near the water and

Gulf Coast ribbon snake

eat aquatic prey—amphibians, fish, crayfish, and aquatic insects. Water snakes often congregate around drying waterholes to feast on all manner of stranded aquatic creatures. Although these snakes have nasty dispositions and readily bite if handled, they are all nonvenomous. Like their relatives the garter and ribbon snakes, water snakes are live-bearers. This entire assemblage of snakes shares another annoying trait: if handled or provoked they give off a sickly sweet, clinging secretion from glands near the anal opening.

Six species of water snakes have been found on the Aransas Refuge, but none is abundant. The diamond-backed water snake is especially adept at catching free-swimming fish and is the kind most often encountered around freshwater sites. Small prey is quickly swallowed, but with larger fish, the snake engulfs the head and gills and holds on until the fish weakens and smothers. Then it performs the singularly serpent feat of disconnecting its lower jaws, allowing it to work the relatively huge morsel down its gullet. Once into the alimentary canal, the food mass creates a conspicuous bulge until digestion gets well along.

The green water snake is occasionally seen in ponds and flooded ditches. Specimens have been observed swimming rapidly back and forth through muddy puddles with mouths agape, sweeping up hapless mosquito fish. Graham's water snake has been documented only twice on the northern edge of Blackjack Peninsula. A single specimen of the colorful broad-banded water snake was seen crossing the road along the Tour Loop in 1981. Although the blotched water snake is quite common in moist habitats throughout the Coastal Bend, only a single specimen has been recorded on the Aransas; it was found dead on the road outside the WIC in 1992. The species is probably more abundant than that lone sighting suggests.

The Gulf saltmarsh snake is the only local species of water snake that prefers a brackish water habitat. This brownish serpent with straw-colored lines down its body and brown half-moons on its belly is the commonest water snake in the tidal-flat community. It haunts the thick vegetation in Cattail Slough and clumps of reeds on the edge of San Antonio Bay—and watch for it from the boardwalk. These snakes forage along the inner perimeter of the tidal flat for frogs and crayfish, and they frequently take advantage of mullet and killifishes trapped in tidal pools. They probably prey on fiddler crabs as well.

The western mud snake is not closely related to the water snakes, but it does live in the same freshwater habitat. This snake prefers heavily vegetated pools with a thick layer of muck on the bottom, where it burrows through the ooze in search of its favorite prey—crayfish and lesser sirens. Mud snakes are a shining, iridescent black above and a startlingly bright carmine below, making them one of the prettiest reptilian species on the refuge. When alarmed, these harmless snakes tuck the head beneath a coil and raise the curled tail to display its brilliant underside. Although most sightings have been at Burgentine Lake on the western side of Blackjack Peninsula, when the swales are brimming with rainwater mud snakes are occasionally seen crossing the road to the observation tower.

The rough green snake is one of the most appealing snakes on the Aransas. Watch for these slender serpents along the Heron Flats Trail. They are abundant, but it may take a sharp eye to spot one amid the shrubs and vines, where they ease along the branches in search of caterpillars, katydids, grasshoppers, and spiders. They have the neat habit of sipping dew drops from leaves. Unfortunately, green snakes are

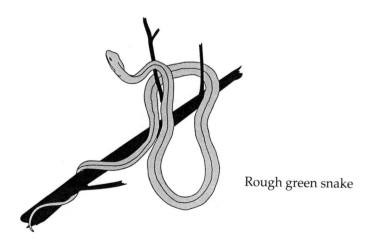

Rough green snake

commonly killed by vehicles when they try to cross roads; watch out for them. If you see a dead one, pause for a second look. Soon after death a biochemical change in the skin transforms their mint green to a turquoise blue.

Kingsnakes are glossy, medium-sized reptiles known especially for their habit of feeding on other snakes, including venomous species. They are immune to the venom. They subdue prey by constriction and also eat lizards and rodents and the eggs of birds and reptiles. Four kinds of kingsnakes occur on the refuge.

The speckled kingsnake is not only the commonest representative of its group on the Aransas but also one of the handsomest large serpents in the Coastal Bend. Each shiny black scale bears a luminous yellow-white dot, giving the snake a salt-and-pepper appearance. Watch for this slow-moving, rather docile snake on the tidal flat and in grassy swales. It is also common on Matagorda Island.

The refuge is on the eastern edge of the range of the closely related desert kingsnake, which has been taken rarely on the dry upland on the Tatton Unit. It is colored like the speckled kingsnake, but with a row of dark blotches down the middle of the back.

It is not certain whether prairie kingsnakes are locally rare or merely so secretive that they are seldom encountered; only two have been seen on the refuge, both in the short-grass upland on the Tatton Unit. These snakes are tan, with a row of squarish brown blotches along the back and sides.

The Louisiana milk snake, a retiring species occasionally found under driftwood on the margins of the bays, is another kind of kingsnake. If you like to pursue myths, find out how it got the name "milk snake." These snakes spend much of their time burrowing through the sand and cordgrass tussocks but are sometimes seen abroad on warm, rainy nights. The prettily ringed milk snake may easily be taken for a coral snake, but remember: "Red and yellow kill a fellow; red and black, venom lack." Milk snakes have the red-touches-black combination. Besides that, the coral snake has a bright yellow band, in contrast to the milk snake's cream-colored one.

The Texas scarlet snake is also brightly ringed in red, cream, and black, and as with the Louisiana milk snake, adjacent red and black bands announce its harmless nature. Another mark is its red snout (black in the coral snake). The scarlet snake spends most of its life burrowing through the loose coastal sand in search of reptile eggs, which seem to be its dietary staple, though it also feeds on small snakes and ground skinks. Only a few specimens have been found in Coastal Texas, four on the Aransas Refuge. The deep sand of the oak-bay forest between the Youth Environmental Training Area and the Big Tree Trail is the preferred habitat of the scarlet snake. The species is on the state threatened list.

Two species of rat snakes are known from the refuge. The fairly common great plains rat snake prefers short-grass prairie and is most often seen in the ridge-and-swale community on Blackjack Peninsula and on the Tatton Unit. It is an arch predator on fulvous harvest mice, young cotton rats, and ground-nesting birds. The Texas rat snake is quite common and can be expected in all communities except the tidal flat. This is one of the largest snakes on the refuge; adults routinely grow six feet long. Although they are not poisonous, a cornered individual puts on an impressive defensive display, rearing the front end to strike repeatedly, hissing and vibrating the tail tip to produce a rasping sound reminiscent of the rattling of an aroused rattlesnake. The lithe constrictors prowl across all types of terrain and spend much time in trees and shrubs. They are relentless predators of rodents and birds, and they are particularly adept at discovering nests. These snakes can detect active bird nests by a sense of smell acute enough for them to determine from the ground whether a climb is worth the effort. Their fondness for eggs has earned them the local name "chicken snake." Your best chance to see one of these large blotched serpents is when an individual crosses the road on the Tour Loop. They are slow-moving, so give them time to pass across.

Racers are slender, large-eyed, alert, and very fast-moving snakes that hunt the grassland and low shrubbery for lizards, mice, birds' nests, and grasshoppers. They are usually abroad during the hottest part of the day and are most often seen on the refuge when they streak across a road. An encounter afoot is usually no more than a startled glimpse and a quick rustle before the speedy reptile has disappeared.

The western coachwhip is a pale brown racer. The sharp outlines of its scales give it the attractive braided appearance that fostered its name. It is one of the few snakes that is fast enough to overtake a prairie racerunner in an open field chase. Like all racers, the western coachwhip is high-strung and irritable. If cornered and threatened, some individuals will raise the fore part of the body and aggressively advance on an intruder. These snakes readily bite when handled, and although nonvenomous, they can cause painful lacerations rather like a cat scratch.

While coachwhips prefer the open grassland of the Tatton and Matagorda units, the eastern yellow-bellied racer ranges throughout the dry interior of the mainland refuge. This is the olive-brown to blue-gray snake that occasionally dashes across the paved road ahead of your vehicle. A closely related variety, the Mexican racer, reaches its northern limit on the Aransas. It cannot be easily distinguished from the eastern

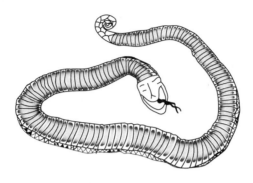

Hognose snake

yellow-bellied racer in the field. Both snakes are locally called blue racers.

Only one specimen of the bullsnake has been seen on the refuge. This large and powerful constrictor (the one discovered in a building at headquarters in 1974 was seven feet long) prefers more open terrain than is offered on Blackjack Peninsula, but it may be a routine resident on the Tatton Unit. Bullsnakes are arch predators on all rodents and ground-living birds.

The loose, sandy terrain of the Aransas Refuge is prime habitat for two interesting species of snakes, the western hognose snake and the more common eastern hognose snake. These harmless serpents are known for their entertaining defensive behavior. When threatened they coil, flatten the body, hiss wickedly, and even engage in sham striking behavior (so the local name, "puff adder"). If its bluff fails, the snake suddenly goes into writhing contortions as though mortally wounded. The act ends with the snake on its back, mouth agape, tongue dragging in the sand. When the source of provocation departs, the snake cautiously rights itself and glides away. Hognose snakes use their upcurved snouts to plow through the sand for resting toads and lizards. How does a hognose snake swallow a defensive toad puffed up with air? Simple: a pair of long teeth located in the back of the snake's mouth pop an inflated toad as easily as a pin pops a balloon.

Five species of venomous snakes have been definitely recorded from the Aransas Refuge. Only two, the cottonmouth moccasin and the western diamondback rattlesnake, need be of concern for routine visitors. Remember, even poisonous snakes are protected here. You are performing no useful service and you may endanger yourself if you molest one of these serpents. Observe it, admire it, and let it be.

The Texas coral snake is rather common on Blackjack Peninsula, but because of its subterranean nature it is seldom seen. It spends most of its time beneath surface debris or in the tangle of roots and maze of rodent burrows beneath the sand, where it ferrets after small snakes and lizards. On the refuge most coral snakes have been found around the watered lawns at headquarters. They are mostly abroad early or late in the day after summer rains. These slender, brightly ringed snakes (adjacent red and yellow rings are distinctive) pack a potent venom, but the likelihood of a person being bitten is virtually nil unless the snake is picked up. Educate the children and you need no further precaution.

The remaining four species of venomous snakes are pit vipers: all have a cavity in front of each eye (the pit) leading to a unique heat-sensing organ. This sense allows the snake to detect warm-blooded prey in the dark at a distance of several feet. Pit vipers also have a large pair of hollow fangs folded in the roof of the mouth. These are swung erect when the snake strikes, and they conduct the venom into the flesh of the prey. Although venom and fangs probably evolved as food-getting mechanisms, the combination works effectively in defense. Unlike the coral snake, pit vipers bear camouflage colors. Because they routinely lie in ambush for their prey, they are apt to be encountered at close range by oblivious hikers or free-ranging children.

Most visitors never see a poisonous snake on the refuge. For hikers, the best way to avoid an encounter is to stay on the marked trails and scan heavily vegetated trailsides before proceeding. Be particularly careful around the margins of pools. Moist, warm weather after a prolonged dry spell brings out the wildlife on the Aransas, including snakes. Your safest and most likely confrontation will be with a poisonous snake crossing the road. Get a good look from your vehicle window and resist any temptation to run over the reptile. Remember, they belong here.

The moist and shaded woods along the first half of the Heron Flats Trail look like good habitat for broad-banded copperheads, but only one individual has been sighted there. Despite the ample litter of oak leaves, Blackjack Peninsula is apparently too sandy and dry for them. Specimens have been seen rarely on the northern edge of the refuge.

Whereas copperheads are uncommon, the closely related western cottonmouth moccasin is the most abundant poisonous snake on the Aransas. These fat-bodied pit vipers are most often seen in and around water, brackish or fresh, but they can be expected in any well-vegetated area, and they are frequently seen crossing roads from one ditch to another. In wet years, cottonmouths disperse across the entire refuge; in dry years they concentrate around the lakes and on the tidal flats.

Moccasins are prone to remain quietly coiled unless approached closely. Then they may vibrate the tail and cock their head back, gaping widely to reveal the white lining of the mouth. If further provoked, some individuals remain immobile or attempt to slither into the vegetation or water, but others strike wickedly. A bite requires the immediate attention of a physician.

Cottonmouths are indiscriminate feeders. Although best adapted for securing fishes, frogs, and crayfish, they will take any creature that their rather potent venom will stop and their jaws can engulf. A stomach analysis of 34 specimens collected on the nearby Welder Wildlife Refuge revealed that the predominant food item was birds. Among the 13 species were red-winged blackbirds and brown-headed cowbirds, which roost in bulrushes, and eastern meadowlarks, which inhabit tidal flats and grassy swales. The young of American coots, soras, and common moorhens were taken, and even mockingbirds and cardinals, probably when the birds were attempting to drink. After birds, other snakes ranked high, mostly water snakes and garter snakes, but one cottonmouth had consumed a diamondback rattlesnake. Certainly the most amazing record was of a 41-inch cottonmouth that had managed to swallow a 49-inch great plains rat snake. How's that for gluttony? The food list continued through lesser sirens, green treefrogs, pigmy mice, and least shrews and even extended to snails, grasshoppers, caterpillars, and sundry aquatic insects. Besides that, cottonmouths occasionally consume fishes and amphibians that have died in drying waterholes. In their turn, adult moccasins are eaten by alligators, and young ones are preyed upon by everything from whooping cranes and great blue herons to raccoons and speckled kingsnakes.

Two species of rattlesnakes are known from the Aransas, the western massasauga and the western diamondback. The little massasauga (mass-ah-SAW-gah, an Indian name) is only occasionally seen on Blackjack Peninsula. It prefers the dense cover of Gulf cordgrass and is especially common in the moist, luxuriant grassland that covers the central portion of the Matagorda Unit. These snakes lie up in animal burrows and beneath clumps of grass until they move out to hunt for mice, shrews, frogs, and other snakes. Although massasaugas are small— adults are seldom over two feet long—they have a feisty disposition and strike readily. Their small rattle produces little more than a soft click.

The western diamondback rattlesnake is at once the best-known and the most systematically persecuted snake in Texas. Certainly it deserves respect. It is large and dangerously poisonous and, if pressured, will readily defend itself, but it hardly merits annihilation. On a refuge, rattlers get the same measure of protection as other wildlife.

There are few natural sights more thrilling and ominously beautiful

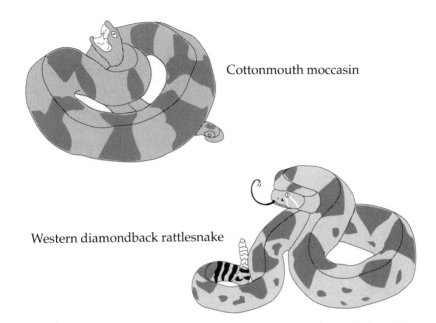

Cottonmouth moccasin

Western diamondback rattlesnake

than a cornered diamondback with the forepart of its air-inflated body drawn into a high S curve, its black tongue flicking methodically and its erect string of vibrating rattles sending out a dry whine that sets every nerve on edge. The alert snake swivels to follow every movement and can instantly strike half its body length. Most of the poisonous snakebites that occur in Texas are due to encounters with this truly spectacular creature.

Western diamondbacks range throughout the refuge. They can be expected in all communities, although they are rare in the oak-bay forest and the interiors of large live oak mottes. The species is especially common in the cordgrass areas that border the tidal flats, among the mesquite and prickly pears on the Tatton Unit, and on the shell ridges of the Matagorda Unit. Although they must be watched for, rattlers are not overabundant in that part of the refuge open to public access.

Diamondbacks are not prone to climb, but they do not hesitate to swim across pools and lakes, and individuals occasionally strike out across the bays. During high water a rattlesnake can coil into a buoyant pile and float until it makes landfall.

Even during January and February, rattlers are not completely dormant, but they do tend to move into armadillo burrows and brushy hideaways in the uplands of Blackjack Peninsula. Individuals often emerge to bask in the winter sun, and they have been found crawling about when the temperature was a chilly 40° F. In the springtime, when they begin moving to their preferred foraging grounds in the cordgrass meadows, rattlesnakes are frequently seen crossing refuge roads. As summer progresses they lie up during the day and hunt at night.

Despite their broad habitat tolerance, western diamondbacks are rather restricted in prey selection, feeding mainly on rodents. On Blackjack Peninsula their staples are cotton rats and rice rats. On the Tatton they certainly take advantage of another favorite, the south plains wood rat. Doubtless rattlers also consume significant numbers of pocket gophers and whatever smaller rodents they come across. They also take small cottontail rabbits as well as meadowlarks, bobwhite quail, and other ground-living birds. Although adult rattlers can fend for themselves, juveniles are commonly eaten by most carnivorous mammals, also by feral hogs, javelinas, wading birds, raptorial birds, kingsnakes, and alligators. Because of its multifarious ecological ties, the western diamondback rattlesnake plays a critical role in the natural balance on the Aransas. If you see one, give it the consideration it so much deserves but so seldom receives.

The Aransas Refuge is on the extreme southern edge of the known range of the western pigmy rattlesnake. There is one refuge record for this species, but the documentation is vague.

Judging by their known distributions in Texas, at least twelve other species of snakes could eventually be added to the refuge list: Texas indigo snake, Texas long-nosed snake, Schott's whipsnake, marsh brown snake, Mexican milk snake, Texas glossy snake, Texas night snake, Texas lined snake, South Texas ground snake, Texas black-headed snake, Texas patch-nosed snake, and canebreak rattlesnake.

CHAPTER 12

Fishes

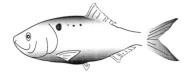 Except for an occasional flash of silver amid the waves or the wriggle of a tail fin when a Forster's tern makes a successful dive, most visitors to the Aransas Refuge seldom actually see a fish. Yet fishes constitute the most abundant and diverse group of backboned creatures in the Coastal Bend. Sixty species are on the refuge checklist of common kinds. One good haul with a twenty-foot minnow seine might net several hundred individual fish, and any enthusiastic high school class can bring in thirty species in an afternoon.

A standard manual for the fishes of the Gulf of Mexico covers more than five hundred species, the majority of which might be expected to invade, at least occasionally, the proclamation boundary of the Aransas Refuge. Some kinds come into the shallows seasonally as juveniles, then return to the Gulf to spawn. Others enter the surrounding grass beds on a flood tide seeking food, then leave on an ebb tide. When the rivers rise, freshwater fishes mingle with the saltwater forms. Even when the weather is benign and the waters are serene, the natural mix of salt, brackish, and fresh water provides a welter of aquatic habitats that are populated with a wide and continually shifting array of fishes.

Strictly freshwater fishes and several tolerant brackish-water forms inhabit the ponds and sloughs that dot the inland parts of the refuge. These sites are depopulated during droughts and revitalized during washovers.

All the fishes are subject to the same recurrent stresses. Change in salt content in the water causes metabolic stress in fish. Normal salinity for San Antonio Bay is 18–22 parts per thousand (ppt); for the Gulf, 32 ppt. But the Coastal Bend is characterized by periods of low rainfall with reduced surface runoff, which translates into increased salinity in the bays and tidal-flat pools. At such times Mustang Lake may get nearly as salty as the Gulf, and the salinity of isolated tidal pools near Long Lake occasionally rises to twice that value. Because of salt in their muddy bottoms, even freshwater ponds become brackish as they evaporate.

Drought is usually accompanied by elevated temperature. On a tor-

rid August afternoon, knee-deep water in Mustang Lake can reach
95° F. Aside from the direct stress on aquatic creatures, such heat drives
virtually all dissolved oxygen out of the water. Unless they are especially adapted, fish must seek deeper, cooler water or asphyxiate.

Local waters are shallow; shallow water is subject to rapid changes in
quality. Local bottoms are muddy; muddy bottoms are easily swirled
to produce muddy water. Muddy water hinders the penetration of sunlight; less sunlight means fewer submerged green plants. Also, shallow
muddy bottoms, constantly shifted by waves and currents, provide
poor footing for rooted aquatic plants. Fewer plants means skimpier
food chains and harder times for herbivorous creatures and consequent
belt-tightening for carnivores. Sparser aquatic vegetation also translates into less submarine cover for prey species and young creatures.
The ecological rules are the same for aquatic communities as for terrestrial ones.

Routine stresses can be aggravated by a blue norther, with its wind-
whipped tides and plunging temperatures, or a hurricane may dash
seawater into freshwater basins and inundate vast stretches of coastline.
Runoff from hurricane-spawned rains restructures local drainage channels and transforms the bays into freshwater lakes for weeks on end.
Local flooding brings a plethora of agricultural chemicals into Burgentine Lake, and an uncharted array of pollutants flushes coastward from
swamped sewage treatment plants. Freshly dredged ooze from the bottom of the Gulf Intracoastal Waterway is laced with a potent mix of
toxic chemicals.

Yet, if not in pristine abundance, the fishes at least thrive. They eat
and are eaten and so compose a vital portion of the food web that suc-
cors the Aransas.

Think about fish connections. A striped mullet scoops a mouthful of
organic muck from the bottom of San Antonio Bay. A Gulf saltmarsh
snake corners and consumes the mullet. That night the snake falls prey
to a raccoon. The raccoon runs afoul of a young alligator, manages to
pull away, but later dies from its wounds. The next morning, turkey
vultures quickly find the body and leave only skin and bones. Later you
see one of these same scavengers wheeling on a rising parcel of warm
air high over headquarters, but because the natural cycles are intricate
and subtle, you never suspect that mullet calories are helping keep the
bird aloft.

We shall mention only the few fish species that you are likely to observe or hear about. To learn more, we recommend *Fishes of the Gulf of
Mexico* by H. D. Hoese and R. H. Moore. Many of the local species as
well as excellent interpretive displays of all of the coastal marine communities can be seen at the Texas State Aquarium in Corpus Christi.

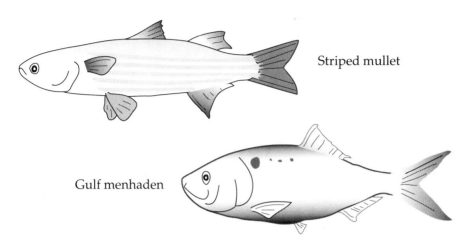

Striped mullet

Gulf menhaden

Table 10. *Fishes That Inhabit Mustang Lake*

Abundant	Common	Occasional
Striped mullet	Bay anchovy	Sheepshead
Sheepshead killifish	Silver jenny	Chain pipefish
Tidewater silverside	Bayou killifish	Black drum
Spot	Silver perch	Naked goby
Gulf killifish	Atlantic croaker	Common jack
Pinfish	Pigfish	Hardhead catfish
Longnose killifish	Gizzard shad	Least puffer
Gulf menhaden		Skipjack
		Atlantic needlefish
		Southern flounder
		Blackcheek tonguefish
		Speckled trout
		Red drum

Well-stocked aquaria are also open to the public at the Marine Institute of the University of Texas at Port Aransas.

During a lull in the traffic of birds at the observation tower, you might gaze across the surface of Mustang Lake and wonder what sorts of fishes swim beneath its turbid water. One way to find out is to drag a seine along the margin. This would miss the larger, quicker species but would get a fair sample of the smaller, more common ones. Table 10 presents an outline, based on actual sampling, of what might be caught; it also suggests what sort of prey the wading-and-spearing birds are after. Although all of the species listed in the table are common enough,

Table 11. *Fishes of Freshwater Ponds*

Sailfin molly	Yellow bullhead
Spotted gar	Bantam sunfish
Warmouth	Sheepshead killifish
Redear sunfish	Rainwater killifish
Carp	Golden topminnow
Mosquito fish	Longear sunfish
Bluegill sunfish	

some kinds are exceptionally numerous. Fully half of each wriggling seine haul would probably be made up of striped mullet and sheepshead killifish; two-thirds would likely be composed of the eight species listed as abundant.

The catch from seining a freshwater pond will be more difficult to predict. Each pond has its own history, water quality, type of vegetation, and assemblage of resident predators. If the site has not dried up in recent years and is not routinely invaded by salt water, then you could expect such fishes as those listed in Table 11.

Killifishes, collectively called mud minnows, constitute a dominant and usually the most abundant group of small fishes in protected shallow waters throughout the Coastal Bend. Adults seldom exceed six inches in length from the tip of their protruding lower jaws to the edge of their squared-off tail fins. They are ecologically important because of their abundance and their position low in the food chain.

On each flood tide, killifishes advance up the shoreline as far as they can, seeking food. Most species are omnivores; they graze the phytoplankton, nibble the bottom-living algae, sort through the muck, snap at amphipods, zap mosquito wigglers, crunch up small snails, slurp up tinier members of their own kind, and avidly tear into bits of carrion. Almost every carnivore gobbles up killifishes when the opportunity arises.

The most remarkable trait of killies is their indestructibility. Of all the local fishes, the killifishes can tolerate (and even thrive on) the greatest extremes in salt concentration, oxygen depletion, and elevated temperature. Although not remarkably cold hardy, they can secrete sugar into their bloodstream to give it an antifreeze quality and then burrow into the bottom mud, where they remain comatose but alive until the water temperature rises. Killies are creatures of shorelines and shallows, and their resultant accessibility to terrestrial predators is another reason they loom large in a diverse assortment of food chains. But these little fishes are also adept at escaping their pursuers, even when seemingly trapped in the shallows. When startled they go scooting off in all directions, leaving little trails of stirred up mud to cover their sudden dive beneath a shell or into a tuft of vegetation.

Seven species of killifishes are resident on the Aransas. Three—the bayou killifish, the golden topminnow, and the rainwater killifish—prefer fresh to slightly brackish water and occur in Thomas Slough and several inland freshwater sites. They move into the bays after heavy freshwater runoff. Another three like distinctly brackish water. The longnose killifish, Gulf killifish, and diamond killifish live in Mustang Lake and in the vegetated shallows around the perimeter of Blackjack Peninsula.

The seventh species of killifish, the sheepshead killifish, is versatile enough to live in every aquatic habitat on the refuge. In a group renowned for its toughness, this is the toughest. If you see an active school of squatty minnows anywhere, they are most likely to be this kind. The shallow tidal pool near the end of the boardwalk, even when reduced to just a fetid puddle, is often aswarm with happy sheepsheads. As the water evaporates the salinity rises to extraordinary levels and the backs of the fish protrude from the ooze. Still they manage. They continue to wriggle valiantly until a raccoon scoops them up or the saline mud finally solidifies around them—tough to the end.

From late March through mid-May, look closely into the pools that constitute Muskgrass Slough, between the middle and outer ridges on the Heron Flats Trail (Mollie Pond and Killifish Pond in Figure 29 in Chapter 14). There male sheepsheads and sailfin mollies will be engaged in setting up breeding territories and in courting females. The peacock-blue backs of the male sheepsheads flash in the sun as the en-

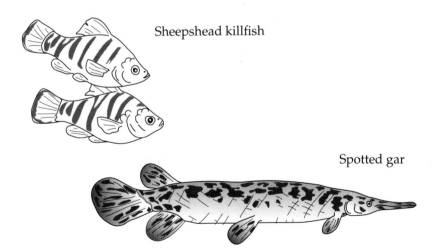

Sheepshead killfish

Spotted gar

ergetic little fish dash about. Male mollies at the peak of mating behavior are less frenzied and even more colorful. They continually sidle
up to each other and erect their large dorsal fins to reveal resplendent
blues, washes of orange, and contrasting rows of black dots. While
watching these fish you may notice the silvery, quick-darting, male
mosquito fish chasing after their own corpulent females in these same
pools. Most visitors pass obliviously by this silent, frantic spectacle.

If you ease up beside Thomas Slough and sit quietly where you can
peer into clear water, you may see one or more species of sunfishes
appear from the submerged vegetation. Bluegill and redear sunfishes
are common and can usually be seen at the alligator observation site
across the road from the WIC. The Big Willow footbridge, at the junc-
ture of the Rail Trail and the Heron Flats Trail, is another good spot.

Consider yourself privileged if one of the neatest predatory fishes on
the refuge slips into view and begins to drift slowly toward a preoccu-
pied sunfish. The spotted gar is well camouflaged with olive-brown
blotches. It is an intriguing fish with strange bony scales, a functional
lung, a mouth full of needle-sharp teeth, and an immensely old ancestry. Hold your breath as the distance between gar and sunfish gradually
shortens. The sunfish may spook, or the gar may get close enough to
make a lightning-fast sidewise snap. Either way you will have had a
revealing experience.

On a larger predatory scale, in Jones Lake, big alligator gars stalk
carp. When the water level drops so they can get at them, alligators feast
on both carp and alligator gars. With a further drop in water level, feral
hogs wade in and chomp up the stranded fish. As the water is gradually
replaced by hard-baked mud, wading birds, raccoons, cottonmouths,
vultures, scavenger beetles, and microbes reroute the dwindling aquatic
resources into the terrestrial food chains.

CHAPTER 13

Invertebrates

In this catchall chapter we include that multitude of creatures without backbones—everything from crayfish to crickets and flies to fritillaries.

Invertebrates are immensely varied in appearance and behavior, rich in numbers of species, countless in numbers of individuals, and mostly small in size. Their huge populations are explained in part by body size and diversity. Small, adaptable bodies make small demands on natural resources—little food, little water, little oxygen, little space. A nook or cranny and a crumb or dewdrop will suffice. Consider how many grasshoppers can live on an acre of ridge-and-swale compared with how many deer are on that same area.

Organisms with the short lifetime that usually goes with small size are compensated by prolific reproduction and rapid development. When a favorable season rolls around, the invertebrates rapidly rise to the occasion. When times get hard, they die wholesale or disappear into dormant stages.

Because they live everywhere and in profusion, invertebrates are involved in practically every aspect of the ecology of the Aransas Refuge. Though only a few species can be ranked as dominant forms, it is the cumulative effect of groups of species that counts—all the crabs, all the beetles, all the spiders, all the ants.

Within these groups there are herbivores, carnivores, omnivores, detritivores, scavengers, and parasites. In many cases the larval stages belong to one feeding category while the adults belong to another—caterpillars and butterflies, for instance. Some kinds filter water; others eat mud; great numbers munch up greenery or suck plant sap. Many invertebrates eat other invertebrates, and a few of them even manage to turn the tables and bring down a backboned creature now and then—a dragonfly larva that catches and consumes a tadpole, for example. Quite a few suck blood, and some act as vectors for disease-producing microorganisms. A few sting. Lots of them fly; many climb; others hop, crawl, or wriggle. Most constitute important fodder, by whatever circuitous loop of the food chain, for the backboned residents on the refuge. Try imagining a food chain that links a cricket with a bobcat, a doodlebug with a red-tailed hawk.

Although the great diversity among invertebrates makes them endlessly fascinating, that same heterogeneity presents a problem: in a general guidebook we can mention only a small fraction of the forms known to occur on the Aransas Refuge. We have chosen those that you are most likely to notice (some perhaps as nuisances) during your visit, a few that are ecologically important, and some that are just downright interesting. Coverage is further limited by touching only lightly on aquatic habitats.

To study the terrestrial invertebrates in more depth, begin with *The Audubon Society Field Guide to North American Insects and Spiders*, by Lorus and Margery Milne. D. J. Borror and R. E. White's *Field Guide to the Insects* is also a good introductory manual. More so than with most animal groups, the overwhelming diversity of kinds of invertebrates makes access to a good picture book necessary for field identification.

Crustaceans

Although these creatures are mostly aquatic in habit, several kinds are frequently observed or leave noticeable evidence of their occurrence. A few constitute significant links between the aquatic and terrestrial food webs.

Of approximately two dozen species of crayfishes known to occur in Texas, only two kinds have been definitely recorded from the Aransas Refuge. One of them, Hedgpeth's crayfish, has been found nowhere else. The southern red crayfish is certainly the most numerous kind on the refuge, but judging from known distributions, at least three other species could be expected on Blackjack Peninsula.

You may not see a southern red crayfish (locally called crawfish) during your visit, but a large population exists. They live in freshwater sloughs and ponds and in scattered burrows that extend down to the water table. Burrow entrances—holes about as big as your index finger, usually rimmed with a platform of mud—can be found around the margins of Jones and Hog lakes and at the edges of roadside ditches. After a good rain you may see southern red crayfish crossing the paved roads.

As you drive the Tour Loop, watch in low-lying grassy areas for crayfish chimneys—vertical tubes four to six inches tall constructed of marble-sized pellets of mud hauled up from extensive burrows. These hardened mud turrets stand out boldly where a swale has been recently burned. Chimneys can be found on the inland fringes of the tidal flats,

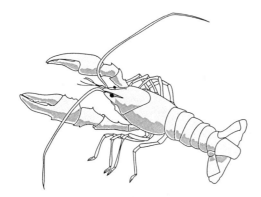

Southern red crayfish

but they do not extend into the saline mud. Holes and loose mud pellets around brackish water are the work of fiddler crabs.

The Southern red crayfish is a keystone species on the Aransas. They are numerous and widespread, occupying the interfaces between water and land and between brackish and fresh water, so they figure in a wide variety of food chains. Although mostly herbivorous, crayfish will eat most small aquatic creatures and also work through detritus, which means they convert a large array of organic materials into animal protoplasm. Virtually every larger animal regards crayfish protoplasm as delicious: fishes, snakes, alligators, raccoons, night-herons, whooping cranes, all actively seek and probe for crayfish. The refuge simply would not be the same without this important crustacean.

The blue crab is one of the ecologically important marine analogs of the crayfish. Although blue crabs must spawn in salt water, juveniles and adults live throughout the brackish-water community and frequently invade freshwater ponds and streams. During wet weather or high tides these crabs readily move overland, so they often populate inland ditches and ponds on Blackjack Peninsula. Wherever they occur they make their presence felt as insatiable omnivores and scavengers.

From early summer into midwinter, there is a steady and plentiful supply of succulent young blue crabs entering the back bays all along the Coastal Bend. They form a staple in the diets of many denizens of the tidal flats. Every bird you see stalking the margin of Mustang Lake would welcome an opportunity to gobble up a tender young blue crab; the same is true for less evident predators—red drum, Gulf saltmarsh snakes, diamondback terrapins, marsh rice rats, raccoons, and coyotes.

The Aransas harbors two common species of fiddler crabs. True to its name, the mud fiddler prefers a muddy substrate and is usually found

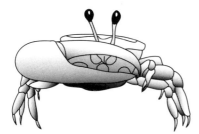

Sand fiddler crab

among stalks of sea ox-eye at the bay's edge. The sand fiddler is partial to wet sand and ranges from the smooth cordgrass margin across the tidal flat. Mud fiddlers are larger and their carapaces are aquamarine; the smaller sand fiddlers are cryptically sand-colored. Both species dig vertical holes and scatter the pellets of excavated material around the entrance. Fiddlers do not build chimneys like crayfish do.

During the warm part of the year you can count on seeing sand fiddler burrows at the end of the boardwalk. At low tide you may see some of the little crabs near their burrows or marching in tight squadrons around the bases of the cordgrass clumps at the edge of the water, busily sifting the sand and mud for organic matter. They leave a scatter of tiny pellets of cleaned sand in their wake. Because they have special chambers for holding water around their gills, fiddlers can spend extended periods on the shoreline and tidal flat. All tidal-flat predators eat them; tiny sand fiddlers are even popped up by Gulf Coast toads or snatched by foraging tiger beetles.

Fiddler crabs live in colonies, and they have interesting social behavior. If you get the chance, observe them with your binoculars and watch the males, perched near their burrow entrances, silently communicating by flicking the oversized pincher. These little semaphores are waved both to keep other males at a distance and to attract a female as a potential mate. If a female shows interest, the male waves more vigorously and begins to bob up and down with excitement. If a male manages to lure a female to the mouth of his burrow, he ducks inside and tries to entice her into his retreat by tapping the wall with his large pincher. At night, when a prospective mate cannot see his waving movements, the male taps a staccato on the rim of his burrow in an attempt to attract her attention. Sand fiddlers are the more demonstrative of the two species, but in both, copulation usually takes place deep within the male's burrow.

To appreciate the importance of fiddlers and other small crustaceans in the diets of creatures on the refuge, you might try dissecting several of the dry regurgitation pellets dropped by birds. (They are clean, dry, and not odorous.) These cylindrical, chalky deposits can usually be found on the ramp to the observation tower, on the boardwalk, and on the bridge over Cattail Slough, where birds often perch. They are composed mostly of flakes of crustacean exoskeletons but also contain identifiable pinchers and other body parts. Carefully picking one apart is a good learning exercise.

In October 1988, in the aftermath of Hurricane Gilbert, a giant land crab was discovered at Hopper's Landing immediately outside the refuge gate. With a carapace width exceeding six inches, this is the largest species of semiterrestrial crab on the Atlantic Coast. More at home among the mangroves in the Caribbean, these crabs rarely occur as far north as South Padre Island. It is exciting to think that there might be a few of these shy nocturnal creatures lurking in burrows among the sea ox-eye thickets bordering the Aransas. The solitary specimen was released in a protected inlet on the refuge.

At low tide, look in the muddy sand along the bayshore off the boardwalk for the many small, volcanolike turrets in all stages of collapse. Each one was constructed by a ghost shrimp, so named for its translucent white color. These burrowing crustaceans, so common across the shallow bay margin and in all brackish pools, are one of the delicacies for which many bird bills probe. Long-billed curlews and marbled godwits are past masters at plucking unwary ghost shrimp from their burrows, and hardhead catfish routinely slurp them out.

The numerous unadorned pinholes in the silty sand between the ghost shrimp burrows are made by several kinds of marine worms (red threadworms and Culver's sandworms are the most common ones), and there are bird bills adept at extracting these slender morsels. Other holes in the mud are made by marine clams, mostly the stout razor, jackknife clam, constricted macoma, and common rangia. At low tide, raccoons are often seen belly-deep in the bay feeling for these bivalves, and at night feral hogs root through the shallows for the same fare. The shorebirds that frequent the wet sand off the end of the boardwalk are searching for them too, each species according to its own taste and ability.

If you continue your bayside walk, stop at a lavender patch of stranded marine algae. Turn it with your toe to uncover a great number of little hopping amphipods, appropriately called beach fleas. Sanderlings, ruddy turnstones, and snowy plovers know how to hustle after amphipods. Try catching and holding a slippery beach flea between your thumb and fingertip to appreciate the dexterity of the feeding birds.

Beach fleas well illustrate the relationship between small body size and large population numbers. If the clumps of these little crustaceans were spread evenly, there would be about twenty individuals per square inch of beach. Consider one hundred yards of beach thirty feet wide, say, from the boardwalk to the Big Tree Trail at medium low tide. That stretch of apparently barren silty sand is home to almost 26 million beach fleas that collectively weigh over two tons! No wonder they attract the birds.

As you move along the beach looking ahead at the strand line, you may spot what appears to be a wave of cockroaches scurrying away from patches of shade cast by driftwood. These are crustaceans akin to pillbugs and aptly named sea roaches. They occasionally wet their gills in salt water, but they live and breed at the water's edge. Like household cockroaches, they are quick and insatiable scavengers.

If you turn over pieces of debris along the strand line (the upper limit of routine high tide), you will surely uncover groups of sowbugs. Like the sea roaches, these animals are relatives of the common pillbug, but when provoked they scurry for cover rather than rolling into a ball. Sowbugs come out at night to feed on decomposing plant and animal matter thrown up by the waves.

Insects

Dragonflies

These fast-flying insects are very common on the Aransas. Adults spend the day cruising through the air or perching on the extreme tips of reeds and branches. Dragonflies are among the most alert and agile of all flying insects. Try catching one, or even getting within arm's reach, and you will prove the point. They hawk after all sorts of flying insects (mosquitoes are favored prey), which they catch with their hairy legs and snip to bits with their strong mouthparts. Some feed on the wing; others return to a favored perch for a leisurely meal.

Male dragonflies patrol territories and do battle with rivals for the attention of females. You may see a pair locked in copulation on the wing. The female will eventually deposit her eggs in the stems of submerged plants. The predaceous aquatic larvae, called naiads (NYE-adds), ambush freshwater insects, minnows, and tadpoles, which they grasp with a remarkable set of flip-out mouthparts. After about a year of aquatic life, the larvae crawl out onto a plant stem and transform into adult dragonflies.

The large brown-spotted yellow-wing, with pale yellow wings shot through with red veins and overlaid with large brown blotches, is one of the most eye-catching of the dragonflies seen around the ponds on the Heron Flats Trail. The most common species on the refuge during the summer is the little saltmarsh dragonfly. The blue-black males and burnt-orange females patrol the tidal flats and swales, often in immense numbers. The huge green darner, with a wingspan of nearly 4½ inches, is the largest dragonfly on the Aransas. Darners pass their larval stage in freshwater ponds, but the strong-flying adults, with emerald-green bodies and turquoise abdomens, range across the entire peninsula and are frequently seen on the tidal flats.

Beetles

Of the welter of beetles on the Aransas, the ones most apt to catch your eye are the several kinds of tiger beetles that scatter before your advancing footsteps along the shoreline or open tidal flat. These fast-moving predators of small insects and amphipods usually run in short spurts but can fly when pressed. Adults are strikingly colored in metallic green or in copper with white-enameled comma marks. The grublike larvae live in vertical burrows in the sand, where they lurk in the openings to snatch passing insects. However, a small wingless wasp seeks out the beetle larva, deftly paralyzes it with a sting, lays an egg on its body, and seals it in its burrow to serve as food for her own larva. Because they are so common, tiger beetles are a significant link in the food web of the tidal flat community. These alert beetles are aware of their surroundings, including each other. You might sit quietly and watch a group of them foraging and settling social disputes among themselves.

Although they are not beetles, there is another group of yet smaller predators that run, hop, and flit across the barren areas on the tidal flat. These little insects are shorebugs, and they behave like pint-sized tiger beetles. They stalk the several species of gnat-sized flies that are so common in their habitat. In their turn, shorebugs are sniped by black-necked stilts and semipalmated plovers.

Butterflies

Butterflies brighten the landscape. They also cross-pollinate flowers in their search for nectar, and of course, they delight visitors. Their caterpillars munch leaves and serve as prey for a variety of insects, spiders, and birds. You can identify quite a few butterflies from your vehicle. Pictures of all species mentioned here are in *The Audubon Society Field Guide to North American Butterflies,* by R. M. Pyle.

A common large black species with blue-green iridescence on the upper surface of the hindwings is the pipevine swallowtail. It dallies over roadside flowers throughout the spring and summer. Its caterpillar, brick red with rows of fleshy, crimson tubercles, feeds on pipevines, from which it absorbs bitter compounds. These substances remain in the adult and render it distasteful to most birds.

When the lavender-flowered thistles and pale blue mistflowers bloom in the spring, the large brown-and-yellow palamedes swallowtails flutter over them in great numbers. The mint-green palamedes caterpillars, which feed almost exclusively on red bay leaves, have a pair of bright orange spots with black centers on their humped thorax. Perhaps these baleful eyespots intimidate some predators.

As summer progresses, eastern tiger swallowtails, eastern black swallowtails, and giant swallowtails appear. The giant swallowtail is the state's largest butterfly, with a wingspan over five inches. Its larva, brownish splotched with beige, bears a striking resemblance to a splatter of bird droppings. If you touch it, the caterpillar will evert two orange horns that release a harmless but unpleasant odor. To witness pure fascination, let a child get the caterpillar to perform.

You may have to wait and observe them during their brief rests to see the distinctive marks of the fast-flitting yellow butterflies common along the roadsides. Among the most abundant are the medium-sized orange sulphur, clouded sulphur, and dogface sulphur, the latter named for the figure silhouetted on its forewings, complete with eye, muzzle, and ear. Look for the larger, all-yellow cloudless giant sulphur and the orangish orange-barred giant sulphur flying high and fast between flowers.

In early spring the white flowers of several wild mustards bring out a cloud of cabbage white butterflies. You might think of this as a pretty example of a natural association, but cabbage whites were unintentionally introduced from Europe over a century ago and have spread across the continent. Watch also for the native checkered whites. By early summer, lazy flutters of great southern whites will be attending the flowers of sea ox-eye on the tidal flats; their larvae munch the succulent leaves of maritime saltwort.

The gulf fritillary, rich russet above with large silver dashes outlined in black on its underwing, is common in summer. Its caterpillar feeds on passion vine. The smaller, tawny brown variegated fritillary is overlaid with an intricate pattern of black lines and spots, and its underwings are not boldly marked.

Hackberry butterflies may invite themselves to your picnic; salad

Pipevine swallowtail

Palamedes swallowtail   Dogface sulphur

dressing is irresistibly attractive to them. Put a daub off to one side and watch the butterfly take a sample with its watchspring tongue.

Of the few butterflies that overwinter as adults, two live on the Aransas. You might see either the red admiral or the buckeye basking in a cold winter sun. Both are bright colored and distinctively patterned. Two other species, the closely related painted lady and American painted lady, are also cold hardy and are occasionally sighted in the wintertime. All four kinds can be expected on the refuge during the warm part of the year too, when they are joined by the West Indian buckeye.

You might suppose that only a serious lepidopterist would be motivated to identify any of the confusing array of little checkered butterflies that flit among the roadside daisies. Yet, with a field guide and a little patience you can distinguish the common species: the silvery crescentspot, bordered patch, Texan crescentspot, and the diminutive pearl crescentspot. These make dainty additions to anyone's life list.

The hairstreaks are a group of small (less than two inches), fast-flying butterflies of particular beauty. Once one stops on a flower it will allow you to approach slowly for a close-up view. On the hindwings are two pairs of hair-thin tails that twiddle constantly. These little butterflies rest with wings folded over their bodies, so you can get a good look at the red, silver, and black tracery that decorates the underside of the hindwing and is used to identify the species. With a picture book in

Flower spider with hairstreak

hand, kneel beside a hairstreak sipping nectar and see if you can distinguish the four common kinds: red-banded, dusky blue, southern, and gray.

One other hairstreak, the great purple, is less common but always claims attention. The underwings of both sexes are purple-gray with red and metallic blue markings; the upper wings of the male are a brilliant, iridescent turquoise, and even his abdomen is showy—blue above and bright red below. The caterpillars of this species feed on mistletoe.

Now and then you will spot a hairstreak resting on a flower in an odd posture. Odder still, it does not fly even when you touch it. Look closely. The little butterfly is probably being held by the head in the clutches of either a bristly flower spider or a squatty ambush bug. With your magnifying glass (which you should bring as faithfully as you bring binoculars) study the floral world of bees, beetles, lacebugs, spiders, butterflies, and caterpillars. You have stumbled upon an unsung fascination of the Aransas—the intricate community of small creatures that live on and within flowers. Indian blankets, thistles, mistflowers, and sunflowers are especially well populated. You may look up to find other visitors curiously watching you, wondering what secret you have discovered.

Most butterflies prefer open sun, but in the shady oak mottes in springtime or after early summer rains, a flutter of little wood satyrs may be startled from the leaf litter; or you may scatter a group of burnt-orange question marks that have been feeding on fermenting mustang grapes. In the fall of a good year you might encounter the zebra longwing, an animated spangle of sunshine wafting slowly through the trailside gloom. Zebras are unique in several ways. They are one of the few butterflies that feed on pollen rather than nectar. Individuals faithfully follow the same foraging paths each day, and they roost in clusters each night.

Monarch butterfly

The Coastal Bend is near the center of one of the two major fly-ways used by monarch butterflies when they migrate across Texas. Migratory monarchs pass across the refuge, northbound in late March, southbound in late October and early November. Sometimes they filter through in unimpressive dozens; other times they arrive by the thousands. Unlike a bird, no individual monarch makes a round-trip from its wintering grounds in Mexico to the northern edge of its summer range in Canada and back again. Eggs are laid, larvae grow, and pupae metamorphose along the way, and several generations transpire during the annual cycle. A marking program has revealed that individual butterflies can move at least one thousand miles along the route. In mild years, a few weather-beaten adult monarchs overwinter on the Aransas.

Although not a close relative, the summer-resident viceroy butterfly resembles the monarch. This is an apparent example of mimicry. Monarch caterpillars pick up foul-tasting chemicals from the milkweeds on which they feed. This repulsive quality is retained by the adult and causes potential bird predators to learn quickly to avoid monarchs. The viceroy also tastes bad (it manufactures its own distasteful ingredient rather than getting it from its diet) and is likewise avoided by most birds. By assuming a common color pattern, both monarch and viceroy benefit from their mutual advertisement of bad taste: a predator that learns to avoid one will probably avoid the other without further tutoring. Check your guide book so you can tell the difference between these two look-alikes.

The queen butterfly, a nonmigratory relative of the monarch, is moderately common on the Aransas throughout the warm part of the year. Although the mahogany-colored adults do not closely resemble the monarch, queen caterpillars do feed on milkweeds, and the species is also distasteful to many birds.

The tiniest butterfly on the Aransas, with a wingspan of barely half an inch, is the western pigmy blue. Aside from a thin white edge, most of the upper surface of the wings is coppery brown, grading into brilliant metallic blue near the body. On the underside, each hind wing bears six iridescent black spots. These tiny butterflies flutter silently over the tidal flats, where they lay their eggs on and sip nectar from the flowers of glasswort plants. If you want to observe pigmy blues, get down on your knees and think small.

The many small to medium-sized butterflies called skippers are recognized by widely spaced antennae terminating in curved knobs. Most kinds of skippers are not easily distinguished, but two common dark species are the funereal duskywing and the common sootywing. A brighter one is the aptly named long-tailed skipper. All three visit a variety of wildflowers.

Snout butterflies, although not migratory like monarchs, do form northbound waves when there has been a good hatch in South Texas. During these outbursts, usually in July or August, snouts pass across the Coastal Bend by the hundreds of thousands daily for a week or more. They are called snouts for their beaklike mouth appendages.

The Aransas Refuge lies close enough to the Rio Grande Valley that in exceptional years one can reasonably hope to catch a glimpse of vagrant tropicals; a malachite, a banded daggerwing, or a crimson-banded black would make anyone's visit a smashing success.

Moths

The Aransas supports a rich fauna of moths, with larvae and adults involved in many ecological relationships: high-flying adults are among the staples for nighthawks and bats, many larvae are caught by wasps for feeding to their own developing offspring, and small birds search out both adults and larvae. But because moths are mainly night fliers, we shall mention only some caterpillars and a few adults that might catch your attention.

At one time or another you are likely to see a woolly bear caterpillar (named for its bottlebrush covering of black hairs) hustling across the road; in some years they become a nuisance. The commonest one, the saltmarsh caterpillar, is not, as its name implies, restricted to the bay margin but rather feeds on a variety of plants throughout the ridge-and-swale community. It metamorphoses into a furry-bodied white moth with a two-inch wingspan.

In spring the handrail on the ramp to the observation tower is sometimes alive with fuzzy caterpillars. Depending on the year, they will likely be the larvae of pale tussock moths or of hickory tussock moths. Both kinds spend the winter as eggs in little fuzzy balls attached to twigs and to the ramp railing. The caterpillars emerge in the spring and ravenously munch tree leaves until they metamorphose into small speckle-winged moths. These caterpillars have short white tufts and long black pencils of hair that look like they might sting, but they are only mildly irritating to some people. However, some look-alike moth caterpillars do have stinging hairs, so best observe and not touch.

In the autumn of a good caterpillar year, the live oaks on the Aransas support a dense population of spiny oak-slug moths. The small brownish moths usually go unnoticed, but visitors should be alert for their caterpillars. These inch-long, mint-green creatures slide slowly along branches and railings. They are covered with macelike knobs of stiff white spines, which cause a burning red rash when touched.

You might notice peculiar little cone-shaped pouches covered with sticks hanging from willow branches along the Heron Flats Trail. These are the cases of bagworms; each contains either the caterpillar or the wingless female of a nondescript little moth.

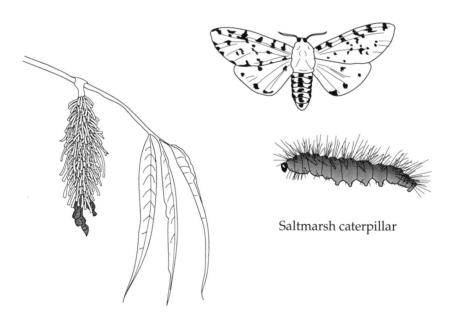

Saltmarsh caterpillar

Bagworm

The refuge hosts a diversity of sphinx moths, but since most are inactive by day, they go unobserved. The group is ecologically important because the strong-flying adults cross-pollinate many kinds of flowering plants, especially mustang grape, peppervine, and evening primrose, and the caterpillars (which all resemble the familiar tomato hornworm, a member of the clan) eat a variety of greenery and are preyed upon by birds. The white-lined sphinx is one of the most common local species. Its narrow, three-inch-long front wings are brown with a beige band from base to tip; the hind wings are orange-pink with dark margins. This moth is often abroad late in the day, hovering above bull thistles, Texas thistles, and coast mistflowers while it probes their depths for nectar with its long tongue. Visitors are often attracted by the heavy whir of the creature's stiff wings, and it is easy to see why some confuse these large insects with hummingbirds. Indeed, they are sometimes called hummingbird moths.

More than one visitor has been startled by what he thought was a bat zooming past his head as he entered the dark concrete archway leading to the ramp at the observation tower. Surprisingly, bats have never been seen at this site, but an occasional black witch moth roosts in the cool gloom. With a wingspan of five inches, this dark tropical species is one of the largest moths on the refuge. Its outsized caterpillars feed on a variety of herbaceous and woody legumes.

Bees and Wasps

You will recognize honeybees and bumblebees on any spring or summer walk. How about leafcutter bees and carpenter bees?

Leaf-cutter bee

Medium-sized leafcutter bees visit flowers to collect pollen, which they carry beneath the abdomen rather than on the hind legs like honeybees. Without realizing it, you may already have noticed evidence of their remarkable habit for provisioning their nests. These bees lay their eggs in holes in the sand lined and partitioned with bits of leaves and stocked with pollen. Pieces are cut from the leaves of various shrubs; each kind of leafcutter bee probably has its own preferred plant. On the Aransas, red bay trees along the Dagger Point Trail are heavily used. Examine some bay branches. If the bees have been at work, half to full circles will be neatly snipped from the edges of leaves; some may have their entire margin disfigured.

You may also see extensive leaf-cutting on rattlepods beside the pier at Jones Lake and along Thomas Slough, but this is beetle work, not bee work. Broad-nosed weevils feed on the edges of the rattlepod leaflets, leaving them scalloped and sometimes nearly defoliating the plants. In late May or early June you can find the little black-and-pink beetles munching away. If you touch a branch the weevils will quickly twirl to the far side or drop off. See if you can catch one of these harmless creatures and hold it to your ear to hear the soft, grinding squeak it makes by rubbing the back of its head against its thorax. Although your beetle will be stridulating in protest, the sound is ordinarily used during courtship.

Eastern carpenter bees lay their eggs in galleries gouged in solid wood and provisioned with pollen. These large, robust bees resemble bumblebees as they zoom around their nest site, buzzing loudly. Such a colony sounds aggressive, but the bees will not sting unless they are handled. Carpenter bees will burrow in dead branches, but they seem to prefer the neat surface of planks, and they always place their entrance hole on the underside of the board. For several years one group of carpenter bees has used the split-rail fence on the middle ridge of the Heron Flats Trail, and another colony is active in the wooden barrier at the alligator observation point on Thomas Slough across from the WIC.

In the spring of 1990, special traps were put up on the refuge to intercept the anticipated arrival of Africanized honeybees moving north through Mexico. In the fall of that year the first colony of this pugnacious strain was discovered in South Texas, and by the summer of 1992, the bees had arrived in Aransas County. They have since pushed north through the state onto the Edwards Plateau; to date, however, the bees have not been documented on the refuge (careful laboratory measurement is necessary to distinguish them from ordinary honeybees). Even if undetected swarms do occur here, the presence of these invaders should cause little concern to visitors to the Aransas. Bees busy on flowers are no hazard, but Africanized honeybees are exceptionally defen-

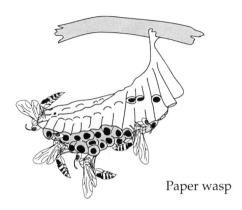

Paper wasp

sive of their hives, so to avoid a confrontation, steer clear of hollow tree limbs or animal burrows buzzing with bees—something you would probably do anyway. Staying on marked trails and roads should assure you of a safe visit.

You may find a palm-sized nest made by paper wasps (locally called yellow jackets) attached by a thin pedicel to a tree branch or beneath an overhang around the refuge buildings. Give the nest arm's-length clearance to avoid arousing the yellow-and-black wasps that are protective of their nest. These natural paper combs are constructed of chewed wood pulp and saliva. What do you suppose paper wasps bring to their developing larvae for food? Hint: if you missed the comment, reread the preceding section on moths.

At least one kind of hornet occurs on the Aransas. In 1985, a volleyball-sized nest was discovered beneath a clump of Gulf cordgrass on the Heron Flats Trail. In 1992, an aggregation of hornets was discovered sipping fluid from the decomposing body of a cottonmouth moccasin.

As you head for the base of the ramp to the observation tower, look up at the ceiling of the concrete archway. The fist-sized blobs of dried mud are the work of the yellow-and-black mud dauber, a thin-waisted wasp. A second, less common wasp, the organ-pipe mud dauber, constructs distinctive parallel columns of mud cells. Finally, a third species, the blue mud dauber, usurps the mud cells built by the yellow-and-black dauber. The energy required to haul so much mud is amazing enough. Just as remarkable is the provisioning of each of the several cells of every mud nest with at least a dozen paralyzed spiders to serve as food for a wasp larva. That means there are a lot of spiders entombed above your head.

In late summer, golden digger wasps excavate their burrows on the sandy barrens in the tidal-flat community. At the bottom of a vertical tunnel the adult wasp, nearly an inch long, with black-tipped orange abdomen, constructs one or more chambers. She provisions each chamber with several green saltmarsh katydids that she has caught in the surrounding grass and paralyzed with her sting. Then she lays one egg and seals the compartment. The larva feeds on the katydids, pupates, metamorphoses, and eventually digs its way to the surface.

Galls are abnormal plant growths caused by the introduction of a chemical substance. Several groups of tiny insects lay their eggs in plant tissue and then induce the formation of these peculiar growths so their larvae will be protected and can feed on the gall tissue. From the viewpoint of the plant, the formation of hardened gall tissue may be a means of restricting deeper invasion by the parasites.

The oak gall wasp leaves abundant evidence of its presence in the marble-sized, black woody galls on live oak trees. Once the wasp larva metamorphoses and gnaws its way out through a round exit hole, the durable gall may become the home of small spiders or of specialized species of carpenter ants.

Another tiny wasp causes the small, fuzzy beige tufts beneath live oak leaves called woolly leaf galls; yet another species stimulates the formation of many spherical red currant galls about ⅜ of an inch in diameter underneath oak leaves. Both types of galls can be seen as you ascend through the oak branches on the ramp to the observation tower.

The only other plant gall that is abundant enough on the refuge to be noticeable is not caused by a wasp, but it is convenient to mention it here. Almost every red bay tree has some abnormally curled leaves with tubular, blisterlike swellings on the margins. The enlargements are galls; they are usually dusty lavender in the springtime and turn brown in late summer. If you slice open a fresh one and peer inside with your hand magnifier, you can make out, among shed exoskeletons and flakes of white wax, a cluster of tiny cottony white insects, the developing nymphs of jumping plant lice. Eventually a slit develops in the gall to allow the adults, which resemble miniature cicadas, to emerge. Perhaps because most of the leaves on any one tree remain unparasitized, these sap-sucking insects seem to cause no lasting damage to their host.

Flies

Flies of one kind or another are everywhere you look: houseflies attend your picnic; gnats persistently attempt to sip moisture from the corners of your eyes; March flies, popularly called lovebugs, smudge your windshield; flotillas of shore flies skitter along the muddy edges of brackish tidepools; picture-winged flies display their metallic bodies and wave their ornamented wings in ecstatic courtship displays; dance flies and long-legged flies pounce upon their pint-sized kin; and robber flies play a falconlike role, snatching all types of flying insects in midair and then retiring to a favorite perch to suck their prey dry. But for all visitors, all personnel, and most wildlife there is only one important fly on the Aransas National Wildlife Refuge—the mosquito. Indeed, just as Aransas whoopers are famous, so Aransas skeeters are notorious; visitors flock to the former and flee the latter.

That importance, of course, is from our point of view; mosquitoes are arch nuisances and potential carriers of disease. But they are ecologically significant. Their teeming aquatic larvae transform microbes, protozoa, algae, and suspended detritus into animal protein to be consumed by the next higher links in the food chain: dragonfly nymphs, predatory water bugs and beetles, killifishes, least sandpipers, and lesser yellowlegs. Many creatures, from spiders and dragonflies to frogs and birds, consume the flying adults. A lot of metabolic machinery on the refuge is fueled by mosquito calories.

Whatever you may think of them, you cannot ignore mosquitoes. At peak seasons the impact of hordes of blood-hungry mosquitoes is enough to alter the habits of both wildlife and men. Deer, birds (especially unprotected nestlings and birds on the roost), and even herptiles engage in whatever escape behavior they can to avoid the misery of repeated mosquito bites. Visitors use chemical sprays and protective clothing or plan to avoid predictable outbreaks and favored feeding times. For the unwary or the unbelieving, what might have been a pleasant hour's ramble along the Heron Flats Trail can degrade into a ten-minute, leg-slapping dash for the car.

At least a few mosquitoes are active during every month of the year on the Aransas. Numbers drop precipitously in January and February but resurge with the earliest spring warm-up and remain bothersome until the first strong northers in late November and early December. Throughout the long mosquito season, day to day abundance depends on rainfall. Wet years spawn unsuppressed multitudes; a string of dry months fosters a truce, immediately broken at the first rain shower or unusually high tide. Strong breezes inhibit the flying adults; calms set them loose in force. Even on windy days, mosquitoes are quick to emerge from disturbed grass and find the downwind side of an exposed patch of skin.

At times it seems that every one of Texas' 76 species of mosquitoes must be on the Aransas Refuge. Judging from mild winters, convenient

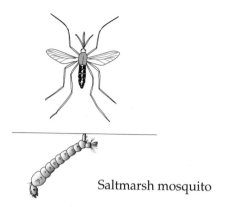

Saltmarsh mosquito

sloughs, exposure to Gulf weather systems, and proximity to the tropics, the local mosquito fauna should be diverse, but no systematic survey has been made. Nevertheless, the majority of the ones that whine around visitors and wildlife belong to just three species: the black and the golden saltmarsh mosquitoes, which breed in brackish water, and the purple rain mosquito, which breeds in fresh water. This trio is quite enough to cause misery for all concerned.

The saltmarsh mosquito you swat at today may well have begun a quiescent life six months previously as one of the fertilized eggs sprinkled across dry depressions in the tidal flats and swales—places that catch temporary puddles after rain showers or high tides. The embryos develop rapidly until they are ready to hatch; then they abruptly cease all activity and wait.

The eggs with their full-term embryos may lie dormant in the soil for weeks. This is how most survive the winter months. Finally, inevitably, the water comes. The puddle fills, and within ten minutes active little mosquito wigglers have popped from their eggshells and begun to feed. In only three to four days, the larvae develop to pupae, and two days later, the pupae metamorphose.

With all the water in the bays and lakes, why do saltmarsh mosquitoes use ephemeral puddles? Their big reward is avoidance of predatory killifish and mosquito fish. Another is a rich source of food confined in a quiet cache free from competition. The price they must pay is that they have to hurry. The wigglers' lives are a race against evaporation. However, they do have a safety net; some of the eggs do not hatch on cue. If the puddle disappears too rapidly, these tardy eggs will have a chance to hatch when the puddle fills the next time. And there is always security in numbers. A square foot of damp marsh sod might be covered with ten thousand speck-like saltmarsh mosquito eggs. In a favorable week hundreds of millions of pupae may metamorphose while millions of eggs still lie in waiting. Dislike them if you will, but you must grudgingly admire mosquitoes for their prodigality in a stressful habitat.

You can usually observe one part of this exaggerated determination to survive by inspecting the small puddles of brackish water left beneath the boardwalk by the last high tide. Many of these will contain swirling black clouds of saltmarsh mosquito larvae and pupae (respectively called wigglers and tumblers for their characteristic movements) in such concentrations that you can easily scoop up a palmful. Least sandpipers, shorebugs, and tiger beetles feast on such congested masses. Even Gulf Coast ribbon snakes purposefully swim through them with their mouths widely gaped.

Smaller depressions will have lost most of their water to evaporation and be reduced to a helpless, quivering amalgam of dark protoplasm. Imported red fire ants are quick to discover this stranded bounty, and their lines of workers resemble animated conveyor belts as they haul the dying larvae to their underground chambers. Yet slighter depressions are lined with a thin black crust composed of the dehydrated remains of mosquito larvae that lost the grim race with desiccation. Marsh crabs and ground beetles will munch at the mummified peel. Most visitors clump along the boardwalk completely oblivious to this life and death struggle being played out beneath their feet.

Five to six days after rain or tide, in brackish pools and grassy puddles all across the refuge, hordes of adult saltmarsh mosquitoes split their floating pupal cases, test their wings, and fly off to shady spots to harden their new cuticles. After a day of rest the newly emerged mosquitoes are hungry. Sugar from flower nectar gives them energy. They mate. Soon the females, swelling with eggs, are possessed with the urge to have a blood meal. Protein from blood is necessary for viable eggs.

So, we have a blood-famished female saltmarsh mosquito clinging to a blade of Gulf cordgrass on the edge of the Heron Flats Trail, and here you come. She prefers to fly at dusk or dawn, but startled from rest in midafternoon, she rouses to the opportunity. She can see you dimly against the sky as she rises and circles downwind. Her antennae bring her vital information—a waft of your carbon dioxide–laden breath, a stream of warm moist air from your active body—and she zigzags quickly upwind following your spoor.

Guided now by eye, the mosquito closes in. The odor of lactic acid from your pores leads her to a patch of exposed skin, where she settles gently. If she is lucky, her proboscis will probe to a capillary without stimulating a pain receptor, and she will gorge in twenty seconds and fly heavily away. If she is unlucky you will spook her or swat her.

If things go well for her, two days after her encounter with you, the mosquito will be scattering components of your blood, neatly encapsulated in little spindle-shaped eggshells, across the tidal flat. Then the waiting begins again.

If you believe the only good mosquito is a dead one, you should learn about the largest, loudest, fiercest-looking mosquito on the Aransas Refuge. It has no common name, so we must refer to it by its tongue-twisting scientific name: *Toxorhynchites rutilis* (Tox-oh-rin-KITE-eez ROOT-i-lis). This beautiful insect, resplendently decked in metallic blues, violets, and coppers, is uncommon, but it sometimes wanders into automobiles and gets trapped inside the windshield. Will you refrain from swatting it when you learn that it never sucks blood and that its larvae feed only on other mosquito larvae?

Grasshoppers and Their Kin

This is a large and important group of herbivores, a staple in the diets of many vertebrates, arachnids, and other insects. The ecological associations of its members are diverse, and most kinds are seasonally abundant.

On any summertime walk, watch for flashes of bright color as grasshoppers take to the air, and notice how these insects abruptly disappear when they fold their wings and crash-land. On sunny stretches of the Heron Flats Trail each footstep may startle the little sulphur-winged grasshopper into crackly-winged flight. The golden-yellow wings of the

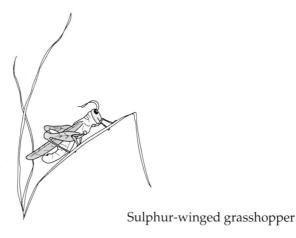

Sulphur-winged grasshopper

mottled sand grasshopper and the delicate orange ones of Caudell's long-horned grasshopper bear a contrasting black band near the tip.

In the tall grass around the Tour Loop the large Carolina grasshoppers and two species of high-flying bird grasshoppers occur. The latter overwinter as adults and are important food items for American kestrels. Many of the grasshoppers of the road- and trailsides belong to the large group called spur-throated grasshoppers.

The Aransas lies in the transition zone between a western and an eastern species of toothpick grasshopper. These insects live in clumps of tall bunchgrasses that cover the ridge-and-swale community. When a flying individual alights in the grass it instantly aligns its body parallel to the stems and completes its camouflage by stiffly stretching its sharp-pointed antennae forward in line with the body. In this posture the creature merits its curious name.

Grasshoppers have quite an array of social mannerisms. Courting males are particularly interesting. Some raise their legs or wings to display bright colors; others produce subtle squeaks, clicks, and chatters. A few engage in brief shuffling dances. Stand still and eavesdrop on them.

As you walk in shaded or moist areas, keep an ear cocked. Many kinds of mostly green and arboreal katydids and grasshoppers with long, hairlike antennae make sounds by day and by night. Most kinds are easier to hear than to see.

Round-winged katydids produce a series of soft "tsips." Angular-winged katydids click. At dusk, leaf katydids high in the live oaks begin their repetitious stuttering. Because of a ventriloquial quality, it may be difficult to locate the penetrating buzz of the cone-headed grasshopper perched in tall grass. All of these songsters are males, and their persistent stridulations are intended to attract mates. The aggregate pandemonium of sound on a summer evening is only part of their output; many species emit frequencies above our hearing threshold.

The daytime call of saltmarsh katydids is a measured sequence of soft trills and clicks. Don't confuse this subtle sound from the depths of cordgrass clumps with the nearly continuous, often overwhelming, dry rasping trills of the dogday cicadas grinding out of the willows along Thomas Slough.

At night the crickets tune up: tree crickets in the willows, field crickets on the ground, and a range of singing cousins in between.

Many visitors see but few appreciate the widespread evidence of the peculiar mole cricket. These burrowing insects leave little meandering ridges in moist soil at the edges of freshwater ponds and roadside ditches. If you move quietly you may hear a mole cricket producing its subdued, groaning chirp from the security of its burrow. Not one per-

Mole cricket

son in a thousand even knows these little creatures exist, yet they are common on the Aransas.

Ants

These insects, abundant in every community type, are ecologically significant as consumers—they feed on everything from honeydew and nectar to insects and carrion as well as harvesting greenery, fruit pulp, and seeds. They are eaten by a variety of animals; narrow-mouthed toads, prairie racerunners, horned lizards, blind snakes, and armadillos are especially fond of them.

The Coastal Bend is rich in ant species, but no one has formally surveyed the kinds on the refuge. Loose sand is poor substrate for tunneling, and level land is subject to swamping and saltwater washover. The Aransas offers few suitable microhabitats—no rocks, no ledges, no cracks, few logs; yet there are plenty of ants, and you can hardly fail to notice some either interesting or pestiferous ones.

Everyone knows that ants love picnics. Is that why the picnic area harbors as great an array of ant species as anywhere on the refuge? Probably not. The ants are more likely attracted by the elevated ground, a tight mixture of shell and sand, and the convenient access to grasses, weeds, and shrubs. Your picnic crumbs are simply an added attraction for them. It is a fact, however, that most of the kinds of ants that we shall mention can be found within a few minutes' stroll from the picnic area.

Harvester ants, the most conspicuous of the seed eaters, are what most people call red ants. A more affectionate nickname is "pogo," a shortened version of their Latin epithet (*Pogonomyrmex*). An individual harvester ant is not long-lived, but a colony may last for years, so nest sites in favorable spots are semipermanent. There are several pogo mounds near the picnic area, another on the slope beside the WIC, and a venerable one at Station 22 midway along the Heron Flats Trail.

Pogos are large enough to be observed from a discreet distance with binoculars. Watch the constant streams of workers hustling along broad pathways out into the grass and back to the nest with seeds to be stored in underground chambers. Continual busy excavating, hauling, scraping, clipping, and grooming goes on even in winter, and this keeps the mound neatly paved with small particles and a wide circle around it free of greenery. Because some of the seeds they discard are still viable, and because the activity of the ants changes the soil texture, the plants growing around the margin of a pogo nest are usually different from those nearby. Maybe you can spot a red-and-yellow assassin bug perched head-down on a weed waiting to reach down and snatch up one hapless pogo from a passing column.

Although pogos are rather docile ants, they can sting, and their venom packs a wallop that is ranked among the most potent in their clan. Stand prudently aside to make your observations, and keep the children off the mound and ant trails.

Look for a second, slimmer species of harvester ant hurrying across the hot sand at the head of the Dagger Point Trail. These ants prefer deep loose sand and do not make a mound at the nest entrance.

Check the mowed roadside on the slope just north of the picnic area for a veritable ant city. The dozen or more tilted craters of excavated sand pellets are the work of a colony of Texas leaf-cutter ants. Other such cities are established along the Big Tree Trail and at the ramp leading to the observation tower. Most of these sites have been in continuous occupation since the refuge was established over half a century ago.

Leaf-cutters look rather like long-legged pogos. They are most active at night, but they work on overcast days and even in sunshine in the spring when new leaves are growing. Workers climb into a variety of shrubs (yaupon is a favorite) to snip fresh greenery and early fruits. They also clip the tiny flowers of live oaks and occasionally gather up fecal pellets dropped by caterpillars that have fed on live oak leaves. This latter type of activity, rather common in nature, is appropriately termed "second harvest."

Long columns of workers protected by a phalanx of large soldiers carry the plant bits deep into the nest, where they are finely minced and spread out in carefully tended chambers. In this meticulously manicured subterranean garden a special fungus grows. The ant colony feeds on the fruiting bodies of this fungus. When a new queen sets out

Texas leaf-cutter ant

she tucks a pellet of the vital fungus into a special cavity in her mouth as seed-stock for the garden of a new colony.

An unseen but fascinating microcommunity haunts the labyrinth of fungal gardens, detritus heaps, brood chambers, and twisting galleries within a busy leaf-cutter mound that may descend more than twenty feet down in the sandy soil. Here, in the perpetual dark, miniature beetles, roaches, silverfish, and crickets live out their lives; the eyeless larvae of minuscule flies and wasps squirm through the debris; near-microscopic mites stalk the passageways; and seething masses of nematode worms and bacteria writhe through the accumulated offal. One species of phorid fly parasitizes the ants. The gnat-sized adult flies hover over the nest entrance or cruise along the foraging trails and suddenly dart down to lay an egg behind an ant's head. The resulting maggot develops inside the ant's head capsule and eventually kills its host. A diminutive cockroach that hitchhikes on the backs of worker ants and a tiny milichiid fly that clings to transported leaf bits to gain entrance into the nest both feed on the fungus garden.

Although you will probably not see any of the small creatures that live within the leaf-cutter nests, you can observe foraging workers and soldiers if they are active. Follow a trail until you discover where the ants are snipping some resource. Does each ant cut and carry, or do individuals have specialized tasks? Incidentally, leaf-cutters are rather mild-mannered. Although a soldier can pinch with its mandibles, these ants do not sting.

Here and there in the grassy expanse between the picnic site and the bay, you can find the shoetop-high craters of the widespread pyramid ant. The insects are just an eighth of an inch long, orange tinted and transparent. Because this species can maintain its nest in shifting sand, it is also common along the Dagger Point Trail and on open sandy terrain across the ridge-and-swale community. The long-legged worker ants move easily over the sliding substrate as they hurry about in search of caterpillars and other soft-bodied insects; they are even known to raid the brood stock of other kinds of ants. Pyramid ants also sip plant sap and nectar (sometimes at second hand, lapping the sweet exudate from aphids), and they will tank up on any sweet liquid spilled at a picnic table. Perhaps because they have an advantage in the dry sand, this is one of the few species of native ants that can hold its own against an invasion of the imported red fire ant. Pyramid ants do not sting.

Sooner or later everyone who goes outdoors in the Coastal Bend runs afoul of fire ants. Most aggressive is the imported red fire ant, a native of Brazil that invaded the refuge in the sixties. However, two native species—the tropical fire ant and southern fire ant—are equally defensive of their nests. Beware of low, irregular earthen domes scattered abundantly along all trailsides and roadsides. One encounter will serve as a lifelong lesson in awareness. The burning sensation is immediate when a fire ant pinches up a bit of skin with its mandibles and plunges in its stinger. If the sting is from an imported red fire ant, a pustule usually appears the next day. This may become infected if scratched, and one person in a hundred develops clinical hypersensitivity to the stings.

Fire ants feed on live and dead insect larvae, soft-bodied adult insects, spiders, centipedes, pillbugs, earthworms, whatever they encounter and can overcome. Although they do not have a sweet tooth, these ants are attracted to oils and tissue fluids, and they quickly find freshly killed creatures. To survive hard times, they will even eat their own brood. Although accounts are often exaggerated, fire ants will occasionally attack pipping eggs and unfeathered young birds. They can be a menace in congested nesting bird colonies on the offshore islands. Either by direct aggression or indirect competition for resources, the imported red fire ant usually causes the reduction or local extinction of most native species of ants with which it comes in contact; the resulting decrease in species diversity must send ripples through the fabric of the affected communities.

Several kinds of ants live in the spherical woody galls that adorn the branches of live oak trees. (The wasp that induces the galls was mentioned earlier.) One species of gall ant occupies several kinds of plant crevices including galls, but the cork-headed ant is adapted especially to living in spherical oak galls. In a few members of the colony, the head is shaped like a bottle cork, and one of these ants dutifully plugs the single entrance hole in the gall until a sister ant, returning to the nest,

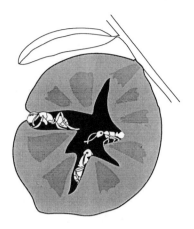

Cork-headed ant

twiddles the corked head with her antennae, bidding the animated portal to open.

The Aransas Refuge even has one species of army ant that sends out columns of eyeless but efficient soldiers to raid the nests of other ants, including those of fire ants. This retiring species does not wreak the same wholesale havoc as its more famous tropical cousins.

Spiders and Their Kin

The most abundant and diversified group of predators on the Aransas is the spiders. On a foggy spring morning, the omnipresence of moisture-laden spiderwebs spread over the grass and adorning shrubs, trees, and weed stalks suggests their abundance. The webs represent only a fraction of the spiders in the area; many spiders build webs out of sight or too small to notice, and others make no web at all.

Sample the treetops, the tidal flat, or the roadside—you will find spiders everywhere. A few sweeps with an insect net or a sift through a handful of leaf litter will have the same result: almost as many tiny spiders as insects. On a breezy afternoon in the spring newly hatched spiderlings disperse by riding delicate strands of silk hundreds of feet into the air. Biologists speak of the feat as ballooning.

All spiders are carnivores, and insects are their principal prey. The collective impact of hundreds of thousands of hungry spiders forges one of the most significant links in the food web on the Aransas. In their turn, spiders are preyed upon by everything from praying mantids, mud dauber wasps, and other spiders to toads, birds, and armadillos.

When a creature finds a new and successful means of making a living (as a spider using webbing), many variations on the same theme soon evolve. The resulting diversification is called *adaptive radiation*—related species pursuing the same essential lifestyle, each in a slightly different way. Recognizing adaptive radiation when you see it is both instructive and fun. The varied ways that spiders use to bring down their prey offer a classic opportunity. Anytime you see a spider during your visit, try to classify its feeding style. Most ground-living species are wandering hunters; they pounce and grapple without resorting to a web. Jumping spiders leap and grab among the plant stems. Flower spiders rely on an ambush strategy. Then there are the web makers: vertical webs, horizontal webs, funnel webs, sheet webs, domed webs, maze webs, and many more. Each web type is designed to capture insects with certain habits. Observe, speculate, and enjoy as you walk.

On a morning with fog or heavy dew the most common medium-sized vertical orb webs that glisten on the weed tops are made by star-bellied spiders and hump-backed orb weavers. In the shrubbery the clusters of peculiar webs resembling inverted bowls are made by basilica spiders. Grass spiders deck the roadsides and short-grass meadows with their handkerchief-sized horizontal sheet webs. On the stalks of smooth cordgrass at the end of the boardwalk, elongate stilt spiders spin their webs to catch dance flies and mosquitoes.

In the summertime you will see large vertical orb webs with a zigzag white zipper in the center strung high in the tops of tall weeds and shrubs. These are spun by black-and-yellow garden spiders. The related banded garden spiders spin a similar, smaller web nearer the ground. It is thought that the purpose of the zipper is to alert small birds, which might otherwise plunge into the web and destroy it.

Watch for spiderwebs in the shade along the first part of the Heron Flats Trail. Here one of the prettiest spiders on the refuge spins her snare. The orchard spider is richly colored in red, yellow, and bright silver. The grotesque spiny-bellied orb weaver and arrow-bellied orb weaver also string webs in the trailside shrubbery. Each has long spines on its enameled abdomen. The curious little caudate orb weaver builds a web at knee level. In the center it fixes a jumble of debris where it sits quietly, camouflaged. Poke a finger at the litter, and the spider will forego its ruse and drop to the ground.

Although the population comes and goes depending upon the severity of the preceding winter, in some years the large webs of the subtropical golden-silk spider are common on shady trails. These webs are made of strong, sticky yellow silk, and several of the hairy-legged female spiders commonly string their orbs next to each other so that it is difficult for a visitor to pass. See if you can duck or dodge and leave the spiders undisturbed.

Black-and-yellow garden spider

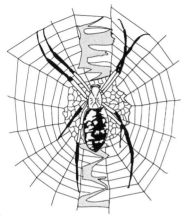

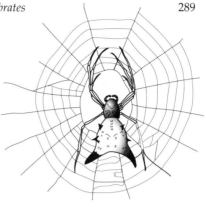

Spiny-bellied orb weaver

Of the spiders that do not capture prey in a web, the most common are wolf spiders. You will see many of these ground dwellers at the inner edge of the tidal flat and throughout the grassland, moving around searching for insects to pounce upon. At night their eyes glow like green gems in the beam of a flashlight. Burrowing wolf spiders live in deep tunnels excavated in the sand in the oak-bay forest community; they snatch small critters that happen past their burrow entrance. Sheet web burrowing wolf spiders dash out of their tunnels to snatch up grasshoppers and crickets that land on the small flat web laid outside the burrow opening.

Although tarantulas have not been documented from the mainland portion of the refuge, the area is within their broad range in Texas, and these large, hairy spiders must surely inhabit the shell ridges and clay soils. They have been seen in the chaparral community on Matagorda Island and probably occur in comparable habitat on the Tatton Unit. Tarantulas live in burrows, from which they make brief sorties to catch passing crickets, grasshoppers, and small snakes and lizards. One of the principal enemies of these large spiders is the tarantula hawk. This large wasp, with a gun-metal-blue body and orange wings, paralyzes the tarantula with a sting, lays an egg on the body, and seals it into a burrow. You are most likely to see a tarantula crossing the road on an early summer evening, when the males emerge in force to seek out the burrows of receptive females.

Trapdoor spiders are one of the most secretive invertebrates on the Aransas. This fat-bodied species is almost never observed unless flushed from its burrow by heavy rains. The nearly invisible entrance to the spider's burrow is artfully closed with a thin wafer of webbing, hinged on one edge and encrusted with sand. When vibrations tell it an insect

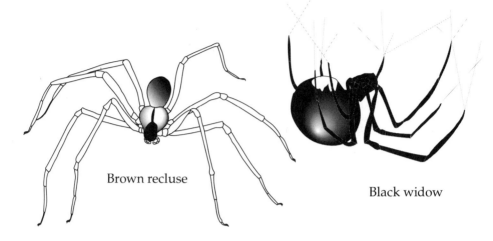

Brown recluse

Black widow

is nearby, the spider pops up the lid, grabs its prey, and reseals the entrance—all in the blink of an eye.

Often colored to blend with their surroundings, flower spiders crouch in blossoms to ambush insects attracted there. The green lynx spider lurks in the foliage with the same purpose.

The emerald-jawed jumping spider is the largest and most often observed member of its clan on the refuge. This is a stocky, hairy black spider with white markings on its abdomen and metallic-green mouthparts. These arachnids commonly live on prickly pear pads, and you may notice their cottony retreats nestled among the thorns.

Two species of North American spiders are dangerously poisonous to man. Both of them catch prey in messy tangles of web spun across crevices and amid plant litter. Both occur on the Aransas, but they live secretive, retiring lives and are not likely to be encountered on a routine visit.

The black widow is common beneath logs and in cracks on standing stumps. The shiny black female has long thin legs, a bulbous abdomen, and a distinctive red hourglass mark on the belly. Although these spiders usually snare insects, one was observed to catch and overpower a newly metamorphosed Gulf Coast toad.

The brown recluse is only occasionally encountered, mostly in surface litter and abandoned dwellings or outbuildings. This medium-sized, long-legged brown spider is rather plain. The slightly darker brown, violin-shaped mark on its back that is supposed to distinguish it is not nearly so clear as the red hourglass of the black widow. Because of the mark, this is also known as a fiddle-backed spider.

Only one species of scorpion has been recorded from the Aransas. It is moderately common beneath surface debris throughout the dry inland areas and along the strand line at the edge of the bay. It is a predator on any small invertebrates that share its sheltered habitat.

With a heavy population of wildlife and a dense, moist vegetative cover, it is not surprising that the refuge harbors several species of ticks. The lone star tick, Gulf Coast tick, and black-legged deer tick are the most common kinds. Biologists refer to all three as three-host parasites. Larvae often infest ground-living birds, especially eastern meadowlarks and bobwhite quail (lone star tick larvae have been recorded on forty species of birds); nymphs seek out small mammals such as cotton rats and cottontail rabbits; and the adults shift to larger mammals: feral hogs, raccoons, and white-tailed deer. Both lone star and Gulf Coast ticks readily parasitize man, and deer ticks sometimes transfer to hunters who are skinning their kill. You may pick up an adult tick during a walk, and if you should brush against the wrong leaf, you may have the demoralizing experience of acquiring a load of several hundred seed ticks (larval ticks). Rid yourself of the parasites by rubbing them with a palmful of sand and consider the experience a part of being outdoors.

You may be aware that two relatively rare tick-borne bacterial diseases, Rocky Mountain spotted fever and Lyme disease, are occasionally reported in Texas. Neither has been definitely documented on the Aransas Refuge, although the lone star tick is known to harbor the infective microorganisms and the deer tick is a suspected vector. Prudently staying on marked trails and prompt search and removal of ticks after your outing should assure you of a safe visit.

If you sit in or walk through tall grass you can anticipate an infesta-

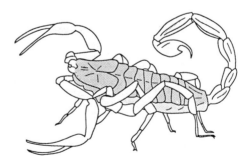

Scorpion

Lone star tick

tion of another pestiferous arachnid—the chigger mite. A soap-and-water scrub after your outing may prevent a bout of itching from these annoying "red bugs."

Many other kinds of invertebrates live on the refuge, from doodle-bugs to earthworms and centipedes to land snails. If you keep alert for them, every walk can become an adventure.

CHAPTER 14

Woody Plants

Most people realize that plants constitute the critical producer level of the food web. Through photosynthesis, green things tap the energy in sunshine and with it manufacture the life-stuff upon which they and ultimately all animals depend. Plants also produce oxygen, provide shade and shelter, hold soil, and influence rainfall and wind currents. In addition, plants have their own lifestyles, secrets, and beauty that make them worthy of attention.

More than 1,500 kinds of native vascular plants grow in the Coastal Bend. The refuge file currently lists about 850 species, and it is continually being adjusted and expanded. Of those, we mention in this and the following chapter only a few conspicuous and ecologically important kinds. Chapter 8 covers those alien plants that were deliberately introduced. The spontaneous appearances of exotic weeds, grasses, and forbs, even those recognizably due to human activity, are too frequent and widespread for more than passing comment.

We have used the accepted common name from botanical texts to refer to each kind of plant; sometimes popular local names are mentioned as well. The formal Latin designation of each species mentioned is given in Appendix D.

To indicate areas where various plants can be located on the refuge, we frequently refer to the biotic communities described in Chapter 3. On the Heron Flats Trail some individual sites are marked with numbered posts (shown in Figure 29) to match the commentary in a trail brochure available at the WIC. Where appropriate, we have referred to those station numbers to direct you to a particular plant. Flowering times for trees, shrubs, and vines on the Heron Flats Trail are presented in Appendix C.

None of the many illustrated books about woody plants deals specifically with those of the Texas Coastal Bend, but for the trees we recommend *Trees of North America*, by C. Frank Brockman; *Texas Trees: A Friendly Guide*, by Paul W. Cox and Patty Leslie; and *A Field Guide to Texas Trees*, by Benny J. Simpson. The single best reference to all of the

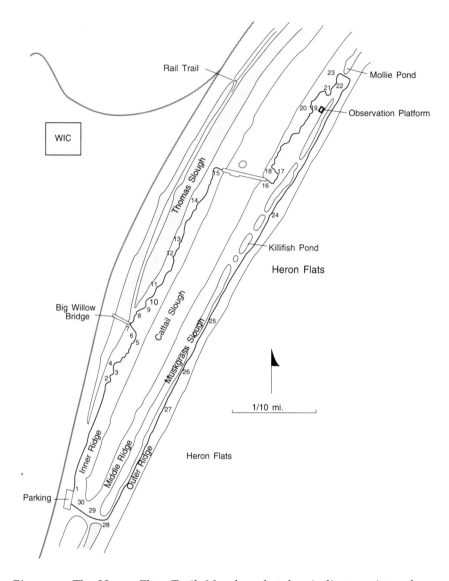

Figure 29. The Heron Flats Trail. Numbered stakes indicate points of interest detailed in a brochure available at the WIC.

vascular plants of the region is *Flora of the Texas Coastal Bend*, by Fred B. Jones, but this work is sparsely illustrated and the text is written for the serious botanical enthusiast.

Trees

Loose porous sand, recurrent dry spells, sporadic waterlogging, and occasional washover by the sea combine to limit the Aransas to a meager twenty or so species of native trees. Actually, you can describe 98 percent of the tree cover on the refuge with one three-letter word: oak.

Hands down, the most abundant and important tree on the Aransas National Wildlife Refuge is the live oak. Technically the local live oaks are an intergrading series of hybrids between the plateau live oak, eastern live oak, and sand dunes live oak. Because of their mongrel nature, the local trees vary from tall individuals that cluster in mottes to chesthigh shrubs crowded in dense thickets.

In previous chapters we have frequently mentioned the outstanding value of live oaks to wildlife, largely by way of their bountiful crop of nutritious acorns, and we commented on the problem of controlling the spread of shrubby oaks. We should also pay homage to the critical role of these trees in holding the sand against buffeting by wind and wave. Certainly one of the live oak's most appealing attributes is its innate beauty. Mottes of live oaks with leaning trunks, arching branches, and alluring shade at headquarters and the picnic area; patriarch trees solemnly defying weather and time on the Big Tree Trail; tiers of windpruned copses marching across the ridge-and-swale on the peninsula; picturesque oaks clinging tenaciously to the tip of Dagger Point: these constitute the pleasant backdrop for every Aransas experience.

Growing among the live oaks, laurel oaks can be distinguished by leaf or acorn. Live oak leaves are stiff and leathery, dark green above and silvery green beneath; the columnar acorn gradually tapers to the tip. Leaves of the laurel oak are thinner and pale green both above and below; the short, fat acorn forms a rounded dome. Laurel oaks never attain the venerable, spreading stature of live oaks. Although laurel oaks can be found intermixed with live oaks across most of Blackjack Peninsula, they are especially characteristic of deep sands in the oakbay community. The best place to observe laurel oaks is along the Dagger Point Trail.

Scattered blackjack oaks are recognized by their black, chunky bark and wide, three-lobed leaves. In the fall, the purple and reddish brown dying leaves of blackjacks stand out amid the evergreen live oaks and laurel oaks. Watch for blackjacks in the oak-bay forest to the east of the road between Dagger Point and the observation tower. Several trees

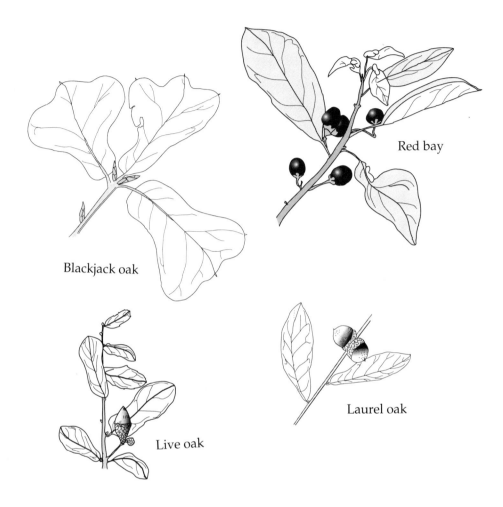

Blackjack oak

Red bay

Live oak

Laurel oak

grow along the paved road between the WIC and the service area at headquarters. The peninsula was named for this oak, probably because of its distinctive appearance rather than its abundance.

There are a few post oaks in the interior of the peninsula, and a small grove of tall laurel-blackjack hybrids is located near the screened shelter at the Youth Environmental Training Area.

When crushed, the lance-shaped, lustrous green leaves of red bay emit a spicy aroma. Every local pioneer housewife kept a jar of dried bay leaves for seasoning. Clusters of small yellow-white flowers bloom in May and develop by autumn into round fruits with a large pit covered by a thin shell of black pulp. Many of the fruits bear the small round exit hole made by a minuscule black seed weevil. Caterpillars of the palamedes swallowtail butterfly feed on the leaves. The swellings on the edges of the leaves are galls caused by jumping plant lice mentioned in Chapter 13. Red bays are at their finest in the oak-bay forest community, best seen along the Dagger Point Trail, and visitors going up the ramp at the observation tower pass through the branches of several specimens. Some of the biggest red bays on the refuge grow in deep sand near the screened shelter in the Youth Environmental Training Area.

Large netleaf hackberries grow beside the observation tower ramp, and smaller ones occur along the Heron Flats Trail (Station 6). Sugar hackberries, with larger, much thinner leaves, are less common (Station 16). Although identification of some trees is difficult because the two species hybridize, if a tree bears pale orange, spherical quarter-inch fruits with a dry rind, little pulp, and a single large seed, it must be a hackberry. Run your finger over the upper surface of a leaf from tip to base; if it feels sandpaper-rough, it is probably a netleaf hackberry. Fox squirrels nibble into green hackberries, and cardinals get what ripe ones they can before waves of robins arrive in the fall to clean out the crop. Feral hogs, javelinas, raccoons, and armadillos pick up fallen fruits.

Numerous black willows (Stations 7 and 15) provide excellent cover, perching sites, and shade along Thomas Slough, and their dense mat of roots helps stabilize the bank.

The only anaqua (ah-NOK-wah) easily accessible to visitors is the lone struggling seedling at Station 4 on the Heron Flats Trail, but healthy mottes of mature trees occur on several upland sites on the western side of Blackjack Peninsula. Their dark, olive-green leaves are perceptibly rough both above and below. Birds, raccoons, and javelina are fond of the juicy yellow fruits, and all sorts of wildlife like to rest in the deep shade cast by a clump of anaquas. Along St. Charles Bay several old house sites are associated with anaqua mottes, and these trees may have been deliberately introduced as windbreaks and shade trees.

Thin mottes of western soapberry are scattered across the uplands on Blackjack Peninsula. Several tall trees grow between the residences and the main road at headquarters. Each compound leaf may be a foot long and is divided into about a dozen pairs of lance-shaped leaflets. In spring the trees display ample panicles of small white flowers. By fall female soapberries bear sprangled clusters of round, translucent, amber-colored fruits, which are toxic and so are avoided by most forms of wildlife. If they are caught by an early frost, soapberries put on a spectacular show of yellow and flame orange before they drop their leaves.

Several species of small trees can be seen on the Heron Flats Trail. Texas persimmon (Station 15) has urn-shaped white flowers in the

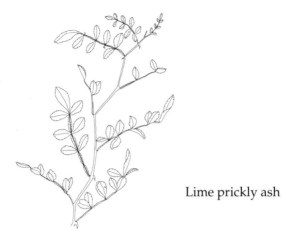

Lime prickly ash

spring, round green fruits by early summer, and edible, fuzzy, black fruits by late summer. Opossums, raccoons, deer, hogs, javelinas, and even armadillos relish juicy persimmons. Although they are messy to peel, you can try a sweet ripe persimmon for yourself. If you like to speculate on how plants get distributed, notice the flat coppery brown persimmon seeds in animal feces along the trail. Texas persimmons do not grow in sand; on the refuge these sturdy little trees are restricted to outcrops of oystershell substrate.

Honey mesquite (muh-SKEET) grows thickly in the mesquite–prickly pear community on the Tatton Unit, and it is also a member of the chaparral community. Mesquites are occasional along the middle and outer ridges of the Heron Flats Trail (Station 18), where you can get a close look at their lacy light-green foliage, cylindrical creamy flower spikes, and woody beige bean pods. The trees are scattered across the ridges and along the Tour Loop in the ridge-and-swale community, and mesquite is the most common species of tree in the open ranchland that you passed through as you approached the refuge. Deer, javelina, coyotes, and rodents crunch up fresh mesquite pods, and scissor-tailed flycatchers, loggerhead shrikes, mourning doves, and mockingbirds frequently choose mesquite branches for nest sites. A variety of insects visit mesquite blossoms (mesquite honey is a local delicacy), and many kinds of beetles invade the pods and seeds.

In the shade along the inside ridge on the Heron Flats Trail crush a leaf of lime prickly ash (Station 12) and inhale the uplifting citruslike odor. Or enjoy the sprays of delicate pink flowers and pendant, three-lobed capsules of the Mexican buckeye (Station 8). In the fall, buckeye leaves turn lemon yellow before they drop, and many of the capsules will have broken open to release their shiny, marble-sized black seeds.

Several chest-high retamas (ray-TAH-mahs) occur between the outer ridge and the edge of Heron Flats. These trees have a smooth green trunk, thorny green branches, and long, ribbonlike drooping leaves edged with many small green leaflets. In the summertime they produce clusters of bright yellow flowers that eventually transform into thin brown bean pods. On the Aransas retamas are most common in the chaparral and the mesquite–prickly pear communities; they avoid deep sand.

A few rather anemic huisache (WEE-satch) occur on the inner and middle ridges on the Heron Flats Trail (Station 14). On the firmer inland soils of the coastal prairie, huisache is abundant and makes a respectable twenty-foot tree. It grows sparingly on shell, but this species does not do well on sand and is uncommon on the refuge.

Salt cedar is native to Western Europe. In the Coastal Bend it was planted as a windbreak and long ago escaped cultivation to grow in thick clumps along bayshores, around fresh and brackish pools, and along roadside ditches. Salt cedars growing on the shoreline of Blackjack Peninsula and several of the islands in San Antonio Bay serve to soften the erosive impact of waves and provide nesting and resting sites for birds. Deer and feral hogs frequently lie up during the day in the dense shade cast by a clump of salt cedars. Unfortunately, saltmarsh mosquitoes choose the same retreats. You can observe salt cedars at Station 27 on the Heron Flats Trail. A second clump grows on the bayshore between the boardwalk and the Big Tree Trail.

Just before you recross Cattail Slough, at the exit end of the Heron Flats Trail, Station 28 marks a fine prickly ash tree with thin, pale bark and catclaw prickles on its branches and leaf stalks. This particular specimen is larger than most local representatives of its kind. Shrub-sized prickly ashes are scattered on sandy mounds across Blackjack Peninsula. White-tailed deer browse its shining aromatic foliage (hold a leaflet up to the sun to see its scatter of tiny oil glands), and bobwhite quail eat the small, spicy, round fruits. An occasional prickly ash trunk is covered with spine-tipped corky projections.

The large sycamore that arches over the road near the picnic area was probably planted. However, the young cottonwood growing in a depression on the east side of the main road, 0.3 mile past the exit from the tour loop, is a volunteer and one of the few of its kind on the Aransas.

Shrubs

Yaupon (YO-pahn) is the commonest shrub on the refuge. It has firm, evergreen leaves with lightly scalloped edges and clusters of white

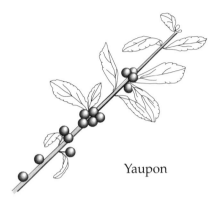

Yaupon

flowers in spring. By autumn the orange-red berries brighten the undergrowth in the oak mottes and feed many mammals and birds. Robins gobble up the fruits each fall and scatter the seeds across the refuge in their droppings. Mockingbirds consider a yaupon shrub heavy with fruit worth fighting over. Caracaras often choose an isolated yaupon copse for a nest site.

The less abundant American beautyberry shares the understory habitat with yaupon. In early summer, clusters of lilac flowers bloom at the bases of the leaves, and by late summer the pairs of thin, ovate leaves are surrounded by globular masses of bright lavender berries. You can judge whether the Aransas is suffering a dry autumn by the status of its beautyberries: round, fat berries mean adequate soil moisture; wrinkled, collapsed fruits speak of drought. Both yaupons and beautyberries line portions of the Big Tree Trail, and they occur together at Station 3 on the Heron Flats Trail.

Tree huckleberry, also called farkleberry, is closely related to blueberries. It reaches the western edge of its range here. In late April bell-shaped white flowers dangle among the ovate leaves at the ends of sprangly twigs; by autumn they have matured into edible (but not tasty) black fruits. The best spot for tree huckleberries is along Blueberry Ridge on the Green Branch of the Dagger Point Trail, where their rich wine-red foliage stands out in the winter.

Several shrubs characteristic of the chaparral community form a dense woody screen along portions of the Heron Flats Trail. Tanglewood (Station 16) anticipates spring in mid-February when its clusters of tiny, greenish yellow flowers with red anthers sprout directly from the still-leafless twigs. From a distance a tanglewood in flower has a fuzzy appearance. Later, the stiff, crooked stems are densely covered

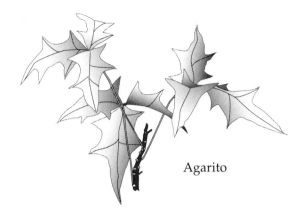

Agarito

with narrow leaves in small clusters or opposite one another. The fruits are pear-shaped, black, and about ⅜ inch long.

By early March bright yellow flowers of agarito (ag-ah-REE-tow) will scent the outer ridge and be eagerly attended by the season's earliest honeybees (Station 17). Each leaf has three stiff leaflets tipped with sharp spines. Spiny hackberry (Station 16) and brasil (bra-SEEL, Station 5) both have thorny stems. In late summer spiny hackberry has round, clear orange fruits ¼ inch in diameter; brasil sets slightly smaller, juicy black fruits after late summer rains. Birds eagerly forage for both kinds. Texas torchwood (Station 20) is a densely branched shrub with numerous shiny, dark green leaves, each made up of three small leaflets with crumpled edges. If you crush a leaf you can detect a distinctive aroma. Torchwood is widespread in Mexico and is near the northern limit of its distribution in the Coastal Bend.

Where fresh water regularly stands, rattlepod is likely to grow. This perennial sprouts from a woody base and occasionally develops into a small tree. Its fine-cut green leaves are brightened in early summer by drooping sprays of golden-yellow, bonnet-shaped flowers, which are later replaced by flat, three-inch pods with four membranous ridges. At Jones Lake and along Thomas Slough, you can hear the summer breeze rattle the dangling dry pods.

Coffee bean, with thin, eight-inch-long pods, and bagpod, with two seeds in each short, inflated pod, are infrequent annuals in low, moist sites. Both are related to the rattlepod, and collectively the three species of legumes are called senna beans (often locally corrupted to "seeny beans").

Buttonbush, another perennial of pond margins and moist depressions, has large leaves (to eight inches long) arising from the stem in

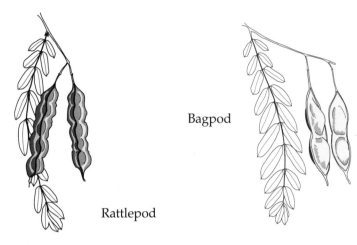

Bagpod

Rattlepod

pairs or triplets. In June you can spot the fuzzy white balls of button-bush flowers in swags between the bay overlook and the Dagger Point turnoff. The fuzz is the flower styles and stigmas, which protrude from each of the many small flowers in the globular cluster.

Wax myrtle is a holdover from the late Pleistocene, when the Aransas was much wetter than it is today. This waist-high shrub with thin, yellow-green leaves is moderately common but spotty; several plants grow near the beginning of the Big Tree Trail. With a magnifying glass, you can see the tiny orange-yellow wax glands profusely dotting the undersides of the leaves. In autumn wax myrtle branches are covered with clusters of small, round, frosted-gray fruits. Cedar waxwings, which occasionally visit the refuge in flocks in the wintertime, are one of the few birds known to feed on the fruits of wax myrtle.

Groundsel may grow to ten feet tall, with abundant narrow leaves and late-summer clusters of fuzzy white flowers. Often surrounded by water, groundsels are favored nesting sites of red-winged blackbirds and great-tailed grackles. Groundsels, along with black willows, border the bridge across Cattail Slough (Station 15) and grow along the inland edge of Heron Flats. The closely related bush baccharis (BACK-ah-ris) is a lower species more adapted to dry conditions, with small, dark green leaves. It prefers the middle and outer ridges on the Heron Flats Trail (Station 17).

Marsh elder closely resembles groundsel and grows in the same habi-tat (Station 26). Distinguish between the two by the arrangement of their leaves: in pairs along the stem in marsh elder, singly in groundsel. Because of its growth habit, marsh elder is sometimes aptly called high-tide bush.

Subshrubs

Five species of ankle- to knee-high plants with weak woody stems dominate the tidal-flat community and can be seen at close range from the boardwalk and at a distance from the observation tower. Most of the gray-tinted growth around Mustang Lake is bushy sea ox-eye. This very common plant grows in nearly pure stands across the tidal flats, where it serves as a natural breakwater, a shelter for marine organisms, a nest site for seaside sparrows, and cover for the ground-nesting willet. The succulent, gray-green leaves are arranged in pairs along the pale stems. Sea ox-eye blooms throughout the summer, but a few plants can usually be found at any time of the year bearing yellow daisy flowers with spiny bases. After the petals fall, the spherical spiny heads remain on the stem tips for weeks. A walk along the boardwalk takes you through a broad band of bushy sea ox-eye.

Whereas sea ox-eye grows in heavy silt, glassworts poke their brittle, nearly leafless stems through the brackish sand. Two species of glassworts grow abundantly to shin height on the tidal flat. The yellow-green stem joints of the upright, sparsely branched annual glasswort are relatively thick; the profusely branching perennial glasswort has rather thin, gray-green stem joints. These plants grow together on the open sand along the boardwalk. Both species are also called pickle-weeds for their crisp texture and salty taste—adaptations to retaining water in their saline habitat. You can safely munch on a stem tip to verify its salty nature.

Whooping cranes and horned larks selectively pluck the growing tips of perennial glasswort while browsing the tidal flat. In early summer a sparkling yellow dust of pollen on the sand is a cue to look for glasswort flowers, tiny yellow dots at the prominent stem joints. As you bend low, you may startle up flutters of western pigmy blue butterflies, which are attracted to flowering glassworts. In the fall the somber tidal flat is brightened as the perennial glasswort turns shades of rose and Indian red; by that time the annual species has died and turned brown.

Tough sprawling stems and erect branchlets of maritime saltwort snake across the sand among the glassworts. Its paired, pale green leaves in the shape of jelly beans are interspersed in summer with pea-sized, lumpy, yellow fruits. Striped caterpillars of great southern white butterflies munch on the fresh foliage.

Scattered through the bushy sea ox-eye zone is Carolina wolfberry, a straggly, drooping plant with sharp thorns and thin green leaves. The sporadic blue-lavender flowers produce bright red berries nearly half an inch across. Look closely at a fruit. Do you see the family resem-

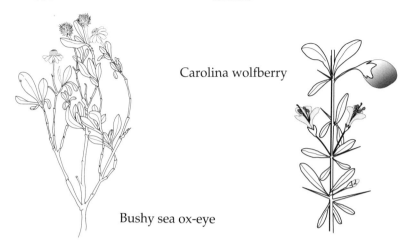

Carolina wolfberry

Bushy sea ox-eye

blance in this miniature pepper? Geese, whooping cranes, and other birds relish these berries, and feces of coyotes and raccoons are sometimes full of the thin yellow seeds. The related Berlandier's wolfberry, sometimes a respectable head-high shrub, grows in the chaparral community and produces smaller, pale orange fruits.

During the first two weeks in April coral beans burst into spectacular bloom. You cannot miss their spikes of sword-shaped, fire truck–red flowers along the roadside between the bay overlook and the observation tower. Each flower secretes a copious supply of sweet nectar that attracts ruby-throated hummingbirds migrating northward across the refuge precisely when the coral beans are at peak bloom. Of course, the timing between plant and bird is not fortuitous. By early summer the flowers have given way to black woody pods that eventually split open to reveal a cache of orange-red beans; the beans stick to the pod margins for some time before they fall to the ground.

You can find the waxy red flowers of Turk's cap (Station 3) in the shade of live oaks along the roads and trails throughout the summer. Hummingbirds and bumblebees probe among the twisted petals beside the protruding column of stamens. The small, apple-shaped fruits that ripen to bright red in late summer are edible but rather bland to our palate.

Lantana blooms throughout the summer with flat clusters of small flowers at the tips of spreading, brittle stems. Blossoms at the outer edge of the cluster are orange, the younger central flowers are butter yellow, and the balls of round fruits are deep blue-black when ripe. Although the plant has a rather unpleasant odor, it is attractive to a variety of butterflies. Lantana is occasional on the roadside, and it grows near the picnic area and along the Heron Flats Trail (Station 21).

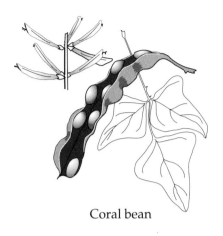

Coral bean   Turk's cap

Wild indigo is a knee-high plant widely scattered in swales along the Tour Loop. It has attractive drooping sprays of soft yellow, bonnet-shaped flowers during March and April. In the fall the dead, blackened plants bounce along in the wind like small tumbleweeds, scattering their beans as they go.

Partridge peas (Station 17) spread their lacy foliage from ankle to chest high, depending on moisture. In favorable years, they dominate the clearings along the roads. From June to the end of warm weather, bees are busy on the thick, dark brown anthers of the abundant, bright yellow flowers, and a variety of wasps and flies hum around the special nectar glands at the bases of the leaves. Each of the three smaller upper petals of the 1¼-inch flowers has a small, intense red spot at the base. The tiny brown beans of partridge pea are favored food for all ground-dwelling birds; flocks of sparrows search them out in the wintertime.

On the Aransas Refuge saltmarsh mallow grows only along Thomas Slough from the big willow tree (Station 7) on the Heron Flats Trail to a point about halfway to the picnic area. These head-high plants with velvety gray-green leaves display their large, soft pink, hibiscuslike flowers before midday throughout the summer. If you see them blooming, pause and enjoy their rare beauty.

Vines

Some 25 kinds of vines twist their way through the vegetation on the Aransas Refuge. Six have woody stems.

The largest species is mustang grape. This common vine clambers through the canopy of most oak mottes, including the one that shades the picnic area. One venerable grapevine in this motte is thought to be

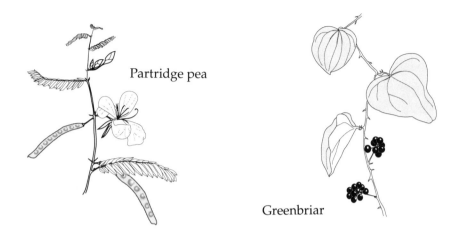

Partridge pea

Greenbriar

the largest of its kind on the refuge. Specimens are noted at Stations 4 and 17 on the Heron Flats Trail, and you can get a close view of the broad leaves with white cobwebby undersides as you ascend the ramp to the observation tower. When the purple-black grapes ripen in early summer they are heavily used by wildlife. If you care for a taste, hold a ripe grape between thumb and forefinger and squeeze it until the pink pulp pops into your mouth. Discard the caustic skin and spit out the seeds. You may be surprised at the delightful taste of the chewy, sweet pulp.

Greenbriar is the most abundant vine on the Aransas Refuge. Curtains of its prickle-studded, wiry, green stems render the undergrowth impenetrable to all but small or low-slung bodies. The spherical clusters of round black fruits that ripen in the fall are relished by the same animals that eat mustang grapes. Catbirds and other winter residents glean the crop throughout the cool months. Although the vine is evergreen, some leaves turn a beautiful orange-bronze in October. By November globules of shiny black greenbriar fruits have appeared amid lavish offerings of orange-red yaupon berries to produce a spectacular autumn display. You can hardly avoid encountering greenbriar along the Big Tree Trail, and one occurs at Station 9 on the Heron Flats Trail. The vine will be outside your car window all along the Tour Loop.

On any summer day the ground at Station 11 on the Heron Flats Trail may be littered with large, orange-red, trumpet-shaped flowers that have fallen from the high-climbing trumpet creeper. The flowers attract hummingbirds (buff-bellied hummers visit it routinely), and the huge olive-green leaves (over a foot long but divided into many leaflets) have special secretory glands that attract ants. Trumpet creeper is not known elsewhere on the refuge.

Just before entering the trees at the start of the Heron Flats Trail (Station 2), the path is bordered with a briar patch of southern dewberry laced through with peppervine. The sprawling prickly stems, white-petaled flowers, and edible black fruits of dewberry make it easily recognizable as a kind of blackberry. Young leaves at the stem tips of peppervine are reddish bronze; older leaves are dark green. The small round fruits change from green to lavender and finally to shiny black, but they are not good to eat.

Happily for visitors, dry summers inhibit the growth of poison ivy on the Aransas. It does occur sparingly in live oak mottes (a specimen is noted at Station 4 on the Heron Flats Trail), where it may appear either as a knee-high sprig or a high-climbing vine, in the latter case referred to as poison oak. Whatever its growth form, the species is easily identified by its smooth, green, three-part leaf with the terminal leaflet on a distinct stalk. As though to atone for its noxious reputation, the tiny pale berries of poison ivy are avidly eaten by most small birds, and in the fall the leaves turn flame red before dropping.

Succulents

Succulents are plants that store water in their tissues as an adaptation to dry conditions. The ability is a boon during Aransas' hot, dry summers and recurrent withering droughts as well as for those plants that live in saline soils, which tend to draw water osmotically from plant tissues.

The huge Spanish daggers (Station 22) on sunny shell ridges of the Heron Flats Trail are impressive at any time of the year, but they are especially so from late February to mid-March when they put up their heavy candelabra of white flowers. Each dagger plant supports a thriving community of insects and arachnids, which come to feed on the flowers and on each other. A second, smaller species, the white-rim yucca, is thinly scattered across the tidal shore community.

Prickly pears are easily recognized by their stems of flat, oblong pads studded with patches of spines. The large Texas prickly pear (Station 22) is one of six kinds of cacti that grow on the Aransas. In April its fresh blossoms open a clear yellow; day-old ones turn orange-gold. Bumble-bees and various beetles are attracted to the flowers. The egg-sized fruits, called tunas, ripen to a rich burgundy color by late summer. Everything from mockingbirds and javelinas to rodents and insects feeds on the juicy tunas. Prickly pears are especially abundant in the mesquite–prickly pear community on the Tatton, where they are a mainstay in the diet of the south plains wood rat.

Tasajillo (tah-sah-HEE-yo), also called pencil cactus, is occasional in

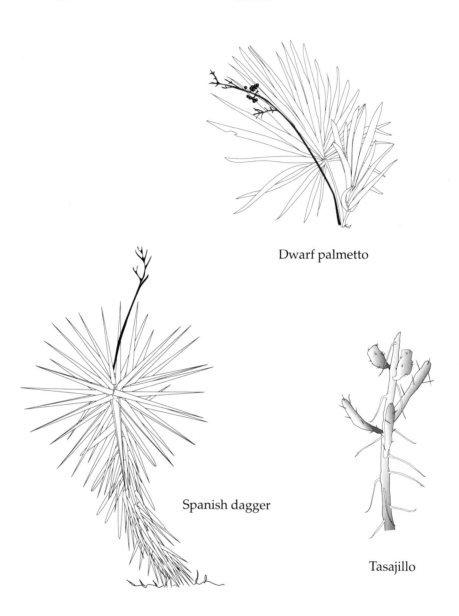

Dwarf palmetto

Spanish dagger

Tasajillo

the chaparral community, and one rather anemic clump grows beside the observation platform at Station 19 on the Heron Flats Trail. Look for waist-high columns of cylindrical green stems covered with stout yellow spines. After summer showers this cactus puts on a few small green-yellow blossoms. The flowers soon transform into bright red, knobby fruits that cling to the stems for weeks. Tasajillo has an efficient means of distributing itself. The spines snag in the flesh or pelt of any animal that brushes against them, and the stem segment readily breaks loose. When scraped off by the irritated animal, the segment falls to the ground and roots.

Grassland prickly pear, a shoetop-high cactus with gray spines, is widespread on clay soil bordering St. Charles Bay. The devil's head, a low, ribbed mound covered with a network of fierce thorns, is common in the mesquite–prickly pear community on the Tatton Unit and along low clay ridges near Burgentine Lake.

The only native palm on the Aransas is the dwarf palmetto. Palmettos become stubby trees along the coastal river bottoms, but on the refuge they are little more than sprays of fan-shaped, pleated leaves springing directly from the ground. These leaves are often bicolored—pale brown at the margin and green centrally—as a consequence of wintertime burning. The brown portion was killed by the fire; the green region is fresh growth. In May palmettos send up tall, slender green stalks of inconspicuous flowers and later set abundant bun-shaped black fruits. Although there seems to be little nourishment in the fruits, palmetto seeds are often abundant in coyote feces. A palmetto is noted at Station 7 on the Heron Flats Trail, and you can see them around Thomas Slough and along the road to the observation tower.

CHAPTER 15

Herbaceous Plants

 This chapter covers an assortment of nonwoody flowering plants arranged into seven groups: wildflowers, aquatic plants, grasses, vines, epiphytes, parasites, and extra specials. *Flora of the Texas Coastal Bend*, by Fred B. Jones, covers all of these groups except the grasses. Grasses are well illustrated and described in *Grasses of the Texas Coastal Bend*, by F. W. Gould and T. W. Box. There is no illustrated wildflower book explicitly for the Texas coast, but three that include many coastal species are *Wildflowers of Texas* by Geyata Ajilvsgi, *Texas Wildflowers* by Campbell and Lynn Loughmiller, and *Roadside Flowers of Texas* by Mary Motz Wills and Howard S. Irwin. You may also find *Plants of the Texas Shore*, by M. M. Cannatella and R. E. Arnold, and *The Smithsonian Guide to Seaside Plants of the Gulf and Atlantic Coasts*, by Wilbur H. and Marion B. Duncan, useful. Also, ask at the WIC for a brochure to the common wildflowers of the Aransas.

Wildflowers

To help you find the common wildflowers, we have tabulated those seen each month on the refuge in three appendices. Appendix A lists wildflowers that routinely appear on the slope beside the WIC, Appendix B covers the roadside between the visitors center and the observation tower, and Appendix C lists the main flowering plants along the Heron Flats Trail. None of these tables includes all of the species that may be in flower. Latin names are given in Appendix D for all species mentioned.

Remember: wildflowers are best enjoyed by simply looking at them. Especially on a wildlife refuge, please refrain from picking them.

Most of the plants on the refuge produce flowers and so could be put into this category, but we have limited the term "wildflower" to its popular use—species that have prominent and usually attractive flowers. Even this restriction leaves well over 100 kinds. The most eye-catching 66 of these are listed here by flower color.

White Flowers

False garlic has a loose bouquet of six to twelve white flowers at the tip of a shin-high stem. Its few thin, grasslike leaves arise directly from a subterranean bulb. Each stalked blossom is about one inch across and has six petallike parts. This plant closely resembles wild onion, but a crushed leaf lacks the distinctive onion odor. In a wet spring, false garlic flowers line the road between headquarters and the picnic area.

Several days after good summer rains, legions of rain lilies rim the roadsides, each ephemeral foot-tall stalk bearing one upright, shining white trumpet two to three inches long. Larger spider lilies are more enduring, but they are rare on the refuge. Their exotic white blossom consists of a central cup surrounded by six drooping, straplike segments that give the flower a spread of six inches. Six thin filaments suspend golden-yellow anthers above the edge of the cup and contribute to the spidery appearance of the flower. Waist-high clumps of spider lilies, with their long, inch-wide leaves, grow in moist depressions; look for one on the edge of the tidal flat between the Heron Flats Trail and the picnic area.

In the fall on the roadside near the entrance to the Heron Flats Trail, watch for wands of green lilies. Each rigidly upright, eighteen-inch stem terminates in a dense cylindrical spike of small greenish white flowers followed by small green fruits. The black spent stems may persist for months.

Late February is the time to get down on your hands and knees to examine the tiny white flowers and downy leaves of whitlow grass sprinkled along the Heron Flats Trail. It is among the first of the early-rising mustard family to celebrate springtime, and it frequently attracts a flutter of equally early sleepy orange butterflies. While you are bent down, check shady spots for chickweed. Each of its five white petals is split nearly to the base, making the little flower appear to have ten thin petals. These early species are soon joined by peppergrass, which holds its many tiny white flowers aloft in dense, shin-level clusters at the ends of the branches.

Old plainsman, like its namesake, stands alone, tall and straight. Look for its waist-high flat clusters of ivory flowers in the clearing near the picnic area. If the spring is a wet one, windflowers will put on an early, ephemeral show. Each blossom, about 1½ inches across, has ten to twenty thin, petallike segments around a central silvery green dome. You may find an occasional lavender windflower.

In early April shin-high prairie bluets begin to appear. One of the most widely distributed wildflowers in the state, they bloom every-

Rain lily

False garlic

where until winter sets in. Each ⅜-inch flower in the loose cluster has four downy, lavender-white petals; the threadlike leaves are in pairs along the stiff stems. On May mornings hoary pea blooms in the deep sand along the road near the Dagger Point turnoff. Each waist-high stalk bears several stems with bonnet-shaped flowers; by afternoon the day-old lower blossoms turn from white to rosy red. Like most legumes, hoary pea has compound leaves composed of many leaflets, and its fruits are unmistakable pea pods.

Beach pimpernel is most at home on the tidal flat, but it also grows profusely in roadside ditches along the Tour Loop. The ¼-inch, urn-shaped flowers with five flaring, pink-tinged lobes dangle from a knee-high stalk. Most of the leaves spread out at ground level.

Summertime white flowers on the Aransas include showy four-inch blossoms of white prickly poppy, crowded pancake-shaped clusters of wild buckwheat, fat cylindrical spikes of pussyfoot, and tiered flower heads of the strong-scented spotted horsemint and lemon horsemint. Two yellow-centered white daisies are also common. The erect stems and 1¾-inch flower heads of lazy daisy sparkle on any sunny afternoon around headquarters and the picnic area. Corpus Christi fleabane is abundant on deep sand near Dagger Point and Jones Lake. Its erect pedicels stand up from prostrate stems and bear ¾-inch flower heads rimmed with numerous thin white petals.

Keep your distance when you inspect the luminous white flowers of bullnettle; the foliage of these waist-high perennials is covered with fierce stinging hairs. Bullnettles grow from enormous subterranean root-stocks that require deep sand, like that around the picnic area.

Shin-high green milkweed produces summertime clusters of numer-

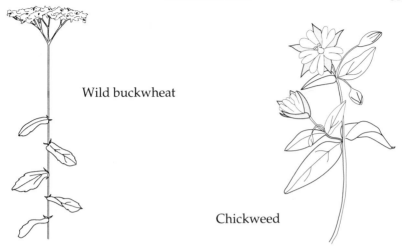

Wild buckwheat

Chickweed

ous green-white flowers. The five erect petals of each ¾-inch blossom form a shallow dish centered by a purple, star-shaped structure called the corona, which incorporates the anthers. Tiny slits in the corona lead to chambers holding saddlebag-shaped packets of pollen grains. When an insect steps into a slit, a saddlebag hangs onto its leg and is withdrawn when the insect moves on. The fragile bag ruptures while the unwitting insect is visiting another flower, thus effecting cross-pollination.

A second kind of common milkweed, called zizote (zeh-ZOH-tay), can be distinguished by its smaller flowers with petals that are bent down at the tips and a greenish white (rather than purple) corona. Both species have viscid white sap and produce banana-shaped pods that contain seeds equipped with exquisitely buoyant parachutes made of soft white hairs.

Watch the roadside of the Tour Loop about a quarter-mile beyond Hog Lake for the impressive head-high stalks of button snakeroot standing bolt upright in moist depressions. A cluster of long, bristly margined leaves is at the base of each stalk, and the tiny flowers are nestled in globular spiny heads at the tips of the branches.

Throughout the summer, in sunny spots along roads and trails, coast germander sends up its spikes. Many flowers open on each leafy vertical branch, and each ¾-inch blossom has one large tonguelike petal and four shorter ones.

Along some stretches of the Tour Loop the edge of the asphalt is hidden beneath the pale green foliage of a prostrate plant with the unlikely name "frogfruit." A crowd of tiny flowers tops each of the dark red, ¾-inch nubbins that arise on long slender stalks from the bases of the paired leaves. Where the plants spread on the dark roadway, the flower clusters stand out. Frogfruit is also a common, but less noticeable, trailside plant. (Frogs do not eat the fruit!)

The singularly flanged stems and large, rough, tobaccolike leaves of frostweed are found in the shade of oak trees, and a stretch of these plants grows in the swag at the parking lot beside the Heron Flats Trail. This chest-high perennial blooms in late summer, when the wide clusters of ½-inch flowers above dark green leaves are attractive to a variety of flies, wasps, and butterflies.

Look for the shade-loving rouge plant in shady nooks along the Heron Flats Trail. The juice of the round, translucent red berries at the bases of the cylindrical flower clusters will stain your fingers or your cheeks. In the fall the leaves of rouge plant turn a striking bronze red.

Seaside heliotrope, a plant of the tidal flat, withstands sun, wind, and salt. Its rubbery stems with their thick, gray-green leaves lie prostrate or are weakly ascending. The ⅛-inch flowers are arranged along pairs of distinctively coiled stem tips. You can find seaside heliotropes beside the boardwalk.

In the fall half a dozen species of asters bloom on the Aransas. All have waist- to chest-high foliage and daisylike flower heads about ½-inch across, with yellow centers and a fringe of numerous white to pale lavender petals. Watch along roadside ditches for the weedy growth and lavender-white flowers of saltmarsh aster, the most common member of the group. A thicket of leafless green stems of spiny aster flanks the west end of the bridge across Cattail Slough, and this plant grows in dense stands on low ground along the tidal flats and around ponds. Saline aster grows in soft mud subject to tidal flooding. Its fleshy leaves and large lavender-white flowers are found sparingly in the tidal-flat community. The knee-high prickly green foliage and small flowers of heath aster are scattered through the inner grasslands.

Pink Flowers

Dainty Drummond's wild onion is sprinkled along the shell ridges on the Heron Flats Trail in March and April. Ten to 25 small flowers, each with six petallike parts on a short pedicel, are loosely clustered on an ankle-high stalk. Crush one of the thin leaves to release the characteristic onion odor.

Bright pink puffball flowers are produced by two different low-growing plants along the road and the Heron Flats Trail. In both species the eye-catching globe is largely composed of numerous spreading, pink filaments tipped with dotlike yellow anthers. To tell the two species apart, feel the stalk beneath a flower cluster: in powderpuff it has soft bristles; in sensitive briar it is covered with stiff prickles. Have you still got enough childlike interest in nature to run your finger gently along the leaves and watch these touch-me-not plants respond by folding their leaflets together?

Meadow pinks are among the most fetching springtime wildflowers on the Aransas. The blossoms are about 1¼ inches wide, with five bubblegum-pink petals and a butter-yellow, star-shaped center. The related grass pink is a miniature version, about half the size of a meadow pink and with a white center. Both species are scattered along the Heron Flats Trail and on roadsides.

Pink evening primroses, a sure sign of spring throughout most of Texas, appear on the roadsides and mowed clearings in February on the refuge. The nodding, showy saucers are 2½ inches across, with four flaring petals and a yellow central blush. The erect flowers of the similar but less common sundrops are only 1¼ inches across.

American germander grows in dense clumps in moist spots along the roads. The rigidly upright, waist-high stalks have erect spires with open flowers at the base and unopened buds at the tips. Each pale pink, lavender-spotted blossom is about ½ inch long, with four small petals and one large tonguelike one.

The similar-looking pink mint blooms on the outer ridge of the Heron Flats Trail in March. These flowers, too, are arranged in a terminal spike with open flowers below, but the buds at the tip are cupped in long, pointed bracts (modified leaves). Each ⅜-inch long flower is flared into a notched upper lip and a large, three-lobed lower lip. The edges of the ovate leaves are neatly pinked.

Round heads of Texas palafoxia in two tones of rose begin to bloom in the summer but are at their peak after fall rains, when they decorate the sandy ridges along the road from the picnic area to the observation tower. The widely branched, semiwoody plant may grow to chest height.

In July, when sharp gayfeathers bloom in a blazing array across the roadside clearings between Dagger Point and the observation tower, you cannot miss them. Their wide-topped spikes of numerous small flowers at the ends of erect, knee-high stems resemble the feathered shafts of innumerable arrows shot from afar by a phalanx of archers.

Purple and Lavender Flowers

Pinkscale gayfeather grows in the sand drifts along the Dagger Point Road. It has a heavy, often foot-long spike of lavender flowers atop a leaning, waist-high stalk.

Several kinds of wild petunias bloom on the refuge in the summer-

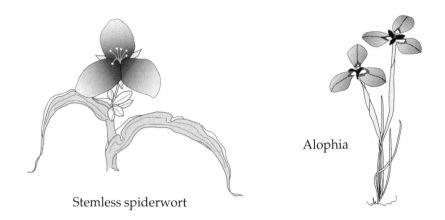

Alophia

Stemless spiderwort

time; all have purple-violet, trumpet-shaped flowers about 1½ inches long. The most common species along the trails is Gulf Coast petunia. If you are in the right place on a hot summer afternoon you may hear pops and clicks as the fruit capsules of petunias burst and catapult their tiny seeds several feet away. Plant ecologists appropriately refer to this as ballistic seed dispersal.

Of the several species of spiderworts on the Aransas, the stemless spiderwort is one of the most common. Its rosettes of long, veined leaves appear in early spring, and the flowers, with three large petals varying from deep orchid through lavender to purple and blue-violet, are at their finest in midmorning.

Although alophias are not especially rare, they are so delicately beautiful that it is always a delight to see them appear after spring showers. Each flower has six petallike parts: three large outer ones that give the flower a two-inch spread, and three small upright central ones. The outer segments are rich purple-violet with a small, white, purple-spotted base. The inner segments are purple with darkened bases. You may recognize the alophia for what it is—a member of the iris family.

Three different kinds of plants on the refuge produce rather similar, shin-high sprays of spotted, two-lipped purplish flowers. The two skullcaps along the Heron Flats Trail can be picked out by their semicircular ridge projecting from the upper side of the green tube beneath the petals. Both kinds of skullcap flowers have a white blotch on the larger blue-violet lower petal. Drummond's skullcap has flowers ½ inch long and leaves no more than one inch long; egg-leaf skullcap has ¾-inch flowers and leaves two inches long or more. The third species, sand brazoria, has a reddish-wine flower with a wide throat that has dark flecks on the inside, and there is no projection on the green tube below the blossom. Sand brazoria sends up its shin-high spires of flowers in the clearing at the picnic area in April.

Waist- to chest-high stems of vervains with small flowers in thin, vertical spikes at the tops of many branches are frequent on the roadsides in the summertime. Texas vervain has thin, smooth stems and pale lavender ¼-inch flowers. Gulf vervain has robust, hairy stems and lilac-pink flowers ⅜ inch wide. Most of the lobed and toothed leaves of vervains are on the lower, unbranched part of the stem. If you roll a stem gently between your fingers you can detect that it is square in cross section.

Lanceleaf loosestrife resembles vervain in its upright growth and vertical flower spikes. It has fewer, larger (½-inch) flowers with six (rather than five) petals and untoothed leaves. Loosestrife also prefers more moist sites than the vervains. A second species, western loosestrife, has darker purple flowers and grows on the perimeter of the tidal flat.

The weak, prostrate, or clambering stems of wine-cup are common around headquarters in the springtime. The rich burgundy flowers, standing on erect, leafless stalks, are cupped in the early morning, but the five broad petals spread widely by noon.

Each flowering branch and distinctive shamrock-shaped leaf of purple woodsorrel springs separately from the ground on a delicate stalk. The flowers, in clusters of two or three, each have five spreading petals. The leaves fold up at night. The upright fruits resemble tiny pickles.

Mats of low-growing sandbells thrive on otherwise barren strips of roadside. The pale purple, ⅜-inch flowers have a spot of yellow in the throat. Sandy road side areas are frequently covered by the prostrate foliage of silverstems. The small, pale flowers are almost lost in the silvery foliage. The hairy leaves of sandbells and the woolly ones of silverstems are adaptations that reduce water loss and shade delicate tissues from the blazing sun; to achieve the same end, the leaves of sandbells curl along their edges in the heat of the day.

Both sand phacelia (fah-SEAL-lee-ah) and bluecurls are shade-loving spring bloomers. The ankle-high sand phacelia has many cup-shaped, one-inch flowers with five white-centered violet petals. Bluecurls stand waist-high and have tight coils of numerous small, violet-blue flowers and white buds. Flowers of both are spangled with bright yellow pollen sacs suspended on slender blue filaments. Both species occur in shaded nooks along the Heron Flats Trail.

Despite its coarse name, toadflax is quite delicate. The pale, ½-inch-long flowers open six or eight at a time on the upper portion of the thin, unbranched, knee-high stem. Each flower has two short, upright upper petals, a broad, three-lobed lower lip, and a distinctive spur (a long, thin tube that curves beneath the petals). Toadflax blooms in small colo-

Toadflax

nies on the roadside and along the Heron Flats Trail in February and March. Despite their beauty, the frail flowers are easily overlooked.

From March through June the large, lilac- to cream-colored shaving-brush heads of bull thistle attract butterflies in sunny upland spots. The robust, prickly plants stand knee-high. Texas thistle is a taller, thinner, less prickly plant with neatly rounded, rose-purple flower heads 1½ inches wide. It too lures butterflies.

The fuzzy, flat-topped clusters of small lilac flowers of coast mistflower are to be seen everywhere on the Aransas throughout the spring and summer. The veiny, wrinkled leaves are arranged in pairs along the sprawling or semierect stems. This is another flower favored by butterflies.

Sea lavender and saltmarsh gerardia (jer-RAR-dee-ah) are tidal-flat inhabitants that can be looked for along the boardwalk and the outer ridge of the Heron Flats Trail. Sea lavender has a rosette of wide, leathery leaves at ground level from which rises a knee-high panicle of ¼-inch violet flowers in late summer. If you look closely, you can see that the little flowers are neatly aligned along one side of each thin flowering branch. From a distance the tiny blossoms look like a thin violet mist suspended in midair. Gerardia has simple fleshy leaves on sprangly stems and produces pinkish purple flowers arranged in a few-flowered spike at knee-level. Each ½-inch flower is tubular with five spreading petal lobes; the lower lobes are noticeably larger.

Blue Flowers

Not even an indigo bunting can out-blue the color of a dayflower in its prime. Below the two sky-blue petals, there is a much smaller, translu-

Blue-eyed grass

cent white one. Dayflowers wither by midday and are replaced each morning by fresh blossoms from the boat-shaped cup of green leaves around the flower buds. This common species is sprinkled through the grassland and is frequent on roadsides.

If you are on the Aransas in January or February, watch for minute, intensely purple-blue dots of tiny bluets in moist sandy openings. You will have to bend low to enjoy the delicate beauty of one of the refuge's smallest wildflowers.

By mid-April there should be several clumps of blue larkspur blooming beside the road near the picnic area. Each knee-high wand supports several beautiful sky-blue blossoms and terminates in frosted blue buds. Like cultivated larkspurs, these have the distinctive curved spur projecting from the back of the flower. The species is rare on the Aransas.

In a wet spring, the trailsides and roadside ditches of the Aransas are awash with blue-eyed grass. Several flattened, unbranched stems arise together in a shin-high tuft on which the bright flowers make a natural bouquet. Despite the name, this is not grass but a member of the iris family. Each yellow-centered, ¾-inch flower has six blue to blue-purple petallike parts that terminate in delicate hairlike bristles.

Probably because of withering summers, bluebonnets are not common on the Aransas. Texas bluebonnets occasionally occur on the dark soil of the Tatton Unit, and they have been introduced several times near headquarters. You may see this species on the roadsides as you approach the refuge.

In ditches along the Tour Loop you will see bluehearts all summer and downy lobelia in the fall. Bluehearts, with only one or two dark blue-violet flowers open at a time on delicate stems, are hard to spot, but the lovely pale blue spikes of lobelia are conspicuous against the backdrop of faded vegetation worn out by the long hot summer.

Red Flowers

Shoetop-high clumps of scarlet pimpernel, a European native that grows widely in South Texas, bloom along the Heron Flats Trail in springtime. The ½-inch-wide flowers, a peculiar shade of salmon-orange, grow on slender pedicels from the bases of the opposite leaves. An occasional plant has vivid blue flowers.

Erect spikes of the pale brick-red, bonnet-shaped flowers of scarlet pea rise from prostrate, grayish green roadside foliage in the summertime. The flowers and leaves of anil indigo resemble those of scarlet pea, but the plant is waist-high and shrubby. Scarlet pea is common along the first open stretch of the Heron Flats Trail (between Stations 1 and 2), while several anil indigo plants grow along the paved road between the Heron Flats Trail and the picnic area. Both are legumes and set small bean pods in late summer.

Cardinal feather is common along roads and trails all summer; look particularly at the picnic area and the head of the Heron Flats Trail. The plants form ankle-high mounds of round, hairy leaves with lobed margins. The tiny red flowers are densely packed into vertical spikes about an inch long. On female plants the groups of long, silky red styles look like a bird feather. Spikes of male flowers are compact.

Woolly globe mallow is not common on the refuge, but where it does grow the distinctive rosy-orange color of its 1¼-inch flowers stands out. The sprawling, shin-high plant is covered with white down, and the flowers are widely spaced on erect stems. Globe mallow occurs sparingly on the slope at the WIC and on sandy sites en route to the tower. It is a spring and early-summer bloomer.

The red-orange of Indian paintbrushes is easily recognized on the roadside just beyond headquarters. A careful examination will show that what appears to be one large flower at the top of each stem is actually a tight cluster of several orange-tipped leaflike bracts. Each bract encloses an inconspicuous greenish yellow flower.

Drummond's phlox is the most common phlox and one of the brightest and most widespread wildflowers on the Aransas. Most of the five-parted blossoms are purple-red with a darker central star, but some are pale purple with a white star. Phlox bloom through spring and into summertime, depending on the rains.

If one wildflower were chosen to be emblematic of the Aransas Wildlife Refuge it might well be Indian blanket. This showy plant blooms nearly the year round, and in an ordinary summer it grows in breath-

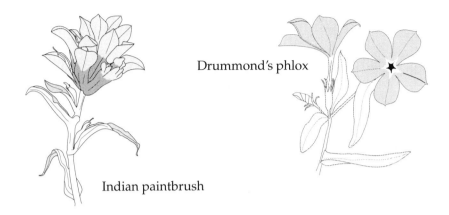

Drummond's phlox

Indian paintbrush

taking abundance. One of its best displays is in the mowed area around headquarters. The flower heads are two inches across, with red-brown centers and numerous red rays tipped with yellow. The proportion of red to yellow varies: many flowers are almost totally red; a rare one is all yellow. If you are sharp-eyed, you may spot one of the curious flower moths that rest on Indian blankets during the daytime. The moth has a yellow head and body and crimson wings, and it artfully positions itself so its colors align with those of the flower.

Yellow Flowers

Stinging nettle is a weedy plant with terminal clusters of small, pale greenish yellow flowers. The paired leaves have toothed margins, and the whole plant is covered with irritating hairs. Stinging nettle is among the earliest plants to bloom, beginning on the refuge in January along the Heron Flats Trail.

The pale yellow flowers of southern corydalis (ko-RID-uh-lis) have a wash of orange-brown at the base. One petal extends into a saclike appendage so that the flowers appear as slightly arched, ⅝-inch tubes positioned horizontally along the upper stems. The bright yellow flowers of puccoon are in clusters, and the five spreading petal lobes have crinkled margins. Both species bloom in early spring: corydalis around headquarters, puccoon at the picnic area.

Both of the species of coreopsis (ko-ree-OP-sis) that begin to flower in April have a red-brown central disk and eight golden-yellow petals with a velvety red-brown spot at the base. The more abundant golden-mane coreopsis has two-inch flowers and decks the roadside near the entrance gate and the slope at the WIC throughout springtime and

Southern corydalis   Puccoon

early summer. Plains coreopsis has flowers about an inch wide and prefers slightly drier ground. In dry spells, stunted individuals of both species get only two to three inches tall and have flowers scarcely ½ inch
across.

On spring mornings, the bright yellow blossoms of square-bud primrose open their four petals early along the outer ridge on the Heron
Flats Trail. The larger (about 2½ inches) flowers of yellow evening
primrose open at dusk and turn a rich golden yellow when they close
at dawn. On moonlit evenings the large saucers of the latter species
glow as though with a soft inner light; they lure sphinx moths to sip
from their long nectar tubes.

Both Texas dandelion and Carolina dandelion are occasional in roadside depressions. In spring and early summer, their two-inch-wide, pale
lemon-yellow flowers, composed of a veritable sunburst of overlapping
tiers of petals and borne on tips of knee-high stems, open early and
close by midday. Texas dandelion has several flowers, and its midstem
leaves are lobed; Carolina dandelion has a solitary flower and unlobed
leaves. Both produce round globes of parachute-bearing seeds, which
invite the passerby to puff them on their way.

Greenthread, like coreopsis, has daisy flowers with purple-brown
centers and eight golden yellow rays. But greenthread is a larger, more
branching plant, sometimes growing chest-high; its leaves are dissected
into thin green segments, and the yellow rays often lack the basal spot
characteristic of coreopsis. Greenthread grows on the outer two ridges
of the Heron Flats Trail (Station 23), where its flowers may be mistaken
for those of the shrubs through which the plant clambers.

Bur clover occurs in all mowed areas at headquarters and along roads
and trails. The small yellow flowers, dark green leaves, and coiled,

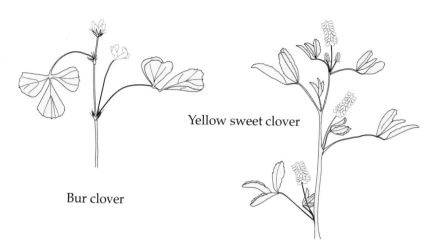

Yellow sweet clover

Bur clover

prickly fruit seldom grow above shoetop level. The related yellow sweet clover has numerous ⅛-inch flowers in erect spikes on knee-high stems. Both of these clovers are introduced.

Ankle-high clumps of the ¾-inch shamrock leaves of yellow wood sorrel appear sparingly from early spring until the dog days of summer. The five-part flowers have fine streaks of orange or red in the throat. The green fruits look like tiny okras and have a sharp sour tang.

Head-high stems and large jagged leaves of wild lettuce grow along shaded parts of the Heron Flats Trail. The small yellow flowers are unremarkable, but the fleecy ¾-inch spheres of parachute seeds that follow are eye-catching.

The flowers of queen's delight are not showy enough to get them into wildflower books, but they are worth knowing for their oddity and because they attract a variety of insects and flower spiders. The plants grow to chest height and stand stiffly erect from a thick base. The numerous stems and dark green leaves exude milky sap if broken. The blossom is held above the abundant, upward-angled leaves on a stout yellow stalk: several round green female flowers beneath a column of small greenish yellow male flowers. In late spring, the female flowers develop into marble-sized, three-lobed green fruits. Queen's delight is best seen on the Tour Loop beyond Hog Lake.

The bronze-centered, soft yellow flowers of stiffstem flax may be first noticed garnishing the ground in the afternoon. The five petals, forming a blossom 1¼ inches in diameter, are barely joined at the base and fall together as pretty little wheels by midday. Pale flax is similar but lacks the bronze center. Both kinds occur on the Heron Flats Trail and at the picnic area in the springtime.

Along shell ridges you may find another of the several plants with

Camphor daisy

long prostrate stems, numerous small leaflets, and sensitive leaves. The leaves of yellowpuff are dark green with a paler central area, and its globose flower heads are bright yellow. Run your finger down a leaf to witness the touch-me-not trait. What advantage might the plant gain from such behavior?

As summertime progresses the proportion of yellow flowers on the refuge increases, and most of them have a daisy anatomy: a central disk surrounded by strap-shaped petals called rays.

Camphorweed is common on the sand around the picnic area and grows to waist or chest height with many bright yellow, one-inch flowers. Camphor daisy grows on the edge of the tidal flat. You will see its 1¼-inch flowers, sticky stems, and sharp-toothed leaves at the end of the boardwalk. It blooms all year long. Bruised leaves of either of these two species emit a strong camphor odor, which probably deters some herbivores.

A tall, columnar brown center and four to eight drooping, brown-based yellow rays easily distinguish Mexican hat. The flowers stand head-high on stout leafless stalks; the lobed leaves are mostly on the lower portion of the stem. Some flowers have all yellow rays, and in immature ones the central column is olive green. In the summertime Mexican hats are common at the end of the Heron Flats Trail.

Rough-hairy, knee-high brown-eyed Susans are common on the roadside all summer. The red-brown central dome of the flower is less than half the height of the center of Mexican hat, and the twenty or so rays are golden yellow and lack a basal spot. The flower is about two inches across.

Three kinds of sunflowers grow on the Aransas, all with the same general appearance: coarse leaves on stout stalks capped by large flow-

Seacoast goldenrod

ers with numerous bright yellow rays surrounding a wide dark center. Well-watered common sunflowers grow over head-high and have two- to four-inch flowers. They like disturbed places and are particularly abundant near the picnic area. Silverleaf sunflower looks much like common sunflower, but its very hairy leaves are noticeably gray-green. The hairs probably retard water loss and shade the leaf surface. Although common on the refuge, it is infrequent in the area of public access. Look for a stand on the roadside about a quarter-mile outside the entrance gate. Well-established plants soar up to fifteen feet. Coast sunflower grows to chest height and has 2¼-inch flowers that are distinctly more orange-yellow than those of the preceding two species. It prefers deep sand and can be seen occasionally along the edges of firebreaks.

What appears to be a waist-high sunflower but with a yellow-centered (rather than dark-centered) blossom is probably rosinweed. These grow sparingly on the roadside between the WIC and the Heron Flats Trail. Cowpen daisy also has yellow rays and a yellow center, but the tips of the rays are deeply notched. The branching plant has toothed, gray-green leaves with basal lobes that clasp the stem. The leaves are aromatic when crushed. Cowpen daisies grow beneath live oaks at the WIC and at the bay overlook parking area.

A thin, solitary stem branching profusely at knee level gives broom-weed its name. The narrow leaves are inconspicuous, while the hundreds of small daisies on the stem tips create a billow of bright yellow dots along firebreaks and roadsides in late summer.

The erect leafy stems of seacoast goldenrod sprout in chest-high clumps from perennial rootstocks. At the top of the stem the narrow leaves angle sharply upwards, and the numerous small, butter-yellow flowers are clustered in a tight six-inch terminal spike. Occasional plants bloom early, but fall (September to November) is the time to enjoy the bright wands of seacoast goldenrods swaying above the russet grasses along the Tour Loop. The more diffuse, flat-topped flower clusters of fragrant goldenrod also appear in the fall; its upper leaves spread widely from the stem. The two species readily hybridize, so intermediate plants are common.

In late summer the roadside clearings between the Dagger Point turn-off and the observation tower are brightened with intermixed expanses of pink sharp gayfeathers and butter-yellow prairie goldenrods. The latter stand stiffly upright to thigh level and support flat-topped clusters of ¼-inch-wide flowers.

Aquatic Plants

Aquatic vegetation is important as shelter and as a food source for wildlife. It contributes to the quality and depth of the water, to firmness and fertility of the bottom, and—as the plants wax and wane and the species composition changes—to the health and longevity of the aquatic community. Most of the aquatic plants on the Aransas have flowers, and we have already mentioned some of those with attractive blossoms. Others can be identified by their growth form or specific growth site. Freshwater plants are best observed along Thomas Slough, from the bridge across Cattail Slough, or from the observation deck at Jones Lake. Brackish-water species can be seen at the end of the boardwalk.

The tall, straplike leaves of cattails erupt thickly from a maze of rhizomes in the rich ooze at the edges of freshwater sites. There is a small gap between the thick, cylindrical female flower spike and the thinner, terminal male part. By early summer the male flowers will have fallen, leaving a naked spire extending above the brown velvety female cluster. In late summer the seed heads get ragged, and seed-carrying cattail fluff fills the air. Red-winged blackbirds nest among the cattails in the springtime, and they visit the stalks in the fall to glean what seeds remain. White-eyed vireos use the fluff to line their nests. Cattail leaves are favorite daytime perches for green treefrogs. The bridge over Cattail Slough affords a good view of a broad expanse of these plants, and the pier on Hog Lake is surrounded by cattails.

The six-foot-tall, slightly curved, cylindrical stems of California bulrush, also called tule (TOOL-eh), grow in dense stands in mucky, shallow fresh water. Chest-high three-square bulrush, with a sharply three-angled erect stem, grows along the banks of ponds and ditches and in moist depressions. Neither of these plants has evident leaves, but in the summertime both produce tufts of brownish flowers near the stem tips. Bulrushes provide cover and foraging sites for red-winged blackbirds,

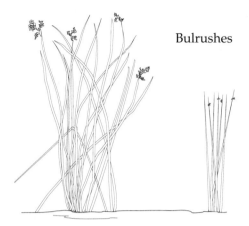

Bulrushes

boat-tailed grackles, sedge wrens, and common moorhens, and their submerged jungle of stems is infiltrated by sunfishes, snails, lesser sirens, yellow mud turtles, alligators, and a host of other creatures.

Common reeds grow in dense leafy stands and send their heavy plumed seed heads twelve feet high to sway in the prevailing wind. A prominent growth of reeds can be seen along the edge of the bay between the Heron Flats Trail and the picnic area. At the same site there are several isolated head-high clumps of sawgrass with lax panicles of rust-brown flowers and leaf margins armed with sharp teeth that can slice an unwary finger. Despite its name, sawgrass is actually one of a large group of grassy-looking plants called sedges. Most wet places are lined with a diversity of ankle- to knee-high kinds of sedges; one that is apt to catch your eye is white-top sedge. At the top of each knee-high stem there is a spray of drooping leaves with chalky white bases that give the appearance of a wide-spread flower.

Rushes are yet another group of abundant, moisture-loving, grasslike plants. There is a welter of species on the Aransas, but most are nondescript. Perhaps you will notice the cherry coke rush, a species that grows abundantly in roadside ditches and is topped by loose clusters of spherical prickly fruits, which ripen to a delicious reddish brown.

On muddy banks and in half-dried ponds the ground is usually covered with the round, umbrellalike leaves of coast pennywort and the prostrate stems and small, paired leaves of waterhyssop. The clusters of tiny flowers of pennywort are white; waterhyssop has cup-shaped lilac flowers. Standing above these are leafy clumps of marsh fleabane with dense heads of purple-pink flowers. All three of these plants can be seen from the bridge over Cattail Slough on the Heron Flats Trail.

The intense yellow four-petaled flowers of narrowleaf water primrose regularly grace Thomas Slough, while a second species, shrubby water primrose, holds its pale yellow blossoms head-high around the margin of Jones Lake.

After a series of wet years water lilies appear in semipermanent freshwater sites on the refuge. The more common species is white water lily, which raises its fetching violet-white blossom above the water on a stout pedicel. The blossom of yellow water lily rides the water surface. At Jones Lake these two species are joined by the striking American lotus, which heaves its huge circular leaves (about two feet in diameter) a foot out of the water on stout stalks and pushes its large (eight inches across) soft-yellow flowers even higher.

Whenever the Guadalupe River floods, it flushes clumps of water hyacinth into San Antonio Bay. As they raft across the brackish bay, these freshwater plants slowly die, and windrows of them, dead and dying, accumulate along the eastern shore of Blackjack Peninsula. An occasional plant may still display an attractive cluster of lavender flowers, and after exceptional floods a broad band of blooming plants may garnish the edge of the bay for several weeks. Water hyacinths can be recognized by the spongy enlargements on the leaf stalks that help to keep the plant afloat.

The only emergent herbaceous brackish-water species of note is smooth cordgrass. This is the dominant grass of the Gulf Coast salt-marsh community, but only relatively small stands occur locally. Smooth cordgrass provides both food and shelter for many small marine creatures, and it buffers the bayshore against wave erosion. At the end of the boardwalk you can see this grass growing in San Antonio Bay, and from the observation tower you can observe it lining the immediate edge of Mustang Lake.

Grasses

Most people think they know a grass when they see one, but few can recognize even half a dozen kinds. Yet grasses make up a large and important fraction of most communities, and on the Gulf Coastal Plain they are vegetative dominants.

Seething generations of insects, arachnids, millipedes, centipedes, nematode worms, fungi, and microbes live and die without ever leaving the microjungle of grass stems. More legions squirm through the grass sod. Even larger creatures, like fulvous harvest mice, eastern meadowlarks, and Great Plains rat snakes, satisfy most of their requirements in grassland. An array of animals from white-tailed deer and bobwhite quail to grasshoppers and caterpillars consume fresh grass; others, like savannah sparrows, pygmy mice, and harvester ants, depend on grass seeds. All of the grass-dependent animals in the countless nests, daytime retreats, and fur-lined nooks hidden among the innumerable grass clumps on the Aransas work their way into other food chains. The grasses rank as significant members of the producer level in the food web.

Aside from their direct contribution to wildlife, grasses mold the terrain by holding topsoil and by inhibiting or at least influencing the growth of woody plants and forbs. Grasslands prosper under a demanding regime of grazing by large herbivores, periodic drought, and occasional wildfire—a combination that must be duplicated in modern grassland management. Finally, more than any other plant group, grasses have swayed the history and the economy of humans on the coastal prairie.

Grasses are flowering plants, but because their wind-pollinated flowers do not need insect lures, they are seldom showy or colorful. However, grasses are not lacking in their own beauty: crisp brown winter foliage, waving heads of silver seed fluff, the poetic arc of a clump of seacoast bluestem braced against the steady onshore breeze, the sweep of a hundred unbroken acres of gossamer-laced, dew-laden culms immobilized in the trance of dawn.

About 85 kinds of grasses are known from the Aransas Refuge. We mention only a few prominent and important ones. Two groups, bluestems and cordgrasses, cover more ground on the Aransas than all the other kinds of grasses combined. Bluestems dominate the sandy interior; cordgrasses take nearly sole possession of the saline flats.

Bluestems

Bluestems are native bunchgrasses, so-named because of the peculiar tint of their foliage, but this distinction is not always evident. About a dozen species grow on the refuge. They make up most of the grass cover in the clearings along the Tour Loop. Most kinds are warm-season perennials. They begin fresh growth tardily in spring, and by early summer they are often overtopped by other, faster-growing grasses and by many tall annuals such as buckwheat, Texas croton, common sunflower, and Texas palafoxia. But as summer progresses the bluestems begin to gain in prominence. By fall (October to November), when most other plants are waning, the bluestems have reached full growth and are heavy with seed. Then there is no question about their claim to dominance.

Bushy bluestem is one of the most prominent grasses on the Aransas Refuge. It grows prolifically in robust, head-high clumps in all lowlying sites along the road. Its whisk broom–like, shaggy seed heads

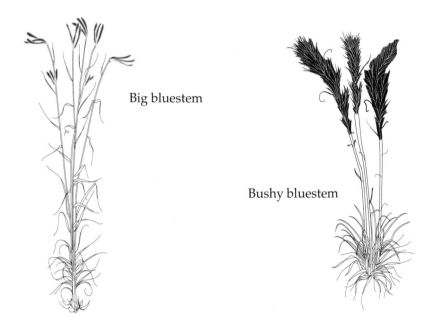

Big bluestem

Bushy bluestem

give it a top-heavy appearance. One of the most attractive displays on the Aransas is a glade of bushy bluestem caught at the peak of its straw-and-russet splendor by the first rays of an October sun.

Broomsedge bluestem resembles bushy bluestem, but it is a shorter, more delicate plant and prefers drier, upland sites. Its winter stalks are straw-colored. Silver bluestem has silvery, tapering seed heads at the ends of thin leafless stalks. Seen against a low sun, an expanse of silver bluestem is dazzling.

The introduced King Ranch bluestem is common on the refuge. Look for its thin purple-brown seed heads in the clearing near the picnic area. In the fall, you may notice violet islands in the purple-brown sea of King Ranch bluestem. These are patches of Roemer tripleawn, a grass with three whisker-thin hairs attached to each slender seed. Because of these hairs, the seed heads ripple continually in the coastal breeze.

Big bluestem is the giant of its clan. This regal grass grows in isolated clumps towering up to ten feet above the surrounding grasses. Despite its impressive appearance, nearly two-thirds of the big bluestem plant is hidden from view as a subterranean maze of thick horizontal rhizomes and a deep fibrous root system. The lilac-tinged heads have a crowfoot arrangement of three thick, seed-laden fingers. Big bluestem disappears quickly when grazed by cattle, so it is seldom seen in its full

Seacoast bluestem

glory anywhere else in the Coastal Bend. Watch for this spectacular grass along roadside ditches and in swales on the Tour Loop and pay it the homage it richly deserves.

Seacoast bluestem is the most widespread member of its group on the refuge. Many upland clearings among the live oaks support nearly pure stands of this native climax bunchgrass. The clumps of foliage are so tightly packed that the thin curling leaves of one plant intermingle with those of adjacent plants to produce a continuous thigh-high sward, while the communal network of rhizomes and fibrous roots holds the sandy soil against both wind and rain. The numerous thin and finely branched flowering stems turn rust-red in the fall, and each is tipped with a small curled tuft of silver-haired seeds. An expanse of seacoast bluestem at its autumnal peak is a rustling conflagration of multiple red tones punctuated with a million wisps of platinum ash. Whooper time is also seacoast bluestem time on the Aransas; every visitor should aspire to experience both.

Cordgrasses

Each of the three species of cordgrasses on the refuge has its own growth zone dictated by the salt and moisture content of the soil.

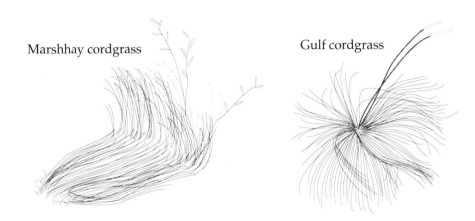

Marshhay cordgrass

Gulf cordgrass

Smooth cordgrass, mentioned among the aquatic plants, grows only along regularly inundated bay margins. The tidal shore community is dominated by marshhay cordgrass, which begins on the inland perimeter of the tidal flat and extends across all low, slightly saline depressions. You can find it on both sides of the path along the outer ridge of the Heron Flats Trail (specifically mentioned at Station 27) and along the bayward end of the boardwalk.

A rank, waist-high clump of Gulf cordgrass, called sacahuista (sah-kah-WEES-tah) by ranchers, makes an apt vegetative symbol for the Gulf Coast. On favorable saline soils above the reach of high tides, such as on the southern third of the Tatton Unit, Gulf cordgrass grows in pure stands. Dark mounds can be observed from the boardwalk, from the observation tower, and along the outer ridge of the Heron Flats Trail (Station 26). Touch your palm gently against the tips of Gulf cordgrass leaves to appreciate why many old-timers called it needle grass.

Marshhay and Gulf cordgrass are not always easy to distinguish from each other. Marshhay is seldom over knee height, and its thin, lax leaves take on a cow-lick curvature, but they are never so evidently bunched as the stiffer Gulf cordgrass. In seed the two species are easily recognized: marshhay has a slender stalk with half a dozen well-separated fingers of seeds; Gulf cordgrass has a single stout stalk terminating in a long spike of numerous overlapping seed branches.

Other Grasses

To strike pure gold on the Aransas, find an expanse of yellow Indian grass in full seed in a late October sun. Although bunches can be found along paved roads, this handsome grass with its gently arched six-foot stems bearing ample tufts of golden grain really catches the eye en masse. Yellow Indian grass frequently gilds clearings a year after they have been burned.

The huge, chest-high, coarse bunchgrass that grows in ditches and swales along the road to the observation tower is switch grass. Its stout, nearly woody stems soar six feet in the air before giving rise to a spreading panicle of tiny seeds. Switch grass, big bluestem, and yellow Indian grass are local outliers from the tallgrass prairie that once swept in uninterrupted grandeur across the wet coastal plain between Galveston and Beaumont in East Texas.

The appealing misty rose-lavender patches that grace the edges of the Tour Loop in autumn are the finely divided seed heads of Gulf muhly (MULE-ee). These fleecy panicles, which seem to float above a dense, waist-high clump of thin leaves, vie with spiderwebs for glistening with dewdrops on cool fall mornings.

Two kinds of low-growing tidal-flat grasses are readily observed along the boardwalk. Shin-high seashore saltgrass thrives in saline muck. It is recognized by its long, keen leaves staggered neatly up opposite sides of the stalk to give a herringbone pattern. The leaves often glisten with salt crystals excreted by the plant to maintain its water balance in its saline habitat. Shoregrass forms a prickly green mat only a few inches high on otherwise barren salty sand. Both of these grasses can withstand occasional tidal overwash. Snow geese feed on the greenery and grub up the rhizomes of saltgrass.

You may discover a carpet of St. Augustine grass beneath some live oak groves. This introduced lawn grass, locally called carpet grass, is common in the Coastal Bend and often survives without care long after the humans who planted it are gone and forgotten. The species belongs to a group of tropical seashore pioneer grasses that originated in southeast Asia. Although there are no definite records, St. Augustine grass was probably brought to the New World by the earliest colonists. Today it has a nearly worldwide distribution along warm coastlines, coastal prairies, and on oceanic islands. On western Atlantic shores it ranges from North Carolina to Argentina.

If you spend much time walking anywhere on the refuge, you are sure to get a shoestring or pants cuff full of sticker burs, compliments of Gulf coast sandbur, a pesky native grass that specializes in hitchhiking on animals.

The common reed, mentioned among the aquatic plants, is actually a huge grass. The refuge also supports many members of other important grass groups, especially dropseeds, paspalums, and panic grasses.

Vines

The strategy of a vine is to reach the sunshine by climbing up some convenient support, usually another plant. Besides the woody vines mentioned in Chapter 14, there is a welter of climbing, clambering, and twining herbaceous vines on the refuge. The ones described here can all be found along the Heron Flats Trail.

Two morning glorys, both with trumpet-shaped flowers, are easily recognizable. In Alamo vine (Station 22) the trumpet is bright white with a purple spot inside the throat. This vine has leaves dissected into fingerlike lobes, and it sets fleshy turnip-shaped fruits. Tievine (Station 19) seldom climbs over chest-high and has lavender trumpets and three-lobed leaves.

You may miss the yellow flowers of melonette and of globeberry (Station 21), but their fruits and their watchspring tendrils are more eye-catching. Melonettes look like inch-long striped watermelons; ripe globeberries resemble orange-red Ping-Pong balls.

The thin green Texas nightshade (Station 20) vine that commonly scrambles in the understory has white, cupped flowers with five petals and red, tomatolike fruits about ⅜ inch in diameter.

There are several different kinds of twining vines with milky sap; all produce horn-shaped fruits that open to release flat brown seeds on silken parachutes. Milkweed vine (Station 24) has pairs of soft, heart-shaped leaves and clusters of small white flowers, and it bears a smooth, four-inch-long pod. Each solitary, pale green flower of pearl milkweed (Station 18) has an opalescent dot in the center. Its six-inch pods are

Alamo vine

Milkweed vine

prickly. Dwarf milkweed vine (Station 23) produces a prodigious number of fragrant, urn-shaped white flowers ⅛ inch long, and its smooth pods are less than two inches long.

Snapdragon vine (Station 24) has a ¾-inch tubular flower that flares into two upper petals and three larger lower ones. The petals are vivid purple, and there is a raised yellow area in the throat of the whitish floral tube. Look for the flowers and the triangular leaves on abundant stems, scrambling among the shrubs and bunchgrasses along the outer ridge of the Heron Flats Trail. There, too, watch at shin-level for the 1¼-inch, pale lavender spoon-shaped flowers of butterfly pea. Before the heat of midday you can also spot butterfly peas from your vehicle gleaming among the live oak thickets along the Tour Loop.

Three species of low twining beans with small, yellow, bonnet-shaped flowers and curved bean pods are common on the refuge. Both Texas snoutbean, with one to three flowers rising from the leaf base, and least snoutbean, with a delicate spike of flowers from the leaf base, have leaves divided into three leaflets. American snoutbean, which often sprawls along the edge of the pavement of the Tour Loop, has fat heart-shaped leaves.

Wild cowpea is another twining vine with a raceme of yellow bonnet-shaped flowers and a three-part leaf. Cowpea has larger flowers, and the leaf segments are lance-shaped rather than triangular as in the snout-beans. It also prefers wetter places. Look for cowpea among the common reeds on the edge of San Antonio Bay.

The stems, leaves, and even parts of the flowers of hairy stylisma (sty-LIZ-mah) are densely covered with soft hairs, a protection against heat and evaporation in the dry, sandy areas it favors. They spread across the ground and clamber in the shrubby oaks and in sandy clearings along the Tour Loop. To see the one-inch white funnel-shaped flowers, you must look before noon.

Epiphytes

Epiphytes are plants that grow, not just climb, on other plants but are not parasitic. An epiphyte merely uses its host plant as a convenient place to sit in the sunshine. On the Aransas, only two species of flowering plants belong in this category: Spanish moss and ball moss.

Since these plants do produce small flowers, they cannot be true mosses. In fact, they are bromeliads, a predominantly tropical group. Both species are composed of tangled masses of thin stems and leaves. They are silver-gray from a snug covering of waxy scales, which prevent water loss but can be raised to absorb water when it is available. Beneath the scales the plants are quite green and carry on routine photosynthesis.

The long stems of Spanish moss hang in swaying festoons, usually from live oak branches. For a few hours after a summer rain, their pale lavender flowers can be seen among the stems. The short, rigid stems of ball moss form a fist-sized mass that sits astride a branch. Its small purple flowers bloom at the ends of wiry pedicels sticking out several inches beyond the leaves. These pedicels remain on the plant for months, so clumps of ball moss almost always have numerous protruding stalks. The minute seeds of both species are wafted to new perches by wisps of fluff.

A fascinating microcommunity of insects, arachnids, millipedes, and other small creatures lives in the moist, shady depths of moss plants,

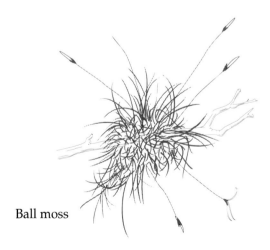

Ball moss

and these clumps are favorite foraging sites for small perching birds. Many birds and some rodents line their nests with the tough fibrous strands of dead moss.

You can see both kinds of mosses in the live oaks on the Heron Flats (Station 13) and Big Tree trails, and ball moss is common in tree branches bordering the ramp to the observation tower. Because it is more tolerant of drought, ball moss is the more common of the two species on the refuge.

Parasites

Parasitic plants not only grow on other plants but also put modified roots into the host's tissue and obtain some or all of their nourishment there.

On the refuge, mistletoe grows mainly on mesquite and net-leaf hackberry. It is not common in the area of public access, but there are small bunches in the hackberries over the picnic table at the alligator observation site across from the WIC. The evergreen clumps of brittle green branches and thick yellow-green leaves are easier to spot in the wintertime on leafless trees. Mistletoe flowers are inconspicuous, but the round, translucent white berries that appear in the wintertime are well known. Seeds wiped from the bill of a bird that has fed on the sticky berries give mistletoe a start in a new spot.

Dodders, with neither green color nor leaves, are more evidently parasitic. They look like loops of pale yellow string tangled through the branches of their host. Dodders sprout from seed and develop a root system, but they have no chlorophyll. To survive, a young dodder must be near enough to a host plant to twine into it. Then it puts fibrils into the host's tissues, severs its own connection with the ground, and thereafter lives entirely on nutrients absorbed from the host. Each kind of dodder parasitizes one species or a select group of plants. Spreading dodder, the most common one on the refuge, can be seen in mats on the branches of marsh elder along the outer ridge of the Heron Flats Trail (Station 24). Its clusters of white flowers appear in late summer. Tree dodder is the species seen tangled in the tops of live oaks, where it leaves brown masses of dead stems in the wintertime. Although the host plants must be weakened by these parasites, they do not usually look disabled.

Extra Specials

Botanists, like birders or butterfly collectors, delight in new, rare, or especially appealing species. The Aransas Refuge harbors a reservoir of such botanical treats. We briefly mention a few that have pleased us.

- Saltmarsh morning glory: an occasional twiner on sea ox-eye on the tidal flats and among sedges in moist ditches; rather common in wet years. The huge (3½-inch) rose-purple trumpets open early and wither by noon.
- Meadow beauty: a plant from the east, reported here for the first time in the Coastal Bend. Showy, two-inch pink flower with four petals and eight curved yellow anthers; rare and restricted.
- Annual sundew: ground-hugging, coin-sized rosettes of paddle-shaped leaves covered with red hairs. Sticky droplets on the hairs catch small insects, which the plant consumes. On open wet sand along roadside ditches.
- Two-flower bladderwort: submerged leaves fashioned into unique traps that capture and digest tiny aquatic creatures; tiny yellow flowers on emergent stalks. Occurs in Thomas Slough.
- Upland ladies' tresses: the only orchid on the refuge. Occasional shin-high stalks in roadside ditches topped with a symmetrical spiral of small white flowers.
- Woods wine-cup: relatively huge wine-cup, with petals spreading over two inches and finely toothed on the tips. An eastern species, rare and restricted.
- Purple pleat leaf: the refuge's finest native iris. A 1½-inch, royal-purple flower on a thin, knee-high stalk, blooms in early summer between Dagger Point and the tower. Common enough but ephemeral.
- Texas bluebell (also called prairie gentian): two-inch indigo flowers on knee-high stems with satiny blue-green foliage. In bud, the petals are twirled into a sharp spiral. Occasional in depression at Station 19 on Heron Flats Trail.
- American cupscale: a species from the southeast not previously reported from the Coastal Bend. An uncommon grass of moist swales (grows beside pier at Jones Lake) with panicle of asymmetrical, inflated flowers.
- Woevine: resembles a giant dodder. Pale green to orange vine snaking through live oak and red bay, at intervals curled around and attached to branches. Occasional on live oaks at the tower and on the Youth Environmental Training Area.
- Maypop passionflower: low-twining vine with tendrils and three-lobed leaves. The male and female floral parts and a lavender wreath of wavy, hairlike segments stand up on a stout central pedestal. Lacy bracts enclose the green fruit but drop off as it matures to orange red. One vine known at bridge over Cattail Slough on Heron Flats Trail.

CHAPTER 16

Nonflowering Plants

 The only trait common to this conglomeration of plants is that they do not have flowers and so never produce either fruits or seeds. Instead, they reproduce by simple cell division, by spores, or by vegetative propagation. Because of their obscure means of reproduction, botanists call such plants *cryptogams*, a term that derives from the Greek and means "secret marriage." Many kinds do not have ordinary roots, stems, or leaves. Even lacking such conventional botanical attributes, they manage the basic life functions. Some carry on routine photosynthesis. Others absorb nourishment from living or dead hosts. Though they lack bright petals, not all kinds are drab, and many of them have peculiar and interesting life cycles.

These plants are low on the evolutionary tree, but some have a high ecological impact. Marine algae are a mainstay in the food web of the bays. Bacteria and fungi are indispensable for recycling nutrients and providing the tons of detritus that feed the smallest of creatures and, by devious branches of the food web, many larger ones as well. Both lichens and mosses serve as food and shelter for an array of minuscule organisms that are preyed upon by larger invertebrates and by small birds.

We will mention only a few conspicuous members of five groups of nonflowering plants: algae, fungi, lichens, mosses, and ferns. *Nonflowering Plants,* by F. S. Shuttleworth and H. S. Zim, is a well-illustrated introductory guide to this frequently overlooked portion of the plant world.

Algae

During the fall and winter, rafts of waterfowl dive, dabble, and graze in the shallows of San Antonio Bay, harvesting bushels of plant material every day. Two species make up the bulk of the birds' fare. One of these, widgeon grass, is actually a flowering plant. Despite its name, it is not a true grass but belongs to its own unique plant family. Its flowers are too tiny to be noticed, and the plant, which is rooted in the bottom and entirely submerged, resembles a thin-leaved seaweed, so we have included it here. Many acres of shallow bay bottom are covered with widgeon grass until the waterfowl mow it down, eagerly consuming fruits, branches, leaves, and even the roots. When the water is clear, from a vantage along the Dagger Point Trail you can see dark patches of widgeon grass dotting the bottom of San Antonio Bay.

The second plant utilized by waterfowl, seahorsetail, is a filmy alga that grows profusely throughout the summer and is available by the ton when the birds arrive. Coots and diving ducks often bob to the surface with long streamers of the alga in their bills. Seahorsetail commonly attaches to widgeon-grass stalks, and the two plants are eaten together. By the time the birds leave, the once luxuriant submarine meadows are virtually barren, but a warm season of growth reconstitutes them. Strong winds sometimes pile windrows of widgeon grass and seahorsetail along the edge of Blackjack Peninsula, and you can usually find evidence of both species at the end of the boardwalk.

Bushy olive to purple-green growths of the alga called sea bush are attached to the muddy bottom and on oyster reefs in San Antonio Bay. Many of these fleshy-textured plants are blown onto the shoreline, where they turn bright lilac. Beach fleas seek food and shelter beneath these rotting algal masses, and you might see a willet or a ruddy turnstone adroitly flip a bit of sea bush to uncover a meal.

In portions of the tidal flat and the brackish pool communities, where there are extreme variations in moisture, temperature, and salinity, rooted plants do not grow at all. But these open stretches of silty sand are often coated with a thin, slick film of blue-green algae, hardy plants quite important to the ecology of the bayshore. The mucus-covered mats retard evaporation, and the blue-green algae not only carry on photosynthesis, producing green matter and oxygen, but also engage in a peculiar activity called nitrogen fixation, which increases the fertility of the soil and the water. Shore flies pass their life cycles on the algal mats, and western sandpipers spend much time probing there for fly larvae. During droughts or prolonged low tides the blue-green algae form an apparently lifeless black crust on the tidal flat; dormant living tissue quickly revives with the return of moisture.

The ponds that constitute Muskgrass Slough between the middle and outer ridges on the Heron Flats Trail support dense tangles of muskgrass (Station 25), a many-celled alga with the joints of its long brittle stems marked by spreading rings of cylindrical leaflike structures. When the water evaporates, the depressions are lined with thick mats of dying muskgrass, brown at first but bleaching nearly white in the sun. When the pond refills, the subterranean portions of the stems quickly revive and regrow. Shorebirds search the foliage of muskgrass for small crustaceans and insects, and the fresh growth and rhizomes are favored food of ducks. You will doubtless be delighted to learn that muskgrass exudes chemicals that not only kill mosquito wrigglers but also make the water less attractive to female mosquitoes about to lay eggs. These potent, garliclike substances also cause the musky odor of the crushed leaves and thus are the basis for the plant's common name.

The most common alga in Thomas Slough is appropriately named pond silk. In early spring, its thin green threads grow at the bottom, but as the season progresses, large verdant swirls of detached filaments cloud the water. As it matures, pond silk rises to the surface, where it forms bubbly, yellow-green mats upon which numerous tiny insects cavort. In late summer, the mats transform into a brown scum covered with blisters of gas from the decomposition of the now dead algae. The mass eventually sinks and disintegrates to become part of the bottom detritus. You can observe pond silk from the Big Willow footbridge.

Coontail is actually a flowering plant, but its minute flowers are seldom observed. The rootless, submerged stems with their rings of thin leaves resemble muskgrass, but coontail is dark green, while muskgrass is yellow-green. A dense growth of coontail clogs Thomas Slough at the head of the Rail Trail.

Fungi

All fungi lack chlorophyll; they absorb their nourishment from living or dead organic matter. A few species cause disease, but the bulk of them are involved in decomposition, the breakdown of plant and animal remains that is crucial for the release of nutrients in both terrestrial and aquatic communities. Sooner or later, the seemingly ageless live oaks will die, and even their iron-hard core will slowly disintegrate before the relentless onslaught of a battery of wood-rot fungi.

Some of the larger kinds of fungi support insect microcommunities, and several species are important seasonal food for mice, squirrels, javelinas, wild hogs, white-tailed deer, and wild turkeys. Quite a few species are colorful, and all of the larger ones are worth pausing to observe for their alien, somewhat mystical habits: abrupt emergence into a dank and gloomy habitat, strange architecture built of cold fleshy tissue, fiber laced with exotic, often toxic secretions, ephemeral existence, sudden disappearance. Little wonder that fungi evoke a morbid fascination in most people.

Mushrooms, puffballs, yeasts, mildews, and sundry "molds" and their spores are everywhere, especially in the soil. Fungi are by far the most abundant and diverse of the nonflowering plants, but most kinds are microscopic or nearly so. *The Audubon Society Field Guide to North American Mushrooms*, by Gary Lincoff, and *Texas Mushrooms: A Field Guide*, by Susan Metzler and Van Metzler, are well-illustrated references to many local species.

Mushrooms

The Aransas Refuge supports a varied array of mushrooms and puffballs, general names for the two main groups of large fungi. But the growth of most kinds is fickle and fleeting, and their distinguishing traits are subtle, so we will mention only a few conspicuous species.

The best time to see mushrooms and puffballs on the Aransas is in late summer or fall, a few days after a good rain. Look for mushrooms in leaf litter on the edges of live oak mottes and around tree stumps. Puffballs often occur on sparsely grassed sand. One of the delights of fungi is that they can pop up unexpectedly most anywhere, so be alert wherever you roam.

Typical mushrooms release microscopic spores from gills, the radiating platelike structures on the underside of the cap. The giant among Aransas species is the green-spored lepiota (lepy-OH-tah), which has gray-green spores. Clusters of these mushrooms appear on the roadsides after heavy spring and summer rains. The flat white cap, up to almost a foot across, stands on a sturdy six-inch stalk.

On a moist day you may encounter the silky, gray-brown, fleshy, two- to four-inch caps of meadow mushrooms along the Big Tree or Dagger Point trails. The gills start out bright pink, becoming rich chocolate-

Fawn mushroom

Meadow mushroom

brown as the spores mature. Fawn mushrooms occur in the same habitat but are more widely scattered. Their stalks are usually attached to dead wood beneath the sand. The three-inch caps, soft brown and slightly sticky, usually grow beneath a cover of yaupon or oak branches. The fresh white gills turn salmon-pink when the spores ripen.

Cool fall days induce from the deep sand along the Dagger Point Trail one of the real gems among Aransas mushrooms—the emetic russula. Watch for the flat-topped, rose-pink caps among the leaf litter; they sit on stout white stalks and may be three inches across. If you find one, others are likely to be nearby.

Inky-cap mushrooms are common on the Aransas, but they are impulsive, springing up suddenly and disappearing in a few hours. Most have long, slender white stalks and parasol-shaped white caps that darken and flatten as they mature. A hallmark of the group is the rapid disintegration of the cap into a glutinous black mass. Though they are capricious, the picnic area is a likely place to watch for inky-caps. Clusters of these black-spored mushrooms commonly sprout from animal feces.

After fall rains, clusters of jack-o-lantern mushrooms, growing on tree stumps and buried wood where oak and bay have been mowed, are often spectacular. The cap is burnt orange, and the orange gills pale to yellow as they blend into the stalk. Mature caps have down-curved edges and a deep depression in the center. It takes a close look in a really dark room to see the ghostly green luminescence of the gills— an appropriate trait for a pumpkin-colored mushroom that grows at Halloween time.

The Aransas Refuge harbors several toxic mushrooms. At least two belong to the infamous amanita (am-ah-NEET-ah) and are called destroying angels. Both of the Aransas species are a beguiling snow white and have a skirtlike ring around the upper portion of the stem. If you merely admire them and pass on, they can do you no harm.

Boletes

Another group of fungi, the boletes (BOW-leets) have no gills but release their spores from an array of pores on the undersurface of the cap. These squatty fungi have bulbous stalks and caps that resemble doorknobs in size and shape. The cap of the common delicate bolete is tinted like a ripe peach, with a bright yellow pore surface below. Boletes are most common in live oak leaf litter. Their caps are frequently gnawed by beetles and mice.

During wet fall months, the old-man-of-the-woods bursts sporadi-

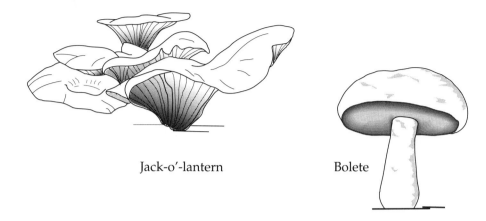

Jack-o'-lantern   Bolete

cally from the leaf litter in the oak-bay forest community. The white cap of this hoary bolete is studded with blackish scales and hairy tufts, and the stem is roughened with fibers and scales.

Shelf Fungi

The semiwoody caps of shelf fungi also release spores from a pored undersurface, but they do not have stalks; the caps grow directly from logs and tree trunks, often in overlapping clusters. Tiers of the orange-and-yellow-banded fans of sulphur shelf fungus grow commonly on live oaks. These and other shelf fungi, most of them creamy white, can be found on dead or dying tree branches along the Big Tree Trail, while the plump beige pads of oyster mushroom bedeck black willow branches along Thomas Slough.

Puffballs

Puffballs are distinguished by having a dense mass of spores enclosed in a parchmentlike cover. Eventually the cover ruptures, and a cloud of dark spores is released. These fungi usually appear following rains in dry, open sandy areas, but the fruiting bodies linger for weeks. Most puffballs are low-growing and globular, but the related stinkhorns are columnar.

White puffballs appear along sandy trails. They grow from pea to golf-ball size; some are smooth, but most kinds have a warty or spiny surface. Some develop a pore at the top when the spores are ripe, and if you press the fruiting body gently, a cloud of dark spores will

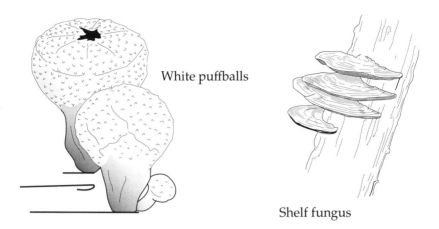

White puffballs

Shelf fungus

spew from the hole. From such forced exhalations we get the name "puffball."

The largest species of puffballs on the refuge, which we have named doughballs for their resemblance to blobs of rising bread dough, are five to six inches in diameter. These are white when young and mature to a well-done crisp brown. Eventually the top splits to reveal a mass of purple or olive-yellow spores. The empty urnlike bases of doughballs sometimes remain along sandy trails for weeks.

Earthballs are hard lumps about the size of a chicken egg with a leathery, straw-colored skin. Lacking a stalk, they are often nearly hidden by windblown sand. When an earthball matures, the top quarter of the tough skin rips open to reveal a powdery mass of purple-brown spores. Raindrops and wind quickly disperse the spores, leaving empty, jagged-edged bowls in the sand.

Earthstars have a thick outer skin over the papery spore case. As the fungus matures, the skin darkens and splits into segments that open into a star shape when the weather is wet and curl back over the spore case when it is dry. Spores are released through a pore in the center of the papery ball, and the drab, deflated spheres with their rim of stiff, starlike petals remain on the ground for weeks. Earthstars are common along the east side of the road between Dagger Point and the tower; they favor one- or two-year-old burns.

Stinkhorns

Stinkhorns are a peculiar type of puffball. They develop in egg-shaped capsules underground and then send up one or more tubes on which

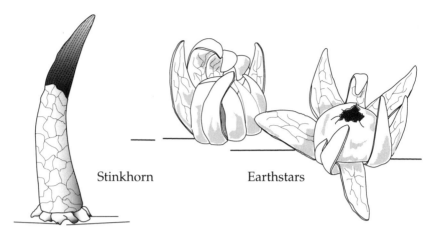

Stinkhorn   Earthstars

the spores are suspended in a smelly slime. The spore-filled slime sticks onto flies that are attracted by the foul odor, and it is spread when the insects alight somewhere else. The combination of slime and flies sounds offensive, but stinkhorns are intriguing if not appealing fungi.

Common stinkhorn is ankle-high. The tapered, spongy tube is salmon-colored and capped with a layer of green-brown slime. The tube lasts only a day and is most commonly seen on sandy sites after fall rains.

Even the cinnabar color of the ankle-high columnar stinkhorn is easily missed in its grassy habitat. The central stalk is split into three segments, which rejoin at their tips in the mass of greenish, fetid spore material. The odor of columnar stinkhorns is attractive to at least one animal besides flies; feral hogs avidly gobble up these fungi.

Stinkhorns are seldom abundant, and the netted stinkhorn is one of the rarest of its clan on the refuge. At some unknown signal, the five-inch white stalk rises rapidly from its subterranean bulb. A wrinkled greenish spore head develops atop the stalk, and a delicate white, net-like veil spreads downward from the head to encircle the upper half of the stalk. The spectacular structure lasts less than a day. Watch for it on damp fall days in the oak-bay forest community. The sight will almost surely be a once-in-a-lifetime experience.

Lichens

Most of the body of these compound plants is fungal tissue, but there is an enclosed layer of algal cells. A lichen (LIE-ken) may be viewed as a fungus that has enslaved an alga to produce carbohydrates for it by photosynthesis. The combination is successful. Lichens are tough

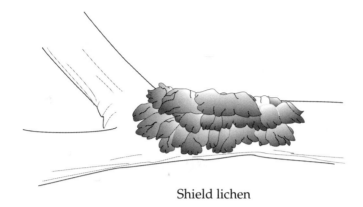

Shield lichen

enough to survive every extreme of the coastal environment except prolonged submersion in salt water or dry, shifting sand.

Typically, lichens are attached to a firm substrate, which limits them on the Aransas Refuge to tree trunks and branches. A watchful eye will perceive that lichens are quite common on most of the trees along every trail; hackberries and live oaks support especially luxuriant growths. Lichens are epiphytes, not parasites.

Several species of foliose lichens contribute to the gray-green patina on the chunky bark of live oak trees. As you walk up the ramp to the observation tower you can closely observe the mineral-gray shield lichens that grow in leaflike layers on the oak branches. Tangled masses of golden lichen droop from tree branches, and streamers of gray-green old-man's-beard wave in the breeze along the shaded portion of the Heron Flats Trail.

Mosses

"Moss" is one of those generalized words taken over from common language by science and sharpened in meaning to limit it to a specific group of plants. Spanish moss and ball moss are epiphytic flowering plants; lichens are frequently called tree moss, and many people refer to marine algae as sea moss. Here we consider true moss—plants that fit the strict botanical designation.

True mosses are delicate and low-growing but always green. They lack true roots and stems and cannot easily draw water into their tiny leaves. Reproduction requires at least a film of water, so mosses grow successfully only in moist habitats. This severely limits the occurrence of mosses on the drought-prone Aransas Refuge.

True moss

Where on the refuge might an immobile, continually thirsty plant find the right combination of partial sunshine and dependable moisture to eke out a living? Only in the bark crevices of the larger live oak trees. That is where to look for the most common species of moss on the Aransas, appropriately named tree moss. Tree moss forms green cushions on favorable live oak limbs on the Big Tree and Heron Flats trails and beneath the observation tower. Station 10 on the Heron Flats Trail marks a growth on a low live oak trunk that is convenient for close examination. You can kneel there and look through your magnifying glass at the diminutive forest of green leaves (they may be curled up if conditions are very dry) and stalked, golden spore capsules. Then you will recognize a true moss the next time you see one.

Ferns

Shifting sand, withering summers, and occasional seawater overwash make the local environment a hostile one for ferns. Only about half a dozen of the approximately one hundred species of ferns recorded from Texas occur in the Coastal Bend, and none of them is widespread. Four kinds of ferns have been found on the Aransas Refuge; two grow in the area of public access.

Water clover is well named for its long-stalked four-part leaves. Colonies of water clover are known from muddy overflows at several windmills in the interior of Blackjack Peninsula.

The smallest species of fern in Texas, mosquito fern, would hardly spread across your thumbnail. During the summer, many plants form extensive floating mats, which turn red as the plants die in the fall. Water fern is spread from one freshwater site to another on the feet of gadwalls, teal, coots, and gallinules, which feed on it. On the Aransas Refuge water fern occurs consistently only at Tule Lake, and it appears sporadically at Thomas Slough.

Resurrection fern is so named because it withers into a brown mound when dry and quickly unfurls its green fronds following rains. This is an epiphytic species that grows on large, well-shaded live oak branches, usually accompanied by mats of tree moss. Resurrection fern is rare on the refuge. It is known from a few live oaks near the Big Tree Trail and should be looked for along the shaded part of the Heron Flats Trail (Station 13).

The wiry stems of bracken fern send a spray of olive-green fronds to chest height. A colony of bracken fern growing on the dam at Big Devil Bayou and another near Johnson Mill are the first of this species reported from the Coastal Bend.

Soaring vultures

Plants in Flower on Slope at WIC

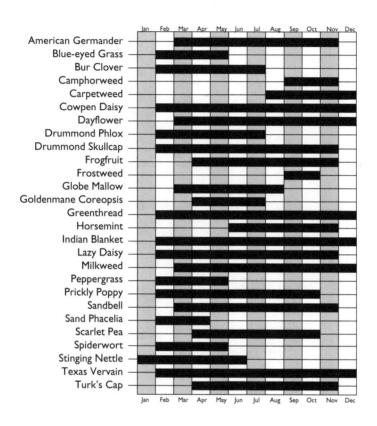

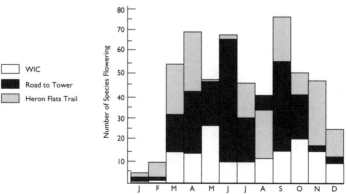

Summary of Flowering Plants 1985–1986

Plants in Flower along Road to Tower

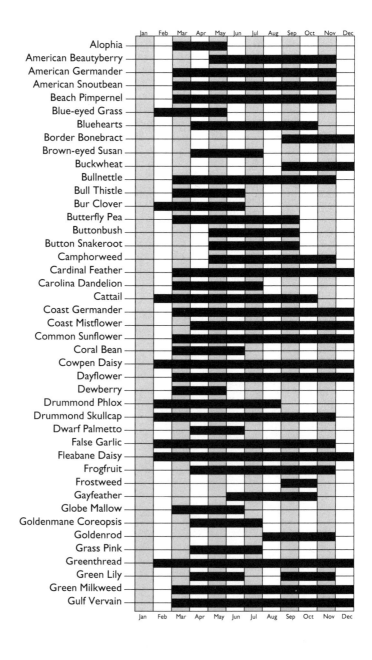

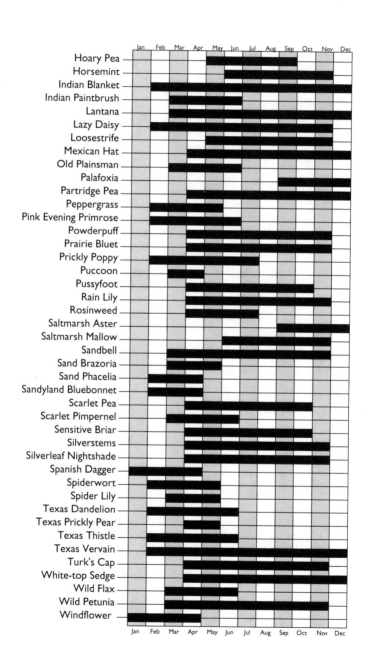

Plants in Flower on Heron Flats Trail

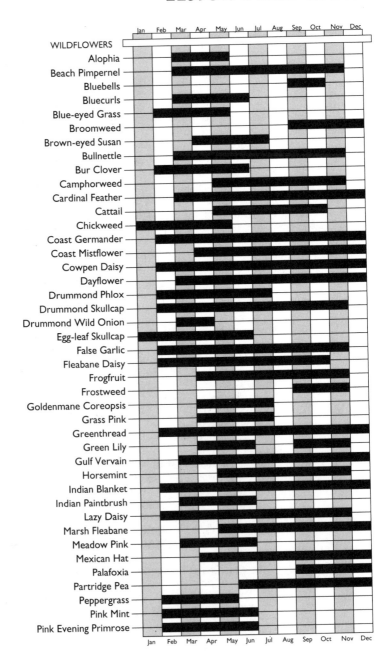

	Jan	Feb	Mar	Apr	May	Jun	Jul	Aug	Sep	Oct	Nov	Dec
WILDFLOWERS												
Alophia												
Beach Pimpernel												
Bluebells												
Bluecurls												
Blue-eyed Grass												
Broomweed												
Brown-eyed Susan												
Bullnettle												
Bur Clover												
Camphorweed												
Cardinal Feather												
Cattail												
Chickweed												
Coast Germander												
Coast Mistflower												
Cowpen Daisy												
Dayflower												
Drummond Phlox												
Drummond Skullcap												
Drummond Wild Onion												
Egg-leaf Skullcap												
False Garlic												
Fleabane Daisy												
Frogfruit												
Frostweed												
Goldenmane Coreopsis												
Grass Pink												
Greenthread												
Green Lily												
Gulf Vervain												
Horsemint												
Indian Blanket												
Indian Paintbrush												
Lazy Daisy												
Marsh Fleabane												
Meadow Pink												
Mexican Hat												
Palafoxia												
Partridge Pea												
Peppergrass												
Pink Mint												
Pink Evening Primrose												

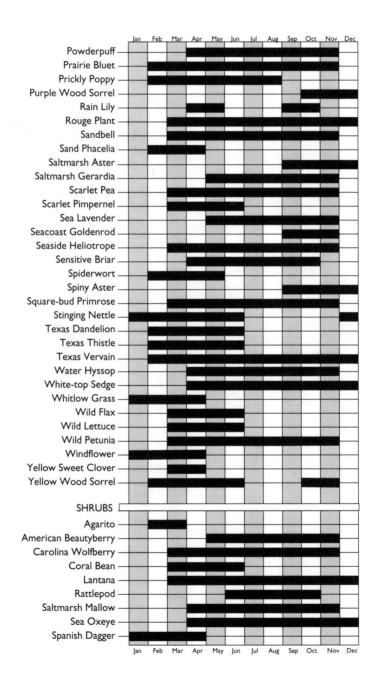

Jan Feb Mar Apr May Jun Jul Aug Sep Oct Nov Dec

Powderpuff
Prairie Bluet
Prickly Poppy
Purple Wood Sorrel
Rain Lily
Rouge Plant
Sandbell
Sand Phacelia
Saltmarsh Aster
Saltmarsh Gerardia
Scarlet Pea
Scarlet Pimpernel
Sea Lavender
Seacoast Goldenrod
Seaside Heliotrope
Sensitive Briar
Spiderwort
Spiny Aster
Square-bud Primrose
Stinging Nettle
Texas Dandelion
Texas Thistle
Texas Vervain
Water Hyssop
White-top Sedge
Whitlow Grass
Wild Flax
Wild Lettuce
Wild Petunia
Windflower
Yellow Sweet Clover
Yellow Wood Sorrel

SHRUBS

Agarito
American Beautyberry
Carolina Wolfberry
Coral Bean
Lantana
Rattlepod
Saltmarsh Mallow
Sea Oxeye
Spanish Dagger

Jan Feb Mar Apr May Jun Jul Aug Sep Oct Nov Dec

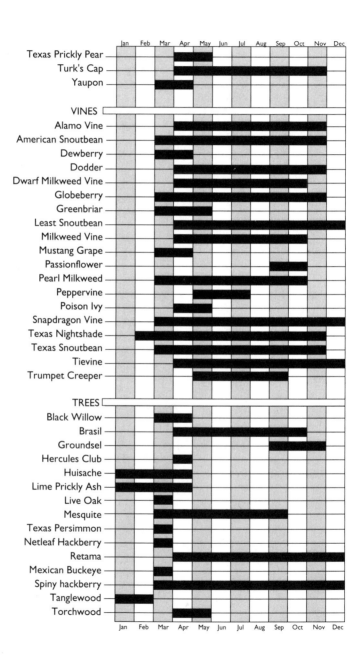

Plants Mentioned in Text

Woody Plants

agarito	*Mahonia trifoliata*
American beautyberry	*Callicarpa americana*
American plum	*Prunus* spp.
anaqua	*Ehretia anacua*
Arizona cypress	*Cupressus arizonica*
athel	*Tamarix aphylla*
bagpod	*Sesbania vesicaria*
Berlandier's wolfberry	*Lycium berlandieri*
blackbrush	*Acacia rigidula*
blackjack oak	*Quercus marilandica*
black willow	*Salix nigra*
bougainvillea	*Bougainvillea glabra*
brasil	*Condalia hookeri*
bumelia	*Bumelia lanuginosa*
bush baccharis	*Baccharis texana*
bushy sea ox-eye	*Borrichia frutescens*
buttonbush	*Cephalanthus occidentalis*
Carolina wolfberry	*Lycium carolinianum*
cenizo	*Leucophyllum frutescens*
chinaberry	*Melia azedarach*
Chinese arbor vitae	*Thuja orientalis*
Chinese tallow	*Sapium sebiferum*
coffee bean	*Sesbania macrocarpa*
coma	*Bumelia celastrina*
coral bean	*Erythrina herbacea*
cottonwood	*Populus deltoides*
devil's head	*Echinocactus texensis*
dwarf palmetto	*Sabal minor*
eastern live oak	*Quercus virginiana*
grassland prickly pear	*Opuntia macrorhiza*
greenbriar	*Smilax bona-nox*
groundsel	*Baccharis halimifolia*
hairy palm	*Trachycarpus caespitosus*

honey mesquite	*Prosopis glandulosa*
huisache	*Acacia farnesiana*
Japanese honeysuckle	*Lonicera japonica*
Kentucky coffee tree	*Gymnocladus dioica*
lantana	*Lantana horrida*
laurel oak	*Quercus hemisphaerica*
lime prickly ash	*Zanthoxylum fagara*
maritime saltwort	*Batis maritima*
marsh elder	*Iva frutescens*
Mexican buckeye	*Ungnadia speciosa*
mustang grape	*Vitis mustangensis*
netleaf hackberry	*Celtis reticulata*
oleander	*Nerium oleander*
partridge pea	*Cassia fasciculata*
peppervine	*Ampelopsis arborea*
petticoat palm	*Washingtonia filifera*
plateau live oak	*Quercus fusiformis*
poison ivy	*Toxicodendron radicans*
post oak	*Quercus stellata*
prickly ash	*Zanthoxylum hirsutum*
rattlepod	*Sesbania drummondii*
red bay	*Persea borbonia*
red gum	*Eucalyptus* sp.
retama	*Parkinsonia aculeata*
Russian olive	*Elaeagnus angustifolia*
sago palm	*Cycas revoluta*
salt cedar	*Tamarix gallica*
saltmarsh mallow	*Kosteletzkya virginica*
sand dunes live oak	*Quercus minima*
slash pine	*Pinus elliottii*
southern dewberry	*Rubus trivialis*
Spanish dagger	*Yucca treculeana*
spiny hackberry	*Celtis pallida*
sugar hackberry	*Celtis laevigata*
sycamore	*Platanus occidentalis*
tanglewood	*Forestiera angustifolia*
tasajillo	*Opuntia leptocaulis*
Texas persimmon	*Diospyros texana*
Texas prickly pear	*Opuntia engelmannii*
Texas torchwood	*Amyris texana*
tree huckleberry	*Vaccinium arboreum*
trumpet creeper	*Campsis radicans*
Turk's cap	*Malvaviscus arboreus*

wax myrtle	*Myrica cerifera*
western soapberry	*Sapindus drummondii*
white mulberry	*Morus alba*
white-rim yucca	*Yucca tenuistyla*
wild indigo	*Baptisia leucophaea*
yaupon	*Ilex vomitoria*

Herbaceous Plants

alamo vine	*Merremia dissecta*
alophia	*Alophia drummondii*
American bulrush	*Scirpus americanus*
American cupscale	*Sacciolepis striata*
American germander	*Teucrium canadense*
American lotus	*Nelumbo lutea*
American snoutbean	*Rhynchosia americana*
anil indigo	*Indigofera suffruticosa*
annual glasswort	*Salicornia bigelovii*
annual sundew	*Drosera annua*
arrowleaf	*Sagittaria* spp.
Bahia grass	*Paspalum notatum*
ball moss	*Tillandsia recurvata*
beach panic grass	*Panicum amarulum*
beach pimpernel	*Samolus ebracteatus*
Bermuda grass	*Cynodon dactylon*
big bluestem	*Andropogon gerardii*
black needlerush	*Juncus roemerianus*
bluecurls	*Phacelia congesta*
blue-eyed grass	*Sisyrinchium pruinosum*
bluehearts	*Buchnera floridana*
blue larkspur	*Delphinium carolinianum*
blue panic	*Panicum antidotale*
border bonebract	*Sclerocerpus uniserialis*
broomsedge bluestem	*Andropogon virginicus*
broomweed	*Amphiachyris dracunculoides*
brown-eyed Susan	*Rudbeckia hirta*
buckwheat	*Eriogonum multiflorum*
buffelgrass	*Cenchrus ciliaris*
bullnettle	*Cnidoscolus texanus*
bull thistle	*Cirsium horridulum*
bur clover	*Medicago polymorpha*
burhead	*Echinodorus rostratus*
bushy bluestem	*Andropogon glomeratus*

butterfly pea	*Centrosema virginianum*
button snakeroot	*Eryngium yuccifolium*
California bulrush	*Scirpus californicus*
carpetweed	*Calyptocarpus vialis*
camphor daisy	*Machaeranthera phyllocephala*
camphorweed	*Heterotheca subaxillaris*
cane bluestem	*Bothriochloa barbinodis*
cardinal feather	*Acalypha radians*
Carolina dandelion	*Pyrrhopappus carolinianus*
cattail	*Typha domingensis*
cherry coke rush	*Juncus validus*
chickweed	*Stellaria media*
chufa	*Cyperus esculentus*
coast germander	*Teucrium cubense*
coast mistflower	*Eupatorium betonicifolium*
coast pennywort	*Hydrocotyle umbellata*
coast sunflower	*Helianthus debilis*
common reed	*Phragmites australis*
common sunflower	*Helianthus annuus*
coontail	*Ceratophyllum demersum*
Corpus Christi fleabane	*Erigeron myrionactis*
cowpen daisy	*Verbesina encelioides*
crinkleawn	*Trachypogon secundus*
dayflower	*Commelina erecta*
doveweed	*Croton* spp.
downy lobelia	*Lobelia puberula*
Drummond's phlox	*Phlox drummondii*
Drummond's skullcap	*Scutellaria drummondii*
Drummond's wild onion	*Allium drummondii*
duck potato	*Sagittaria latifolia*
duckweed	*Lemna perpusilla*
dwarf milkweed vine	*Cynanchum barbigerum*
Eastern gamagrass	*Tripsacum dactyloides*
egg-leaf skullcap	*Scutellaria ovata*
Egyptian panic grass	*Panicum geminatum*
false garlic	*Nothoscordum bivalve*
fleabane daisy	*Erigeron myrionactis*
fragrant goldenrod	*Solidago odora*
fringed windmill grass	*Chloris ciliata*
frogfruit	*Phyla incisa*
frostweed	*Verbesina microptera*
giant bristle grass	*Setaria magna*
globeberry	*Ibervillea lindheimeri*

golden aster	*Heterotheca subaxillaris*
goldenmane coreopsis	*Coreopsis basalis*
grama grass	*Bouteloua* spp.
grass pink	*Centaurium calycosum*
green lily	*Schoenocaulon drummondii*
green milkweed	*Asclepias viridis*
greenthread	*Thelesperma filifolium*
ground cherry	*Physalis* spp.
Gulf Coast petunia	*Ruellia yucatana*
Gulf Coast sandbur	*Cenchrus incertus*
Gulf cordgrass	*Spartina spartinae*
Gulf muhly	*Muhlenbergia capillaris*
Gulf vervain	*Verbena xutha*
hairy stylisma	*Stylisma villosa*
heath aster	*Aster ericoides*
hoary pea	*Tephrosia onobrychoides*
hornwort	*Ceratophyllum demersum*
Indian blanket	*Gaillardia pulchella*
Indian paintbrush	*Castilleja indivisa*
King Ranch bluestem	*Bothriochloa ischaemum*
Knotroot bristle grass	*Setaria geniculata*
lanceleaf loosestrife	*Lythrum alatum* var. *lanceolatum*
lazy daisy	*Aphanostephus skirrobasis*
least snoutbean	*Rhynchosia minima*
lemon horsemint	*Monarda citriodora*
longtom	*Paspalum lividum*
manatee grass	*Cymodocea filiformis*
marsh fleabane	*Pluchea odorata*
marshhay cordgrass	*Spartina patens*
maypop passionflower	*Passiflora incarnata*
meadow beauty	*Rhexia mariana*
meadow pink	*Sabatia campestris*
melonette	*Melothria pendula*
Mexican hat	*Ratibida peduncularis*
milkweed vine	*Sarcostemma cynanchoides*
mistletoe	*Phoradendron tomentosum*
narrowleaf water primrose	*Ludwigia linearis*
nut rush	*Scleria triglomerata*
old plainsman	*Hymenopappus artemisiifolius*
pale flax	*Linum alatum*
passion vine	*Passiflora foetida*
pearl milkweed	*Matelea reticulata*
peppergrass	*Lepidium virginicum*

perennial glasswort	*Salicornia virginica*
pink evening primrose	*Oenothera speciosa*
pink mint	*Stachys drummondii*
pinkscale gayfeather	*Liatris elegans*
pipevine	*Aristolochia longiflora*
plains coreopsis	*Coreopsis tinctoria*
pondweed	*Potamogeton diversifolius*
powderpuff	*Mimosa strigillosa*
prairie bluet	*Hedyotis nigricans*
prairie goldenrod	*Euthamia leptocephala*
puccoon	*Lithospermum incisum*
purple pleatleaf	*Eustylis purpurea*
purple wood sorrel	*Oxalis drummondii*
pussyfoot	*Dalea obovata*
queen's delight	*Stillingia sylvatica*
rain lily	*Cooperia drummondii*
Roemer tripleawn	*Aristida roemeriana*
rosinweed	*Silphium asperrimum*
rouge plant	*Rivina humilis*
ryegrass	*Lolium perenne*
sago pondweed	*Potamogeton pectinatus*
saline aster	*Aster tenuifolius*
saltmarsh aster	*Aster subulatus*
saltmarsh bulrush	*Scirpus maritimus*
saltmarsh gerardia	*Agalinis maritima*
saltmarsh morning glory	*Ipomoea sagittata*
sandbell	*Nama hispidum*
sand brazoria	*Brazoria arenaria*
sand love grass	*Eragrostis trichodes*
sand phacelia	*Phacelia patuliflora*
sandyland bluebonnet	*Lupinus subcarmosus*
saw grass	*Cladium jamaicensis*
scarlet pea	*Indigofera miniata*
scarlet pimpernel	*Anagallis arvensis*
seacoast bluestem	*Schizachyrium scoparium*
seacoast goldenrod	*Solidago sempervirens*
sea lavender	*Limonium carolinianum* var. *nashii*
seashore dropseed	*Sporobolus virginicus*
seashore paspalum	*Paspalum vaginatum*
seashore saltgrass	*Distichlis spicata*
seaside heliotrope	*Heliotropium curassavicum*
sensitive briar	*Schrankia latidens*
sharp gayfeather	*Liatris acidota*

shoalgrass	*Halodule beaudettei*
shoregrass	*Monanthochloe littoralis*
shrubby water primrose	*Ludwigia octovalvis*
silver bluestem	*Bothriochloa laguroides*
silverleaf nightshade	*Solanum elaeagnifolium*
silverleaf sunflower	*Helianthus argophyllus*
silverstem	*Stemodia tomentosa*
smartweed	*Persicaria* spp.
smooth cordgrass	*Spartina alterniflora*
snapdragon vine	*Maurandya antirrhiniflora*
southern corydalis	*Corydalis micrantha*
southern naiad	*Najas guadalupensis*
spadeleaf	*Centella erecta*
Spanish moss	*Tillandsia usneoides*
spider lily	*Hymenocallis liriosome*
spike rush	*Eleocharis* spp.
spiny aster	*Aster spinosus*
splitbeard bluestem	*Andropogon ternarius*
spotted horsemint	*Monarda punctata*
spreading dodder	*Cuscuta indecora*
square-bud primrose	*Calylophus berlandieri*
St. Augustine grass	*Stenotaphrum secundatum*
stemless spiderwort	*Tradescantia subacaulis*
stiffstem flax	*Linum rigidum*
stinging nettle	*Urtica chamidryoides*
sundrops	*Oenothera kunthiana*
switch grass	*Panicum virgatum*
tanglehead	*Heteropogon contortus*
Texas bluebell	*Eustoma exaltatum*
Texas bluebonnet	*Lupinus texensis*
Texas dandelion	*Pyrrhopappus multicaulis*
Texas nightshade	*Solanum triquetrum*
Texas palafoxia	*Palafoxia texana*
Texas snoutbean	*Rhynchosia senna*
Texas thistle	*Cirsium texanum*
Texas vervain	*Verbena halei*
Texas wintergrass	*Stipa leucotricha*
tievine	*Ipomoea trichocarpa*
tiny bluet	*Hedyotis crassifolia*
toadflax	*Linaria texana*
tree dodder	*Cuscuta exaltata*
two-flower bladderwort	*Utricularia biflora*
upland ladies' tresses	*Spiranthes vernalis*

water hyacinth	*Eichornia crassipes*
water hyssop	*Bacopa monnieri*
water penny	*Hydrocotyle umbellata*
weeping love grass	*Eragrostis curvula*
western loosestrife	*Lythrum californicum*
western ragweed	*Ambrosia psilostachya*
white prickly poppy	*Argemone albiflora*
white-top sedge	*Dichromena colorata*
white tridens	*Tridens albescens*
white water lily	*Nymphaea elegans*
Whitlow grass	*Draba cuneifolia*
widgeon grass	*Ruppia maritima*
wild buckwheat	*Eriogonum multiflorum*
wild celery	*Vallisneria americana*
wild iris	*Alophia drummondii*
wild lettuce	*Lactuca ludoviciana*
wild millet	*Panicum* spp.
wild petunia	*Ruellia* spp.
windflower	*Anemone berlandieri*
wine-cup	*Callirhoe involucrata*
woevine	*Cassytha filiformis*
woods wine-cup	*Callirhoe papaver*
woolly globe mallow	*Sphaeralcea lindheimeri*
yellow cowpea	*Vigna luteola*
yellow evening primrose	*Oenothera grandis*
yellow Indian grass	*Sorghastrum nutans*
yellow nutgrass	*Cyperus esculentus*
yellowpuff	*Neptunia pubescens*
yellow sweet clover	*Melilotus indicus*
yellow water lily	*Nymphaea mexicana*
yellow wood sorrel	*Oxalis dillenii*
zizote	*Asclepias oenotheroides*

Nonflowering Plants

blue-green algae	*Lyngbya* spp. and *Microcoleus* spp.
bracken fern	*Pteridium aquilinum*
columnar stinkhorn	*Clathrus columnatus*
common stinkhorn	*Mutinus caninus*
delicate bolete	*Boletus sensibilis*
destroying angel	*Amanita bisporigera* and *A. virosa*
doughball	*Calvatia craniformis* and *C. cyathiformis*

earthball	*Scleroderma bovista*
earthstar	*Astraeus hygrometricus*
emetic russula	*Russula emetica*
fawn mushroom	*Pluteus cervinus*
foliose lichen	*Physcia* spp.
golden lichen	*Teloschistes flavicans*
green-spored lepiota	*Chlorophyllum molybdites*
inky-cap mushroom	*Coprinus* spp.
jack-o'-lantern mushroom	*Omphalotus olearius*
meadow mushroom	*Agaricus campestris*
mosquito fern	*Azolla caroliniana*
muskgrass	*Chara* spp.
netted stinkhorn	*Dictyophora duplicata*
old-man's-beard	*Usnea strigosa*
old-man-of-the-woods	*Strobilomyces floccopus*
oyster mushroom	*Pleurotus ostreatus*
pond silk	*Spirogyra* spp.
resurrection fern	*Polypodium polypodioides*
sea bush	*Gracilaria verrucosa*
seahorsetail	*Cladophora delicatula*
shield lichen	*Parmelia perforata*
sulphur shelf fungus	*Laetiporus sulphureus*
tree moss	*Leucodon julaceus*
water clover	*Marsilea uncinata*
white puffball	*Lycoperdon* spp.

Vertebrates Mentioned in Text

Mammals

armadillo	*Dasypus novemcinctus*
Attwater's pocket gopher	*Geomys attwateri*
axis deer	*Cervus axis*
badger	*Taxidea taxus*
big free-tailed bat	*Tadarida macrotis*
black rat	*Rattus rattus*
black-tailed jackrabbit	*Lepus californicus*
bobcat	*Felis rufus*
coati	*Nasua nasua*
cougar	*Felis concolor*
coyote	*Canis latrans*
deer mouse	*Peromyscus maniculatus*
domestic cow	*Bos taurus*
eastern cottontail	*Sylvilagus floridanus*
eastern mole	*Scalopus aquaticus*
eastern pipistrelle	*Pipistrellus subflavus*
evening bat	*Nycticeius humeralis*
fallow deer	*Cervus dama*
feral hog	*Sus scrofa*
fox squirrel	*Sciurus niger*
fulvous harvest mouse	*Reithrodontomys fulvescens*
gray fox	*Urocyon cinereoargenteus*
gray wolf	*Canis lupus*
Gulf Coast hog-nosed skunk	*Conepatus leuconotus*
hispid cotton rat	*Sigmodon hispidus*
hispid pocket mouse	*Perognathus hispidus*
hoary bat	*Lasiurus cinereus*
house mouse	*Mus musculus*
jaguar	*Felis onca*
jaguarundi	*Felis jaguarondi*
javelina	*Dicotyles tajacu*
least shrew	*Cryptotis parva*
long-tailed weasel	*Mustela frenata*

marsh rice rat	*Oryzomys palustris*
Mexican free-tailed bat	*Tadarida brasiliensis*
Mexican ground squirrel	*Spermophilus mexicanus*
mink	*Mustela vison*
mule deer	*Odocoileus hemionus*
northern grasshopper mouse	*Onychomys leucogaster*
northern yellow bat	*Lasiurus intermedius*
Norway rat	*Rattus norvegicus*
nutria	*Myocastor coypus*
ocelot	*Felis pardalis*
opossum	*Didelphis virginiana*
pigmy mouse	*Baiomys taylori*
raccoon	*Procyon lotor*
red bat	*Lasiurus borealis*
red wolf	*Canis rufus*
ringtail	*Bassariscus astutus*
silky pocket mouse	*Perognathus flavus*
silver-haired bat	*Lasionycteris noctivagans*
south plains wood rat	*Neotoma micropus*
southwestern short-tailed shrew	*Blarina hylophaga*
spotted skunk	*Spilogale putorius*
striped skunk	*Mephitis mephitis*
swamp rabbit	*Sylvilagus aquaticus*
Texas gray wolf	*Canis lupus monstrabilis*
West Indian manatee	*Trichechus manatus*
white-footed mouse	*Peromyscus leucopus*
white-tailed deer	*Odocoileus virginianus*

Birds

American avocet	*Recurvirostra americana*
American bittern	*Botaurus lentiginosus*
American coot	*Fulica americana*
American crow	*Corvus brachyrhynchos*
American kestrel	*Falco sparverius*
American oystercatcher	*Haematopus palliatus*
American peregrine falcon	*Falco peregrinus anatum*
American robin	*Turdus migratorius*
American swallow-tailed kite	*Elanoides forficatus*
American tree sparrow	*Spizella arborea*
American wigeon	*Anas americana*
American woodcock	*Scolopax minor*
anhinga	*Anhinga anhinga*

aplomado falcon	*Falco femoralis*
arctic peregrine falcon	*Falco peregrinus tundrius*
ash-throated flycatcher	*Myiarchus cinerascens*
Attwater's greater prairie chicken	*Tympanuchus cupidos attwateri*
Baird's sandpiper	*Calidris bairdii*
bald eagle	*Haliaeetus leucocephalus*
band-tailed pigeon	*Columba fasciata*
bank swallow	*Riparia riparia*
barn owl	*Tyto alba*
barn swallow	*Hirundo rustica*
barred owl	*Strix varia*
Bell's vireo	*Vireo bellii*
belted kingfisher	*Megaceryle alcyon*
Bewick's wren	*Thryomanes bewickii*
black-and-white warbler	*Mniotilta varia*
black-bellied plover	*Pluvialis squatarola*
black-bellied whistling duck	*Dendrocygna autumnalis*
black-billed cuckoo	*Coccyzus erythropthalmus*
black-chinned hummingbird	*Archilochus alexandri*
black-crowned night-heron	*Nycticorax nycticorax*
black-headed grosbeak	*Pheucticus melanocephalus*
black-necked stilt	*Himantopus mexicanus*
black rail	*Laterallus jamaicensis*
black-shouldered kite	*Elanus caeruleus*
black skimmer	*Rynchops niger*
black tern	*Chlidonias niger*
black vulture	*Coragyps atratus*
blue jay	*Cyanocitta cristata*
blue-gray gnatcatcher	*Polioptila caerulea*
blue grosbeak	*Guiraca caerulea*
blue-winged teal	*Anas discors*
boat-tailed grackle	*Quiscalus major*
bobwhite quail	*Colinus virginianus*
Bonaparte's gull	*Larus philadelphia*
Botteri's sparrow	*Aimophila botterii*
Brewer's blackbird	*Euphagus cyanocephalus*
broad-tailed hummingbird	*Selasphorus platycercus*
broad-winged hawk	*Buteo platypterus*
bronzed cowbird	*Molothrus aeneus*
brown-crested flycatcher	*Myiarchus tyrannulus*
brown-headed cowbird	*Molothrus ater*
brown pelican	*Pelecanus occidentalis*
brown thrasher	*Toxostoma rufum*

buff-bellied hummingbird	*Amazilia yucatanensis*
bufflehead	*Bucephala albeola*
burrowing owl	*Speotyto cunicularia*
cactus wren	*Campylorhynchus brunneicapillus*
California quail	*Callipepla californica*
Canada goose	*Branta canadensis*
canvasback	*Aythya valisineria*
Carolina chickadee	*Parus carolinensis*
Carolina wren	*Thryothorus ludovicianus*
Caspian tern	*Sterna caspia*
Cassin's sparrow	*Aimophila cassinii*
catbird	*Dumetella carolinensis*
cattle egret	*Bubulcus ibis*
cedar waxwing	*Bombycilla cedrorum*
chimney swift	*Chaetura pelagica*
chipping sparrow	*Spizella passerina*
chuck-will's-widow	*Caprimulgus carolinensis*
cinnamon teal	*Anas cyanoptera*
clapper rail	*Rallus longirostris*
clay-colored sparrow	*Spizella pallida*
cliff swallow	*Hirundo pyrrhonota*
common goldeneye	*Bucephala clangula*
common grackle	*Quiscalus quiscula*
common loon	*Gavia immer*
common merganser	*Mergus merganser*
common moorhen	*Gallinula chloropus*
common nighthawk	*Chordeiles minor*
common snipe	*Gallinago gallinago*
common tern	*Sterna hirundo*
common yellowthroat	*Geothlypis trichas*
Cooper's hawk	*Accipiter cooperii*
crested caracara	*Polyborus plancus*
curve-billed thrasher	*Toxostoma curvirostre*
dickcissel	*Spiza americana*
double-crested cormorant	*Phalacrocorax auritus*
downy woodpecker	*Picoides pubescens*
dunlin	*Calidris alpina*
eared grebe	*Podiceps nigricollis*
eastern bluebird	*Sialia sialis*
eastern kingbird	*Tyrannus tyrannus*
eastern meadowlark	*Sturnella magna*
eastern screech owl	*Otus asio*
eastern wood pewee	*Contopus virens*

Eskimo curlew	*Numenius borealis*
European starling	*Sturnus vulgaris*
ferruginous hawk	*Buteo regalis*
field sparrow	*Spizella pusilla*
Forster's tern	*Sterna forsteri*
Franklin's gull	*Larus pipixcan*
fulvous whistling duck	*Dendrocygna bicolor*
gadwall	*Anas strepera*
golden-crowned kinglet	*Regulus satrapa*
golden-crowned sparrow	*Zonotrichia atricapilla*
golden eagle	*Aquila chrysaetos*
golden-fronted woodpecker	*Melanerpes aurifrons*
golden-winged warbler	*Vermivora chrysoptera*
grasshopper sparrow	*Ammodramus savannarum*
gray-cheeked thrush	*Catharus minimus*
great blue heron	*Ardea herodias*
great crested flycatcher	*Myiarchus crinitus*
great egret	*Casmerodius albus*
greater roadrunner	*Geococcyx californianus*
greater scaup	*Aythya marila*
greater yellowlegs	*Tringa melanoleuca*
great horned owl	*Bubo virginianus*
great kiskadee	*Pitangus sulphuratus*
great-tailed grackle	*Quiscalus mexicanus*
green-backed heron	*Butorides striatus*
green kingfisher	*Chloroceryle americana*
green-tailed towhee	*Chlorura chlorura*
green-winged teal	*Anas crecca*
grooved-billed ani	*Crotophaga sulcirostris*
gull-billed tern	*Sterna nilotica*
Harris hawk	*Parabuteo unicinctus*
herring gull	*Larus argentatus*
hooded merganser	*Lophodytes cucullatus*
horned grebe	*Podiceps auritus*
horned lark	*Eremophila alpestris*
house sparrow	*Passer domesticus*
house wren	*Troglodytes aedon*
Inca dove	*Columbina inca*
indigo bunting	*Passerina cyanea*
killdeer	*Charadrius vociferus*
king rail	*Rallus elegans*
ladder-backed woodpecker	*Picoides scalaris*
lark bunting	*Calamospiza melanocorys*

lark sparrow	*Chondestes grammacus*
laughing gull	*Larus atricilla*
least bittern	*Ixobrychus exilis*
least grebe	*Tachybaptus dominicus*
least sandpiper	*Calidris minutilla*
least tern	*Sterna antillarum*
Le Conte's sparrow	*Ammodramus leconteii*
lesser golden plover	*Pluvialis dominica*
lesser nighthawk	*Chordeiles acutipennis*
lesser scaup	*Aythya affinis*
lesser yellowlegs	*Tringa flavipes*
Lincoln's sparrow	*Melospiza lincolnii*
little blue heron	*Egretta caerulea*
loggerhead shrike	*Lanius ludovicianus*
long-billed curlew	*Numenius americanus*
long-billed dowitcher	*Limnodromus scolopaceus*
long-billed thrasher	*Toxostoma longirostre*
magnificent frigate-bird	*Fregata magnificens*
mallard	*Anas platyrhynchos*
marbled godwit	*Limosa fedoa*
marsh wren	*Cistothorus palustris*
masked duck	*Oxyura dominica*
merlin	*Falco columbarius*
Mississippi kite	*Ictinia misisippiensis*
mottled duck	*Anas fulvigula*
mourning dove	*Zenaida macroura*
neotropic cormorant	*Phalacrocorax brasilianus*
northern cardinal	*Cardinalis cardinalis*
northern flicker	*Colaptes auratus*
northern harrier	*Circus cyaneus*
northern mockingbird	*Mimus polyglottos*
northern oriole	*Icterus galbula*
northern parula	*Parula americana*
northern pintail	*Anas acuta*
northern shoveler	*Anas clypeata*
oldsquaw	*Clangula hyemalis*
olivaceous flycatcher	*Myiarchus tuberculifer*
olive-sided flycatcher	*Contopus borealis*
olive sparrow	*Arremonops rufivirgatus*
orange-crowned warbler	*Vermivora celata*
orchard oriole	*Icterus spurius*
osprey	*Pandion haliaetus*
painted bunting	*Passerina ciris*

pauraque	*Nyctidromus albicollis*
pectoral sandpiper	*Chalidris melanotos*
peregrine falcon	*Falco peregrinus*
phainopepla	*Phainopepla nitens*
Philadelphia vireo	*Vireo philadelphicus*
pied-billed grebe	*Podilymbus podiceps*
pileated woodpecker	*Dryocopus pileatus*
piping plover	*Charadrius melodus*
poor-will	*Phalaenoptilus nuttallii*
purple gallinule	*Porphyrula martinica*
purple martin	*Progne subis*
pyrrhuloxia	*Cardinalis sinuatus*
red-bellied woodpecker	*Melanerpes carolinus*
red-breasted merganser	*Mergus serrator*
red-breasted nuthatch	*Sitta canadensis*
reddish egret	*Egretta rufescens*
red-eyed vireo	*Vireo olivaceus*
redhead	*Aythya americana*
red-headed woodpecker	*Melanerpes erythrocephalus*
red-shouldered hawk	*Buteo lineatus*
red-tailed hawk	*Buteo jamaicensis*
red-winged blackbird	*Agelaius phoeniceus*
ring-billed gull	*Larus delawarensis*
ring-necked duck	*Aythya collaris*
ring-necked pheasant	*Phasianus colchicus*
Roadrunner	*Geococcyx californianus*
Rockdove	*Columba livia*
Rock wren	*Salpinctes obsoletus*
roseate spoonbill	*Ajaia ajaja*
rose-breasted grosbeak	*Pheucticus ludovicianus*
ross goose	*Chen rossii*
rough-legged hawk	*Buteo lagopus*
rough-winged swallow	*Stelgidopteryx serripennis*
royal tern	*Sterna maxima*
ruby-crowned kinglet	*Regulus calendula*
ruby-throated hummingbird	*Archilochus colubris*
ruddy duck	*Oxyura jamaicensis*
ruddy turnstone	*Arenaria interpres*
rufous hummingbird	*Selasphorus rufus*
rufous-sided towhee	*Pipilo erythrophthalmus*
sanderling	*Calidris alba*
sandhill crane	*Grus canadensis*
Sandwich tern	*Sterna sandvicensis*

savannah sparrow	*Passerculus sandwichensis*
scarlet tanager	*Piranga olivacea*
scissor-tailed flycatcher	*Tyrannus forficatus*
seaside sparrow	*Ammodramus maritimus*
sedge wren	*Cistothorus platensis*
semipalmated plover	*Charadrius semipalmatus*
semipalmated sandpiper	*Chalidris pusilla*
sharp-shinned hawk	*Accipiter striatus*
short-billed dowitcher	*Limnodromus griseus*
short-eared owl	*Asio flammeus*
snow goose	*Chen caerulescens*
snowy egret	*Egretta thula*
snowy plover	*Charadrius alexandrinus*
solitary sandpiper	*Tringa solitaria*
song sparrow	*Melospiza melodia*
sooty tern	*Sterna fuscata*
sora	*Porzana carolina*
spotted sandpiper	*Actitis macularia*
stilt sandpiper	*Calidris himantopus*
summer tanager	*Piranga rubra*
Swainson's hawk	*Buteo swainsoni*
Swainson's thrush	*Catharus ustulatus*
Swainson's warbler	*Limnothlypis swainsonii*
swamp sparrow	*Melospiza georgiana*
tree swallow	*Tachycineta bicolor*
tricolored heron	*Egretta tricolor*
tropical parula	*Parula pitiayumi*
tufted titmouse	*Parus bicolor*
tundra swan	*Cygnus columbianus*
turkey vulture	*Cathartes aura*
upland sandpiper	*Bartramia longicauda*
veery	*Catharus fuscescens*
verdin	*Auriparus flaviceps*
vesper sparrow	*Pooecetes gramineus*
Virginia rail	*Rallus limicola*
western grebe	*Aechmophorus occidentalis*
western kingbird	*Tyrannus verticalis*
western meadowlark	*Sturnella neglecta*
western sandpiper	*Calidris mauri*
winter wren	*Troglodytes troglodytes*
whimbrel	*Numenius phaeopus*
whip-poor-will	*Caprimulgus vociferus*
white-crowned sparrow	*Zonotrichia leucophrys*

white-eyed vireo	*Vireo griseus*
white-faced ibis	*Plegadis chihi*
white-fronted goose	*Anser albifrons*
white ibis	*Eudocimus albus*
white pelican	*Pelecanus erythrorhynchos*
white-tailed hawk	*Buteo albicaudatus*
white-throated sparrow	*Zonotrichia albicollis*
white-throated swift	*Aeronautes saxatalis*
white-winged dove	*Zenaida asiatica*
white-winged scoter	*Melanitta fusca*
whooping crane	*Grus americana*
wild turkey	*Meleagris gallopavo*
willet	*Catoptrophorus semipalmatus*
Wilson's phalarope	*Phalaropus tricolor*
Wilson's plover	*Charadrius wilsonia*
wood duck	*Aix sponsa*
wood stork	*Mycteria americana*
wood thrush	*Hylocichla mustelina*
yellow-bellied sapsucker	*Sphyrapicus varius*
yellow-billed cuckoo	*Coccyzus americanus*
yellow-crowned night-heron	*Nyctanassa violacea*
yellow rail	*Coturnicops noveboracensis*
yellow-rumped warbler	*Dendroica coronata*
yellowthroat	*Geothlypis trichas*
yellow-throated warbler	*Dendroica dominica*
zone-tailed hawk	*Buteo albonotatus*

Herptiles

American alligator	*Alligator mississippiensis*
Atlantic hawksbill sea turtle	*Eretmochelys imbricata*
Atlantic loggerhead sea turtle	*Caretta caretta*
Atlantic ridley sea turtle	*Lepidochelys kempi*
Blanchard's cricket frog	*Acris crepitans*
blotched water snake	*Nerodia erythrogaster transversa*
broad-banded copperhead	*Agkistrodon contortrix laticinctus*
broad-banded water snake	*Nerodia fasciata confluens*
bullfrog	*Rana catesbeiana*
bullsnake	*Pituophis melanoleucus*
checkered garter snake	*Thamnophis marcianus*
common snapping turtle	*Chelydra serpentina*
Couch's spadefoot	*Scaphiopus couchi*

desert kingsnake	*Lampropeltis getulus splendida*
diamond-backed water snake	*Nerodia rhombifera*
eastern garter snake	*Thamnophis sirtalis*
eastern green toad	*Bufo debilis*
eastern hognose snake	*Heterodon platyrhinos*
eastern narrow-mouthed toad	*Gastrophryne carolinensis*
eastern red-spotted newt	*Notophthalmus viridescens*
eastern tiger salamander	*Ambystoma tigrinum*
eastern yellow-bellied racer	*Coluber constrictor flaviventris*
five-lined skink	*Eumeces fasciatus*
flat-headed snake	*Tantilla gracilis*
Graham's crayfish snake	*Regina grahami*
gray treefrog	*Hyla chrysoscelis*
Great Plains narrow-mouthed toad	*Gastrophryne olivacea*
Great Plains rat snake	*Elaphe guttata*
green anole	*Anolis carolinensis*
green sea turtle	*Chelonia mydas*
green treefrog	*Hyla cinerea*
green water snake	*Nerodia cyclopion*
ground skink	*Scincella lateralis*
Guadalupe spiny softshell	*Trionyx spiniferus guadalupensis*
Gulf Coast ribbon snake	*Thamnophis proximus orarius*
Gulf Coast toad	*Bufo valliceps*
Gulf saltmarsh snake	*Nerodia fasciata clarki*
Hurter's spadefoot	*Scaphiopus holbrooki*
keeled earless lizard	*Holbrookia propinqua*
leatherback sea turtle	*Dermochelys coriacea*
lesser siren	*Siren intermedia*
Louisiana milk snake	*Lampropeltis triangulum amaura*
marsh brown snake	*Storeria dekayi limnetes*
Mediterranean gecko	*Hemidactylus turcicus*
Mexican milk snake	*Lampropeltis triangulum annulata*
Mexican racer	*Coluber constrictor oaxaca*
Mississippi mud turtle	*Kinosternon subrubrum*
northern fence lizard	*Sceloporus undulatus*
ornate box turtle	*Terrapene ornata*
prairie kingsnake	*Lampropeltis calligaster*
prairie racerunner	*Cnemidophorus sexlineatus*
red-eared slider	*Trachemys scripta*
Rio Grande leopard frog	*Rana berlandieri*
rough earth snake	*Virginia striatula*
rough green snake	*Opheodrys aestivus*

Schott's whipsnake	*Masticophis taeniatus schotti*
sheep frog	*Hypopachus variolosus*
slender glass lizard	*Ophisaurus attenuatus*
small-mouthed salamander	*Ambystoma texanum*
southern black-spotted newt	*Notophthalmus meridionalis*
southern crawfish frog	*Rana areolata*
southern leopard frog	*Rana sphenocephala*
southern prairie skink	*Eumeces septentrionalis*
South Texas ground snake	*Sonora Semiannulata taylori*
speckled kingsnake	*Lampropeltis getulus holbrooki*
spotted chorus frog	*Pseudacris clarki*
spotted whiptail	*Cnemidophorus gularis*
squirrel treefrog	*Hyla squirella*
Strecker's chorus frog	*Pseudacris streckeri*
Texas black-headed snake	*Tantilla nigriceps fumiceps*
Texas blind snake	*Leptotyphlops dulcis*
Texas brown snake	*Storeria dekayi texana*
Texas coral snake	*Micrurus fulvius tenere*
Texas diamondback terrapin	*Malaclemys terrapin littoralis*
Texas garter snake	*Thamnosis sirtalis annectans*
Texas glossy snake	*Arizona elegans*
Texas horned lizard	*Phrynosoma cornutum*
Texas indigo snake	*Drymarchon corais*
Texas lined snake	*Tropidoclonion lineatum*
Texas long-nosed snake	*Rhinocheilus lecontei*
Texas night snake	*Hypsiglena torquata*
Texas patch-nosed snake	*Salvadora grahamiae lineata*
Texas rat snake	*Elaphe obsoleta*
Texas scarlet snake	*Cemophora coccinea*
Texas slider	*Chrysemys concinna*
Texas spiny lizard	*Sceloporus olivaceus*
Texas toad	*Bufo speciosus*
Texas tortoise	*Gopherus berlandieri*
three-toed box turtle	*Terrapene carolina triunguis*
timber rattlesnake	*Crotalus horridus*
upland chorus frog	*Pseudacris triseriata*
western coachwhip	*Masticophis flagellum*
western cottonmouth moccasin	*Agkistrodon piscivorus leucostoma*
western diamondback rattlesnake	*Crotalus atrox*
western hognose snake	*Heterodon nasicus*
western massasauga	*Sistrurus catenatus*
western mud snake	*Farancia abacura*

western pigmy rattlesnake	*Sistrurus miliarius streckeri*
Woodhouse's toad	*Bufo woodhousei*
yellow mud turtle	*Kinosternon flavescens*

Fish

alligator gar	*Lepisosteus spatula*
Atlantic croaker	*Micropogonias undulatus*
Atlantic needlefish	*Strongylura marina*
bantam sunfish	*Lepomis symmetricus*
bay anchovy	*Anchoa mitchilli*
bayou killifish	*Fundulus pulvereus*
blackcheek tonguefish	*Symphurus plagiusa*
black drum	*Pogonias cromis*
bluegill sunfish	*Lepomis macrochirus*
carp	*Cyprinus carpio*
chain pipefish	*Syngnathus louisianae*
common jack	*Caranx hippos*
diamond killifish	*Adinia xenica*
gizzard shad	*Dorosoma cepedianum*
golden topminnow	*Fundulus chrysotus*
Gulf killifish	*Fundulus grandis*
Gulf menhaden	*Brevoortia patronus*
hardhead catfish	*Arius felis*
least puffer	*Sphoeroides parvus*
longear sunfish	*Lepomis megalotis*
longnose killifish	*Fundulus similis*
mosquito fish	*Gambusia affinis*
naked goby	*Gobiosoma bosci*
pigfish	*Orthopristis chrysoptera*
pinfish	*Lagodon rhomboides*
rainwater killifish	*Lucania parva*
red drum	*Sciaenops ocellata*
redear sunfish	*Lepomis microlophus*
sailfin molly	*Poecilia latipinna*
sheepshead	*Archosargus probatocephalus*
sheepshead killifish	*Cyprinodon variegatus*
silver jenny	*Eucinostomus gula*
silver perch	*Bairdiella chrysura*
skipjack	*Elops saurus*
southern flounder	*Paralichthys lethostigma*
speckled trout	*Cynoscion nebulosus*

spot	*Leiostomus xanthurus*
spotted gar	*Lepisosteus oculatus*
striped mullet	*Mugil cephalus*
tidewater silverside	*Menidia beryllina*
warmouth	*Lepomis gulosus*
yellow bullhead	*Ictalurus natalis*

Invertebrates Mentioned in Text

acorn moth	*Valentinia glandulella*
ambush bug	*Phymata erosa*
American painted lady	*Vanessa virginensis*
angular-winged katydid	*Microcentrum rhombifolium*
army ant	*Neviamyrmex pilosum*
arrow-bellied orb weaver	*Micrathena sagittata*
assassin bug	*Apiomerus sessipes*
bagworm	*Oiketicus abbotti*
banded daggerwing	*Marpesia chiron*
banded garden spider	*Argiope trifasciata*
basilica spider	*Mecynogea lemniscata*
beach flea	*Orchestia platensis*
bird grasshopper	*Schistocerca americana* and *S. alutacea*
black-and-yellow garden spider	*Argiope aurantia*
black-legged deer tick	*Ixodes scapularis*
black saltmarsh mosquito	*Aedes taeniorhynchus*
black widow	*Latrodectus mactans*
black witch moth	*Ascalapha odorata*
blowfly	Family Calliphoridae
blue crab	*Callinectes sapidus*
blue mud dauber	*Chalybion californicum*
bordered patch	*Chlosyne lacinia*
bristly flower spider	*Misumenops asperatus*
broad-nosed weevil	*Eudiagogus pulcher*
brown recluse	*Loxosceles reclusa*
brown shrimp	*Penaeus aztecus*
brown-spotted yellow-wing	*Celithemis eponina*
buckeye	*Junonia coenia*
bumblebee	*Bombus* spp.
burrowing wolf spider	*Geolycosa missouriensis*
cabbage white	*Artogeia rapae*
Carolina grasshopper	*Dissosteira carolina*
carrion beetle	*Silpha* spp.
caudate orb weaver	*Cyclosa caroli*

Caudell's long-horned grasshopper	*Isinidia amplicornis*
cayenne tick	*Amblyomma cajennense*
checkered white	*Pontia protodice*
chigger mite	*Trombicula* spp.
clouded sulphur	*Colias philodice*
cloudless giant sulphur	*Phoebis sennae*
common rangia	*Rangia cuneata*
common sootywing	*Pholisora catullus*
cone-headed grasshopper	*Neoconocephalus triops*
constricted macoma	*Macoma constricta*
cork-headed ant	*Camponotus etiolata*
crimson-banded black	*Biblis hyperia*
Culver's sandworm	*Laeonereis culveri*
currant gall wasp	*Belenocnema fossoria*
dance fly	Family Empididae
deer liver fluke	*Fascioloides magna*
diminutive cockroach	*Attaphila fungicola*
dogday cicada	*Tibicen* spp.
dogface sulphur	*Zerene cesonia*
dusky blue hairstreak	*Calycopis isobeon*
eastern black swallowtail	*Papilio polyxenes*
eastern carpenter bee	*Xylocopa virginica*
eastern tiger swallowtail	*Pterourus glaucus*
elongate stilt spider	*Tetragnatha elongata*
emerald-jawed jumping spider	*Phiddipus audax*
field cricket	*Gryllus pennsylvanicus*
flower moth	*Schinia masoni*
flower spider	*Misumena vatia* and *Misumenoides formosipes*
funereal duskywing	*Erynnis funeralis*
gall ant	*Camponotus rasilis*
ghost shrimp	*Callianassa jamaicense*
giant land crab	*Cardiosoma guanhumi*
giant swallowtail	*Heraclides cresphontes*
gnat	*Liohippelates pusio*
golden digger wasp	*Sphex ichneumoneus*
golden saltmarsh mosquito	*Aedes sollicitans*
golden-silk spider	*Nephila clavipes*
grass shrimp	*Palaemonetes* spp.
grass spider	*Agelenopsis* spp.
gray hairstreak	*Strymon melinus*
great purple hairstreak	*Atlides halesus*
great southern white butterfly	*Ascia monuste*

green darner	*Anax junius*
green lynx spider	*Peucetia viridans*
Gulf Coast tick	*Amblyomma maculatum*
Gulf fritillary	*Agraulis vanillae*
hackberry butterfly	*Asterocampa celtis*
harvester ant	*Pogonomyrmex barbatus* and
	P. occidentalis
Hedgpeth's crayfish	*Cambarus hedgpethi*
hickory tussock moth	*Lophocampa caryae*
honeybee	*Apis mellifera*
hornet	*Vespula squamosa*
hornshell snail	*Cerithidea pliculosa*
housefly	*Musca domestica*
hump-backed orb weaver	*Eustala anastera*
imported red fire ant	*Solenopsis invicta*
jackknife clam	*Ensis minor*
jumping plant louse	*Trioza magnoliae*
leaf katydid	*Pterophylla camellifolia*
leaf-cutter bee	*Megachile* spp.
lichen moth	*Clemensia albata*
little wood satyr	*Megisto cymela*
lone star tick	*Amblyomma americanum*
long-legged fly	Family Dolichopodidae
long-tailed skipper	*Urbanus proteus*
malachite	*Spiroeta stelenes*
march fly	*Plecia nearctica*
marsh crab	*Sesarma reticulatum*
marsh periwinkle	*Littorina irrorata*
milichiid fly	*Pholeomyia texensis*
mole cricket	*Gryllotalpa hexadactyla*
monarch	*Danaus plexippus*
mottled sand grasshopper	*Spharagemon collare*
mud fiddler crab	*Uca rapax*
oak gall wasp	*Holcaspis cinerosus*
orange sulphur	*Colias eurytheme*
orange-barred giant sulphur	*Phoebis philea*
orchard spider	*Leucauge venusta*
organ-pipe mud dauber	*Trypoxylon politum*
painted lady	*Vanessa cardui*
palamedes swallowtail	*Pterourus palamedes*
pale tussock moth	*Halysidota tessellarius*
paper wasp	*Polistes exclamans*
pearl crescentspot	*Phyciodes tharos*

phorid fly	*Myrmosicarius texanus*
picture-winged fly	Family Otitidae
pipevine swallowtail	*Battus philenor*
pistol shrimp	*Alpheus heterochaelis*
purple rain mosquito	*Psorophora cyanescens*
pyramid ant	*Conomyrma flava*
queen	*Danaus glippus*
question mark	*Polygonia interrogationis*
red admiral	*Vanessa atalanta*
red-banded hairstreak	*Calycopis cecrops*
red threadworm	*Heteromastus filiformis*
robber fly	*Efferia pogonias*
round-winged katydid	*Amblycorypha rotundifolia*
saltmarsh caterpillar	*Estigmene acraea*
saltmarsh dragonfly	*Erythrodiplax berenice*
saltmarsh katydid	*Orchelium vulgare* and
	Conocephalus spp.
saltmarsh snail	*Melampus bidentatus*
sand fiddler crab	*Uca panacea*
scorpion	*Centruroides vittatus*
sea roach	*Ligia exotica*
sheet web burrowing spider	*Sosippus texanus*
shorebug	*Pentacora* spp.
shore fly	*Ephydra* spp.
silvery crescentspot	*Charidryas nycteis*
sleepy orange butterfly	*Eurema nicippe*
snout butterfly	*Libytheana bachmanii*
southern fire ant	*Solenopsis xyloni*
southern hairstreak	*Euristrymon ontario*
southern red crayfish	*Procambarus clarki*
sowbug	*Porcellionides pruinosus*
spiny-bellied orb weaver	*Micrathena gracilis*
spiny oak-slug moth	*Euclea delphinii*
spur-throated grasshopper	*Melanoplus* spp.
star-bellied spider	*Acanthepeira stellata*
stone crab	*Menippe mercenaria*
stout razor clam	*Tagelus plebius*
sulphur-winged grasshopper	*Arphia sulphurea*
tarantula	*Dugesiella hentzi*
tarantula hawk	*Pepsis* spp.
Texan crescentspot	*Anthanassa texana*
Texas leaf-cutter ant	*Atta texana*

tiger beetle	*Megacephala carolina* and *Cicindela* spp.
tiger beetle wasp	*Methocha* spp.
toothpick grasshopper	*Achurum sumichrasti* and *A. hilliardi*
trapdoor spider	*Myrmeciophila fluviatilis*
tree cricket	*Decanthus* spp.
tropical fire ant	*Solenopsis geminata*
variegated fritillary	*Eupoieta claudia*
viceroy	*Limenitis archippus*
western pigmy blue	*Brepidium exilis*
West Indian buckeye	*Junonia evarete*
white-lined sphinx	*Hyles lineata*
wolf spider	*Lycosa* spp.
woolly leaf gall wasp	*Andricus laniger*
yellow-and-black mud dauber	*Sceliphron cementarium*
zebra longwing	*Heliconius charitonius*

Bibliography

Introduction

Bedichek, Roy 1950. *Karankaway Country.* Austin: University of Texas Press.
———. 1961. *Adventures with a Texas Naturalist.* Austin: University of Texas Press.
Graham, G. L. 1992. *Texas Wildlife Viewing Guide.* Helena and Billings, Montana: Falcon Press Publishing Co.

1. The Land—How It Came to Be

Finsley, C. 1989. *A Field Guide to Fossils of Texas.* Austin: Texas Monthly Press.
Kurten, B. 1988. *Before the Indians.* New York: Columbia University Press.
Kurten, B., and E. Anderson. 1980. *Pleistocene Mammals of North America.* New York: Columbia University Press.
Matthews, W. H. 1960. *Texas Fossils: An Amateur Collectors Handbook.* Austin: Bureau of Economic Geology.
McGowen, J. H., et al. 1976. *Environmental Geologic Atlas of the Texas Coastal Zone—Port Lavaca Area.* Austin: Bureau of Economic Geology.
Spearing, D. 1991. *Roadside Geology of Texas.* Missoula: Mountain Press Publishing Co.

2. The Land—Where It Fits

Bomar, G. W. 1983. *Texas Weather.* Austin: University of Texas Press.
Gehlbach, F. R. 1981. *Mountain Islands and Desert Seas.* College Station: Texas A&M University Press.
Lockwood, C. C. 1984. *The Gulf Coast: Where the Land Meets the Sea.* Baton Rouge: Louisiana State University Press.
Phelan, R. 1976. *Texas Wild: The Land, Plants, and Animals of the Lone Star State.* New York: E. P. Dutton & Co.
Tveten, J. L. 1982. *Coastal Texas: Water, Land, and Wildlife.* College Station: Texas A&M University Press.

3. The Land—How It Works

Amos, W. H., and S. H. Amos. 1985. *Atlantic and Gulf Coasts.* New York: Alfred A. Knopf.
Britton, J. C., and B. Morton. 1989. *Shore Ecology of the Gulf of Mexico.* Austin: University of Texas Press.
Kendeigh, S. C. 1961. *Animal Ecology.* Englewood Cliffs, N.J: Prentice-Hall.

Smith, R. L. 1966. *Ecology and Field Biology.* New York: Harper & Row.
Teal, J., and M. Teal. 1969. *Life and Death of the Salt Marsh.* New York: Random House.

4. The Land—What We Have Made of It

Hester, Thomas R. 1980. *Digging into South Texas Prehistory: A Guide for Amateur Archaeologists.* San Antonio: Corona Publishing Co.
The History of Refugio County, Texas. 1985. Dallas: Refugio County History Books Committee of Texas Extension Homemakers Council of Refugio County, Curtis Media Corp.
Huson, Hobart. 1953. *Refugio: A Comprehensive History of Refugio County from Aboriginal Times to 1953.* Woodsboro, Tex.: Rooke Foundation.
Kingston, M., ed. 1988. *A Concise History of Texas.* Austin: Texas Monthly Press.
Newcomb, W. W. Jr. 1961. *The Indians of Texas.* Austin: University of Texas Press.
Weniger, D. 1984. *The Explorers' Texas: The Lands and Waters.* Austin: Eakin Publishing.

5. The Whooping Crane

Allen, R. P. 1952. *The Whooping Crane.* New York: National Audubon Society.
Doughty, Robin W. 1989. *Return of the Whooping Crane.* Austin: University of Texas Press.
McNulty, F. 1986. *The Whooping Crane: The Bird that Defies Extinction.* New York: Dutton.

6. The Endangered Ones

Brown, J. E. 1983. *The Return of the Brown Pelican.* Baton Rouge: Louisiana State University Press.
Doughty, Robin W. 1983. *Wildlife and Man in Texas: Environmental Change and Conservation.* College Station: Texas A&M University Press.
Doughty, Robin W., and Barbara M. Parmenter. 1989. *Endangered Species: Disappearing Animals and Plants in the Lone Star State.* Austin: Texas Monthly Press.
Matthews, J. R., and C. J. Moseley, eds. 1991. *The Official World Wildlife Fund Guide to Endangered Species of North America.* Washington D.C.: Beacham Publishing.
National Research Council. 1990. *Decline of the Sea Turtles: Causes and Prevention.* Washington, D.C.: National Academy Press.

9. Mammals

Baumgardner, G. D., et al. 1992. Distributional status of short-tailed shrews (genus *Blarina*) in Texas. *Southwestern Naturalist* 37(3): 326–328.
Davis, W. B. 1960. *The Mammals of Texas.* Austin: Texas Parks & Wildlife Dept.
Lowery, G. H. Jr. 1981. *Mammals of Louisiana and Its Adjacent Waters.* Baton Rouge: Louisiana State University Press.

Schmidly, D. J. 1983. *Texas Mammals East of the Balcones Fault Zone.* College Station: Texas A&M University Press.

———. 1993. *The Bats of Texas.* College Station: Texas A&M University Press.

Whitaker, J. O. Jr. 1980. *The Audubon Society Field Guide to North American Mammals.* New York: Alfred A. Knopf.

10. Birds

Chandler, R. J. 1987. *The Facts on File Guide to North Atlantic Shorebirds.* New York: Facts on File.

Ehrlich, P. R., et al. 1988. *The Birder's Handbook.* New York: Simon & Schuster.

Hammerstrom, F. 1986. *Harrier, Hawk of the Marshes.* Washington, D.C.: Smithsonian Institution Press.

Jones, Barry. 1992. *A Birder's Guide to Aransas National Wildlife Refuge.* Albuquerque: Southwest Natural & Cultural Heritage Association.

Kutac, E. A. *Birder's Guide to Texas.* Houston: Gulf Publishing Co.

Meanley, B. 1985. *The Marsh Hen.* Centreville, Md.: Tidewater Publishing.

National Geographic Society. 1983. *Field Guide to the Birds of North America.* Washington, D.C.: National Geographic Society.

Peterson, Roger Tory. 1963. *A Field Guide to the Birds of Texas and Adjacent States.* Boston: Houghton Mifflin Co.

Rappole, J. H., and G. W. Blacklock. 1985. *Birds of the Texas Coastal Bend: Abundance and Distribution.* College Station: Texas A&M University Press.

Telfair, R. C. 1983. *The Cattle Egret: A Texas Focus and World View.* College Station: Texas Agricultural Experimental Station.

11. Herptiles

Conant, Roger. 1975. *A Field Guide to Reptiles and Amphibians of Eastern and Central North America.* Boston: Houghton Mifflin Co.

Dixon, J. R. 1987. *Amphibians and Reptiles of Texas.* College Station: Texas A&M University Press.

Raun, G. G. 1965. *A Guide to Texas Snakes.* Austin: Texas Memorial Museum.

Tennant, Alan. 1984. *The Snakes of Texas.* Austin: Texas Monthly Press.

12. Fish

Hoese, H. D., and R. H. Moore. 1977. *Fishes of the Gulf of Mexico.* College Station: Texas A&M University Press.

Robins, C. R., et al. 1986. *A Field Guide to Atlantic Coast Fishes of North America.* Boston: Houghton Mifflin Co.

13. Invertebrates

Borror, Donald J., and Richard E. White. 1970. *A Field Guide to the Insects of America North of Mexico.* Boston: Houghton Mifflin Co.

Milne, Lorus, and Margery Milne. 1980. *The Audubon Society Field Guide to North American Insects and Spiders.* New York: Alfred A. Knopf.

Mitchell, R. T., and H. S. Zim. 1964. *Butterflies and Moths*. New York: Golden Press.

Pyle, R. M. 1981. *The Audubon Society Field Guide to North American Butterflies*. New York: Alfred A. Knopf.

14. Woody Plants

Brockman, C. F. 1968. *Trees of North America*. New York: Western Publishing Co.

Cox, P. W., and P. Leslie. 1988. *Texas Trees: A Friendly Guide*. San Antonio: Corona Publishing Co.

Everitt, J. H., and D. L. Drawe. 1993. *Trees, Shrubs, and Cacti of South Texas*. Lubbock: Texas Tech University Press.

Jones, F. B. 1982. *Flora of the Texas Coastal Bend*. Corpus Christi: Mission Press.

Simpson, Benny J. 1988. *A Field Guide to Texas Trees*. Austin: Texas Monthly Press.

15. Herbaceous Plants

Ajilvsgi, Geyata. 1984. *Wildflowers of Texas*. Bryan: Shearer Publishing.

Cannatella, M. M., and R. E. Arnold. 1985. *Plants of the Texas Shore*. College Station: Texas A&M University Press.

Duncan, W. H., and M. B. Duncan. 1987. *The Smithsonian Guide to Seaside Plants of the Gulf and Atlantic Coasts*. Washington, D.C.: Smithsonian Institution Press.

Eleuterius, L. N. 1990. *Tidal Marsh Plants*. Gretna, La.: Pelican Publishing Co.

Gould, Frank W., 1978. *Common Texas Grasses: An Illustrated Guide*. College Station: Texas A&M University Press.

Gould, Frank W., and T. W. Box. 1965. *Grasses of the Texas Coastal Bend*. College Station: Texas A&M University Press.

Jones, F. B. 1982. *Flora of the Texas Coastal Bend*. Corpus Christi: Mission Press.

Loughmiller, Campbell, and Lynn Loughmiller. 1984. *Texas Wildflowers: A Field Guide*. Austin: University of Texas Press.

Niehaus, T. F. 1984. *A Field Guide to Southwestern and Texas Wildflowers*. Boston: Houghton Mifflin Co.

Wills, Mary Motz, and Howard S. Irwin. 1961. *Roadside Flowers of Texas*. Austin: University of Texas Press.

16. Nonflowering Plants

Lincoff, G. H. 1981. *The Audubon Society Field Guide to North American Mushrooms*. New York: Alfred A. Knopf.

Metzler, S., and V. Metzler. 1992. *Texas Mushrooms: A Field Guide*. Austin: University of Texas Press.

Phillips, R. 1991. *Mushrooms of North America*. Boston: Little, Brown & Co.

Reese, W. D. 1984. *Mosses of the Gulf South*. Baton Rouge: Louisiana State University Press.

Shuttleworth, F. S., and H. S. Zim. 1967. *Non-flowering Plants*. New York: Golden Press.

Index